PHILIP'S

MODERN SCHOOL ATLAS

93rd edition

IN ASSOCIATION WITH
THE ROYAL GEOGRAPHICAL SOCIETY
WITH THE INSTITUTE OF BRITISH GEOGRAPHERS

CONTENTS

Note: Each section is colour-coded on this contents page and on the heading of each page for ease of reference.

Published in Great Britain in 2000
by George Philip Limited,
a division of Octopus Publishing Group Limited,
2–4 Heron Quays, London E14 4JP

Cartography by Philip's

Ninety-third edition
© 2000 George Philip Limited

ISBN 0–540–07784–4 Paperback edition
ISBN 0–540–07783–6 Hardback edition

BRITISH ISLES MAPS

A separate map key is provided on the first page of the World Maps section.

SETTLEMENTS

◼ **LONDON**   ▣ **GLASGOW**   ▣ **BRADFORD**   ▢ **Brighton**   ◉ Gateshead

◉ *Aylesbury*   ◎ *Sligo*   ⊙ *Selkirk*   ○ *Burford*   ○ *Lampeter*

Settlement symbols and type styles vary according to the population and importance of towns

Built up areas   ▢ London Boroughs

ADMINISTRATION

——— International boundaries   **W A L E S**   Country names

——— National boundaries   KENT   Administrative area names

——— Administrative boundaries   *EXMOOR*   National park names

COMMUNICATIONS

=== Motorways
=== *under construction*

——— Major roads
——— *under construction*
⇥——⇤ *in tunnels*

——— Other important roads
——— *under construction*
⇥——⇤ *in tunnels*

⊕ Major airports

——— Main passenger railways
——— *under construction*
⇥——⇤ *in tunnels*

——— Other passenger railways
——— *under construction*
⇥——⇤ *in tunnels*

—— Canals
—— *in tunnels*

⊕ Other airports

PHYSICAL FEATURES

〰 Perennial rivers

〜 Tidal flats

⬭ Lakes or reservoirs

⬚ Reservoirs under construction

▲ 444   Elevations in metres

▼ 38   Depths below sea level in metres

ELEVATION AND DEPTH TINTS

Height of Land above Sea Level   Land below Sea Level   Depth of Sea

in metres	1000	750	500	400	200	100	0	150	300	600	1500	3000	6000	in feet
in feet	3000	2250	1500	1200	600	300								
							0	20	50	100	200	500	1000	2000	in metres

SHETLAND ISLANDS
on same scale

ORKNEY ISLANDS on same scale

CARTOGRAPHY BY PHILIP'S.

1:1 000 000

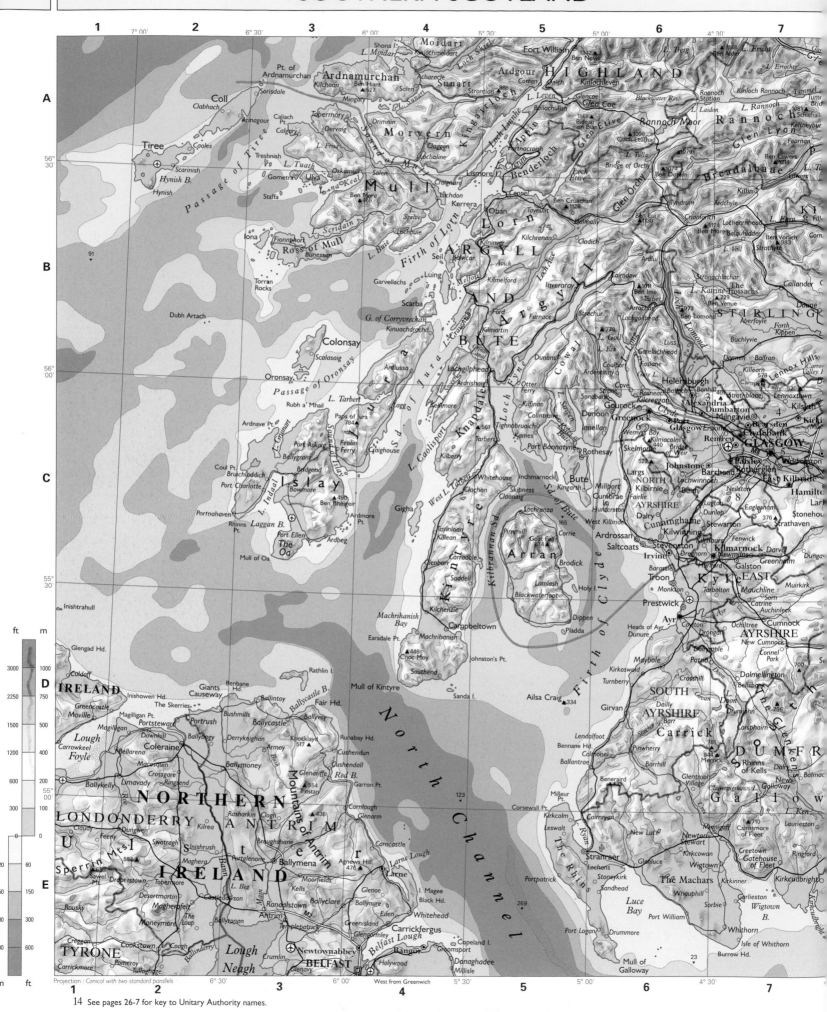

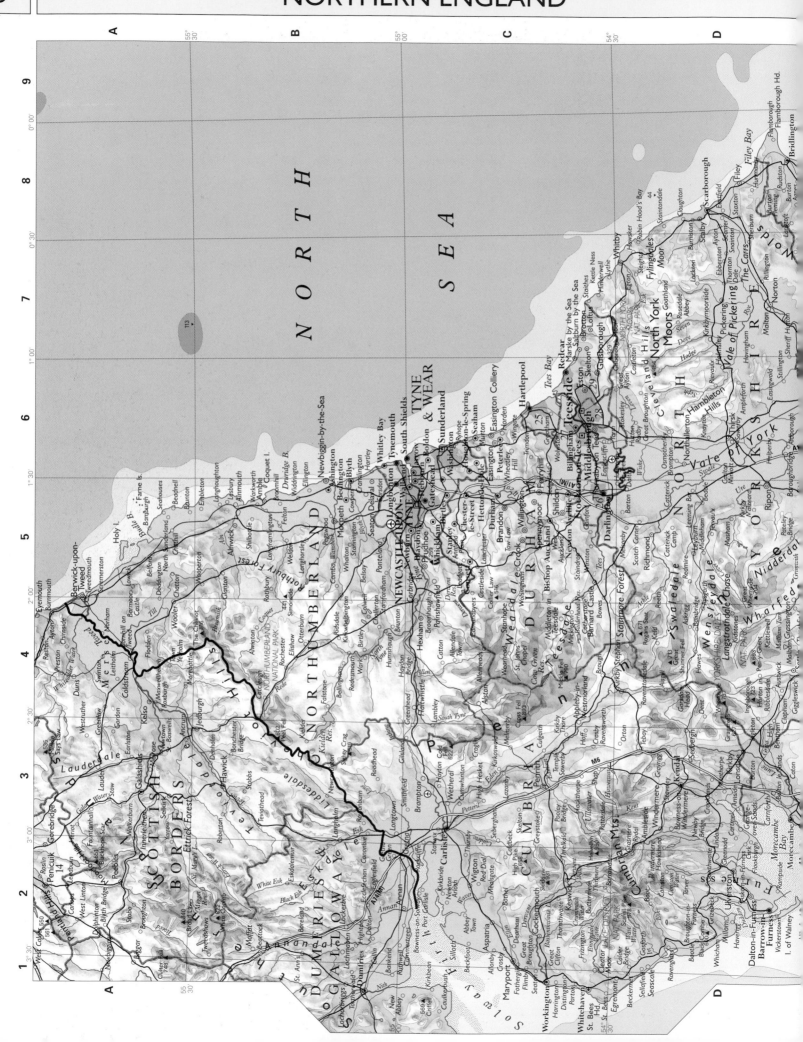

See pages 26-7 for key to Unitary Authority names.

1:1 000 000

Projection : Conical with two standard parallels

West from Greenwich

SOUTH AND SOUTH-EAST ENGLAND

Projection : Conical with two standard parallels

West from Greenwich

20 See pages 26-7 for key to Unitary Authority names.

Grid columns: 7 8 9 10 11 12

0° 30' 0° 00' 0° 30' 1° 00'

Grid rows: A B C D

52° 30' 52° 00' 51° 30' 51° 00' 1° 00'

LINCOLNSHIRE

The Wash

NORFOLK

NORFOLK BROADS NAT. PARK

CAMBRIDGESHIRE

The Fens

Breckland

SUFFOLK

BEDFORDSHIRE

HERTFORDSHIRE

ESSEX

GREATER LONDON

LONDON

SURREY

KENT

WEST SUSSEX

EAST SUSSEX

The Weald

North Downs

South Downs

Romney Marsh

Thames Estuary

Strait of Dover

FRANCE

Selected towns and cities:
Grantham, Boston, Hunstanton, Wells-next-the-Sea, Cromer, Sheringham, Great Yarmouth, Lowestoft, King's Lynn, Norwich, Peterborough, Wisbech, Ely, Newmarket, Bury St. Edmunds, Thetford, Diss, Beccles, Halesworth, Southwold, Cambridge, Bedford, Ipswich, Woodbridge, Felixstowe, Harwich, Colchester, Clacton-on-Sea, Milton Keynes, Luton, Stevenage, Harlow, Chelmsford, Maldon, Southend-on-Sea, Watford, LONDON, Basildon, Brentwood, Gravesend, Rochester, Gillingham, Chatham, Sittingbourne, Margate, Broadstairs, Ramsgate, Herne Bay, Whitstable, Canterbury, Deal, Dover, Folkestone, Maidstone, Ashford, Guildford, Dorking, Reigate, Crawley, Royal Tunbridge Wells, Hythe, New Romney, Horsham, Haywards Heath, Burgess Hill, Uckfield, Hastings, Bexhill, Eastbourne, Brighton, Hove, Worthing, Bognor Regis, Chichester, Arundel, Newhaven, Seaford, Lewes

Straits: Strait of Dover, C. Gris-Nez, Calais, Boulogne-sur-Mer, FRANCE

East from Greenwich

COPYRIGHT GEORGE PHILIP LTD.

1:1 000 000

10   0   10   20 miles
10   0   10   20   30 km

IRISH SEA

St. George's Channel

Cardigan Bay

Liverpool Bay

Caernarfon Bay

Tremadog Bay

LIVERPOOL

CHESHIRE

SHROPSHIRE

HEREFORDSHIRE

WORCESTER

GLOUCESTERSHIRE

MONMOUTHSHIRE

POWYS

GWYNEDD

CLWYD

DYFED

CEREDIGION

CARMARTHENSHIRE

PEMBROKESHIRE

FLINTSHIRE

DENBIGHSHIRE

WREXHAM

ANGLESEY

ISLE OF ANGLESEY

STAFFS.

W. MIDS.

SNOWDONIA NATIONAL PARK

BRECON BEACONS NATIONAL PARK

PEMBROKESHIRE NATIONAL PARK

Black Mountains

Malvern Hills

Forest of Dean

Clee Hills

Mynydd Preseli

Holyhead

Chester

Shrewsbury

Hereford

Gloucester

Aberystwyth

Carmarthen

Pembroke

Brecon

Llandudno

Colwyn Bay

Bangor

Caernarfon

Conwy

Severn

FRANCE

CHANNEL ISLANDS
on same scale

Jersey

Guernsey

Alderney

Sark

St. Peter Port

St. Helier

CHANNEL ISLANDS

Passage de la Déroute

COPYRIGHT GEORGE PHILIP LTD.

ISLES OF SCILLY
on same scale

Isles of Scilly

St. Mary's

Tresco

St. Martin's

St. Agnes

Bishop Rk.

Wolf Rock

Land's End

C. Cornwall

St. Just

Newlyn

Penzance

Sennen

St. Levan

Bristol Channel

BRISTOL

CARDIFF

Newport

VALE OF GLAMORGAN

Weston-super-Mare

Bath

SOMERSET

Exmoor National Park

DEVON

Dartmoor National Park

DARTMOOR NATIONAL PARK

CORNWALL

DORSET

Plymouth

Exeter

Taunton

Yeovil

Barnstaple

Bideford

Bodmin

Truro

Torquay

Torbay

Paignton

Brixham

Newton Abbot

Teignmouth

Dawlish

Sidmouth

Lyme Bay

Weymouth

Portland Bill

I. of Portland

Bridport

Sherborne

Minehead

Ilfracombe

Lundy

Falmouth

Penzance

St. Ives

Redruth

Camborne

Helston

Lizard Pt.

Land's End

Wolf Rock

Start Pt.

Bolt Head

Eddystone

Projection: Conical with two standard parallels

57 See pages 26-7 for key to Unitary Authority names.

1:1 000 000

West from Greenwich

10 miles 0 10 20 miles

10 0 10 20 30 km

m	ft
3000	
2250	
1500	
1200	
600	
300	
150	
60	
20	
0	

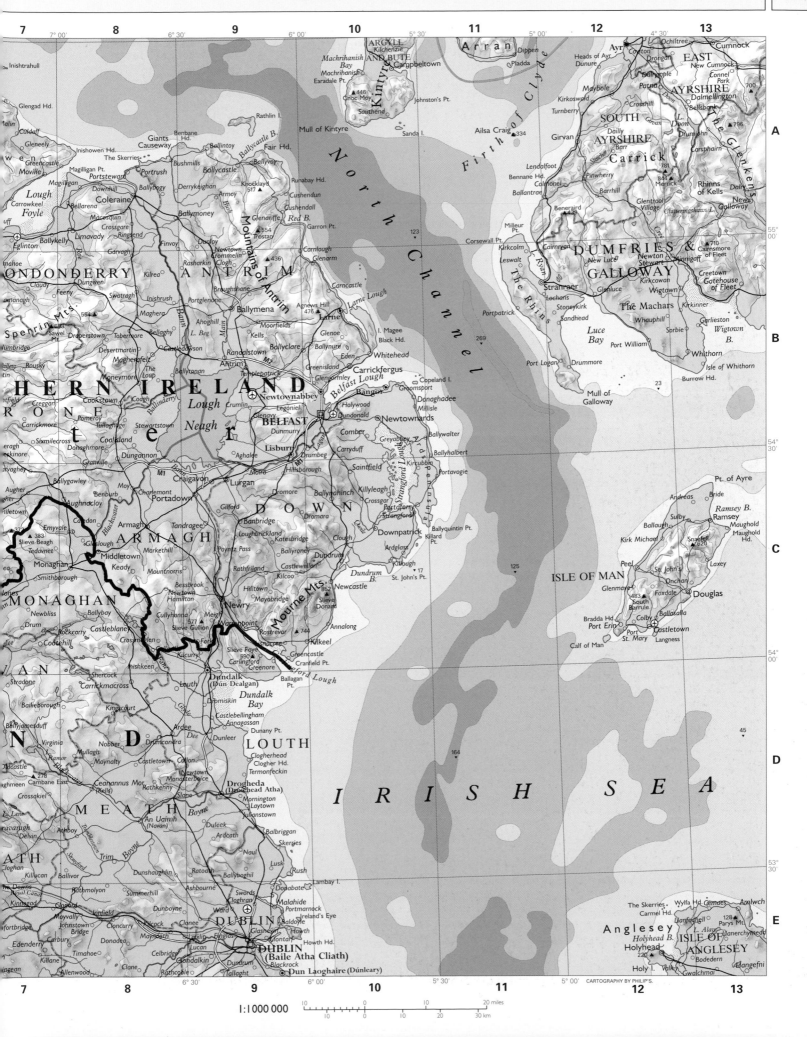

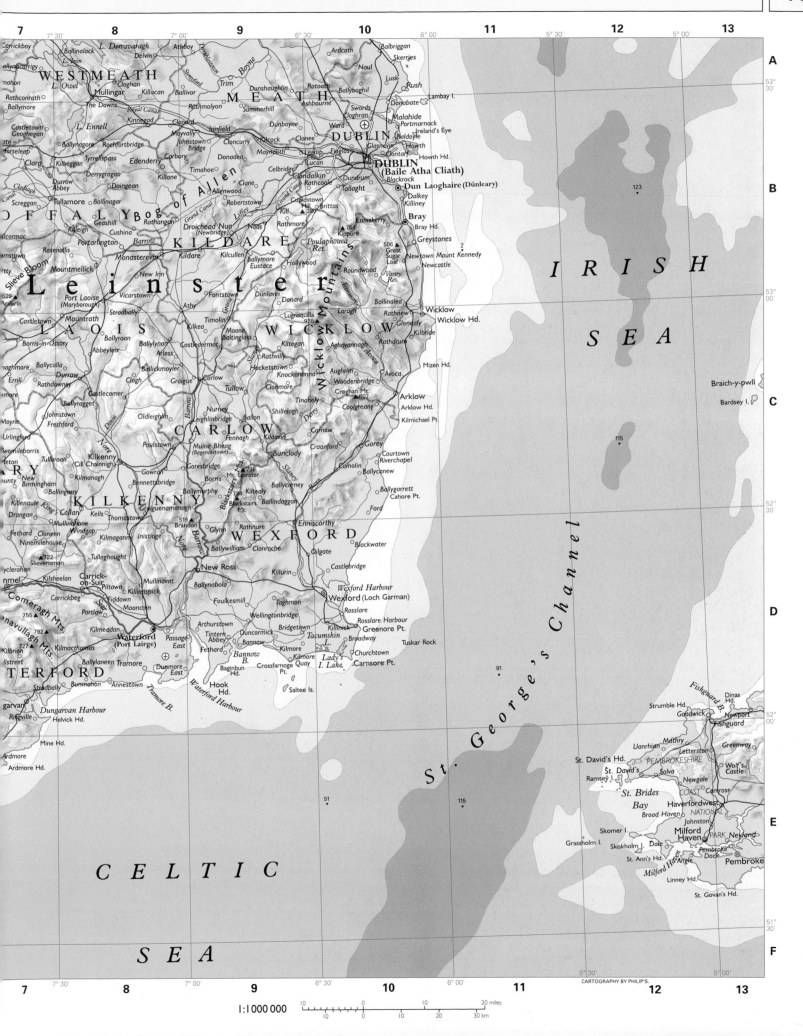

1:1 000 000

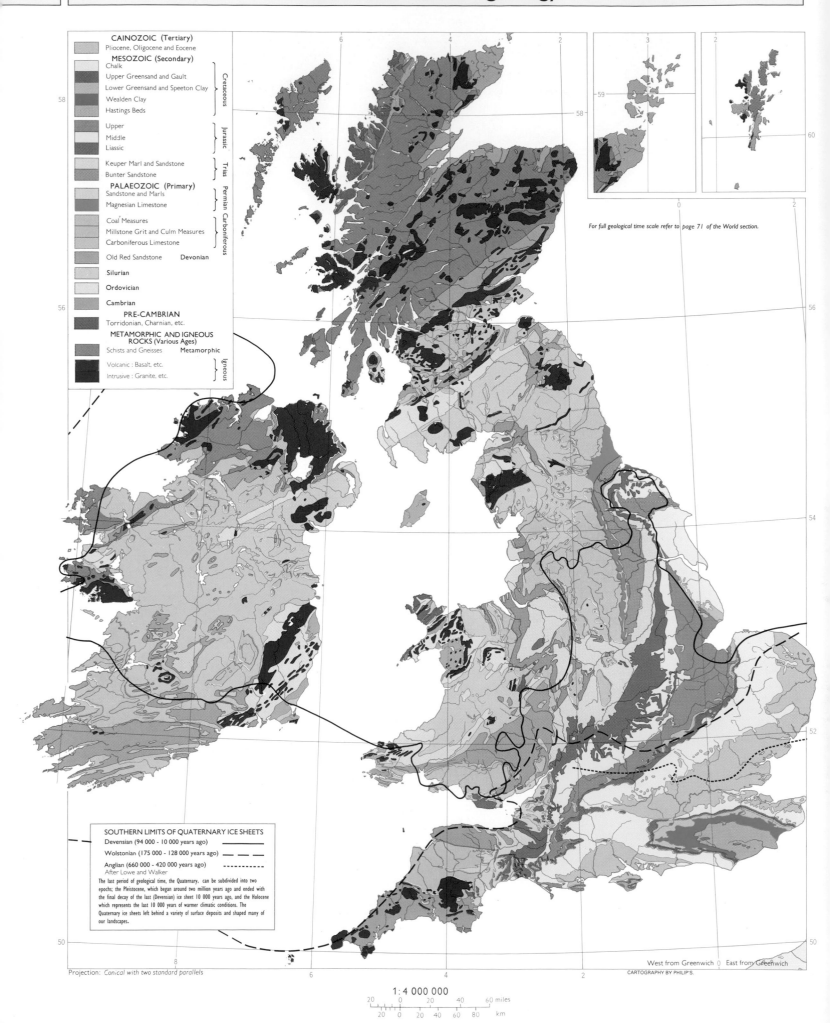

CAINOZOIC (Tertiary)
Pliocene, Oligocene and Eocene

MESOZOIC (Secondary)
Chalk
Upper Greensand and Gault
Lower Greensand and Speeton Clay   *Cretaceous*
Wealden Clay
Hastings Beds

Upper
Middle   *Jurassic*
Liassic

Keuper Marl and Sandstone   *Trias*
Bunter Sandstone

PALAEOZOIC (Primary)
Sandstone and Marls   *Permian*
Magnesian Limestone

Coal Measures
Millstone Grit and Culm Measures   *Carboniferous*
Carboniferous Limestone

Old Red Sandstone   **Devonian**

Silurian

Ordovician

Cambrian

PRE-CAMBRIAN
Torridonian, Charnian, etc.

METAMORPHIC AND IGNEOUS ROCKS (Various Ages)
Schists and Gneisses   **Metamorphic**

Volcanic : Basalt, etc.   *Igneous*
Intrusive : Granite, etc.

For full geological time scale refer to page 71 of the World section.

SOUTHERN LIMITS OF QUATERNARY ICE SHEETS
Devensian (94 000 - 10 000 years ago) ————
Wolstonian (175 000 - 128 000 years ago) — — —
Anglian (660 000 - 420 000 years ago) ·········
After Lowe and Walker

The last period of geological time, the Quaternary, can be subdivided into two epochs; the Pleistocene, which began around two million years ago and ended with the final decay of the last (Devensian) ice sheet 10 000 years ago, and the Holocene which represents the last 10 000 years of warmer climatic conditions. The Quaternary ice sheets left behind a variety of surface deposits and shaped many of our landscapes.

West from Greenwich   0   East from Greenwich

Projection: *Conical with two standard parallels*

CARTOGRAPHY BY PHILIP'S.

1 : 4 000 000

20   0   20   40   60 miles
20 0 20 40 60 80
km

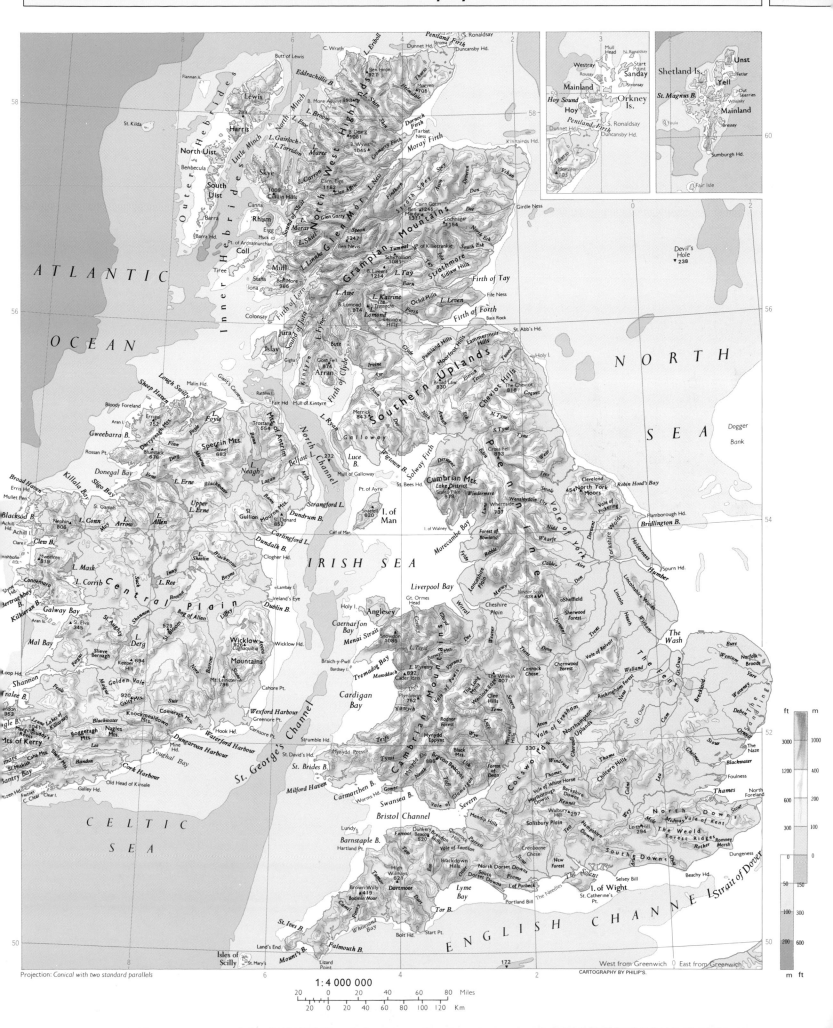

Projection: Conical with two standard parallels

CARTOGRAPHY BY PHILIP'S.

1 : 4 000 000

20   0   20   40   60   80   Miles

20   0   20   40   60   80   100   120   Km

JANUARY TEMPERATURE
Actual surface temperature

°C
7
6
5
4
3
2
1
0

SUNSHINE

453 Average duration of bright sunshine in hours November - April

— January isotherms reduced to sea-level °*Celsius*

Stornoway 418
Braemar 352
Oban 416
Edinburgh 488
Tynemouth 443
Belfast 451
Ambleside 397
Scarborough 453
Colwyn Bay 496
Skegness 511
Dublin 497
Shannon 493
Birmingham 424
Valencia 483
Cardiff 527
Kew 476
Bournemouth 593
Newquay 575

JULY TEMPERATURE
Actual surface temperature

°C
17
16
15
14
13
12
11
10

SUNSHINE

944 Average duration of bright sunshine in hours May - October

— July isotherms reduced to sea-level °*Celsius*

Stornoway 816
Braemar 768
Oban 825
Edinburgh 836
Tynemouth 887
Belfast 834
Ambleside 792
Scarborough 944
Colwyn Bay 995
Skegness 1019
Dublin 883
Shannon 893
Birmingham 875
Valencia 878
Cardiff 1025
Kew 1056
Bournemouth 1125
Newquay 1089

ANNUAL RAINFALL

mm
2500
2000
1500
1000
750
625

Stornoway
Wick
Lerwick 4.5
Tiree 6.8
Turnhouse
Belmullet 2.1
Tynemouth
Dublin 5.7
Ringway 8.2
Manby 6.5
Aberporth 5.6
Valencia 1.1
Dungeness
Exeter 2.1

WIND

% calms in a year

Direction the wind blows from

% frequency of wind from a direction

Force of wind (Beaufort scale)

BEAUFORT FORCE	SPEED (K.P.H.)	CATEGORY
1 - 3	1-20	Light breeze
4	21-29	Moderate breeze
5-6	30-50	Fresh to strong wind
7	51-61	Moderate gale
8-12	over 62	Gale, storm or hurricane

SNOW

Average number of mornings with snow cover per year

more than 50
20-50
15-20
10-15
5-10
less than 5

(after Manley, 1970)

FROST

—5— Mean length of frost free period in months

VARIABILITY OF RAIN

The percentage frequency with which rainfall varies from the normal rainfall regime in an area: the higher the percentage figure, the more variable the rainfall.

over 20%
18-20%
16-18%
14-16%
12-14%
10-12%
under 10%

(after Gregory, 1955)

CLIMATE STATIONS

•T Climate stations which appear on page 19

Regions of reliably high rainfall (more than 1250mm in at least 70% of the years)

Regions of occasionally low rainfall (less than 750mm in at least 30% of the years)

1 : 12 000 000

SYNOPTIC CHART FOR A TYPICAL WINTER DEPRESSION
21st January 1971

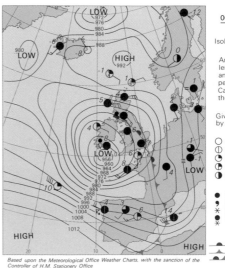

HOUR OF OBSERVATION
06h00 GREENWICH MEAN TIME

PRESSURE
Isobars are drawn at intervals of 4 mb.

WIND
Arrows fly with the wind. A full length feather represents 18 k.p.h. and a short feather 9 k.p.h. A solid pennant represents 90 k.p.h. Calm is indicated by a circle outside the weather symbol

TEMPERATURE
Given in °C and is shown on the charts by a figure alongside the station circle.

CLOUD SYMBOLS

○ Clear sky	◐ Sky ⅝ covered
① Sky 1⁄10 covered	◑ Sky ⅞ covered
◔ Sky 2⁄10 covered	◕ Sky 9⁄10 covered
◔ Sky 3⁄10 covered	● Sky 10⁄10 covered
◑ Sky covered	⊗ Sky obscured

WEATHER SYMBOLS

● Rain	△ Hail
⦂ Drizzle	▽ Shower
✳ Snow	⦑ Thunderstorm
✴ Rain and Snow	≡ Fog
	= Mist

FRONTS
Warm front on the surface
Cold front on the surface
Occluded front

Based upon the Meteorological Office Weather Charts, with the sanction of the Controller of H.M. Stationery Office

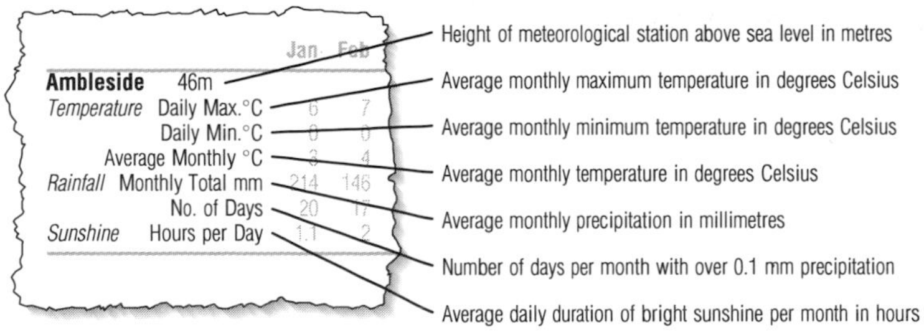
Ambleside 46m
Temperature Daily Max.°C
Daily Min.°C
Average Monthly °C
Rainfall Monthly Total mm
No. of Days
Sunshine Hours per Day
Height of meteorological station above sea level in metres
Average monthly maximum temperature in degrees Celsius
Average monthly minimum temperature in degrees Celsius
Average monthly temperature in degrees Celsius
Average monthly precipitation in millimetres
Number of days per month with over 0.1 mm precipitation
Average daily duration of bright sunshine per month in hours

		Jan	Feb	Mar	Apr	May	June	July	Aug	Sep	Oct	Nov	Dec	Year
Ambleside 46m														
Temperature	Daily Max.°C	6	7	9	12	16	19	20	19	17	13	9	7	13
	Daily Min.°C	0	0	2	4	6	9	11	11	9	6	3	1	5
	Average Monthly °C	3	4	6	8	11	14	15	15	13	10	6	4	9
Rainfall	Monthly Total mm	214	146	112	101	90	111	134	139	184	196	209	215	1851
	No. of Days	20	17	15	15	14	15	18	17	18	19	19	21	208
Sunshine	Hours per Day	1.1	2	3.2	4.5	6	5.7	4.5	4.2	3.3	2.2	1.4	1	3.3
Belfast 4m														
Temperature	Daily Max.°C	6	7	9	12	15	18	18	18	16	13	9	7	12
	Daily Min.°C	2	2	3	4	6	9	11	11	9	7	4	3	6
	Average Monthly °C	4	4	6	8	11	13	15	15	13	10	7	5	9
Rainfall	Monthly Total mm	80	52	50	48	52	68	94	77	80	83	72	90	845
	No. of Days	20	17	16	16	15	16	19	17	18	19	19	21	213
Sunshine	Hours per Day	1.5	2.3	3.4	5	6.3	6	4.4	4.4	3.6	2.6	1.8	1.1	3.5
Belmullet 9m														
Temperature	Daily Max.°C	8	9	10	12	14	16	17	17	16	14	10	9	12
	Daily Min.°C	3	4	4	6	8	10	11	11	10	8	5	4	7
	Average Monthly °C	5	6	7	9	11	13	14	14	13	11	8	6	10
Rainfall	Monthly Total mm	108	64	82	70	75	80	76	95	108	116	127	131	1132
	No. of Days	18	13	16	15	14	12	14	17	16	18	20	22	195
Sunshine	Hours per Day	1.9	2.5	3.4	5.2	7	6	4.6	5.1	3.9	2.9	1.9	1.3	3.8
Birkenhead 60m														
Temperature	Daily Max.°C	6	6	9	11	15	17	19	19	16	13	9	7	12
	Daily Min.°C	2	2	3	5	8	11	13	13	11	8	5	3	7
	Average Monthly °C	4	4	6	8	11	14	16	16	14	10	7	5	10
Rainfall	Monthly Total mm	64	46	40	41	55	55	67	80	66	71	76	65	726
	No. of Days	18	13	13	13	13	13	15	15	15	17	17	19	181
Sunshine	Hours per Day	1.6	2.4	3.5	5.3	6.3	6.7	5.7	5.4	4.2	2.9	1.8	1.3	3.9
Birmingham 163m														
Temperature	Daily Max.°C	5	6	9	12	16	19	20	20	17	13	9	6	13
	Daily Min.°C	2	2	3	5	7	10	12	12	10	7	5	3	7
	Average Monthly °C	3	4	6	8	11	15	16	16	14	10	7	5	10
Rainfall	Monthly Total mm	74	54	50	53	64	50	69	69	61	69	84	67	764
	No. of Days	17	15	13	13	14	13	15	14	14	15	17	18	178
Sunshine	Hours per Day	1.4	2.1	3.2	4.6	5.4	6	5.4	5.1	3.9	2.8	1.6	1.2	3.6
Cambridge 12m														
Temperature	Daily Max.°C	6	7	11	14	17	21	22	22	19	15	10	7	14
	Daily Min.°C	1	1	2	4	7	10	12	12	10	6	4	2	6
	Average Monthly °C	3	4	6	9	12	15	17	17	14	10	7	5	10
Rainfall	Monthly Total mm	49	35	36	37	45	45	58	55	51	51	54	41	558
	No. of Days	15	13	10	11	11	11	12	12	11	13	14	14	147
Sunshine	Hours per Day	1.7	2.5	3.8	5.1	6.2	6.7	6	5.7	4.6	3.4	1.9	1.4	4.1
Cardiff 62m														
Temperature	Daily Max.°C	7	7	10	13	16	19	20	21	18	14	10	8	14
	Daily Min.°C	2	2	3	5	8	11	12	13	11	8	5	3	7
	Average Monthly °C	4	5	7	9	12	15	16	17	14	11	8	6	10
Rainfall	Monthly Total mm	108	72	63	65	76	63	89	97	99	109	116	108	1065
	No. of Days	18	14	13	13	13	13	14	15	16	16	17	18	180
Sunshine	Hours per Day	1.7	2.7	4	5.6	6.4	6.9	6.2	6	4.7	3.4	1.9	1.5	4.3
Craibstone 91m														
Temperature	Daily Max.°C	5	6	8	10	13	16	18	17	15	12	8	6	11
	Daily Min.°C	0	0	2	3	5	8	10	10	8	6	3	1	5
	Average Monthly °C	3	3	5	7	9	12	14	13	12	9	6	4	8
Rainfall	Monthly Total mm	78	55	53	51	63	54	95	75	67	92	93	80	856
	No. of Days	19	16	15	15	14	14	18	15	16	18	19	18	197
Sunshine	Hours per Day	1.8	2.9	3.5	4.9	5.9	6.1	5.1	4.8	4.3	3.1	2	1.5	3.8
Cromer 54m														
Temperature	Daily Max.°C	6	7	9	12	15	18	21	20	18	14	10	8	13
	Daily Min.°C	1	1	3	5	7	10	12	13	11	8	5	3	7
	Average Monthly °C	4	4	6	8	11	14	16	16	15	11	7	5	10
Rainfall	Monthly Total mm	58	46	37	39	48	39	63	56	54	61	64	53	618
	No. of Days	18	16	13	13	11	11	13	12	14	16	18	18	173
Sunshine	Hours per Day	1.8	2.6	4	5.4	6.4	6.8	6.3	5.8	5	3.6	2	1.9	4.3
Dublin 47m														
Temperature	Daily Max.°C	8	8	10	13	15	18	20	19	17	14	10	8	14
	Daily Min.°C	1	2	3	4	6	9	11	11	9	6	4	3	6
	Average Monthly °C	4	5	7	8	11	14	15	15	13	10	7	6	10
Rainfall	Monthly Total mm	67	55	51	45	60	57	70	74	72	70	67	74	762
	No. of Days	13	10	10	11	10	11	13	12	12	11	12	14	139
Sunshine	Hours per Day	1.9	2.5	3.4	5	6.2	6	4.8	4.9	3.9	3.2	2.1	1.6	3.8
Durham 102m														
Temperature	Daily Max.°C	6	6	9	12	15	18	20	19	17	13	9	7	13
	Daily Min.°C	0	0	1	3	6	9	11	10	9	6	3	2	5
	Average Monthly °C	3	3	5	7	10	13	15	15	13	9	6	4	9
Rainfall	Monthly Total mm	59	51	38	38	51	49	61	67	60	63	66	55	658
	No. of Days	17	15	14	13	13	14	15	14	14	16	17	17	179
Sunshine	Hours per Day	1.7	2.5	3.3	4.6	5.4	6	5.1	4.8	4.1	3	1.9	1.4	3.6
Lerwick 82m														
Temperature	Daily Max.°C	5	5	6	8	11	13	14	14	13	10	8	6	9
	Daily Min.°C	1	1	2	3	5	7	10	10	8	6	4	3	5
	Average Monthly °C	3	3	4	5	8	10	12	12	11	8	6	4	7
Rainfall	Monthly Total mm	109	87	69	68	52	55	72	71	87	104	111	118	1003
	No. of Days	25	22	20	21	15	15	17	17	19	23	24	25	243
Sunshine	Hours per Day	0.8	1.8	2.9	4.4	5.3	5.3	4	3.8	3.5	2.2	2.2	0.5	3
London (Kew) 5m														
Temperature	Daily Max.°C	6	7	10	13	17	20	22	21	19	14	10	7	14
	Daily Min.°C	2	2	3	6	8	12	14	13	11	8	5	4	7
	Average Monthly °C	4	5	7	9	12	16	18	17	15	11	8	5	11
Rainfall	Monthly Total mm	54	40	37	37	46	45	57	59	49	57	64	48	593
	No. of Days	15	13	11	12	12	11	12	11	13	13	15	15	153
Sunshine	Hours per Day	1.5	2.3	3.6	5.3	6.4	7.1	6.4	6.1	4.7	3.2	1.8	1.3	4.1
Oxford 63m														
Temperature	Daily Max.°C	7	7	11	14	17	20	22	22	19	14	10	8	14
	Daily Min.°C	1	1	2	5	7	10	12	12	10	7	4	2	6
	Average Monthly °C	4	4	6	9	12	15	17	17	14	11	7	5	10
Rainfall	Monthly Total mm	61	44	43	41	55	52	55	60	59	64	69	57	660
	No. of Days	13	10	9	9	10	9	10	10	10	11	12	13	126
Sunshine	Hours per Day	1.7	2.6	3.9	5.3	6.1	6.6	5.9	5.7	4.4	3.2	2.1	1.6	4.1
Plymouth 27m														
Temperature	Daily Max.°C	8	8	10	12	15	18	19	19	18	15	11	9	14
	Daily Min.°C	4	4	5	6	8	11	13	13	12	9	7	5	8
	Average Monthly °C	6	6	7	9	12	15	16	16	15	12	9	7	11
Rainfall	Monthly Total mm	99	74	69	53	63	53	70	77	78	91	113	110	950
	No. of Days	19	15	14	12	12	12	14	14	15	16	17	18	178
Sunshine	Hours per Day	1.9	2.9	4.3	6.1	7.1	7.4	6.4	6.4	5.1	3.7	2.2	1.7	4.6
Renfrew 6m														
Temperature	Daily Max.°C	5	7	9	12	15	18	19	19	16	13	9	7	12
	Daily Min.°C	1	1	2	4	6	9	11	11	9	6	4	2	6
	Average Monthly °C	3	4	6	8	11	14	15	15	13	9	7	4	9
Rainfall	Monthly Total mm	111	85	69	67	63	70	97	93	102	119	106	127	1109
	No. of Days	19	16	15	15	14	15	17	17	17	18	18	20	201
Sunshine	Hours per Day	1.1	2.1	2.9	4.7	6	6.1	5.1	4.4	3.7	2.3	1.4	0.8	3.4
St Helier 9m														
Temperature	Daily Max.°C	9	8	11	13	16	19	21	21	19	16	12	10	15
	Daily Min.°C	5	4	6	7	10	13	15	15	14	11	8	6	9
	Average Monthly °C	7	6	8	10	13	16	18	18	17	13	10	8	12
Rainfall	Monthly Total mm	89	68	57	43	44	39	48	67	69	77	101	99	801
	No. of Days	19	15	13	12	11	10	11	12	15	15	17	19	169
Sunshine	Hours per Day	2.3	3.1	5	6.7	7.8	8.5	7.8	7.6	5.6	4.1	2.5	1.8	5.3
St Mary's 50m														
Temperature	Daily Max.°C	9	9	11	12	14	17	19	19	18	15	12	10	14
	Daily Min.°C	6	6	7	7	9	12	13	14	13	11	9	7	9
	Average Monthly °C	8	7	9	10	12	14	16	16	15	13	10	9	12
Rainfall	Monthly Total mm	91	71	69	46	56	49	61	64	67	80	96	94	844
	No. of Days	22	17	16	13	14	14	16	15	16	17	19	21	200
Sunshine	Hours per Day	2	2.9	4.2	6.4	7.6	7.6	6.7	6.7	5.2	3.9	2.5	1.8	4.8
Southampton 20m														
Temperature	Daily Max.°C	7	8	11	14	17	20	22	22	19	15	11	8	15
	Daily Min.°C	2	2	3	5	8	11	13	13	11	7	5	3	7
	Average Monthly °C	5	5	7	10	13	16	17	17	15	11	8	6	11
Rainfall	Monthly Total mm	83	56	52	45	56	49	60	69	70	86	94	84	804
	No. of Days	17	13	13	12	12	12	13	13	14	14	16	17	166
Sunshine	Hours per Day	1.8	2.6	4	5.7	6.7	7.2	6.5	6.4	4.9	3.6	2.2	1.6	4.5
Tiree 9m														
Temperature	Daily Max.°C	7	7	9	10	13	15	16	16	15	12	10	8	12
	Daily Min.°C	4	3	4	5	7	10	11	11	10	8	6	5	7
	Average Monthly °C	5	5	6	8	10	12	14	14	13	10	8	6	9
Rainfall	Monthly Total mm	117	77	67	64	55	70	91	90	118	129	122	128	1128
	No. of Days	23	19	17	17	15	16	20	18	20	23	22	24	234
Sunshine	Hours per Day	1.3	2.6	3.7	5.7	7.5	6.8	5.2	5.3	4.2	2.6	1.6	0.9	4
Valencia 9m														
Temperature	Daily Max.°C	9	9	11	13	15	17	18	18	17	14	12	10	14
	Daily Min.°C	5	4	5	6	8	11	12	13	11	9	7	6	8
	Average Monthly °C	7	7	8	9	11	0	15	15	14	12	9	8	11
Rainfall	Monthly Total mm	165	107	103	75	86	81	107	95	122	140	151	168	1400
	No. of Days	20	15	14	13	13	13	15	15	16	17	18	21	190
Sunshine	Hours per Day	1.6	2.5	3.5	5.2	6.5	5.9	4.7	4.9	3.8	2.8	2	1.3	3.7
York 17m														
Temperature	Daily Max.°C	6	7	10	13	16	19	21	21	18	14	10	7	13
	Daily Min.°C	1	1	2	4	7	10	12	12	10	7	4	2	6
	Average Monthly °C	3	4	6	9	12	15	17	16	14	10	7	5	10
Rainfall	Monthly Total mm	59	46	37	41	50	50	62	68	55	56	65	50	639
	No. of Days	17	15	13	13	13	14	15	14	14	15	17	17	177
Sunshine	Hours per Day	1.3	2.1	3.2	4.7	6.1	6.4	5.6	5.1	4.1	2.8	1.6	1.1	3.7

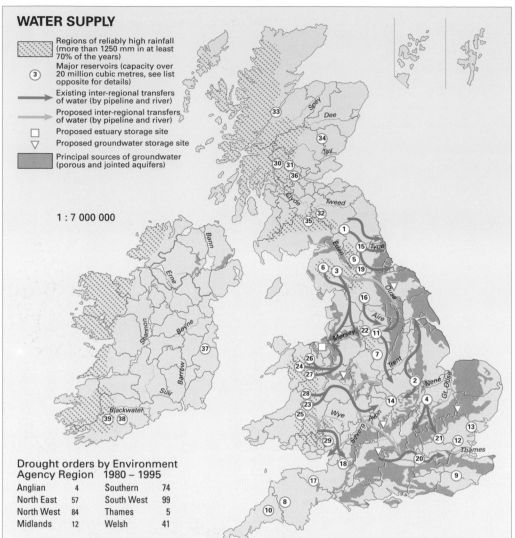

WATER SUPPLY

Regions of reliably high rainfall (more than 1250 mm in at least 70% of the years)

③ Major reservoirs (capacity over 20 million cubic metres, see list opposite for details)

→ Existing inter-regional transfers of water (by pipeline and river)

→ Proposed inter-regional transfers of water (by pipeline and river)

□ Proposed estuary storage site

▽ Proposed groundwater storage site

Principal sources of groundwater (porous and jointed aquifers)

1 : 7 000 000

Drought orders by Environment Agency Region 1980 – 1995

Anglian	4	Southern	74
North East	57	South West	99
North West	84	Thames	5
Midlands	12	Welsh	41

Major reservoirs (with capacity in million m³)

England
1	Kielder Res.	198
2	Rutland Water	123
3	Haweswater	85
4	Grafham Water	59
5	Cow Green Res.	41
6	Thirlmere	41
7	Carsington Res.	36
8	Roadford Res.	35
9	Bewl Water Res.	31
10	Colliford Lake	29
11	Ladybower Res.	28
12	Hanningfield Res.	27
13	Abberton Res.	25
14	Draycote Water	23
15	Derwent Res.	22
16	Grimwith Res.	22
17	Wimbleball Lake	21
18	Chew Valley Lake	20
19	Balderhead Res.	20
20	Thames Valley (linked reservoirs)	
21	Lea Valley (linked reservoirs)	
22	Longendale (linked reservoirs)	

Wales
23	Elan Valley	9?
24	Llyn Celyn	7?
25	Llyn Brianne	62
26	Llyn Brenig	6?
27	Llyn Vyrnwy	6?
28	Llyn Clywedog	4?
29	Llandegfedd Res.	22

Scotland
30	Loch Lomond	8?
31	Loch Katrine	6?
32	Megget Res.	6?
33	Loch Ness	2?
34	Blackwater Res.	2?
35	Daer Res.	2?
36	Carron Valley Res.	2?

Ireland
37	Poulaphouca Res.	168
38	Inishcarra Res.	57
39	Carrigadrohid Res.	3?

Average daily domestic water use in England and Wales

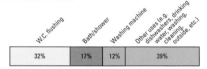

W.C. flushing	Bath/shower	Washing machine	Other uses (e.g. dishwashers, drinking water, washing, cleaning, outside, etc.)
32%	17%	12%	39%

Water abstractions in England and Wales (1995) 55 970 megalitres per day* of which:

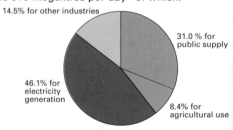

- 14.5% for other industries
- 31.0 % for public supply
- 46.1% for electricity generation
- 8.4% for agricultural use

*average daily domestic consumption per head 380 litres.

WATER ABSTRACTIONS   1 : 12 000 000

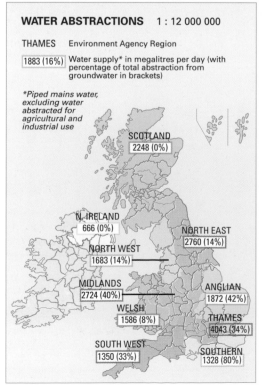

THAMES   Environment Agency Region

1883 (16%)   Water supply* in megalitres per day (with percentage of total abstraction from groundwater in brackets)

*Piped mains water, excluding water abstracted for agricultural and industrial use

- SCOTLAND 2248 (0%)
- N. IRELAND 666 (0%)
- NORTH EAST 2760 (14%)
- NORTH WEST 1683 (14%)
- MIDLANDS 2724 (40%)
- ANGLIAN 1872 (42%)
- WELSH 1586 (8%)
- THAMES 4043 (34%)
- SOUTH WEST 1350 (33%)
- SOUTHERN 1328 (80%)

WATER QUALITY   1 : 12 000 000

The percentage of all rivers and canals of poor or bad quality within each Environment Agency Region 1993 – 1995

- Over 15%
- 10% – 15%
- 5% – 10%
- Under 5%

The percentage of bathing beaches complying with E.C. standards in 1996

- Over 95%
- 75% – 95%
- Under 75%

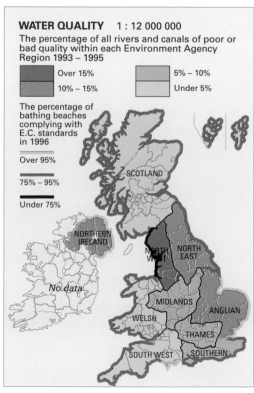

No data

SCOTLAND

NORTHERN IRELAND

NORTH WEST NORTH EAST

MIDLANDS ANGLIAN

WELSH

THAMES

SOUTH WEST SOUTHERN

SOILS   1 : 12 000 000

- Calcareous brown earth
- Brown earth
- Acid brown earth
- Podsol
- Peaty podsol
- Grey-brown podso?
- Gley
- Basin peat and alluvial gleys
- Peaty gley and blanket peat

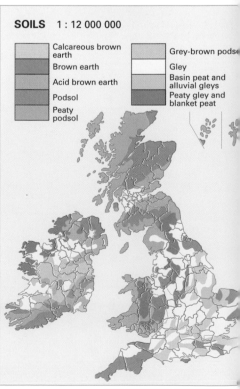

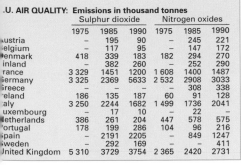

.U. AIR QUALITY: Emissions in thousand tonnes

	Sulphur dioxide			Nitrogen oxides		
	1975	1985	1990	1975	1985	1990
ustria	–	195	90	–	245	221
elgium	–	117	95	–	147	172
enmark	418	339	183	182	294	270
inland	–	382	260	–	252	290
rance	3 329	1451	1200	1 608	1400	1487
ermany	3 325	2369	5633	2 532	2908	3033
reece	–	–	–	–	308	338
eland	186	135	187	60	91	128
aly	3 250	2244	1682	1 499	1736	2041
uxembourg	–	17	10	–	22	–
etherlands	386	261	204	447	578	575
ortugal	178	199	286	104	96	216
pain	–	2191	2205	–	849	1247
weden	–	292	169	–	–	411
United Kingdom	5 310	3729	3754	2 365	2420	2731

FORESTRY   1 : 12 000 000

The percentage of the total area covered by woodland and forest

- Over 20%
- 15% – 20%
- 10% – 15%
- 5% – 10%
- Under 5%
- △ 50%-80% coniferous
- △ Over 80% coniferous

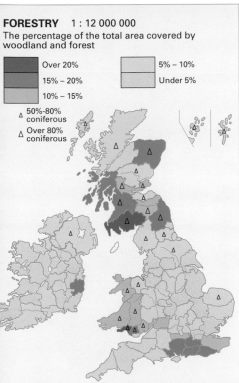

NATURAL VEGETATION   1 : 12 000 000

The plant cover associated with a particular environment if it is unaffected by human activity

- Oak
- Beech and Oak
- Ash and Oak
- Birch and Oakwood
- Scots Pine
- Heath, moorland, water meadows, fen, bog and marsh

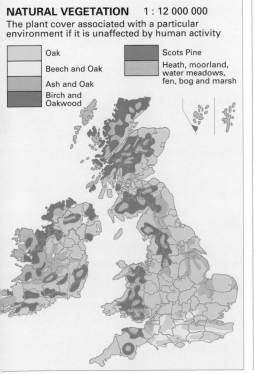

ACID RAIN   1 : 12 000 000

Average acidity of precipitation in the U.K. (pH scale)

- 4.29 and under (most acidic)
- 4.30 – 4.39
- 4.40 – 4.49
- 4.50 – 4.59
- 4.60 – 4.69
- 4.70 – 4.79
- 4.80 and over (least acidic)

No data

E.S.As.
Environmentally Sensitive Areas in the U.K.

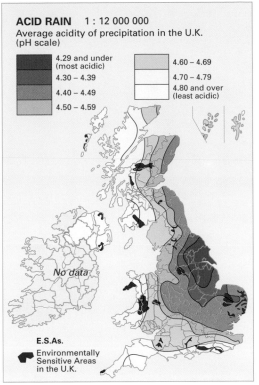

AIR QUALITY   1 : 12 000 000

Hourly average of tropospheric ozone (O$_3$) exceeding 100 parts per billion (summer 1990)*

- Over 45
- 30 – 45
- 15 – 30
- Under 15

Ground-level concentrations of smoke in the U.K., by region
U.K. average: 12 micrograms per m^3

- Less than the U.K. average
- More than the U.K. average
- Over 3x the U.K. average

SCOTLAND
NORTHERN IRELAND
NORTH
YORKSHIRE AND HUMBERSIDE
NORTH WEST
EAST MIDLANDS
WALES
WEST MIDLANDS
EAST ANGLIA
SOUTH WEST
SOUTH EAST

* W.H.O. recommends 75-100 ppb maximum

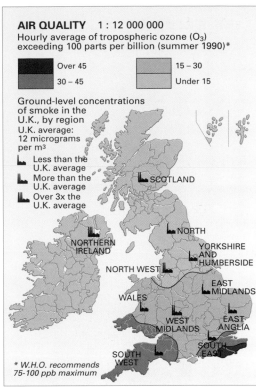

CONSERVATION

- National Parks
- Areas of Outstanding Natural Beauty
- National Scenic Areas
- Forest Parks and Special Protected Areas
- Green Belts (and the urban areas they surround)
- Heritage Coast (England and Wales)/Coastal Conservation Zones (Scotland)

1 : 7 000 000

N. W Sutherland
Assynt-Coigach
South Lewis, Harris and North Uist
Wester Ross
South Uist Machair
Cuillin Hills
Glen Affric
Cairngorms
Deeside
Ben Nevis and Glencoe
Loch Rannoch and Glen Lyon
Argyll
Loch Lomond
Jura
Kyles of Bute
North Arran
Hoy and West Mainland
Shetland

Glenveagh
Antrim Coast and Glens
Sperrin
Galloway Forest Park
The Border Forest Park
Northumberland
North Pennines
Lake District
Yorkshire Dales
North York Moors
Forest of Bowland
Mourne
Connemara
Lincolnshire Wolds
Peak District
Norfolk Coast
Snowdonia
The Broads
Shropshire Hills
Suffolk Coast and Heaths
Killarney
Pembrokeshire Coast
Brecon Beacons
Cotswolds
Chilterns
North Wessex Downs
Surrey Hills
Kent Downs
Exmoor
Cranborne Chase and Wiltshire Downs
New Forest
South Downs
High Weald
North Devon
Dorset
Isle of Wight
Dartmoor
Cornwall
South Devon

✴ World Heritage Sites in the U.K.

(also designated, but not shown, St. Kilda, Outer Hebrides and Henderson Island, South Pacific Ocean)

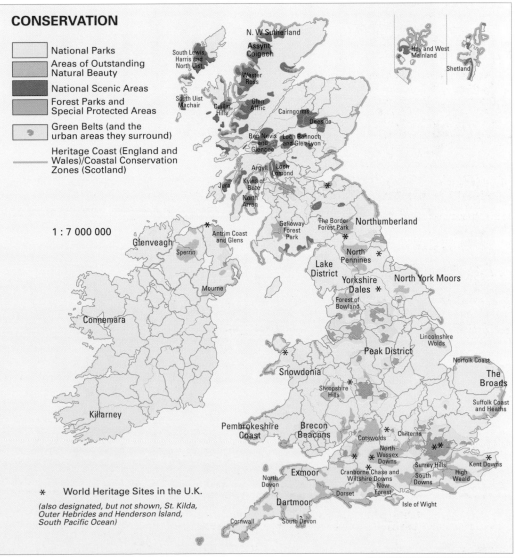

TYPES OF FARM

- Dairy cattle
- Beef cattle
- Sheep
- ● Pigs and/or Poultry
- Mixed farming
- Market gardening (fruit and vegetables)
- Cereals
- Other crops (mainly potatoes, sugar beet)
- Northern limit of 9 month growing season
- Forests
- Built-up areas

1 : 7 000 000

Areas with over 1000mm rainfall per year

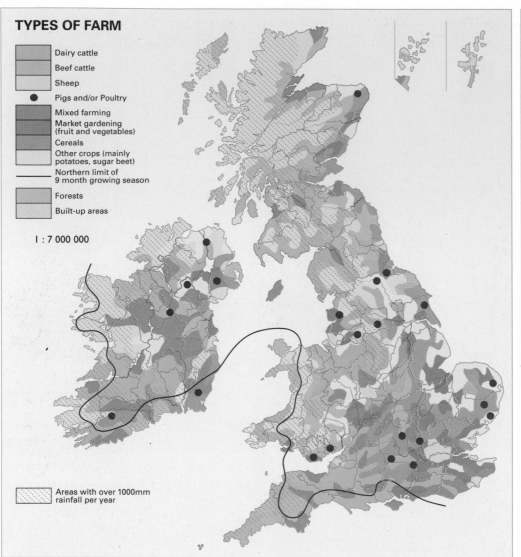

LAND UNDER AGRICULTURE 1 : 12 000 000

The percentage of the total land area used for farming in 1995

- Over 80%
- 60% – 80%
- 40% – 60%
- 20% – 40%
- 0 – 20%

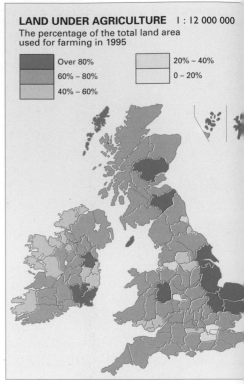

AGRICULTURAL LAND USE 1995 (U.K. only)

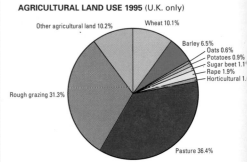

Other agricultural land 10.2%
Wheat 10.1%
Barley 6.5%
Oats 0.6%
Potatoes 0.9%
Sugar beet 1.1%
Rape 1.9%
Horticultural 1.
Rough grazing 31.3%
Pasture 36.4%

WHEAT 1 : 12 000 000

The percentage of the total farmland used for growing wheat in 1995

- Over 40%
- 30% – 40%
- 20% – 30%
- 10% – 20%
- 0 – 10%

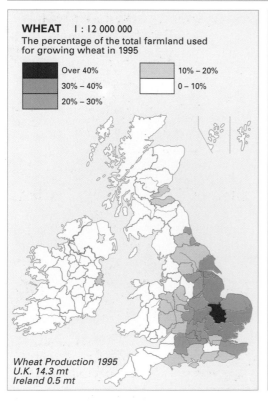

Wheat Production 1995
U.K. 14.3 mt
Ireland 0.5 mt

BARLEY 1 : 12 000 000

The percentage of the total farmland used for growing barley in 1995

- Over 20%
- 10% – 20%
- 0 – 10%

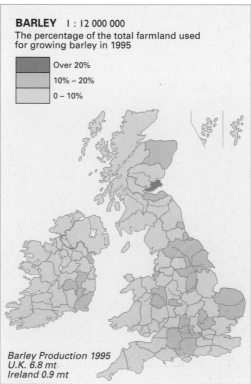

Barley Production 1995
U.K. 6.8 mt
Ireland 0.9 mt

PASTURE 1 : 12 000 000

The percentage of the total farmland used for grazing livestock in 1995

- 80% – 100%
- 60% – 80%
- 40% – 60%
- 20% – 40%
- 0 – 20%

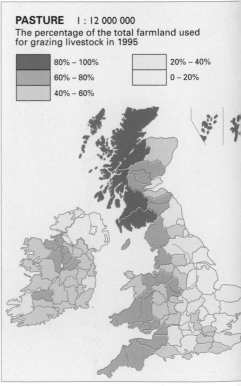

NUMBER AND SIZE OF AGRICULTURAL HOLDINGS IN THE U.K.

Average size of holdings (hectares)

	1940	1980	1995
England & Wales	33.8	60.2	61.7
Scotland	81.8	96.2	160.2
Northern Ireland	13.7	24.2	35.9

Over 100 hectares
50 – 100 hectares
40 – 50 hectares
20 – 40 hectares
5 – 20 hectares
2 – 5 hectares
Under 2 hectares

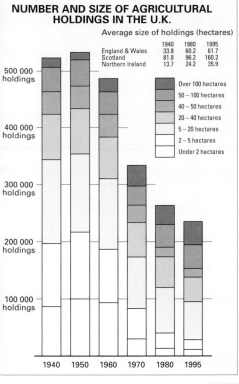

500 000 holdings
400 000 holdings
300 000 holdings
200 000 holdings
100 000 holdings

1940 1950 1960 1970 1980 1995

POTATOES   1 : 12 000 000

The percentage of the total farmland used for growing potatoes in 1995

Over 3%
2% – 3%
1% – 2%
Under 1%

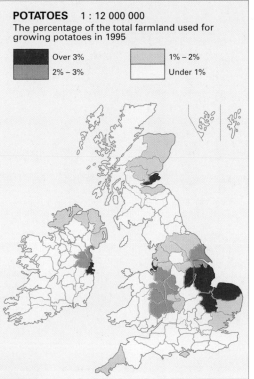

MARKET GARDENING   1 : 12 000 000

The percentage of the total farmland used for market gardening in 1995

Over 4%
3% – 4%
2% – 3%
1% – 2%
Under 1%

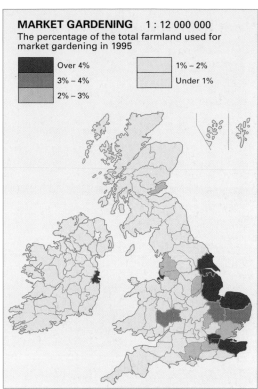

FISHING

Quantities of fish landed at major ports (port districts in Scotland) in 1995

('000 tonnes)
100
50
25
10
5

Type of fish landed

Demersal (Deep Sea Fish)
Pelagic (Shallow Water Fish)
Shellfish

Fishing Regions

IV	North Sea
VIa	West Scotland
VIIa	Irish Sea
VIIb/h/j	W. Ireland & Sole Bank
VIId/e	English Channel
VIIf/g	Bristol Ch. & S. E. Ireland

Fish landed according to region of capture (1995)

Demersal
Pelagic

1 fish represents 10 000 tonnes caught

Region boundary

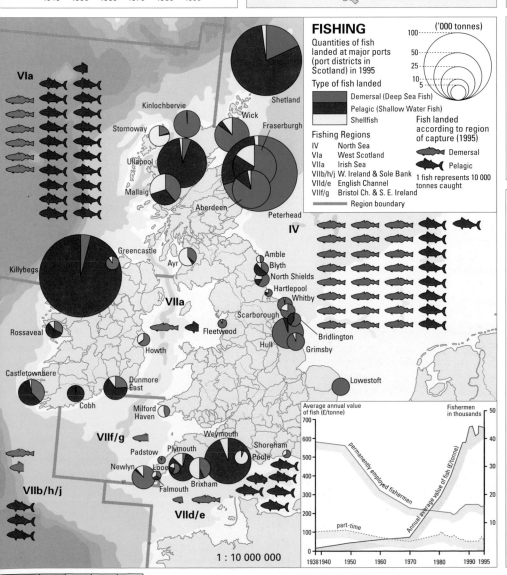

VIa

Kinlochbervie
Shetland
Wick
Stornoway
Fraserburgh
Ullapool
Mallaig
Aberdeen
Peterhead
Greencastle
IV
Killybegs
Ayr
Amble
Blyth
North Shields
Hartlepool
Whitby
Rossaveal
Scarborough
VIIa
Fleetwood
Bridlington
Howth
Hull
Grimsby
Castletownbere
Dunmore East
Lowestoft
Cobh
Milford Haven
VIIf/g
Weymouth
Shoreham
Padstow
Plymouth
Poole
Newlyn
Looe
VIIb/h/j
Brixham
Falmouth
VIId/e

1 : 10 000 000

1000 500 200 100 50 m

Average annual value of fish (£/tonne)

permanently employed fishermen

Fishermen in thousands

Annual average value of fish (£/tonne)

part-time

1938 1940 1950 1960 1970 1980 1990 1995

VALUE OF AGRICULTURAL OUTPUT (U.K. only)

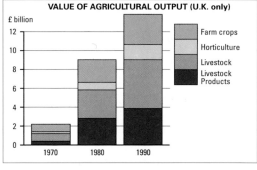

£ billion

Farm crops
Horticulture
Livestock
Livestock Products

12
10
8
6
4
2
0

1970 1980 1990

AGRICULTURAL LAND & LIVESTOCK, 1970-90 (U.K. only)

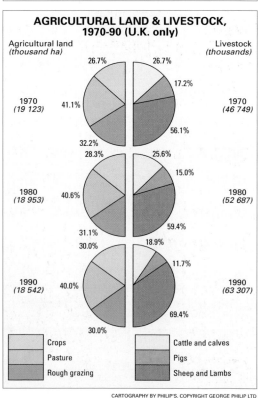

Agricultural land (thousand ha)

Livestock (thousands)

1970 (19 123)
26.7% 41.1% 32.2%

1970 (46 749)
26.7% 17.2% 56.1%

1980 (18 953)
28.3% 40.6% 31.1%

1980 (52 687)
25.6% 15.0% 59.4%

1990 (18 542)
30.0% 40.0% 30.0%

1990 (63 307)
18.9% 11.7% 69.4%

Crops
Pasture
Rough grazing

Cattle and calves
Pigs
Sheep and Lambs

CARTOGRAPHY BY PHILIP'S. COPYRIGHT GEORGE PHILIP LTD

EMPLOYMENT IN MANUFACTURING

The percentage of the workforce employed in manufacturing in 1996

- Over 30%
- 25% – 30%
- 20% – 25%
- 15% – 20%
- 12.5% – 15%
- Under 12.5%

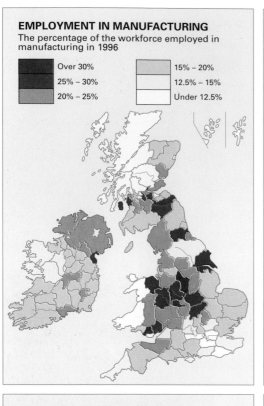

CHANGE IN MANUFACTURING EMPLOYMENT

The percentage change in the number of people employed in manufacturing 1980-89*

- Over 10% gain
- 0 – 10% gain
- 0 – 10% loss
- 10% – 20% loss
- 20% – 30% loss
- Over 30% loss

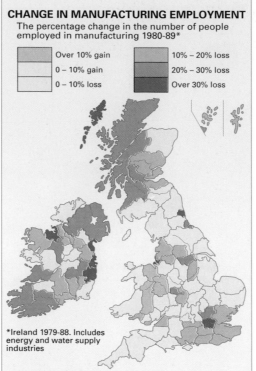

*Ireland 1979-88. Includes energy and water supply industries

LOCATION OF MANUFACTURING INDUSTRY

Heavy Industry
- ▲ Chemicals
- ■ Iron and Steel
- ● Motor vehicles

Light Industry
- ◆ Electrical Engineering

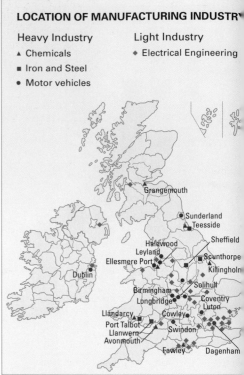

EMPLOYMENT IN AGRICULTURE

The percentage of the workforce employed in agriculture in 1996

- Over 25%
- 10% – 25%
- 2.5% – 10%
- 1% – 2.5%
- 0 – 1%

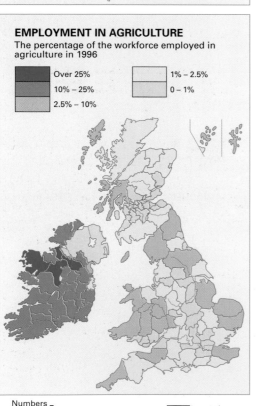

EMPLOYMENT IN SERVICES

The percentage of the workforce employed in the service industry in 1996

- Over 80%
- 70% – 80%
- 60% – 70%
- 50% – 60%
- Less than 50%

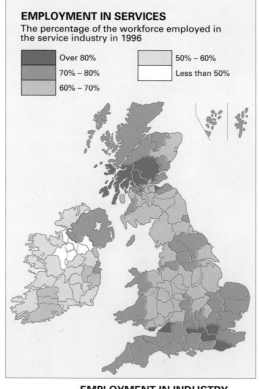

ASSISTED AREAS

These are areas in which extra financial support is focused to encourage economic growth

- Development areas in the U.K.
- Intermediate areas in the U.K.

* Separate legislation applies to the whole of N.Ireland

1 Forres	23 Barnsley
2 Arbroath	24 Doncaster
3 Kirkaldy	25 Mansfield
4 Dunfermline	26 Liverpool
5 Greenock	27 Wigan & St Helens
6 Irvine	28 Wirral
7 Glasgow	29 Holyhead
8 Kilmarnock	30 Wolverhampton
9 Bathgate	31 Birmingham
10 Lanarkshire	32 Fishguard
11 Cumnock & Sanquhar	33 Haverfordwest
12 Girvan	34 South Pembrokeshire
13 Newton Stewart	35 Aberdare
14 Morpeth & Ashington	36 Pontypridd & Rhondda
15 Newcastle-upon-Tyne	37 Merthyr & Rhymney
16 South Tyneside	38 Blaenau Gwent & Abergaven
17 Sunderland	39 Newquay
18 Hartlepool	40 Redruth & Camborne
19 Stockton-on-Tees	41 Penzance & St. Ives
20 Bishop Auckland	42 Helston
21 Middlesbrough	43 Falmouth
22 Rotherham & Mexborough	44 Thanet

EMPLOYMENT IN INDUSTRY

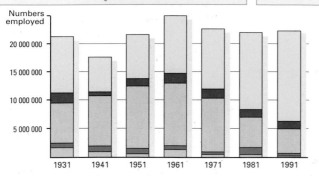

Numbers employed

20 000 000
15 000 000
10 000 000
5 000 000

1931 1941 1951 1961 1971 1981 1991

Employment in the U.K. by industry

- Services
- Transport
- Manufacturing
- Mining & energy supply
- Agriculture, forestry and fishing

1 : 12 000 000

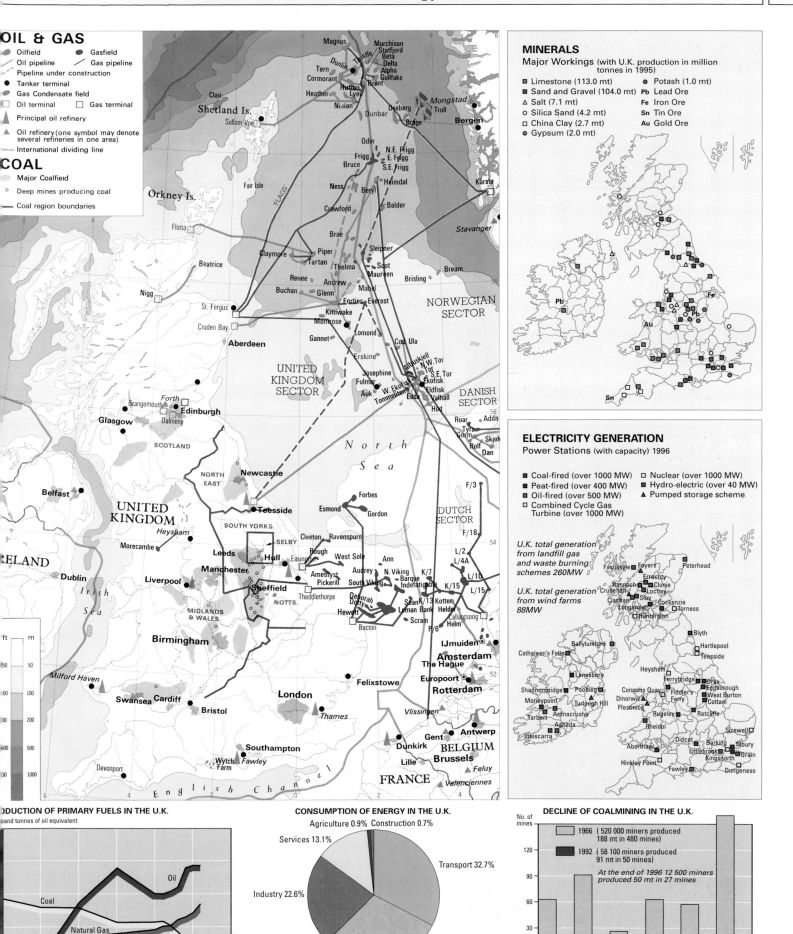

OIL & GAS

- ● Oilfield
- ⬤ Gasfield
- — Oil pipeline
- — Gas pipeline
- -- Pipeline under construction
- ● Tanker terminal
- Gas Condensate field
- ◻ Oil terminal
- ◻ Gas terminal
- ▲ Principal oil refinery
- ▲ Oil refinery (one symbol may denote several refineries in one area)
- — International dividing line

COAL

- Major Coalfield
- ○ Deep mines producing coal
- — Coal region boundaries

MINERALS
Major Workings (with U.K. production in million tonnes in 1995)

- ■ Limestone (113.0 mt)
- ■ Sand and Gravel (104.0 mt)
- △ Salt (7.1 mt)
- ○ Silica Sand (4.2 mt)
- ◻ China Clay (2.7 mt)
- ◉ Gypsum (2.0 mt)
- ● Potash (1.0 mt)
- **Pb** Lead Ore
- **Fe** Iron Ore
- **Sn** Tin Ore
- **Au** Gold Ore

ELECTRICITY GENERATION
Power Stations (with capacity) 1996

- ■ Coal-fired (over 1000 MW)
- ■ Peat-fired (over 400 MW)
- ■ Oil-fired (over 500 MW)
- ◻ Combined Cycle Gas Turbine (over 1000 MW)
- ◻ Nuclear (over 1000 MW)
- ■ Hydro-electric (over 40 MW)
- ▲ Pumped storage scheme

U.K. total generation from landfill gas and waste burning schemes 260MW

U.K. total generation from wind farms 88MW

PRODUCTION OF PRIMARY FUELS IN THE U.K.
sand tonnes of oil equivalent

Oil
Coal
Natural Gas
Hydro/Nuclear

1970 1975 1980 1985 1990 1995 1996 2000

CONSUMPTION OF ENERGY IN THE U.K.

- Agriculture 0.9%
- Construction 0.7%
- Services 13.1%
- Transport 32.7%
- Industry 22.6%
- Domestic 29.9%

Total consumption 1996 160.8 million tonnes of oil equivalent

DECLINE OF COALMINING IN THE U.K.

No. of mines

- 1966 (520 000 miners produced 188 mt in 480 mines)
- 1992 (58 100 miners produced 91 mt in 50 mines)

At the end of 1996 12 500 miners produced 50 mt in 27 mines

SCOTLAND | NORTH EAST | SELBY | SOUTH YORKSHIRE | NOTTS | MIDLANDS AND WALES

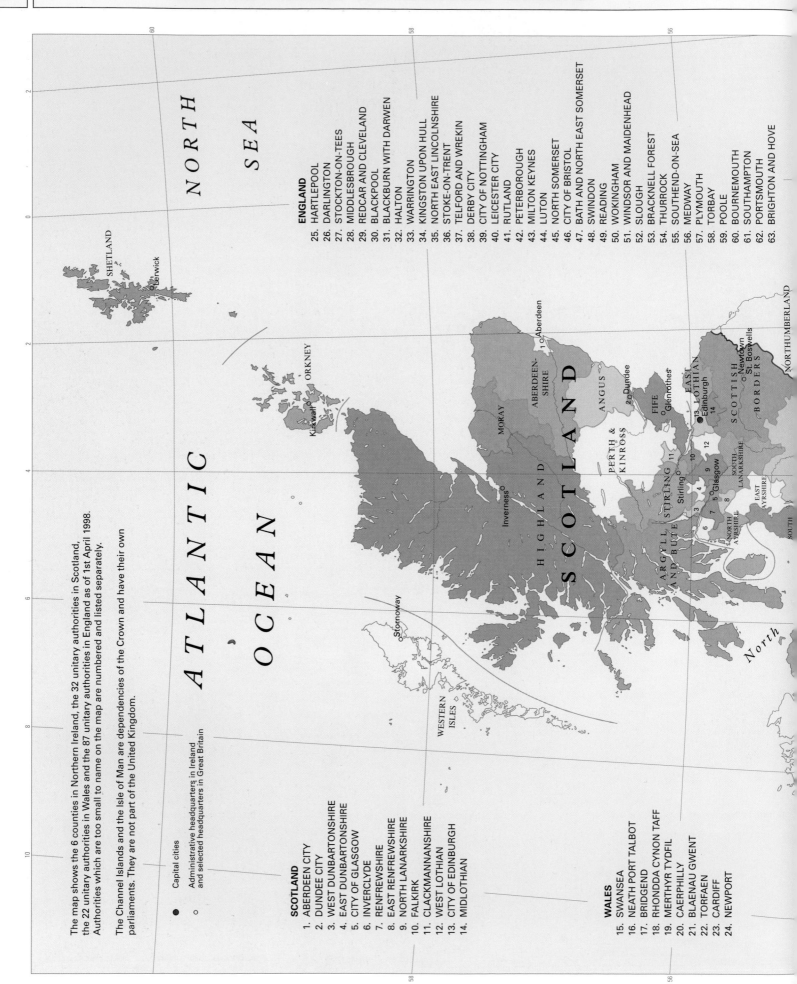

The map shows the 6 counties in Northern Ireland, the 32 unitary authorities in Scotland, the 22 unitary authorities in Wales and the 87 unitary authorities in England as of 1st April 1998. Authorities which are too small to name on the map are numbered and listed separately.

The Channel Islands and the Isle of Man are dependencies of the Crown and have their own parliaments. They are not part of the United Kingdom.

● Capital cities
○ Administrative headquarters in Ireland and selected headquarters in Great Britain

SCOTLAND
1. ABERDEEN CITY
2. DUNDEE CITY
3. WEST DUNBARTONSHIRE
4. EAST DUNBARTONSHIRE
5. CITY OF GLASGOW
6. INVERCLYDE
7. RENFREWSHIRE
8. EAST RENFREWSHIRE
9. NORTH LANARKSHIRE
10. FALKIRK
11. CLACKMANNANSHIRE
12. WEST LOTHIAN
13. CITY OF EDINBURGH
14. MIDLOTHIAN

WALES
15. SWANSEA
16. NEATH PORT TALBOT
17. BRIDGEND
18. RHONDDA CYNON TAFF
19. MERTHYR TYDFIL
20. CAERPHILLY
21. BLAENAU GWENT
22. TORFAEN
23. CARDIFF
24. NEWPORT

ENGLAND
25. HARTLEPOOL
26. DARLINGTON
27. STOCKTON-ON-TEES
28. MIDDLESBROUGH
29. REDCAR AND CLEVELAND
30. BLACKPOOL
31. BLACKBURN WITH DARWEN
32. HALTON
33. WARRINGTON
34. KINGSTON UPON HULL
35. NORTH EAST LINCOLNSHIRE
36. STOKE-ON-TRENT
37. TELFORD AND WREKIN
38. DERBY CITY
39. CITY OF NOTTINGHAM
40. LEICESTER CITY
41. RUTLAND
42. PETERBOROUGH
43. MILTON KEYNES
44. LUTON
45. NORTH SOMERSET
46. CITY OF BRISTOL
47. BATH AND NORTH EAST SOMERSET
48. SWINDON
49. READING
50. WOKINGHAM
51. WINDSOR AND MAIDENHEAD
52. SLOUGH
53. BRACKNELL FOREST
54. THURROCK
55. SOUTHEND-ON-SEA
56. MEDWAY
57. PLYMOUTH
58. TORBAY
59. POOLE
60. BOURNEMOUTH
61. SOUTHAMPTON
62. PORTSMOUTH
63. BRIGHTON AND HOVE

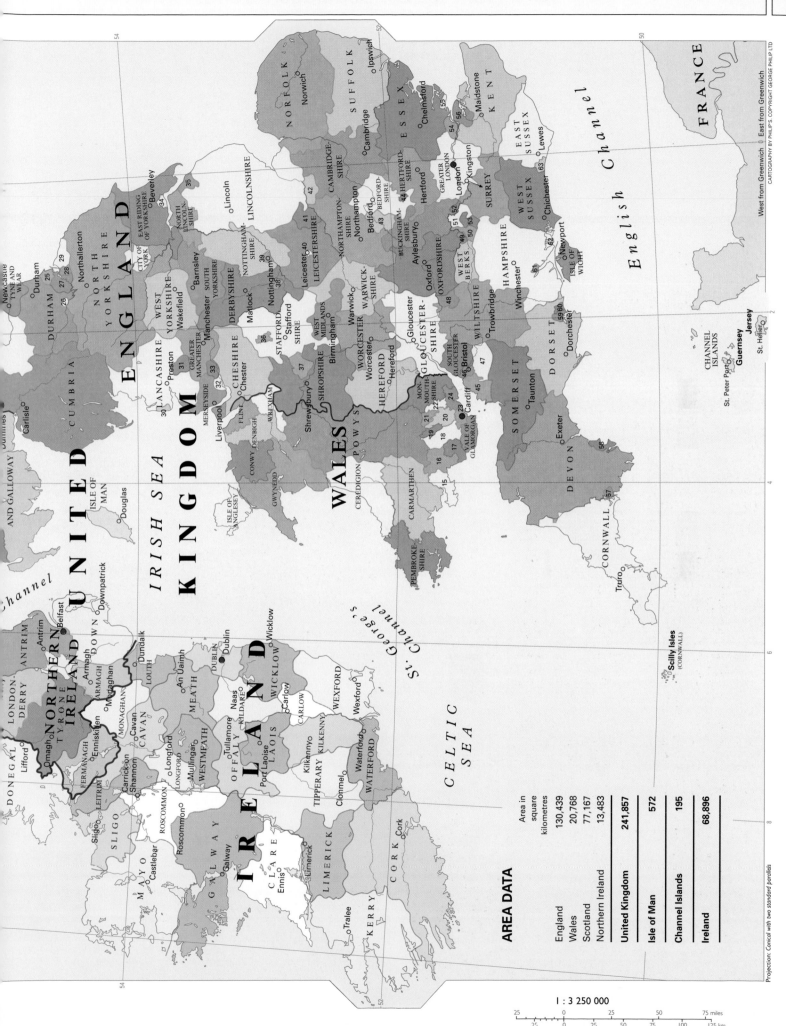

FRANCE

UNITED KINGDOM

ENGLAND

WALES

KINGDOM

IRELAND

NORTHERN IRELAND

English Channel

IRISH SEA

St. George's Channel

CELTIC SEA

Channel

POWYS

CUMBRIA

DURHAM

NORTH YORKSHIRE

WEST YORKSHIRE

SOUTH YORKSHIRE

NORTH LINCOLNSHIRE

LINCOLNSHIRE

NORFOLK

SUFFOLK

ESSEX

KENT

EAST SUSSEX

WEST SUSSEX

SURREY

GREATER LONDON

HERTFORD-SHIRE

BEDFORD-SHIRE

NORTHAMPTON-SHIRE

CAMBRIDGE-SHIRE

LEICESTERSHIRE

NOTTINGHAM-SHIRE

DERBYSHIRE

STAFFORD-SHIRE

CHESHIRE

GREATER MANCHESTER

LANCASHIRE

MERSEYSIDE

SHROPSHIRE

WEST MIDLANDS

WARWICK-SHIRE

WORCESTER-SHIRE

HEREFORD

GLOUCESTER-SHIRE

SOUTH GLOUCESTER

OXFORDSHIRE

BUCKINGHAM-SHIRE

WEST BERKS

HAMPSHIRE

WILTSHIRE

SOMERSET

DORSET

DEVON

CORNWALL

ISLE OF WIGHT

MON-MOUTH-SHIRE

CEREDIGION

CARMARTHEN

PEMBROKE-SHIRE

GWYNEDD

CONWY

DENBIGH

FLINT

WREXHAM

ISLE OF ANGLESEY

VALE OF GLAMORGAN

TYNE AND WEAR

Newcastle
Durham
Northallerton
Beverley
Lincoln
Norwich
Ipswich
Cambridge
Chelmsford
Maidstone
Lewes
Chichester
Newport
Hertford
Bedford
Northampton
Aylesbury
Oxford
London
Kingston
Winchester
Trowbridge
Dorchester
Taunton
Exeter
Truro
Bristol
Gloucester
Worcester
Hereford
Birmingham
Warwick
Stafford
Matlock
Nottingham
Barnsley
Wakefield
Preston
Manchester
Chester
Liverpool
Shrewsbury
Cardiff
Carlisle
Douglas

ISLE OF MAN

Belfast
Antrim
Downpatrick
Armagh
Omagh
Lifford
Enniskillen
Monaghan
Downpatrick

LONDON-DERRY
TYRONE
ANTRIM
DOWN
ARMAGH
FERMANAGH

DONEGAL
SLIGO
LEITRIM
CAVAN
MONAGHAN
MAYO
ROSCOMMON
LONGFORD
WESTMEATH
MEATH
LOUTH
GALWAY
OFFALY
LAOIS
KILDARE
DUBLIN
WICKLOW
CLARE
TIPPERARY
KILKENNY
CARLOW
WEXFORD
LIMERICK
KERRY
CORK
WATERFORD

Dublin
Naas
Dundalk
An Uaimh
Tullamore
Mullingar
Longford
Carrick-on-Shannon
Sligo
Castlebar
Roscommon
Galway
Ennis
Tralee
Limerick
Cork
Waterford
Clonmel
Kilkenny
Carlow
Wexford
Wicklow
Port Laoise

CHANNEL ISLANDS
Guernsey
Jersey
St. Peter Port
St. Helier

Scilly Isles (CORNWALL)

AREA DATA	Area in square kilometres
England	130,439
Wales	20,768
Scotland	77,167
Northern Ireland	13,483
United Kingdom	**241,857**
Isle of Man	572
Channel Islands	195
Ireland	68,896

1 : 3 250 000

miles 25 0 25 50 75 miles

25 0 25 50 75 100 125 km

Projection: Conical with two standard parallels

West from Greenwich 0 East from Greenwich

CARTOGRAPHY BY PHILIP'S. COPYRIGHT GEORGE PHILIP LTD

POPULATION DENSITY 1891

See map at right for reference to colours

Density in 1891 by country :
U.K. 142 people per km²
Ireland 49 people per km²

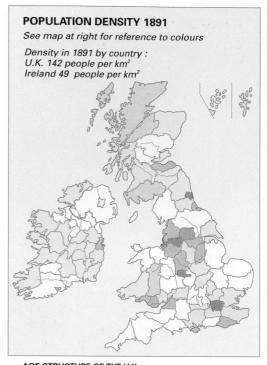

POPULATION DENSITY 1995

Persons per km²

	Over 1000
	500 – 1000
	200 – 500
	100 – 200
	50 – 100
	25 – 50
	Under 25

The density for the whole of the U.K. is 241 people per km², the density for Ireland is 53.

1 : 7 000 000

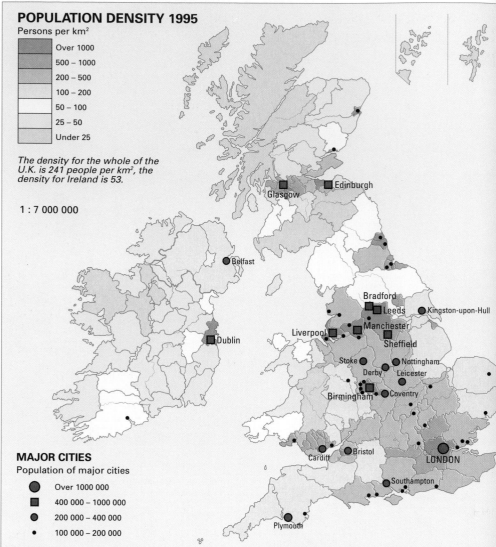

MAJOR CITIES
Population of major cities

●	Over 1000 000
■	400 000 – 1000 000
●	200 000 – 400 000
•	100 000 – 200 000

AGE STRUCTURE OF THE U.K.

The bars represent the percentage of males and the percentage of females in the age group shown

☐ 1901   ☐ 1990   — Projected 2150

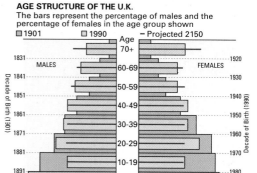

YOUNG PEOPLE   1 : 12 000 000

The percentage of the population under 15 years old in 1995 (Ireland 1991)

	Over 30%		19% – 20%
	25% – 30%		18% – 19%
	20% – 25%		Under 18%

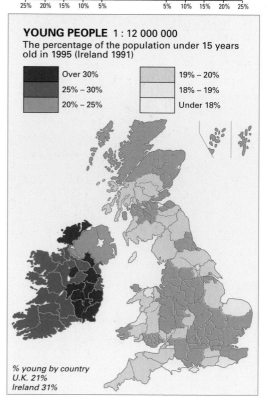

% young by country
U.K. 21%
Ireland 31%

OLD PEOPLE   1 : 12 000 000

The percentage of the population over pensionable age* in 1995 (Ireland 1991)

	Over 20%		12.5% – 15%
	17.5% – 20%		10% – 12.5%
	15% – 17.5%		Under 10%

*Pensionable age is 65 for males, 60 for females

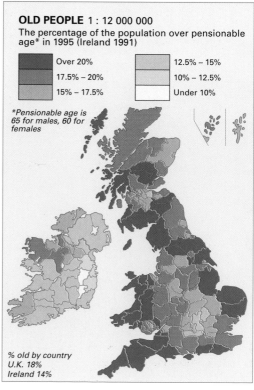

% old by country
U.K. 18%
Ireland 14%

URBANIZATION   1 : 12 000 000

The percentage of the population living in towns and cities (latest available year)

	Over 90%		60% – 70%
	80% – 90%		50% – 60%
	70% – 80%		Under 50%

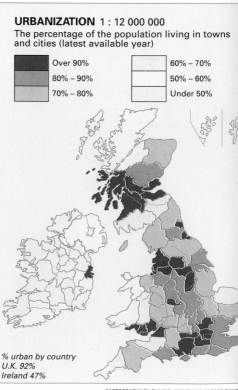

% urban by country
U.K. 92%
Ireland 47%

NATURAL POPULATION CHANGE

The difference between the number of births and the number of deaths per thousand inhabitants in 1995

- Over 10 more births
- 5 – 10 more births
- 2.5 – 5 more births
- 0 – 2.5 more births
- 0 – 2.5 more deaths
- Over 2.5 more deaths

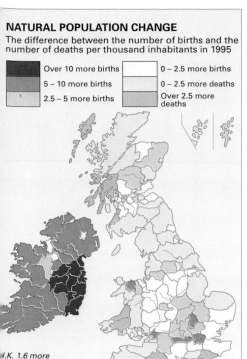

U.K. 1.6 more births than deaths
Ireland 22.7 more births than deaths

ETHNIC GROUP

Ethnic minorities as a % of total population in 1995/1996

- Over 6%
- 4% – 6%
- 2% – 4%
- 0 – 2%

Ethnic minority groups

- Indian/ Pakistani/ Bangladeshi
- W. Indian/ African
- Other

77 000 Total number of ethnic minority people in each region

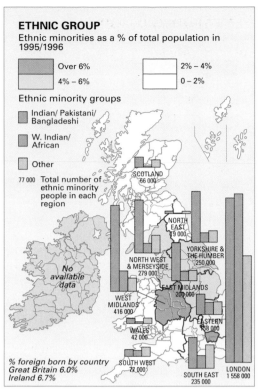

SCOTLAND 66 000

NORTH EAST 9 000

YORKSHIRE & THE HUMBER 250 000

NORTH WEST & MERSEYSIDE 279 000

EAST MIDLANDS 200 000

WEST MIDLANDS 416 000

EASTERN 58 000

WALES 42 000

No available data

SOUTH WEST 77 000

SOUTH EAST 235 000

LONDON 1 558 000

% foreign born by country
Great Britain 6.0%
Ireland 6.7%

MIGRATION 1 : 12 000 000

The difference between the number moving in and the number moving away (per 1000 inhabitants)*

- Over 15 moved in
- 10 – 15 moved in
- 5 – 10 moved in
- 0 – 5 moved in
- 0 – 5 moved away
- 5 – 10 moved away

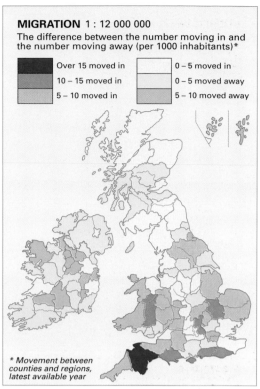

* Movement between counties and regions, latest available year

U.K. VITAL STATISTICS, 1900-2000

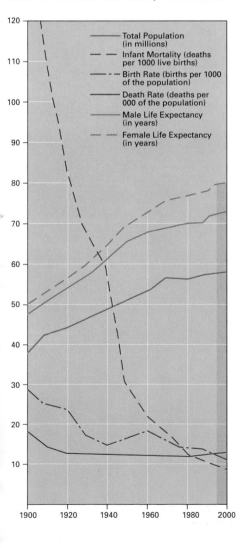

- Total Population (in millions)
- Infant Mortality (deaths per 1000 live births)
- Birth Rate (births per 1000 of the population)
- Death Rate (deaths per 000 of the population)
- Male Life Expectancy (in years)
- Female Life Expectancy (in years)

POPULATION CHANGE 1961-1991

The percentage change in the number of people between 1961 and 1991

- Over 30% gain
- 25% – 30% gain
- 20% – 25% gain
- 15% – 20% gain
- 10% – 15% gain
- 5% – 10% gain
- 0 – 5% gain

- 0 – 5% loss
- 5% – 10% loss
- Over 10% loss

1 : 7 000 000

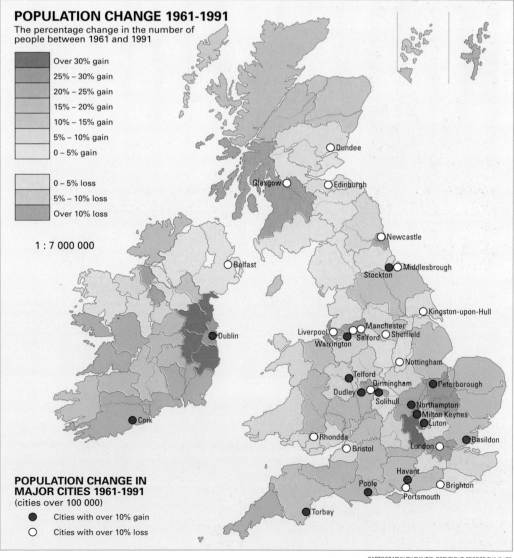

Dundee
Glasgow
Edinburgh
Newcastle
Belfast
Middlesbrough
Stockton
Kingston-upon-Hull
Liverpool
Manchester
Salford
Sheffield
Warrington
Nottingham
Dublin
Telford
Birmingham
Peterborough
Dudley
Solihull
Northampton
Milton Keynes
Luton
Rhondda
London
Basildon
Bristol
Cork
Havant
Poole
Brighton
Portsmouth
Torbay

POPULATION CHANGE IN MAJOR CITIES 1961-1991

(cities over 100 000)

- Cities with over 10% gain
- Cities with over 10% loss

HOUSE OWNERSHIP

The percentage of dwellings which are owner-occupied in 1990 (Ireland 1985)

- Over 80%
- 70% – 80%
- 60% – 70%
- 50% – 60%
- Under 50%

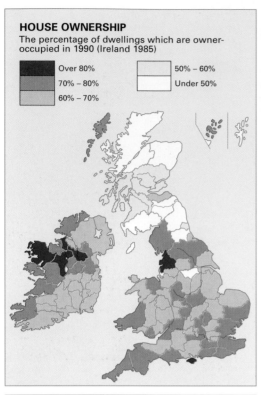

CAR OWNERSHIP

The number of new* cars per thousand people in 1990

- Over 50
- 40 – 50
- 30 – 40
- 20 – 30
- 10 – 20

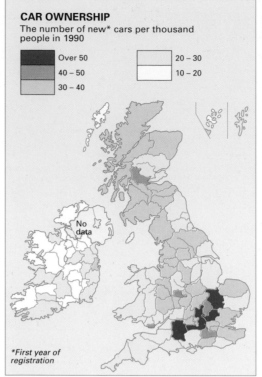

No data

*First year of registration

INCOME

The average gross weekly earnings of males and females in full employment in 1996 (U.K. only)*

- Over £400
- £375 – £400
- £350 – £375
- £325 – £350
- £300 – £325
- Under £300

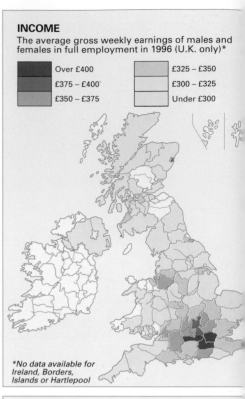

*No data available for Ireland, Borders, Islands or Hartlepool

HEALTH

The number of doctors per 100 000 people (by health authority, latest available year)

- Over 90
- 80 – 90
- 70 – 80
- 60 – 70
- 50 – 60
- Under 50

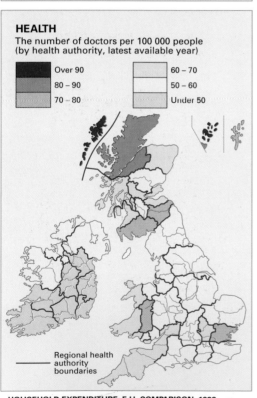

— Regional health authority boundaries

EDUCATION

The percentage of pupils aged 16 staying on in education in 1994/1995 (U.K. only)

- Over 90%
- 85% – 90%
- 80% – 85%
- 75% – 80%
- 70% – 75%
- Under 70%

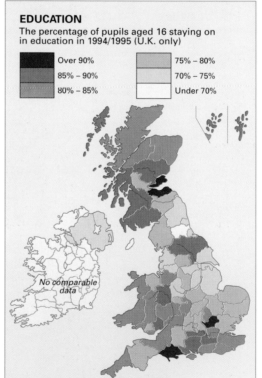

No comparable data

UNEMPLOYMENT

The percentage of the workforce unemployed in 1995 (Ireland 1992)

- Over 15.0%
- 12.5% – 15.0%
- 10.0% – 12.5%
- 7.5% – 10.0%
- 5% – 7.5%
- Under 5.0%

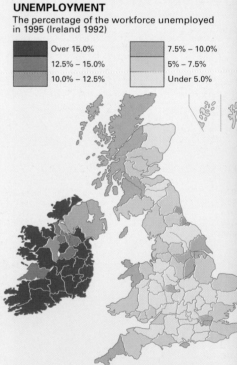

HOUSEHOLD EXPENDITURE: E.U. COMPARISON, 1992

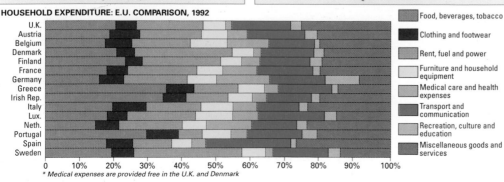

U.K.
Austria
Belgium
Denmark
Finland
France
Germany
Greece
Irish Rep.
Italy
Lux.
Neth.
Portugal
Spain
Sweden

0   10%   20%   30%   40%   50%   60%   70%   80%   90%   100%

* Medical expenses are provided free in the U.K. and Denmark

- Food, beverages, tobacco
- Clothing and footwear
- Rent, fuel and power
- Furniture and household equipment
- Medical care and health expenses
- Transport and communication
- Recreation, culture and education
- Miscellaneous goods and services

% OF U.K. HOUSEHOLDS OWNING DOMESTIC APPLIANCES

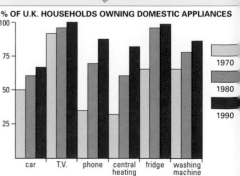

100
75
50
25

car   T.V.   phone   central heating   fridge   washing machine

- 1970
- 1980
- 1990

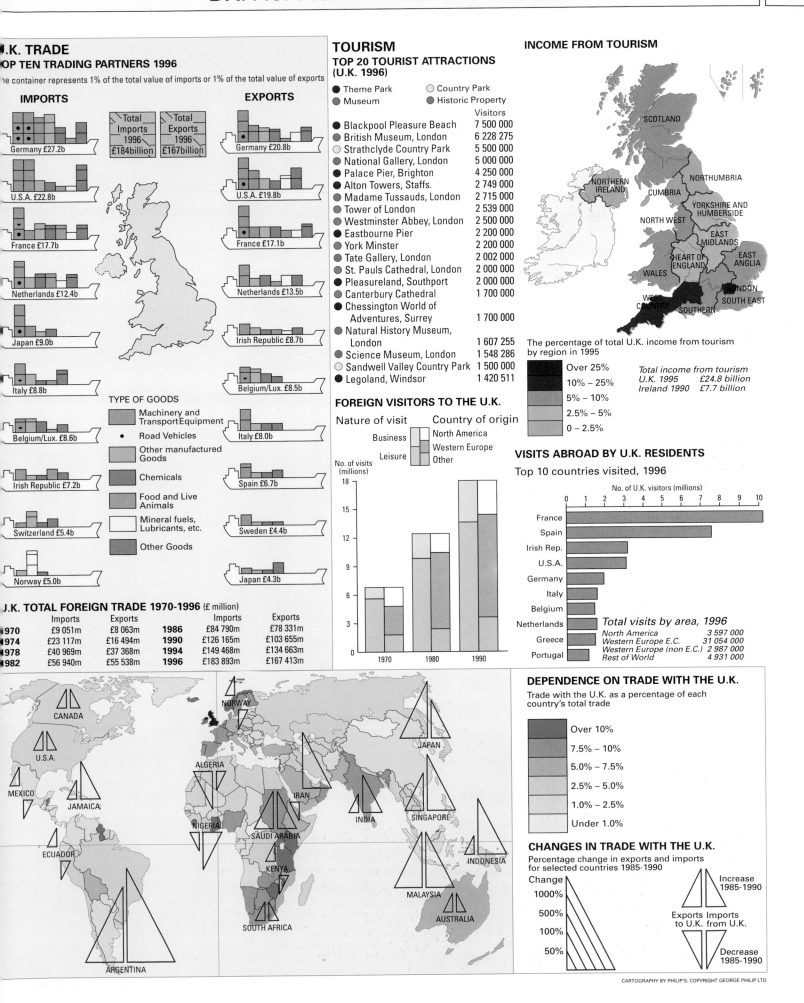

U.K. TRADE
TOP TEN TRADING PARTNERS 1996

The container represents 1% of the total value of imports or 1% of the total value of exports

IMPORTS

Total Imports 1996 £184billion

Total Exports 1996 £167billion

- Germany £27.2b
- U.S.A. £22.8b
- France £17.7b
- Netherlands £12.4b
- Japan £9.0b
- Italy £8.8b
- Belgium/Lux. £8.6b
- Irish Republic £7.2b
- Switzerland £5.4b
- Norway £5.0b

EXPORTS

- Germany £20.8b
- U.S.A. £19.8b
- France £17.1b
- Netherlands £13.5b
- Irish Republic £8.7b
- Belgium/Lux. £8.5b
- Italy £8.0b
- Spain £6.7b
- Sweden £4.4b
- Japan £4.3b

TYPE OF GOODS

- Machinery and Transport Equipment
- • Road Vehicles
- Other manufactured Goods
- Chemicals
- Food and Live Animals
- Mineral fuels, Lubricants, etc.
- Other Goods

U.K. TOTAL FOREIGN TRADE 1970-1996 (£ million)

	Imports	Exports		Imports	Exports
1970	£9 051m	£8 063m	1986	£84 790m	£78 331m
1974	£23 117m	£16 494m	1990	£126 165m	£103 655m
1978	£40 969m	£37 368m	1994	£149 468m	£134 663m
1982	£56 940m	£55 538m	1996	£183 893m	£167 413m

TOURISM
TOP 20 TOURIST ATTRACTIONS (U.K. 1996)

- ● Theme Park
- ● Museum
- ○ Country Park
- ● Historic Property

	Visitors
● Blackpool Pleasure Beach	7 500 000
● British Museum, London	6 228 275
○ Strathclyde Country Park	5 500 000
● National Gallery, London	5 000 000
● Palace Pier, Brighton	4 250 000
● Alton Towers, Staffs.	2 749 000
● Madame Tussauds, London	2 715 000
● Tower of London	2 539 000
● Westminster Abbey, London	2 500 000
● Eastbourne Pier	2 200 000
● York Minster	2 200 000
● Tate Gallery, London	2 002 000
● St. Pauls Cathedral, London	2 000 000
● Pleasureland, Southport	2 000 000
● Canterbury Cathedral	1 700 000
● Chessington World of Adventures, Surrey	1 700 000
● Natural History Museum, London	1 607 255
● Science Museum, London	1 548 286
○ Sandwell Valley Country Park	1 500 000
● Legoland, Windsor	1 420 511

FOREIGN VISITORS TO THE U.K.

Nature of visit
- Business
- Leisure

Country of origin
- North America
- Western Europe
- Other

No. of visits (millions)

1970 1980 1990

INCOME FROM TOURISM

SCOTLAND
NORTHERN IRELAND
NORTHUMBRIA
CUMBRIA
NORTH WEST
YORKSHIRE AND HUMBERSIDE
EAST MIDLANDS
HEART OF ENGLAND
EAST ANGLIA
WALES
WEST COUNTRY
SOUTHERN
LONDON
SOUTH EAST

The percentage of total U.K. income from tourism by region in 1995

- Over 25%
- 10% – 25%
- 5% – 10%
- 2.5% – 5%
- 0 – 2.5%

Total income from tourism
U.K. 1995   £24.8 billion
Ireland 1990   £7.7 billion

VISITS ABROAD BY U.K. RESIDENTS

Top 10 countries visited, 1996

No. of U.K. visitors (millions)
0 1 2 3 4 5 6 7 8 9 10

- France
- Spain
- Irish Rep.
- U.S.A.
- Germany
- Italy
- Belgium
- Netherlands
- Greece
- Portugal

Total visits by area, 1996
North America   3 597 000
Western Europe E.C.   31 054 000
Western Europe (non E.C.) 2 987 000
Rest of World   4 931 000

DEPENDENCE ON TRADE WITH THE U.K.

Trade with the U.K. as a percentage of each country's total trade

- Over 10%
- 7.5% – 10%
- 5.0% – 7.5%
- 2.5% – 5.0%
- 1.0% – 2.5%
- Under 1.0%

CANADA
U.S.A.
MEXICO
JAMAICA
ECUADOR
ARGENTINA
NORWAY
ALGERIA
NIGERIA
SAUDI ARABIA
KENYA
SOUTH AFRICA
IRAN
INDIA
SINGAPORE
MALAYSIA
INDONESIA
JAPAN
AUSTRALIA

CHANGES IN TRADE WITH THE U.K.

Percentage change in exports and imports for selected countries 1985-1990

Change
- 1000%
- 500%
- 100%
- 50%

Increase 1985-1990

Exports Imports to U.K. from U.K.

Decrease 1985-1990

CARTOGRAPHY BY PHILIP'S. COPYRIGHT GEORGE PHILIP LTD

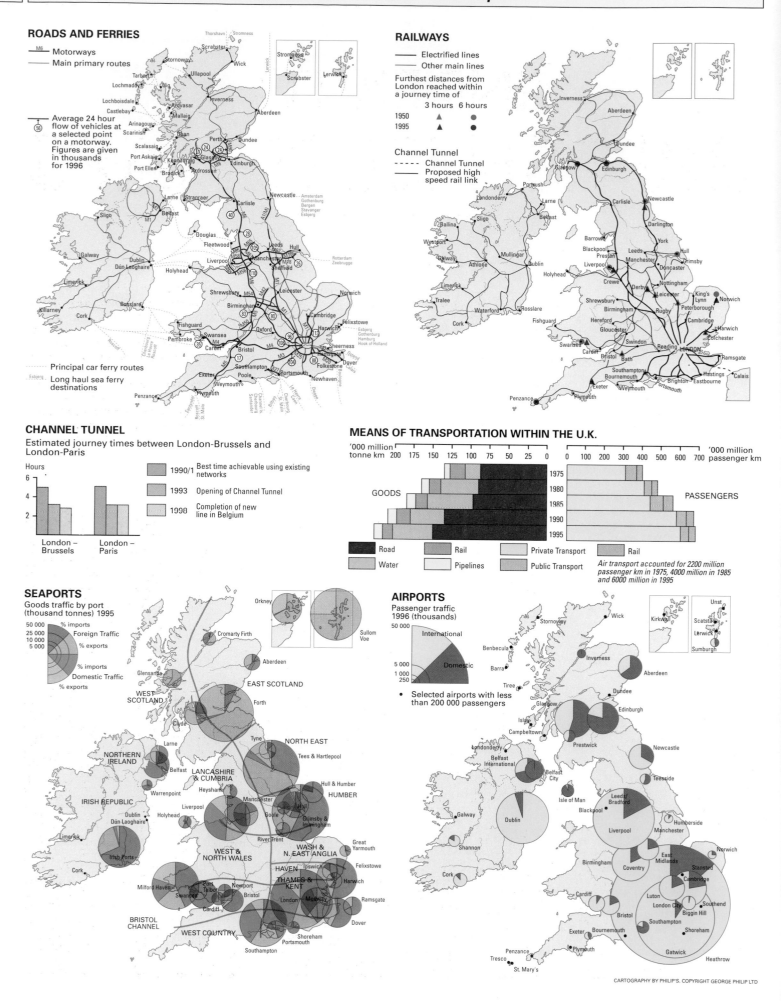

ROADS AND FERRIES

— M6 — Motorways
— Main primary routes

(56) Average 24 hour flow of vehicles at a selected point on a motorway. Figures are given in thousands for 1996

----- Principal car ferry routes
Esbjerg Long haul sea ferry destinations

RAILWAYS

— Electrified lines
— Other main lines

Furthest distances from London reached within a journey time of
 3 hours   6 hours
1950   ▲   ●
1995   ▲   ●

Channel Tunnel
- - - - Channel Tunnel
——— Proposed high speed rail link

CHANNEL TUNNEL

Estimated journey times between London-Brussels and London-Paris

Hours
6
4
2

London – Brussels   London – Paris

■ 1990/1 Best time achievable using existing networks
■ 1993 Opening of Channel Tunnel
□ 1998 Completion of new line in Belgium

MEANS OF TRANSPORTATION WITHIN THE U.K.

'000 million tonne km 200 175 150 125 100 75 50 25 0   0 100 200 300 400 500 600 700 '000 million passenger km

GOODS   PASSENGERS

1975
1980
1985
1990
1995

■ Road   ■ Rail   □ Private Transport   ■ Rail
□ Water   □ Pipelines   ■ Public Transport

Air transport accounted for 2200 million passenger km in 1975, 4000 million in 1985 and 6000 million in 1995

SEAPORTS

Goods traffic by port (thousand tonnes) 1995

50 000
25 000
10 000
5 000

% imports
Foreign Traffic
% exports

% imports
Domestic Traffic
% exports

AIRPORTS

Passenger traffic 1996 (thousands)

50 000
International
5 000
Domestic
1 000
250

• Selected airports with less than 200 000 passengers

CARTOGRAPHY BY PHILIP'S. COPYRIGHT GEORGE PHILIP LTD

INDEX TO BRITISH ISLES MAPS

This index lists the major placenames which appear on the large-scale maps of the British Isles (pages *2–15* with the yellow band). Placenames for the rest of the world can be found in the World Index, with the turquoise band.

The first number beside each name in the index gives the map page on which that feature or place will be found. The letter and figure immediately after the page number give the grid square within which the feature is situated. The letter represents the latitude and the figure the longitude. In some cases the feature may fall within the specified square, while the name is outside. This is usually the case only with very large features. Rivers are indexed to their mouths or confluence.

The 'geographical co-ordinates' which follow the letter-figure references give the latitude and longitude of each place. The first co-ordinate indicates latitude – the distance north of the Equator. The second co-ordinate indicates longitude – the distance east or west of the Greenwich Meridian. Both latitude and longitude are measured in degrees and minutes (there are 60 minutes in a degree).

Thus the entry in the index for Runcorn reads:

Runcorn............ **7 F3** 53 20N 2 44W

This indicates that Runcorn appears on map page 7 in grid square F3 at latitude 53 degrees, 20 minutes north and at longitude 2 degrees, 44 minutes west. To find Runcorn by using the geographical co-ordinates, look at the edges of the map. The degrees of latitude are indicated by blue figures on the left-hand edge of the map and the degrees of longitude are marked on the bottom edge of the map. Runcorn will be found where lines extended from the two points on the map edge would cross on the map.

An open square □ indicates that the name refers to an administrative unit such as a county or region; rivers are indicated by an arrow →. Names composed of a proper name (Wight) and a description (Isle of) are positioned alphabetically by the proper name. All names beginning St. are alphabetized under Saint. A list of abbreviations used can be found in the World Index at the end of the atlas.

A

Abberton Res. . . . **9 C10** 51 50N 0 52 E
Abbeyfeale **14 D4** 52 23N 9 20W
Aberaeron **10 C5** 52 15N 4 16W
Aberayron =
Aberaeron **10 C5** 52 15N 4 16W
Abercarn **10 D7** 51 39N 3 9W
Aberchirder **3 G12** 57 34N 2 40W
Aberdare **10 D7** 51 43N 3 27W
Aberdeen **3 H13** 57 9N 2 6W
Aberdeenshire □ . **3 H12** 57 17N 2 36W
Aberdovey =
Aberdyfi **10 B5** 52 33N 4 3W
Aberdyfi **10 B5** 52 33N 4 3W
Aberfeldy **5 A8** 56 37N 3 50W
Abergavenny **10 D7** 51 49N 3 1W
Abergele **10 A6** 53 17N 3 35W
Abersychan **10 D7** 51 44N 3 3W
Abertillery **10 D7** 51 44N 3 9W
Aberystwyth **10 C5** 52 25N 4 6W
Abingdon **8 C6** 51 40N 1 17W
Aboyne **3 H12** 57 4N 2 48W
Accrington **7 E4** 53 46N 2 22W
Achill Hd. **12 D1** 53 59N 10 15W
Achill I. **12 D1** 53 58N 10 5W
A'Chralaig **2 H7** 57 11N 5 10W
Adlington **7 E3** 53 36N 2 36W
Adwick le Street . **7 E6** 53 35N 1 12W
Agnews Hill **13 B10** 54 51N 5 55W
Ailsa Craig **4 D5** 55 15N 5 7W
Ainsdale **7 E2** 53 37N 3 2W
Aird Brenish **2 F3** 58 8N 7 8W
Airdrie **5 C8** 55 53N 3 57W
Aire → **7 E7** 53 42N 0 55W
Alcester **8 B5** 52 13N 1 52W
Aldbrough **7 E8** 53 50N 0 7W
Aldeburgh . . . . **9 B12** 52 9N 1 35 E
Alderley Edge . . . **7 F4** 53 18N 2 15W
Alderney **11 H9** 49 42N 2 12W
Aldershot **9 D7** 51 15N 0 43W
Aldridge **7 G5** 52 36N 1 55W
Alexandria **4 C6** 55 59N 4 40W
Alford, *Aberds.* . . **3 H12** 57 13N 2 42W
Alford, *Lincs.* . . . . **7 F9** 53 16N 0 10 E
Alfreton **7 F6** 53 6N 1 22W
Allen, Bog of **15 B9** 53 15N 7 0W
Allen, L. **12 C5** 54 12N 8 5W
Alloa **5 B8** 56 7N 3 49W
Alness **3 G9** 57 41N 4 15W
Alnmouth **6 B5** 55 24N 1 37W
Alnwick **6 B5** 55 25N 1 42W
Alsager **7 F4** 53 7N 2 20W
Alsh, L. **2 H6** 57 15N 5 39W
Alston **6 C4** 54 48N 2 26W
Alton **9 D7** 51 8N 0 59W
Altrincham **7 F4** 53 25N 2 21W
Alva **5 B8** 56 9N 3 49W
Alyth **5 A9** 56 38N 3 15W
Amble **6 B5** 55 20N 1 36W
Ambleside **6 D3** 54 26N 2 58W
Amersham **9 C7** 51 40N 0 38W
Amesbury **8 D5** 51 10N 1 46W
Amlwch **10 A5** 53 24N 4 21W
Ammanford **10 D5** 51 48N 4 0W
Ampthill **9 B8** 52 3N 0 30W
An Teallach **2 G7** 57 49N 5 18W
An Uaimh **13 D8** 53 39N 6 40W
Andover **8 D6** 51 13N 1 29W
Anglesey, Isle of □ **10 A5** 53 16N 4 18W
Angus □ **5 A10** 56 46N 2 56W
Angus, Braes of . . **3 J11** 56 51N 3 10W
Annagh Hd. **12 C1** 54 15N 10 5W
Annalee → **13 C7** 54 3N 7 15W
Annan **5 E9** 54 57N 3 17W
Annan → **5 E9** 54 58N 3 18W
Annandale **5 D9** 55 10N 3 25W
Anstey **7 G6** 52 41N 1 14W
Anstruther **5 B10** 56 14N 2 40W
Antrim **13 B9** 54 43N 6 13W
Antrim □ **13 B9** 54 55N 6 20W
Antrim, Mts. of . . . **13 B9** 54 57N 6 8W
Appin **4 A5** 56 37N 5 20W
Appleby-in-
Westmorland . . **6 C4** 54 35N 2 29W
Appledore **11 E5** 51 3N 4 12W
Aran Fawddwy . . . **10 B6** 52 48N 3 40W
Aran I. **12 B4** 55 0N 8 30W
Aran Is. **14 B3** 53 5N 9 42W
Arbroath **5 A10** 56 34N 2 35W
Arbury Hill **8 B6** 52 13N 1 12W
Ardee **13 D8** 53 51N 6 32W
Arderin **15 B7** 53 3N 7 40W
Ardgour **4 A5** 56 45N 5 25W
Ardivachar Pt. . . . **2 H3** 57 23N 7 25W
Ardmore Hd. **15 E7** 51 58N 7 43W
Ardmore Pt. **4 C3** 55 40N 6 2W
Ardnamurchan . . . **4 A4** 56 43N 6 0W
Ardnamurchan, Pt.
of **4 A3** 56 44N 6 14W
Ardnave Pt. **4 C3** 55 54N 6 20W
Ardrossan **4 C6** 55 39N 4 50W
Ards Pen. **13 B10** 54 30N 5 30W
Arenig Fawr **10 B6** 52 56N 3 45W
Argyll **4 B5** 56 14N 5 10W
Argyll & Bute □ . . **4 B5** 56 13N 5 28W
Arisaig **2 J6** 56 55N 5 50W
Arisaig, Sd. of . . . **2 J6** 56 50N 5 50W
Arkaig, L. **2 J7** 56 58N 5 10W
Arklow **15 C10** 52 48N 6 10W
Arklow Hd. **15 C10** 52 46N 6 10W
Armadale **5 C8** 55 54N 3 42W
Armagh **13 C8** 54 22N 6 40W
Armagh □ **13 C8** 54 18N 6 37W
Armthorpe **7 E6** 53 32N 1 3W
Arnold **7 F6** 53 2N 1 8W
Arran **4 C5** 55 34N 5 12W
Arrow, L. **12 C5** 54 3N 8 20W
Arun → **9 E7** 50 48N 0 33W
Arundel **9 E7** 50 52N 0 32W
Ascot **9 D7** 51 24N 0 41W
Ash **9 D7** 51 14N 0 43W
Ashbourne **7 F5** 53 2N 1 44W
Ashburton **11 F6** 50 31N 3 45W
Ashby de la Zouch **7 G6** 52 45N 1 29W
Ashdown Forest . **9 D9** 51 4N 0 2 E
Ashford . . . . **9 D10** 51 8N 0 53 E
Ashington **6 B5** 55 12N 1 35W
Ashton-in-
Makerfield **7 F3** 53 29N 2 39W
Ashton under Lyne **7 F4** 53 30N 2 8W
Aspatria **6 C2** 54 45N 3 20W
Assynt **2 F7** 58 20N 5 10W
Athboy **13 D8** 53 37N 6 55W
Athenry **14 B5** 53 18N 8 45W
Atherstone **7 G5** 52 35N 1 32W
Atherton **7 E3** 53 32N 2 30W
Athlone **14 B7** 53 26N 7 57W
Atholl, Forest of . . **3 J10** 56 51N 3 50W
Athy **15 C9** 53 0N 7 0W
Attleborough . . . . **9 A11** 52 32N 1 1 E
Auchterarder **5 B8** 56 18N 3 43W
Auchtermuchty . . **5 B9** 56 18N 3 15W
Aughnacloy **13 C8** 54 25N 6 58W
Aviemore **3 H10** 57 11N 3 50W
Avoca **15 C10** 52 52N 6 13W
Avoca → **15 C10** 52 48N 6 9W
Avon →, *Bristol* **8 D3** 51 30N 2 43W
Avon →, *Hants.* **8 E5** 50 44N 1 45W
Avon →, *Warks.* **8 C4** 51 57N 2 9W
Avonmouth **8 C3** 51 30N 2 42W
Awe, L. **4 B5** 56 15N 5 15W
Axe Edge **7 F5** 53 14N 1 59W
Axminster **11 F7** 50 47N 3 1W
Aylesbury **9 C7** 51 48N 0 49W
Aylsham . . . . **9 A11** 52 48N 1 16 E
Ayr **4 D6** 55 28N 4 37W
Ayr → **4 D6** 55 29N 4 40W
Ayr, Heads of **4 D6** 55 25N 4 43W
Ayr, Pt. of **10 A7** 53 21N 3 19W
Ayre, Pt. of **3 E12** 58 55N 2 43W

B

Bacton . . . . **9 A11** 52 50N 1 29 E
Bacup **7 E4** 53 42N 2 12W
Badenoch **3 J9** 56 59N 4 15W
Bagenalstown =
Muine Bheag . . **15 C9** 52 42N 6 57W
Baggy Pt. **11 E5** 51 11N 4 12W
Bagh nam
Faoileann **2 H3** 57 22N 7 13W
Baginbun Hd. **15 D9** 52 10N 6 50W
Bagshot **9 D7** 51 22N 0 41W
Baildon **7 E5** 53 52N 1 46W
Baile Atha Cliath =
Dublin **15 B10** 53 20N 6 18W
Bakewell **7 F5** 53 13N 1 40W
Bala **10 B6** 52 54N 3 36W
Bala, L. **10 B6** 52 53N 3 38W
Balbriggan **13 D9** 53 35N 6 10W
Baldock **9 C8** 51 59N 0 11W
Ballachulish **4 A5** 56 40N 5 10W
Ballagan Pt. **13 D9** 54 0N 6 6W
Ballaghaderreen . . **12 D4** 53 55N 8 35W
Ballater **3 H11** 57 2N 3 2W
Ballina, *Mayo,* . . . **12 C3** 54 7N 9 10W
Ballina, *Tipp.,* **14 C6** 52 49N 8 27W
Ballinasloe **14 B6** 53 20N 8 12W
Ballinderry → . . **13 B8** 54 40N 6 32W
Ballinrobe **12 D3** 53 36N 9 13W
Ballinskelligs B. . . **14 E2** 51 46N 10 11W
Ballybunion **14 C3** 52 30N 9 40W
Ballycastle **13 A9** 55 12N 6 15W
Ballyclare **13 B10** 54 46N 6 0W
Ballyconneely B. . **14 B2** 53 23N 10 8W
Ballydavid Hd. . . . **14 D2** 52 15N 10 20W
Ballydonegan B. . **14 E2** 51 38N 10 6W
Ballyhaunis **12 D4** 53 47N 8 47W
Ballyhoura Mts. . . **14 D5** 52 18N 8 33W
Ballymena **13 B9** 54 53N 6 18W
Ballymoney **13 A8** 55 5N 6 30W
Ballymote **12 C4** 54 5N 8 31W
Ballynahinch **13 C10** 54 24N 5 55W
Ballyquintin Pt. . . . **13 C11** 54 20N 5 30W
Ballyshannon **12 B5** 54 30N 8 10W
Balmoral Forest . . **3 J11** 57 0N 3 15W
Baltimore **14 F4** 51 29N 9 22W
Bamber Bridge . . **7 E3** 53 44N 2 39W
Bamburgh **6 A5** 55 36N 1 42W
Banbridge **13 C9** 54 21N 6 17W
Banbury **8 B6** 52 4N 1 21W
Banchory **3 H13** 57 3N 2 30W
Bandon **14 E5** 51 44N 8 45W
Bandon → **14 E5** 51 40N 8 41W
Banff **3 G12** 57 40N 2 32W
Bangor, *Down* . . . **13 B10** 54 40N 5 40W
Bangor, *Gwynedd* **10 A5** 53 13N 4 9W
Bann →, *Down* **13 C8** 54 30N 6 31W
Bann →, *L'derry.* **13 A8** 55 10N 6 40W
Bannockburn **5 B8** 56 5N 3 55W
Bannow B. **15 D9** 52 13N 6 48W
Banstead **9 D8** 51 19N 0 10W
Bantry **14 E4** 51 40N 9 28W
Bantry B. **14 E3** 51 35N 9 50W
Bard Hd. **2 B15** 60 6N 1 5W
Bardsey Sd. **10 B4** 52 47N 4 46W
Bargoed **10 D7** 51 42N 3 22W
Barking and
Dagenham . . . . **9 C9** 51 31N 0 10 E
Barmouth **10 B5** 52 44N 4 3W
Barnard Castle . . . **6 C5** 54 33N 1 55W
Barnet **9 C8** 51 37N 0 15W
Barnoldswick **7 E4** 53 55N 2 11W
Barns Ness **5 C11** 55 59N 2 27W
Barnsley **7 E6** 53 33N 1 29W
Barnstaple **11 E5** 51 5N 4 3W
Barnstaple B. **11 E5** 51 5N 4 20W
Barra **2 J3** 57 0N 7 30W
Barra Hd. **2 J2** 56 47N 7 40W
Barrhead **4 C7** 55 48N 4 23W
Barrow → **15 D9** 52 14N 6 58W
Barrow-in-Furness **6 D2** 54 8N 3 15W
Barrow upon
Humber **7 E8** 53 41N 0 22W
Barrowford **7 E4** 53 51N 2 14W
Barry **11 E7** 51 23N 3 19W
Barry I. **11 E7** 51 23N 3 17W
Barry's Pt. **14 E5** 51 36N 8 40W
Barton upon
Humber **7 E8** 53 41N 0 27W
Basildon . . . . **9 C9** 51 34N 0 29 E
Basingstoke **8 D6** 51 15N 1 5W
Bass Rock **5 B10** 56 5N 2 40W
Bath **8 D4** 51 22N 2 22W
Bathgate **5 C8** 55 54N 3 38W
Batley **7 E5** 53 43N 1 38W
Battle . . . . **9 E9** 50 55N 0 30 E
Beachy Hd. . . . . . . **9 E9** 50 44N 0 16 E
Beaconsfield **9 C7** 51 36N 0 39W
Beaminster **8 E3** 50 48N 2 44W
Bearsden **4 C7** 55 55N 4 21W
Beauly **3 H9** 57 29N 4 27W
Beauly → **3 H9** 57 26N 4 28W
Beauly Firth **3 H9** 57 30N 4 20W
Beaumaris **10 A5** 53 16N 4 7W
Bebington **7 F2** 53 23N 3 1W
Beccles . . . . **9 B12** 52 27N 1 33 E
Bedford **9 B8** 52 8N 0 29W
Bedford Level . . . **9 A8** 52 35N 0 15W
Bedfordshire □ . . **9 B8** 52 4N 0 28W
Bedlington **6 B5** 55 8N 1 35W
Bedwas **11 D7** 51 36N 3 10W
Bedworth **8 B6** 52 28N 1 29W
Bee, L. **2 H3** 57 22N 7 21W
Beeston **7 G6** 52 55N 1 11W
Beighton **7 F6** 53 21N 1 21W
Beinn a' Ghlo **3 J10** 56 51N 3 42W
Beinn Mhor **2 G4** 57 59N 6 39W
Beith **4 C6** 55 45N 4 38W
Belfast **13 B10** 54 35N 5 56W
Belfast L. **13 B10** 54 40N 5 50W
Belmullet **12 C2** 54 13N 9 58W
Belper **7 F6** 53 2N 1 29W
Belturbet **12 C7** 54 6N 7 28W
Bembridge **8 E6** 50 41N 1 4W
Ben Alder **3 J9** 56 50N 4 30W
Ben Avon **3 H11** 57 6N 3 28W
Ben Bheigeir **4 C3** 55 43N 6 6W
Ben Chonzie **5 B8** 56 27N 4 0W
Ben Cruachan . . . **4 B5** 56 26N 5 8W
Ben Dearg, *Highl.* **3 G8** 57 47N 4 58W
Ben Dearg,
Perth & Kinr. . . **3 J10** 56 52N 3 52W
Ben Dhorain **3 F10** 58 7N 3 50W
Ben Dorain **4 A6** 56 32N 4 42W
Ben Eighie **2 G7** 57 37N 5 30W
Ben Hee **3 F8** 58 16N 4 43W
Ben Hiant **4 A3** 56 42N 6 1W
Ben Hope **3 F8** 58 24N 4 36W
Ben Ime **4 B6** 56 14N 4 49W

Place names on the turquoise-coded World Map section are to be found in the index at the rear of the book.

Ben Klibreck **3 F9** 58 14N 4 25W
Ben Lawers **4 A7** 56 33N 4 13W
Ben Lomond **4 B6** 56 12N 4 39W
Ben Loyal **3 F9** 58 25N 4 25W
Ben Lui **4 B6** 56 24N 4 50W
Ben Macdhui **3 H10** 57 4N 3 40W
Ben Mholach **2 F4** 58 14N 6 33W
Ben Mhor **2 H3** 57 16N 7 21W
Ben More, *Arg. & Bute* **4 B3** 56 26N 6 2W
Ben More, *Stirl.* **4 B6** 56 23N 4 31W
Ben More Assynt **3 F8** 58 7N 4 51W
Ben Nevis **3 J7** 56 48N 5 2W
Ben Rinnes **3 H11** 57 25N 3 15W
Ben Stack **3 F8** 58 20N 4 58W
Ben Tharsuinn **3 G9** 57 47N 4 20W
Ben Venue **4 B7** 56 13N 4 28W
Ben Vorlich **4 B7** 56 22N 4 15W
Ben Wyvis **3 G8** 57 40N 4 35W
Benbane Hd. **13 A9** 55 15N 6 30W
Benbaun **12 D2** 53 30N 9 50W
Benbecula **2 H3** 57 26N 7 21W
Benderloch **4 A5** 56 30N 5 22W
Beneraird **4 D6** 55 4N 4 57W
Bennane Hd. **4 D6** 55 8N 4 59W
Bentley **7 E6** 53 33N 1 9W
Benwee Hd. **12 C2** 54 20N 9 50W
Berkeley **8 C4** 51 41N 2 28W
Berkhamsted **9 C7** 51 45N 0 33W
Berkshire Downs **8 C5** 51 30N 1 30W
Berry Hd. **11 G7** 50 24N 3 29W
Berst Ness **3 D12** 59 16N 3 0W
Bertraghboy B. **14 B3** 53 22N 9 54W
Berwick-upon-Tweed **6 A5** 55 47N 2 0W
Berwyn Mts. **10 B7** 52 54N 3 26W
Betws-y-Coed **10 A6** 53 4N 3 49W
Beverley **7 E8** 53 52N 0 26W
Bewdley **8 B4** 52 23N 2 19W
Bexhill **9 E9** 50 51N 0 29 E
Bexley **9 D9** 51 26N 0 10 E
Bicester **8 C6** 51 53N 1 9W
Biddulph **7 F4** 53 8N 2 11W
Bidean nam Bian **4 A5** 56 39N 5 6W
Bideford **11 E5** 51 1N 4 13W
Bideford B. = Barnstaple B. **11 E5** 51 5N 4 20W
Bigbury B. **11 G6** 50 18N 3 58W
Biggar **5 C8** 55 38N 3 31W
Biggleswade **9 B8** 52 6N 0 16W
Billericay **9 C9** 51 38N 0 25 E
Billinge Hill **7 E3** 53 32N 2 42W
Billingham **6 C6** 54 36N 1 18W
Billingshurst **9 D8** 51 2N 0 28W
Bilston **7 G4** 52 34N 2 5W
Bingley **7 E5** 53 51N 1 50W
Birdlip **8 C4** 51 50N 2 7W
Birkenhead **7 F2** 53 24N 3 1W
Birmingham **8 B5** 52 30N 1 53W
Birr **14 B7** 53 7N 7 55W
Birtley **6 C5** 54 53N 1 34W
Bishop Auckland **6 C5** 54 40N 1 40W
Bishop's Stortford **9 C9** 51 52N 0 11 E
Bishop's Waltham **8 E6** 50 57N 1 13W
Bla Bheinn **2 H5** 57 14N 6 7W
Black Combe **6 D2** 54 16N 3 20W
Black Hd., *Ant.* **13 B10** 54 56N 5 42W
Black Hd., *Clare* **14 B4** 53 9N 9 18W
Black Hd., *Corn.* **11 H3** 50 0N 5 6W
Black Isle **3 G9** 57 35N 4 15W
Black Mts. **10 D7** 51 52N 3 5W
Black Mt. = Mynydd Du **10 D6** 51 45N 3 45W
Blackburn **7 E4** 53 44N 2 30W
Blackdown Hill **8 D7** 51 4N 0 41W
Blackdown Hills **8 E2** 50 57N 3 15W
Blackhill **7 E5** 53 32N 1 53W
Blackhope Scar **5 C9** 55 44N 3 5W
Blackmoor Vale **8 E4** 50 54N 2 28W
Blackpool **7 E2** 53 48N 3 3W
Blacksod B. **12 C2** 54 6N 10 0W
Blacksod Pt. **12 C1** 54 7N 10 5W
Blackstairs Mt. **15 C9** 52 33N 6 50W
Blackwater →, *Essex* **9 C10** 51 44N 0 53 E
Blackwater →, *Munst.* **14 E7** 51 55N 7 50W
Blackwater →, *Tyrone* **13 B8** 54 31N 6 35W
Blackwood **10 D7** 51 40N 3 13W
Blaenau Ffestiniog **10 B6** 52 59N 3 57W
Blaenau Gwent □ **10 D7** 51 47N 3 12W
Blaenavon **10 D7** 51 46N 3 5W
Blaina **10 D7** 51 46N 3 10W
Blair Atholl **3 J10** 56 46N 3 50W
Blairgowrie **5 A9** 56 36N 3 20W
Blakeney **9 A11** 52 57N 1 0 E
Blandford Forum **8 E4** 50 52N 2 10W
Blarney **14 E5** 51 57N 8 35W
Blaydon **6 C5** 54 56N 1 47W
Bletchley **9 C7** 51 59N 0 44W
Bloody Foreland **12 A5** 55 10N 8 18W
Bluemull Sd. **2 A16** 60 45N 1 0W
Blyth **6 B5** 55 8N 1 32W
Blyth Bridge **7 G4** 52 58N 2 4W
Boderg, L. **12 D6** 53 55N 8 0W
Bodmin **11 G4** 50 28N 4 44W
Bodmin Moor **11 F4** 50 33N 4 36W
Boggeragh Mts. **14 D5** 52 2N 8 55W
Bognor Regis **9 E7** 50 47N 0 40W
Bogrie Hill **5 D8** 55 8N 3 54W
Boisdale, L. **2 H3** 57 9N 7 19W
Boldon **6 C6** 54 57N 1 26W
Bolsover **7 F6** 53 14N 1 18W
Bolt Hd. **11 G6** 50 13N 3 48W
Bolt Tail **11 G6** 50 13N 3 55W
Bolton **7 E4** 53 35N 2 26W
Bolus Hd. **14 E2** 51 48N 10 20W
Bo'ness **5 B8** 56 1N 3 38W
Bonnyrigg **5 C9** 55 52N 3 8W
Bootle, *Cumb.* **6 D2** 54 17N 3 24W
Bootle, *Mersey.* **7 F2** 53 28N 3 1W
Borehamwood **9 C8** 51 40N 0 15W
Boroughbridge **6 D6** 54 6N 1 23W
Borth **10 C5** 52 29N 4 3W
Boscastle **11 F4** 50 42N 4 42W
Boston **7 G8** 52 59N 0 2W
Bourne **7 G8** 52 46N 0 22W
Bournemouth **8 E5** 50 43N 1 53W
Bourton-on-the-Water **8 C5** 51 53N 1 45W
Bowland, Forest of **7 E3** 54 0N 2 30W
Bowmore **4 C3** 55 45N 6 18W
Bowness-on-Windermere **6 D3** 54 22N 2 56W
Box Hill **9 D8** 51 16N 0 16W
Boyle **12 D5** 53 58N 8 19W
Boyne → **13 D9** 53 43N 6 15W
Bracadale, L. **2 H4** 57 20N 6 30W
Brackley **8 B6** 52 3N 1 9W
Bracknell **9 D7** 51 24N 0 45W
Bradda Hd. **13 C12** 54 6N 4 46W
Bradford **7 E5** 53 47N 1 45W
Bradford on Avon **8 D4** 51 20N 2 15W
Bradwell-on-Sea **9 C10** 51 44N 0 55 E
Braemar **3 J11** 57 0N 3 25W
Braeriach **3 H10** 57 4N 3 44W
Braich-y-pwll **10 B4** 52 47N 4 46W
Braintree **9 C10** 51 53N 0 34 E
Brampton **6 C3** 54 56N 2 43W
Branderburgh **3 G11** 57 43N 3 17W
Brandon, *Durham* **6 C5** 54 46N 1 37W
Brandon, *Kilk.* **15 C9** 52 31N 6 58W
Brandon, *Suffolk* **9 B10** 52 27N 0 37 E
Brandon B. **14 D2** 52 17N 10 8W
Brandon Mt. **14 D2** 52 15N 10 15W
Brandon Pt. **14 D2** 52 18N 10 10W
Braunton **11 E5** 51 6N 4 9W
Bray **15 B10** 53 12N 6 6W
Bray Hd., *Kerry* **14 E2** 51 52N 10 26W
Bray Hd., *Wick.* **15 B10** 53 12N 6 2W
Breadalbane **4 A7** 56 30N 4 15W
Brechin **5 A10** 56 44N 2 40W
Breckland **9 B10** 52 30N 0 40 E
Brecon **10 D7** 51 57N 3 23W
Brecon Beacons **10 D7** 51 53N 3 27W
Bredon Hill **8 B4** 52 3N 2 2W
Brendon Hills **8 D2** 51 6N 3 25W
Brenig, L. **10 A6** 53 6N 3 30W
Brent **9 C8** 51 33N 0 18W
Brentwood **9 C9** 51 37N 0 19 E
Bressay Sd. **2 B15** 60 8N 1 10W
Brianne, L. **10 C6** 52 8N 3 45W
Bridge of Don **3 H13** 57 10N 2 8W
Bridgend **11 D6** 51 30N 3 35W
Bridgnorth **7 G4** 52 33N 2 25W
Bridgwater **8 D3** 51 7N 3 0W
Bridlington **6 D8** 54 6N 0 11W
Bridport **8 E3** 50 43N 2 45W
Brierfield **7 E4** 53 49N 2 15W
Brierley Hill **8 B4** 52 29N 2 7W
Brigg **7 E8** 53 33N 0 30W
Brighouse **7 E5** 53 42N 1 47W
Brightlingsea **9 C11** 51 49N 1 1 E
Brighton **9 E8** 50 50N 0 9W
Bristol **8 D3** 51 26N 2 35W
Bristol Channel **11 E4** 51 18N 4 30W
Brixham **11 G6** 50 24N 3 31W
Brize Norton **8 C5** 51 46N 1 35W
Broad Bay **2 F5** 58 14N 6 16W
Broad Haven **12 C2** 54 20N 9 55W
Broad Law **5 C9** 55 31N 3 22W
Broad Sd. **11 H1** 49 56N 6 19W
Broadstairs **9 D11** 51 21N 1 28 E
Broadway **8 B5** 52 2N 1 51W
Broadwindsor **8 E3** 50 49N 2 49W
Brockenhurst **8 E5** 50 49N 1 34W
Brodick **4 C5** 55 34N 5 9W
Bromfield **8 B3** 52 25N 2 45W
Bromley **9 D9** 51 20N 0 5 E
Bromsgrove **8 B4** 52 20N 2 3W
Bromyard **8 B4** 52 12N 2 30W
Broom, L. **2 G7** 57 55N 5 15W
Brora **3 F10** 58 3N 3 50W
Brosna → **14 B7** 53 8N 8 0W
Brotton **6 C7** 54 34N 0 55W
Brough **6 C4** 54 32N 2 19W
Brough Hd. **3 D11** 59 8N 3 20W
Broughty Ferry **5 B10** 56 29N 2 50W
Brown Clee Hill **8 B3** 52 28N 2 36W
Brown Willy **11 F4** 50 35N 4 34W
Brownhills **7 G5** 52 38N 1 57W
Broxburn **5 C9** 55 56N 3 23W
Bruernish Pt. **2 J3** 57 0N 7 22W
Bruton **8 D4** 51 6N 2 28W
Brynmawr **10 D7** 51 48N 3 11W
Buchan **3 G13** 57 32N 2 8W
Buchan Ness **3 H14** 57 29N 1 48W
Buckfastleigh **11 G6** 50 28N 3 47W
Buckhaven **5 B9** 56 10N 3 2W
Buckie **3 G12** 57 40N 2 58W
Buckingham **9 C7** 52 0N 0 59W
Buckinghamshire □ **9 C7** 51 50N 0 55W
Buckley **10 A7** 53 10N 3 5W
Buddon Ness **5 B10** 56 29N 2 42W
Bude **11 F4** 50 49N 4 33W
Budle B. **6 A5** 55 37N 1 45W
Budleigh Salterton **11 F7** 50 37N 3 19W
Buie, L. **4 B4** 56 20N 5 55W
Builth Wells **10 C7** 52 10N 3 26W
Bulkington **8 B6** 52 29N 1 25W
Bunclody **15 C9** 52 40N 6 40W
Buncrana **12 A7** 55 8N 7 28W
Bundoran **12 C5** 54 24N 8 17W
Bungay **9 B11** 52 27N 1 26 E
Burford **8 C5** 51 48N 1 38W
Burgess Hill **9 E8** 50 57N 0 7W
Burghead B. **3 G10** 57 40N 3 33W
Burnham **9 C7** 51 32N 0 40W
Burnham Market **9 A10** 52 57N 0 43 E
Burnham-on-Crouch **9 C10** 51 37N 0 50 E
Burnham-on-Sea **8 D3** 51 14N 3 0W
Burnley **7 E4** 53 47N 2 15W
Burntisland **5 B9** 56 4N 3 14W
Burntwood **7 G5** 52 41N 1 55W
Burrow Hd. **4 E7** 54 40N 4 23W
Burry Port **10 D5** 51 41N 4 17W
Burscough Bridge **7 E3** 53 36N 2 52W
Burton Latimer **9 B7** 52 23N 0 41W
Burton upon Trent **7 G5** 52 48N 1 39W
Bury **7 E4** 53 36N 2 19W
Bury St. Edmunds **9 B10** 52 15N 0 42 E
Bushey **9 C8** 51 38N 0 20W
Bushmills **13 A8** 55 14N 6 32W
Bute **4 C5** 55 48N 5 2W
Bute, Kyles of **4 C5** 55 55N 5 10W
Bute, Sd. of **4 C5** 55 43N 5 8W
Buttevant **14 D5** 52 14N 8 40W
Buxton **7 F5** 53 16N 1 54W
Byfleet **9 D7** 51 20N 0 32W

C

Cader Idris **10 B6** 52 43N 3 56W
Caernarfon **10 A5** 53 8N 4 17W
Caernarfon B. **10 A4** 53 4N 4 40W
Caernarvon = Caernarfon **10 A5** 53 8N 4 17W
Caerphilly **11 D7** 51 34N 3 13W
Caha Mts. **14 E3** 51 45N 9 40W
Caher **14 D7** 52 23N 7 56W
Cahirciveen **14 E2** 51 57N 10 13W
Cahore Pt. **15 C10** 52 34N 6 11W
Cairn Gorm **3 H10** 57 7N 3 40W
Cairn Table **5 C8** 55 30N 4 0W
Cairngorm Mts. **3 H10** 57 6N 3 42W
Cairnsmore of Fleet **4 E7** 54 59N 4 20W
Caister-on-Sea **9 A12** 52 38N 1 43 E
Caithness **3 F10** 58 25N 3 35W
Caithness, Ord of **3 F10** 58 9N 3 37W
Calder → **7 E6** 53 44N 1 21W
Caledonian Canal **2 J7** 56 50N 5 6W
Caliach Pt. **4 A3** 56 37N 6 20W
Callan **15 C8** 52 33N 7 25W
Callander **4 B7** 56 15N 4 14W
Calne **8 D5** 51 26N 2 0W
Cam → **9 B9** 52 21N 0 16 E
Camberley **9 D7** 51 20N 0 44W
Camborne **11 G3** 50 13N 5 18W
Cambrian Mts. **10 C6** 52 25N 3 52W
Cambridge **9 B9** 52 13N 0 8 E
Cambridgeshire □ **9 B9** 52 12N 0 7 E
Camden **9 C8** 51 33N 0 10W
Camelford **11 F4** 50 37N 4 41W
Campbeltown **4 D4** 55 25N 5 36W
Canbane East **13 D7** 53 45N 7 6W
Canna, Sd. of **2 H5** 57 1N 6 30W
Cannock **7 G4** 52 42N 2 2W
Cannock Chase **7 G5** 52 43N 2 0W
Canterbury **9 D11** 51 17N 1 5 E
Canvey **9 C10** 51 32N 0 35 E
Caolisport, L. **4 C4** 55 54N 5 40W
Cardiff **11 E7** 51 28N 3 11W
Cardigan **10 C4** 52 6N 4 41W
Cardigan B. **10 B4** 52 30N 4 30W
Carisbrooke **8 E6** 50 42N 1 19W
Carlingford L. **13 C9** 54 2N 6 5W
Carlisle **6 C3** 54 54N 2 55W
Carlow **15 C9** 52 50N 6 58W
Carlow □ **15 C9** 52 43N 6 50W
Carlton **7 G6** 52 58N 1 6W
Carluke **5 C8** 55 44N 3 50W
Carmarthen **10 D5** 51 52N 4 20W
Carmarthen B. **10 D4** 51 40N 4 30W
Carmarthenshire □ **10 D5** 51 55N 4 13W
Carmel Hd. **10 A4** 53 24N 4 34W
Carn Ban **3 H9** 57 6N 4 15W
Carn Eige **2 H7** 57 17N 5 9W
Carn Glas-choire **3 H10** 57 20N 3 50W
Carn Mor **3 H11** 57 14N 3 13W
Carn na Saobhaidhe **3 H9** 57 12N 4 20W
Carndonagh **13 A7** 55 15N 7 16W
Carnedd Llewelyn **10 A6** 53 9N 3 58W
Carnforth **6 D3** 54 8N 2 47W
Carnoustie **5 A10** 56 30N 2 41W
Carnsore Pt. **15 D10** 52 10N 6 20W
Carra, L. **12 D3** 53 41N 9 12W
Carrauntoohill **14 E3** 52 0N 9 49W
Carrick **4 D6** 55 12N 4 38W
Carrick-on-Shannon **12 D5** 53 57N 8 7W
Carrick-on-Suir **15 D8** 52 22N 7 30W
Carrickfergus **13 B10** 54 43N 5 50W
Carrickmacross **13 D8** 53 58N 6 43W
Carrigan Hd. **12 B4** 54 38N 8 40W
Carron → **2 H7** 57 30N 5 30W
Carron, L. **2 H6** 57 22N 5 35W
Carstairs **5 C8** 55 42N 3 41W
Cashel **14 C7** 52 31N 7 53W
Cashla B. **14 B3** 53 12N 9 37W
Castle Cary **8 D3** 51 5N 2 32W
Castle Donington **7 G6** 52 50N 1 20W
Castle Douglas **5 E8** 54 57N 3 57W
Castlebar **12 D3** 53 52N 9 17W
Castleblaney **13 C8** 54 7N 6 44W
Castlederg **12 B6** 54 43N 7 35W
Castleford **7 E6** 53 43N 1 21W
Castleisland **14 D4** 52 14N 9 28W
Castlemaine Harbour **14 D3** 52 8N 9 50W
Castlepollard **12 D7** 53 40N 7 20W
Castlerea **12 D5** 53 47N 8 30W
Castletown **13 C12** 54 4N 4 40W
Castletown Bearhaven **14 E3** 51 40N 9 54W
Caterham **9 D8** 51 16N 0 4W
Cavan **12 D7** 54 0N 7 22W
Cavan □ **13 D7** 53 58N 7 10W
Ceanannus Mor **13 D8** 53 42N 6 53W
Cefn-mawr **10 B7** 52 58N 3 3W
Cefnfford **10 D6** 51 42N 3 39W
Celbridge **15 B9** 53 20N 6 33W
Cellar Hd. **2 F5** 58 25N 6 10W
Celyn, L. **10 B6** 52 56N 3 42W
Cemaes Hd. **10 C4** 52 7N 4 44W
Ceredigion □ **10 C6** 52 16N 3 58W
Chadwell St. Mary **9 D9** 51 28N 0 22 E
Chandler's Ford **8 E6** 50 59N 1 23W
Channel Is. **11 J9** 49 30N 2 40W
Chapel en le Frith **7 F5** 53 19N 1 54W
Chard **8 E3** 50 52N 2 59W
Charlbury **8 C6** 51 52N 1 29W
Charlestown of Aberlour **3 H11** 57 27N 3 13W
Charleville = Rath Luirc **14 D5** 52 21N 8 40W
Charlton Kings **8 C4** 51 52N 2 3W
Charnwood Forest **7 G6** 52 43N 1 18W
Chatham **9 D10** 51 22N 0 32 E
Chatteris **9 B9** 52 27N 0 3 E
Cheadle, *Gt. Man.* **7 F4** 53 23N 2 14W
Cheadle, *Staffs.* **7 G5** 52 59N 1 59W
Cheddar **8 D3** 51 16N 2 47W
Chelmsford **9 C9** 51 44N 0 29 E
Cheltenham **8 C4** 51 55N 2 5W
Chepstow **10 D8** 51 38N 2 40W
Chertsey **9 D7** 51 23N 0 30W
Cherwell → **8 C6** 51 46N 1 18W
Chesham **9 C7** 51 42N 0 36W
Cheshire □ **7 F3** 53 14N 2 30W
Cheshunt **9 C8** 51 42N 0 1W
Chesil Beach **11 F8** 50 37N 2 33W
Chester **7 F3** 53 12N 2 53W
Chester-le-Street **6 C5** 54 53N 1 34W
Chesterfield **7 F6** 53 14N 1 26W
Cheviot Hills **6 B3** 55 20N 2 30W
Chichester **9 E7** 50 50N 0 47W
Chicken Hd. **2 F5** 58 10N 6 15W
Chigwell **9 C9** 51 37N 0 4 E
Chiltern Hills **9 C7** 51 44N 0 42W
Chippenham **8 D4** 51 27N 2 7W
Chipping Norton **8 C5** 51 56N 1 32W
Chipping Ongar **9 C9** 51 42N 0 11 E
Chipping Sodbury **8 C4** 51 31N 2 23W
Chobham **9 D7** 51 20N 0 36W
Chorley **7 E3** 53 39N 2 39W
Chorleywood **9 C8** 51 39N 0 29W
Christchurch **8 E5** 50 44N 1 45W
Chulmleigh **11 F6** 50 55N 3 52W
Church Stretton **8 A3** 52 32N 2 49W
Churchdown **8 C4** 51 53N 2 9W
Chwarel y Fan **10 D7** 51 56N 3 5W
Cill Chainnigh = Kilkenny **15 C8** 52 40N 7 17W
Cinderford **8 C3** 51 49N 2 30W
Cirencester **8 C5** 51 43N 1 59W
Clach Leathad **4 A6** 56 36N 4 52W
Clackmannan □ **5 B8** 56 9N 3 49W
Clacton-on-Sea **9 C11** 51 47N 1 10 E
Clara **15 B7** 53 20N 7 38W
Clare □ **14 C4** 52 45N 9 0W
Clare → **14 B4** 53 22N 9 5W
Clare I. **12 D2** 53 48N 10 0W
Clay Cross **7 F6** 53 11N 1 26W
Clear, C. **14 F3** 51 26N 9 30W
Cleator Moor **6 C2** 54 31N 3 30W
Clee Hills **8 B3** 52 26N 2 35W
Cleethorpes **7 E8** 53 33N 0 2W
Cleeve Cloud **8 C5** 51 56N 1 57W
Clent Hills **8 B4** 52 25N 2 6W
Clevedon **8 D3** 51 26N 2 52W
Cleveland Hills **6 D6** 54 25N 1 11W
Cleveleys **7 E2** 53 53N 3 3W
Clew B. **12 D2** 53 54N 9 50W
Clifden **12 E1** 53 30N 10 2W
Clifden B. **12 E1** 53 29N 10 5W
Clift Sd. **2 B15** 60 4N 1 17W
Clisham **2 G4** 57 57N 6 50W
Clitheroe **7 E4** 53 52N 2 23W
Clogher Hd. **13 D9** 53 48N 6 15W
Clonakilty **14 E5** 51 37N 8 53W
Clondalkin **15 B10** 53 20N 6 25W
Clones **13 C7** 54 10N 7 13W
Clonmel **15 D7** 52 22N 7 42W
Clovelly **11 F5** 51 0N 4 25W
Clun Forest **8 B2** 52 27N 3 7W
Clwyd → **10 A6** 53 20N 3 30W
Clydach **10 D6** 51 42N 3 54W
Clyde → **4 C7** 55 56N 4 29W
Clyde, Firth of **4 D6** 55 20N 5 0W
Clydebank **4 C7** 55 54N 4 25W
Clydesdale **5 C8** 55 42N 3 50W
Clywedog, L. **10 C6** 52 29N 3 40W
Cnoc Moy **4 D4** 55 23N 5 44W
Coalisland **13 B8** 54 33N 6 42W
Coalville **7 G6** 52 43N 1 21W
Coatbridge **4 C7** 55 52N 4 2W
Cóbh **14 E6** 51 50N 8 18W
Cockenzie **5 C10** 55 58N 2 59W
Cockermouth **6 C2** 54 40N 3 22W
Cods Hd. **14 E2** 51 40N 10 7W
Coigach **2 G7** 57 55N 5 10W
Colchester **9 C10** 51 54N 0 55 E
Cold Fell **6 C3** 54 54N 2 40W
Coldstream **5 C11** 55 39N 2 14W
Coleraine **13 A8** 55 8N 6 40W
Coleshill **8 B5** 52 30N 1 42W
Colgrave Sd. **2 A16** 60 35N 1 0W
Colinton **5 C9** 55 54N 3 15W
Coll **4 A2** 56 40N 6 35W
Collier Law **6 C5** 54 47N 1 59W
Collooney **12 C5** 54 11N 8 28W
Colne **7 E4** 53 51N 2 11W
Colonsay **4 B3** 56 4N 6 12W
Colwyn Bay **10 A6** 53 17N 3 44W
Combe Martin **11 E5** 51 12N 4 2W
Comber **13 B10** 54 33N 5 45W
Comeragh Mts. **15 D7** 52 17N 7 35W
Congleton **7 F4** 53 10N 2 12W
Conisbrough **7 F6** 53 29N 1 12W
Coniston **6 D2** 54 22N 3 6W
Conn, L. **12 C3** 54 3N 9 15W
Connacht **12 D4** 53 45N 8 40W
Connah's Quay **10 A7** 53 13N 3 6W
Connel **4 B5** 56 27N 5 24W
Connemara **12 E2** 53 29N 9 45W
Cononbridge **3 G9** 57 32N 4 30W
Consett **6 C5** 54 52N 1 50W
Conway = Conwy **10 A6** 53 17N 3 50W
Conwy **10 A6** 53 17N 3 50W
Conwy □ **10 A6** 53 10N 3 44W
Conwy B. **10 A6** 53 17N 3 57W
Cookstown **13 B8** 54 40N 6 43W
Cootehill **13 C7** 54 5N 7 5W
Coquet → **6 B5** 55 18N 1 45W
Corbridge **6 C5** 54 58N 2 0W
Corby **9 A7** 52 30N 0 41W
Corby Glen **7 G7** 52 49N 0 31W
Corcaigh = Cork **14 E6** 51 54N 8 30W
Corfe Castle **8 E4** 50 37N 2 3W
Cork **14 E6** 51 54N 8 30W
Cork □ **14 E5** 51 50N 8 50W
Cork Harbour **14 E6** 51 46N 8 16W
Corn Hill **12 D6** 53 48N 7 43W
Cornwall □ **11 G4** 50 26N 4 40W
Cornwall, C. **11 G2** 50 8N 5 42W
Corrib, L. **14 B4** 53 5N 9 10W
Corringham **9 C10** 51 30N 0 26 E
Corry Mt. **12 C5** 54 8N 8 8W
Corryvreckan, G. of **4 B4** 56 10N 5 44W
Corsewall Pt. **4 E5** 55 0N 5 10W
Corsham **8 D4** 51 25N 2 11W
Coseley **7 G4** 52 33N 2 6W
Cot Nab **7 D7** 54 1N 0 45W
Cotswold Hills **8 C4** 51 42N 2 10W
Cottingham **7 E8** 53 47N 0 23W
Coul Pt. **4 C2** 55 50N 6 30W
Coupar Angus **5 A9** 56 33N 3 17W
Courtmacsherry B. **14 E5** 51 37N 8 37W
Cove **4 B6** 56 2N 4 50W
Coventry **8 B6** 52 25N 1 28W
Cow Green Res. **6 C4** 54 40N 2 20W
Cowal **4 B5** 56 5N 5 8W
Cowdenbeath **5 B9** 56 7N 3 20W
Cowes **8 E6** 50 45N 1 18W
Craigavon **13 C9** 54 28N 6 20W
Craignish, L. **4 B4** 56 11N 5 32W
Crail **5 B10** 56 16N 2 38W
Cramlington **6 B5** 55 5N 1 36W
Cranborne Chase **8 E4** 50 56N 2 6W
Cranbrook **9 D10** 51 6N 0 33 E
Cranfield Pt. **13 C9** 54 1N 6 3W
Cranleigh **9 D8** 51 8N 0 29W
Crawley **9 D8** 51 7N 0 10W
Creag Meagaidh **3 J8** 56 57N 4 38W
Crediton **11 F6** 50 47N 3 39W
Cree → **4 E7** 54 51N 4 24W
Creran, L. **4 A5** 56 30N 5 20W
Crewe **7 F4** 53 6N 2 28W
Crewkerne **8 E3** 50 53N 2 48W
Criccieth **10 B5** 52 55N 4 15W
Cricklade **8 C5** 51 38N 1 50W
Crieff **5 B8** 56 22N 3 50W
Criffell **5 E8** 54 56N 3 38W
Crinan Canal **4 B5** 56 4N 5 30W
Croagh Patrick **12 D2** 53 46N 9 40W
Croghan Mt. **15 C10** 52 48N 6 20W
Crohy Hd. **12 B5** 54 55N 8 28W
Cromarty **3 G9** 57 40N 4 2W
Cromarty Firth **3 G9** 57 40N 4 15W
Cromdale, Hills of **3 H11** 57 20N 3 28W
Cromer **9 A11** 52 56N 1 18 E
Crook **6 C5** 54 43N 1 45W
Crosby **7 E2** 53 30N 3 2W
Cross Fell **6 C4** 54 44N 2 29W
Crossfarnoge Pt. **15 D9** 52 10N 6 37W
Crosshaven **14 E6** 51 48N 8 19W
Crossmaglen **13 C8** 54 5N 6 37W
Crow Hd. **14 E2** 51 34N 10 9W
Crow Sd. **11 H1** 49 56N 6 16W
Crowborough **9 D9** 51 3N 0 9 E
Crowthorne **9 D7** 51 22N 0 50W
Croydon **9 D8** 51 18N 0 5W
Cruden Bay **3 H14** 57 25N 1 50W
Cuckfield **9 D8** 51 1N 0 8W
Cuffley **9 C8** 51 43N 0 9W
Cuilcagh **12 C6** 54 12N 7 50W
Cuillin Hills **2 H5** 57 14N 6 15W
Cuillin Sd. **2 H5** 57 4N 6 20W
Cullen **3 G12** 57 45N 2 50W
Cullin, L. **12 D3** 53 58N 9 12W
Culloden **3 H9** 57 29N 4 7W
Cullompton **11 F7** 50 52N 3 23W
Culm → **11 F6** 50 46N 3 31W
Culter Fell **5 C8** 55 35N 3 30W
Cults **3 H13** 57 8N 2 10W
Culvain **2 J7** 56 55N 5 19W
Cumbernauld **5 C8** 55 57N 3 58W
Cumbrae Is. **4 C6** 55 46N 4 54W
Cumbria □ **6 C3** 54 35N 2 55W
Cumbrian Mts. **6 D2** 54 30N 3 0W
Cumnock **4 D7** 55 27N 4 18W
Cunninghame **4 C6** 55 38N 4 35W
Cupar **5 B9** 56 20N 3 3W
Cupidstown Hill **15 B9** 53 15N 6 31W
Currane, L. **14 E2** 51 50N 10 8W
Cwmbran **10 D7** 51 39N 3 3W

D

Daingean **15 B8** 53 18N 7 15W
Dalbeattie **5 E8** 54 55N 3 50W
Dalkeith **5 C9** 55 54N 3 5W
Dalmellington **4 D7** 55 20N 4 25W
Dalry **4 C6** 55 44N 4 42W
Dalton-in-Furness **6 D2** 54 9N 3 10W
Danbury **9 C10** 51 43N 0 34 E
Darlington **6 C5** 54 33N 1 33W
Dart → **11 G6** 50 24N 3 36W
Dartford **9 D9** 51 26N 0 15 E
Dartmoor **11 F6** 50 36N 4 0W
Dartmouth **11 G6** 50 21N 3 35W
Darton **7 E5** 53 36N 1 32W

Place names on the turquoise-coded World Map section are to be found in the index at the rear of the book.

Darvel   **Hunterston**

Place names on the turquoise-coded World Map section are to be found in the index at the rear of the book.

36 INDEX TO BRITISH ISLES MAPS

Huntingdon **Narberth**

Huntingdon **9 B8** 52 20N 0 11W
Huntly **3 H12** 57 27N 2 48W
Hurstpierpoint **9 E8** 50 56N 0 11W
Husinish Pt. **2 G3** 57 59N 7 6W
Huyton **7 F3** 53 25N 2 52W
Hyde **7 F4** 53 26N 2 6W
Hynish B. **4 B2** 56 29N 6 40W
Hythe, *Hants.* **8 E6** 50 51N 1 23W
Hythe, *Kent* **9 D11** 51 4N 1 5 E

I

Ibstock **7 G6** 52 42N 1 23W
Ilchester **8 E3** 51 0N 2 41W
Ilfracombe **11 E5** 51 13N 4 8W
Ilkeston **7 G6** 52 59N 1 19W
Ilkley **7 E5** 53 56N 1 49W
Ilmington Downs **8 B5** 52 5N 1 41W
Ilminster **8 E3** 50 55N 2 56W
Immingham **7 E8** 53 37N 0 12W
Inchard, L. **2 F7** 58 28N 5 2W
Indaal, L. **4 C3** 55 44N 6 20W
Ingleborough **6 D4** 54 11N 2 23W
Inishfree B. **12 A5** 55 4N 8 20W
Inishmore **14 B3** 53 8N 9 45W
Inishowen Hd. **13 A8** 55 14N 6 56W
Inishowen Pen. **13 A7** 55 14N 7 15W
Innellan **4 C6** 55 54N 4 58W
Inner Hebrides **2 J4** 57 0N 6 30W
Inner Sd. **2 H6** 57 30N 5 55W
Innerleithen **5 C9** 55 37N 3 4W
Inver B. **12 B5** 54 35N 8 28W
Inveraray **4 B5** 56 13N 5 5W
Inverbervie **3 J13** 56 50N 2 17W
Inverclyde □ **4 C6** 55 57N 4 46W
Invergordon **3 G9** 57 41N 4 10W
Inverkeithing **5 B9** 56 2N 3 24W
Inverness **3 H9** 57 29N 4 12W
Inverurie **3 H13** 57 15N 2 21W
Iona **4 B3** 56 20N 6 25W
Ipswich **9 B11** 52 4N 1 9 E
Irlam **7 F4** 53 26N 2 27W
Ironbridge **7 G4** 52 38N 2 29W
Irthlingborough **9 B7** 52 20N 0 37W
Irvine **4 C6** 55 37N 4 40W
Irvinestown **12 C6** 54 28N 7 38W
Islay **4 C3** 55 46N 6 10W
Islay, Sd. of **4 C3** 55 45N 6 5W
Isle of Wight □ **8 E6** 50 40N 1 20W
Islington **9 C8** 51 32N 0 6W
Ithon → **10 C7** 52 16N 3 23W
Ivybridge **11 G6** 50 24N 3 56W

J

Jarrow **6 C6** 54 58N 1 28W
Jedburgh **5 D10** 55 28N 2 33W
Jersey **11 J9** 49 13N 2 7W
John o' Groats **3 E11** 58 39N 3 3W
Johnstone **4 C6** 55 50N 4 31W
Johnston's Pt. **4 D4** 55 20N 5 32W
Jura **4 C4** 56 0N 5 50W
Jura, Paps of **4 C4** 55 55N 6 0W

K

Kanturk **14 D5** 52 10N 8 55W
Katrine, L. **4 B6** 56 15N 4 30W
Keady **13 C8** 54 15N 6 42W
Keal, L. na **4 B3** 56 30N 6 5W
Kebock Hd. **2 F5** 58 1N 6 20W
Keen, Mt. **3 J12** 56 58N 2 54W
Keeper Hill **14 C6** 52 46N 8 17W
Kegworth **7 G6** 52 50N 1 17W
Keighley **7 E5** 53 52N 1 54W
Keith **3 G12** 57 33N 2 58W
Kells = Ceanannus
Mor **13 D8** 53 42N 6 53W
Kells, Rhinns of **4 D7** 55 9N 4 22W
Kelso **5 C11** 55 36N 2 27W
Kelty **5 B9** 56 8N 3 23W
Kempston **9 B7** 52 7N 0 30W
Ken, L. **4 E7** 55 0N 4 8W
Kendal **6 D3** 54 19N 2 44W
Kenilworth **8 B5** 52 22N 1 35W
Kenmare **14 E3** 51 52N 9 35W
Kenmare R. → **14 E3** 51 40N 10 0W
Kennet → **9 D7** 51 24N 0 58W
Kensington and
Chelsea **9 C8** 51 30N 0 12W
Kent □ **9 D10** 51 12N 0 40 E
Kerry □ **14 D3** 52 7N 9 35W
Kerry Hd. **14 D3** 52 26N 9 56W
Keswick **6 C2** 54 35N 3 9W
Kettering **9 B7** 52 24N 0 44W
Kettla Ness **2 B15** 60 3N 1 20W
Kettle Ness **6 C7** 54 32N 0 41W
Key, L. **12 D5** 54 0N 8 15W
Keymer **9 E8** 50 55N 0 5W
Keynsham **8 D4** 51 25N 2 29W
Keyworth **7 G6** 52 52N 1 8W
Kidderminster **8 B4** 52 24N 2 13W
Kidlington **8 C6** 51 49N 1 18W
Kidsgrove **7 F4** 53 6N 2 15W
Kidwelly **10 D5** 51 44N 4 20W
Kielder Res. **6 B3** 55 11N 2 31W
Kilbirnie **4 C6** 55 46N 4 42W
Kilbrannan Sd. **4 C5** 55 40N 5 23W
Kilcreggan **4 C6** 55 59N 4 50W
Kildare **15 B9** 53 10N 6 50W
Kildare □ **15 B9** 53 10N 6 50W
Kilfinnane **14 D6** 52 21N 8 30W
Kilkee **14 C3** 52 41N 9 40W
Kilkeel **13 C9** 54 4N 6 0W
Kilkenny **15 C8** 52 40N 7 17W
Kilkenny □ **15 C8** 52 35N 7 15W
Kilkieran B. **14 B3** 53 18N 9 45W
Killala **12 C3** 54 13N 9 12W
Killala B. **12 C3** 54 20N 9 12W
Killaloe **14 C6** 52 48N 8 28W
Killard, Pt. **13 C10** 54 18N 5 31W
Killarney **14 D3** 52 2N 9 31W
Killary Harbour **12 D2** 53 38N 9 52W
Killin **4 B7** 56 28N 4 20W
Killorglin **14 D3** 52 6N 9 48W
Killybegs **12 B5** 54 38N 8 26W
Killyleagh **13 C10** 54 24N 5 40W
Kilmallock **14 D5** 52 22N 8 35W
Kilmarnock **4 C7** 55 36N 4 30W
Kilmaurs **4 C6** 55 37N 4 33W
Kilmichael Pt. **15 C10** 52 44N 6 8W
Kilrenny **5 B10** 56 15N 2 40W
Kilrush **14 C4** 52 39N 9 30W
Kilsyth **4 C7** 55 58N 4 3W
Kilwinning **4 C6** 55 40N 4 41W
Kincardine **3 J13** 56 57N 2 30W
Kinder Scout **7 F5** 53 24N 1 53W
Kingairloch **4 A4** 56 37N 5 30W
Kinghorn **5 B9** 56 4N 3 10W
King's → **15 C8** 52 32N 7 12W
Kings Langley **9 C8** 51 43N 0 27W
King's Lynn **9 A9** 52 45N 0 25 E
Kingsbridge **11 G6** 50 17N 3 46W
Kingscourt **13 D8** 53 55N 6 48W
Kingsteignton **11 F6** 50 32N 3 35W
Kingston upon Hull **7 E8** 53 45N 0 20W
Kingston-upon-
Thames **9 D8** 51 23N 0 20W
Kingswear **11 G6** 50 21N 3 33W
Kingswood **8 D3** 51 26N 2 31W
Kingussie **3 H9** 57 5N 4 2W
Kinlochleven **4 A6** 56 42N 4 59W
Kinnairds Hd. **3 G14** 57 40N 2 0W
Kinross **5 B9** 56 13N 3 25W
Kinsale **14 E5** 51 42N 8 31W
Kinsale, Old Hd. of **14 E5** 51 37N 8 32W
Kintore **3 H13** 57 14N 2 20W
Kintyre **4 C4** 55 30N 5 35W
Kintyre, Mull of **4 D4** 55 17N 5 55W
Kippure **15 B10** 53 11N 6 23W
Kirkburton **7 E5** 53 36N 1 42W
Kirkby **7 F3** 53 29N 2 54W
Kirkby-in-Ashfield **7 F6** 53 6N 1 15W
Kirkby Lonsdale **6 D3** 54 13N 2 36W
Kirkby Stephen **6 D4** 54 27N 2 23W
Kirkbymoorside **6 D7** 54 16N 0 56W
Kirkcaldy **5 B9** 56 7N 3 10W
Kirkconnel **5 D8** 55 23N 4 0W
Kirkcudbright **4 E7** 54 50N 4 3W
Kirkcudbright B. **4 E7** 54 46N 4 1W
Kirkham **7 E3** 53 47N 2 52W
Kirkintilloch **4 C7** 55 57N 4 10W
Kirkwall **3 E12** 58 59N 2 59W
Kirriemuir **5 A9** 56 41N 3 1W
Kishorn, L. **2 H6** 57 22N 5 40W
Knapdale **4 C4** 55 55N 5 30W
Knaresborough **7 E6** 54 1N 1 31W
Knighton **10 C7** 52 21N 3 2W
Knockalongy **12 C4** 54 12N 8 45W
Knockboy **14 E4** 51 49N 9 27W
Knocklayd **13 A9** 55 10N 6 15W
Knockmealdown **14 D7** 52 14N 7 55W
Knockmealdown
Mts. **14 D7** 52 16N 8 0W
Knocknaskagh **14 D6** 52 7N 8 25W
Knottingley **7 E6** 53 42N 1 15W
Knoydart **2 H6** 57 3N 5 33W
Knutsford **7 F4** 53 18N 2 22W
Kyle **4 C7** 55 32N 4 25W
Kyle of Lochalsh **2 H6** 57 17N 5 43W

L

Laceby **7 E8** 53 32N 0 10W
Ladder Hills **3 H11** 57 14N 3 13W
Ladhar Bheinn **2 H6** 57 5N 5 37W
Ladybank **5 B9** 56 16N 3 8W
Lady's Island L. **15 D10** 52 12N 6 23W
Lagan → **13 B10** 54 35N 5 55W
Laggan B. **4 C3** 55 40N 6 20W
Lairg **3 F9** 58 1N 4 24W
Lake District **6 C2** 54 30N 3 10W
Lamb Hd. **3 D12** 59 5N 2 32W
Lambeth **9 D8** 51 27N 0 7W
Lamb's Hd. **14 E2** 51 44N 10 10W
Lammermuir **5 C11** 55 50N 2 25W
Lammermuir Hills **5 C10** 55 50N 2 40W
Lampeter **10 C5** 52 6N 4 6W
Lanark **5 C8** 55 40N 3 48W
Lancashire □ **7 E3** 53 40N 2 30W
Lancaster **6 D3** 54 3N 2 48W
Lancing **9 E8** 50 49N 0 19W
Land's End **11 G2** 50 4N 5 43W
Langholm **5 D10** 55 9N 2 59W
Langness **13 C12** 54 3N 4 37W
Laois □ **15 C8** 53 0N 7 20W
Largs **4 C6** 55 48N 4 51W
Larkhall **5 C8** 55 44N 3 58W
Larne **13 B10** 54 52N 5 50W
Larne L. **13 B10** 54 52N 5 50W
Lasswade **5 C9** 55 53N 3 8W
Lauder **5 C10** 55 43N 2 45W
Launceston **11 F5** 50 38N 4 21W
Laune → **14 D3** 52 5N 9 40W
Laurencekirk **3 J13** 56 50N 2 30W
Lavagh More **12 B5** 54 47N 8 7W
Laxford, L. **2 F7** 58 25N 5 10W
Leadhills **5 D8** 55 25N 3 47W
Leamington Spa =
Royal
Leamington Spa **8 B5** 52 18N 1 32W
Leane, L. **14 D3** 52 2N 9 32W
Leatherhead **9 D8** 51 18N 0 20W
Lechlade **8 C5** 51 42N 1 40W
Ledbury **8 B4** 52 3N 2 25W
Lee → **14 E5** 51 50N 8 30W
Leeds **7 E5** 53 48N 1 34W
Leek **7 F4** 53 7N 2 2W
Leicester **7 G6** 52 39N 1 9W
Leicestershire □ **7 G6** 52 40N 1 10W
Leigh **7 F3** 53 29N 2 31W
Leighton Buzzard **9 C7** 51 55N 0 39W
Leinster **15 C8** 53 0N 7 10W
Leinster, Mt. **15 C9** 52 38N 6 47W
Leiston **9 B12** 52 13N 1 35 E
Leith **5 C9** 55 59N 3 10W
Leith Hill **9 D8** 51 10N 0 23W
Leitrim **12 D5** 54 0N 8 5W
Leitrim □ **12 C6** 54 8N 8 0W
Lenadoon Pt. **12 C3** 54 19N 9 3W
Lennox Hills **4 B7** 56 3N 4 12W
Lennoxtown **4 C7** 55 58N 4 14W
Leominster **8 B3** 52 15N 2 43W
Lerwick **2 B15** 60 10N 1 10W
Leslie **5 B9** 56 12N 3 12W
Letchworth **9 C8** 51 58N 0 13W
Letterkenny **12 B6** 54 57N 7 42W
Leven **5 B10** 56 12N 3 0W
Leven, L., *Highl.* **4 A5** 56 42N 5 2W
Leven, L.,
Perth & Kinr. **5 B9** 56 12N 3 22W
Lewes **9 E9** 50 53N 0 2 E
Lewis **2 F4** 58 10N 6 40W
Lewis, Butt of **2 E5** 58 30N 6 12W
Lewisham **9 D8** 51 27N 0 1W
Leyburn **6 D5** 54 19N 1 50W
Leyland **7 E3** 53 41N 2 42W
Lichfield **7 G5** 52 40N 1 50W
Liffey → **15 B10** 53 21N 6 20W
Lifford **12 B7** 54 50N 7 29W
Lilleshall **7 G4** 52 45N 2 22W
Limavady **13 A8** 55 3N 6 58W
Limerick **14 C5** 52 40N 8 38W
Limerick □ **14 C5** 52 30N 8 50W
Lincoln **7 F7** 53 14N 0 32W
Lincolnshire □ **7 F8** 53 14N 0 30W
Lincolnshire Wolds **7 F8** 53 20N 0 5W
Lingfield **9 D8** 51 11N 0 0 E
Linlithgow **5 C8** 55 58N 3 38W
Linney Hd. **11 D3** 51 37N 5 4W
Linnhe, L. **4 A5** 56 36N 5 25W
Lisburn **13 B9** 54 30N 6 9W
Liscannor B. **14 C4** 52 57N 9 24W
Liskeard **11 G5** 50 27N 4 29W
Lismore **14 D7** 52 8N 7 58W
Listowel **14 D4** 52 27N 9 30W
Litherland **7 F3** 53 29N 3 0W
Little Minch **2 G4** 57 35N 6 45W
Littleborough **7 E4** 53 39N 2 6W
Littlehampton **9 E7** 50 48N 0 32W
Littleport **9 B9** 52 27N 0 18 E
Liverpool **7 F3** 53 25N 3 0W
Livingston **5 C8** 55 52N 3 33W
Lizard **11 H3** 49 58N 5 10W
Lizard Pt. **11 H3** 49 57N 5 11W
Llanberis **10 A5** 53 7N 4 7W
Llandeilo **10 D6** 51 53N 3 59W
Llandovery **10 D6** 51 59N 3 49W
Llandrindod Wells **10 C7** 52 15N 3 23W
Llandudno **10 A6** 53 19N 3 51W
Llanelli **10 D5** 51 41N 4 11W
Llanfairfechan **10 A6** 53 15N 3 58W
Llanfairpwllgwyngyll **10 A5** 53 13N 4 11W
Llangefni **10 A5** 53 15N 4 20W
Llangollen **10 B7** 52 58N 3 10W
Llanidloes **10 C6** 52 28N 3 31W
Llanrwst **10 A6** 53 8N 3 49W
Llantrisant **11 D7** 51 33N 3 22W
Llantwit-Major **11 E7** 51 24N 3 29W
Llanwrtyd Wells **10 C6** 52 6N 3 39W
Llethr **10 B6** 52 47N 3 58W
Lleyn Peninsula **10 B4** 52 55N 4 35W
Loanhead **5 C9** 55 53N 3 10W
Loch Garman =
Wexford **15 D10** 52 20N 6 28W
Lochaber **3 J8** 56 55N 5 0W
Locharbriggs **5 D8** 55 7N 3 37W
Lochcarron **2 H6** 57 25N 5 30W
Lochgelly **5 B9** 56 7N 3 18W
Lochgilphead **4 B5** 56 2N 5 27W
Lochinver **2 F7** 58 9N 5 15W
Lochmaben **5 D9** 55 8N 3 27W
Lochnagar **3 J11** 56 57N 3 14W
Lochwinnoch **4 C6** 55 47N 4 39W
Lochy → **2 J7** 56 52N 5 3W
Lochy, L. **3 J8** 56 58N 4 55W
Lockerbie **5 D9** 55 7N 3 21W
Loftus **6 C7** 54 33N 0 52W
Lomond, L. **4 B6** 56 8N 4 38W
London **9 D8** 51 30N 0 5W
London Colney **9 C8** 51 43N 0 18W
Londonderry **12 B7** 55 0N 7 23W
Londonderry □ **12 B7** 55 0N 7 10W
Long, L. **4 B6** 56 4N 4 50W
Long Eaton **7 G6** 52 54N 1 16W
Long Mt. **10 B7** 52 38N 3 7W
Longbenton **6 B5** 55 2N 1 34W
Longford **12 D6** 53 43N 7 50W
Longford □ **12 D6** 53 42N 7 45W
Longridge **7 E3** 53 50N 2 37W
Longtown, *Cumb.* **6 B3** 55 1N 2 59W
Longtown,
Hereford **8 C3** 51 58N 2 59W
Looe **11 G5** 50 24N 4 25W
Loop Hd. **14 C3** 52 34N 9 55W
Lorn **4 B5** 56 26N 5 10W
Lorn, Firth of **4 B4** 56 20N 5 40W
Lossie → **3 G11** 57 42N 3 20W
Lossiemouth **3 G11** 57 43N 3 17W
Lostwithiel **11 G4** 50 24N 4 41W
Loughborough **7 G6** 52 46N 1 11W
Loughrea **14 B5** 53 11N 8 33W
Loughros More B. **12 B4** 54 48N 8 30W
Loughton **9 C9** 51 38N 0 4 E
Louth, *Lincs.* **7 F9** 53 23N 0 0 E
Louth, *Louth* **13 D8** 53 47N 6 33W
Louth □ **13 D8** 53 55N 6 30W
Lowestoft **9 B12** 52 29N 1 44 E
Lowther Hills **5 D8** 55 20N 3 40W
Luce Bay **4 E6** 54 45N 4 48W
Ludlow **8 B3** 52 23N 2 42W
Lugnaquilla **15 C10** 52 58N 6 28W
Luimneach =
Limerick **14 C5** 52 40N 8 38W
Lunan B. **5 A11** 56 40N 2 25W
Lundy **11 E4** 51 10N 4 41W
Lune → **7 D3** 54 0N 2 51W
Lunna Ness **2 B15** 60 27N 1 4W
Lurgan **13 C9** 54 28N 6 25W
Luton **9 C8** 51 53N 0 24W
Lutterworth **8 B6** 52 28N 1 12W
Lybster **3 F11** 58 18N 3 16W
Lydd **9 E10** 50 57N 0 56 E
Lydney **8 C3** 51 43N 2 32W
Lyme B. **11 F8** 50 36N 2 55W
Lyme Regis **11 F8** 50 44N 2 57W
Lymington **8 E5** 50 46N 1 32W
Lymm **7 F4** 53 23N 2 30W
Lyndhurst **8 E5** 50 53N 1 33W
Lynher → **11 G5** 50 30N 4 21W
Lynton **11 E6** 51 14N 3 50W
Lytham St. Anne's **7 E2** 53 45N 3 0W

M

Mablethorpe **7 F9** 53 21N 0 14 E
Mc Swyne's B. **12 B5** 54 37N 8 25W
Macclesfield **7 F4** 53 16N 2 9W
Macduff **3 G13** 57 40N 2 30W
Macgillycuddy's
Reeks **14 E3** 51 57N 9 45W
Machen **11 D7** 51 35N 3 8W
Machrihanish B. **4 D4** 55 28N 5 50W
Machynlleth **10 B6** 52 36N 3 51W
Macnean, L. **12 C6** 54 19N 7 52W
Macroom **14 E5** 51 54N 8 57W
Maddy, L. **2 G3** 57 36N 7 8W
Madley **8 B3** 52 3N 2 51W
Maesteg **11 D6** 51 36N 3 40W
Magherafelt **13 B8** 54 44N 6 37W
Maghull **7 E3** 53 31N 2 56W
Magilligan Pt. **13 A8** 55 10N 6 58W
Maidenhead **9 C7** 51 31N 0 42W
Maidstone **9 D10** 51 16N 0 31 E
Maigue → **14 C5** 52 39N 8 48W
Main → **13 B9** 54 49N 6 20W
Maine → **14 D3** 52 10N 9 40W
Mainland, *Orkney* **3 E11** 59 0N 3 10W
Mainland, *Shet.* **2 B15** 60 15N 1 22W
Mal B. **14 C3** 52 50N 9 30W
Malahide **15 B10** 53 26N 6 10W
Maldon **9 C10** 51 43N 0 41 E
Malham Tarn **6 D4** 54 6N 2 11W
Malin Hd. **12 A7** 55 18N 7 24W
Malin Pen. **13 A7** 55 20N 7 17W
Mallaig **2 H6** 57 0N 5 50W
Mallow **14 D5** 52 8N 8 40W
Malltraeth B. **10 A5** 53 7N 4 30W
Malmesbury **8 C4** 51 35N 2 5W
Malpas **7 F3** 53 3N 2 47W
Maltby **7 F6** 53 25N 1 12W
Malton **6 D7** 54 9N 0 48W
Malvern Hills **8 B4** 52 5N 2 20W
Man, I. of **13 C13** 54 15N 4 30W
Manchester **7 E4** 53 30N 2 15W
Mangerton Mt. **14 E4** 51 57N 9 30W
Mangotsfield **8 D4** 51 29N 2 29W
Manningtree **9 C11** 51 56N 1 3 E
Mansfield **7 F6** 53 8N 1 12W
Mansfield
Woodhouse **7 F6** 53 11N 1 11W
Mar **3 H12** 57 11N 2 53W
March **7 G9** 52 33N 0 5 E
Maree, L. **2 G7** 57 40N 5 30W
Margam **11 D6** 51 33N 3 45W
Margate **9 D11** 51 23N 1 24 E
Margery Hill **7 F5** 53 27N 1 43W
Market Deeping **7 G8** 52 40N 0 20W
Market Drayton **7 G4** 52 55N 2 29W
Market Harborough **9 B7** 52 29N 0 55W
Market Rasen **7 F8** 53 24N 0 20W
Market Weighton **7 E7** 53 52N 0 40W
Markinch **5 B9** 56 12N 3 9W
Marlborough **8 D5** 51 26N 1 44W
Marlborough
Downs **8 D5** 51 25N 1 55W
Marlow **9 C7** 51 34N 0 47W
Marple **7 F4** 53 23N 2 5W
Marske by the Sea **6 C7** 54 35N 1 0W
Maryborough =
Port Laoise **15 B8** 53 2N 7 20W
Maryport **6 C2** 54 43N 3 30W
Mask, L. **12 D3** 53 36N 9 24W
Matlock **7 F5** 53 8N 1 32W
Mauchline **4 C7** 55 31N 4 23W
Maughold Hd. **13 C13** 54 18N 4 17W
Maumturk Mts. **12 D2** 53 32N 9 42W
Maybole **4 D6** 55 21N 4 41W
Mayfield **9 D9** 51 1N 0 17 E
Maynooth **15 B9** 53 22N 6 38W
Mayo □ **12 D3** 53 47N 9 7W
Mealfuarvonie **3 H8** 57 15N 4 34W
Mearns, Howe of
the **3 J13** 56 52N 2 26W
Measham **7 G5** 52 43N 1 30W
Meath □ **13 D8** 53 32N 6 40W
Medway → **9 D10** 51 28N 0 45 E
Medway Towns □ **9 D10** 51 22N 0 33 E
Megget Res. **5 D9** 55 29N 3 18W
Melfort, L. **4 B4** 56 13N 5 33W
Melksham **8 D4** 51 22N 2 9W
Melrose **5 C10** 55 35N 2 44W
Meltham **7 E5** 53 35N 1 51W
Melton Mowbray **7 G7** 52 46N 0 52W
Melvin, L. **12 C5** 54 26N 8 10W
Menai Bridge **10 A5** 53 14N 4 11W
Menai Strait **10 A5** 53 14N 4 10W
Mendip Hills **8 D3** 51 17N 2 40W
Mere **8 D4** 51 5N 2 16W
Meriden **8 B5** 52 27N 1 36W
Merrick **4 D7** 55 8N 4 28W
Merse **5 C11** 55 40N 2 30W
Mersea I. **9 C10** 51 48N 0 55 E
Mersey → **7 F3** 53 20N 2 56W
Merseyside □ **7 F3** 53 25N 2 55W
Merthyr Tydfil **10 D7** 51 45N 3 23W
Merton **9 D8** 51 25N 0 13W
Methil **5 B9** 56 10N 3 1W
Mevagissey **11 G4** 50 16N 4 48W
Mexborough **7 E6** 53 31N 1 18W
Mickle Fell **6 C4** 54 38N 2 16W
Mickleover **7 G5** 52 55N 1 32W
Middlesbrough **6 C6** 54 35N 1 14W
Middleton **7 E4** 53 33N 2 12W
Middleton in
Teesdale **6 C4** 54 38N 2 5W
Middleton-on-Sea **9 E7** 50 48N 0 37W
Middletown **13 C8** 54 18N 6 50W
Middlewich **7 F4** 53 12N 2 28W
Midhurst **9 E7** 50 59N 0 44W
Midleton **14 E6** 51 52N 8 12W
Midlothian □ **5 C9** 55 51N 3 2W
Midsomer Norton **8 D4** 51 17N 2 29W
Mildenhall **9 B10** 52 20N 0 30 E
Milford **9 D7** 51 10N 0 38W
Milford Haven **10 D3** 51 43N 5 2W
Milford on Sea **8 E5** 50 44N 1 36W
Milleur Pt. **4 D5** 55 2N 5 5W
Millom **6 D2** 54 13N 3 16W
Millport **4 C6** 55 45N 4 55W
Milltown Malbay **14 C4** 52 51N 9 25W
Milngavie **4 C7** 55 57N 4 20W
Milton Keynes **9 B7** 52 3N 0 45W
Mine Hd. **15 E7** 52 0N 7 37W
Minehead **8 D2** 51 12N 3 29W
Minginish **2 H5** 57 14N 6 15W
Mirfield **7 E5** 53 41N 1 42W
Mitchelstown **14 D6** 52 16N 8 18W
Mizen Hd., *Cork* **14 F3** 51 27N 9 50W
Mizen Hd., *Wick.* **15 C10** 52 52N 6 4W
Moate **15 B7** 53 25N 7 43W
Moffat **5 D9** 55 20N 3 27W
Moher, Cliffs of **14 C4** 52 58N 9 27W
Moidart **2 J6** 56 49N 5 41W
Moidart, L. **2 J6** 56 47N 5 40W
Mold **10 A7** 53 10N 3 10W
Monach, Sd. of **2 G2** 57 34N 7 30W
Monadhliath Mts. **3 H9** 57 10N 4 4W
Monaghan **13 C8** 54 15N 6 58W
Monaghan □ **13 C8** 54 15N 7 0W
Monar, L. **2 H7** 57 26N 5 8W
Monasterevin **15 B8** 53 10N 7 5W
Monavullagh Mts. **15 D7** 52 14N 7 35W
Moneymore **13 B8** 54 42N 6 40W
Monifieth **5 B10** 56 30N 2 48W
Monmouth **10 D8** 51 48N 2 43W
Monmouthshire □ **10 D8** 51 48N 2 54W
Montgomery **10 B7** 52 34N 3 9W
Montrose **5 A11** 56 43N 2 28W
Moorfoot Hills **5 C9** 55 44N 3 8W
Morar, L. **2 J6** 56 57N 5 40W
Moray □ **3 G11** 57 31N 3 18W
Moray Firth **3 G10** 57 50N 3 30W
Morecambe **6 D3** 54 5N 2 52W
Morecambe B. **6 D3** 54 7N 3 0W
Moreton-in-Marsh **8 C5** 51 59N 1 42W
Moretonhampstead **11 F6** 50 39N 3 45W
Morley **7 E5** 53 45N 1 36W
Morpeth **6 B5** 55 11N 1 41W
Morte B. **11 E5** 51 10N 4 13W
Morte Pt. **11 E5** 51 13N 4 14W
Morven, *Gramp.* **3 H11** 57 8N 3 1W
Morven, *Highl.* **3 F10** 58 15N 3 40W
Morvern **4 A4** 56 38N 5 44W
Mossley **7 E4** 53 31N 2 1W
Motherwell **5 C8** 55 48N 4 0W
Mountain Ash **10 D7** 51 42N 3 22W
Mountmellick **15 B8** 53 7N 7 20W
Mountrath **15 C8** 53 0N 7 30W
Mount's Bay **11 G3** 50 3N 5 27W
Mourne → **12 B7** 54 45N 7 25W
Mourne Mts. **13 C10** 54 10N 6 0W
Moville **13 A7** 55 11N 7 3W
Mu Ness **2 A16** 60 41N 0 50W
Muckle Flugga **2 A16** 60 51N 0 54W
Muckros Hd. **12 B4** 54 37N 8 35W
Muine Bheag **15 C9** 52 42N 6 57W
Mull **4 B4** 56 27N 6 0W
Mull, Sd. of **4 A4** 56 30N 5 50W
Mull Hd. **3 E12** 58 59N 2 51W
Mullaghareirk Mts. **14 D4** 52 20N 9 10W
Mullardoch, L. **3 H7** 57 23N 5 0W
Mullet Pen. **12 C1** 54 10N 10 2W
Mullingar **12 D7** 53 31N 7 20W
Mulroy B. **12 A6** 55 15N 7 45W
Mumbles Hd. **11 D6** 51 33N 4 0W
Mundesley **9 A11** 52 53N 1 24 E
Munster **14 D5** 52 20N 8 40W
Murton **6 C6** 54 51N 1 22W
Musselburgh **5 C9** 55 57N 3 3W
Mutton I. **14 C3** 52 50N 9 31W
Mweelrea **12 D2** 53 37N 9 48W
Mynydd Du **10 D6** 51 45N 3 45W
Mynydd Eppynt **10 C6** 52 4N 3 30W
Mynydd Preseli **10 D4** 51 57N 4 48W

N

Naas **15 B9** 53 12N 6 40W
Nagles Mts. **14 D5** 52 8N 8 30W
Nailsea **8 D3** 51 25N 2 44W
Nailsworth **8 C4** 51 41N 2 12W
Nairn **3 G10** 57 35N 3 54W
Nairn → **3 G10** 57 32N 3 58W
Nantwich **7 F3** 53 5N 2 31W
Narberth **10 D4** 51 48N 4 45W

Place names on the turquoise-coded World Map section are to be found in the index at the rear of the book.

INDEX TO BRITISH ISLES MAPS

37

Narrows **Slieve Elva**

Narrows **2 H5** 57 20N 6 5W
Nash Pt. **11 E6** 51 24N 3 34W
Navan = An Uaimh **13 D8** 53 39N 6 40W
Naver —► **3 E9** 58 34N 4 15W
Neagh, L. **13 B9** 54 35N 6 25W
Neath **10 D6** 51 39N 3 49W
Neath —► **10 D6** 51 38N 3 35W
Neist Pt. **2 H4** 57 24N 6 48W
Nelson **7 E4** 53 50N 2 14W
Nenagh **14 C6** 52 52N 8 11W
Nenagh —► **14 C6** 52 56N 8 16W
Nene —► **9 A9** 52 38N 0 13 E
Nephin **12 C3** 54 1N 9 21W
Nephin Beg Range **12 D2** 54 0N 9 40W
Ness **2 F5** 58 27N 6 20W
Ness, L. **3 H8** 57 15N 4 30W
Neston **7 F2** 53 17N 3 3W
Nevis, L. **2 J6** 57 0N 5 43W
New Alresford **8 D6** 51 6N 1 10W
New Bedford R. —► **9 A9** 52 34N 0 20 E
New Forest **8 E5** 50 53N 1 40W
New Galloway **4 D7** 55 4N 4 10W
New Holland **7 E8** 53 42N 0 22W
New Mills **7 F5** 53 22N 2 0W
New Milton **8 E5** 50 45N 1 40W
New Quay **10 C5** 52 13N 4 21W
New Radnor **10 C7** 52 15N 3 10W
New Romney **9 E10** 50 59N 0 57 E
New Ross **15 D9** 52 24N 6 58W
New Rossington **7 F6** 53 30N 1 4W
New Scone **5 B9** 56 25N 3 26W
New Tredegar **10 D7** 51 43N 3 15W
Newark-on-Trent **7 F7** 53 6N 0 48W
Newbiggin-by-the-Sea **6 B5** 55 12N 1 31W
Newbridge = Droichead Nua **15 B9** 53 11N 6 50W
Newburgh **5 B9** 56 21N 3 15W
Newburn **6 C5** 54 57N 1 45W
Newbury **8 D6** 51 24N 1 19W
Newcastle **13 C10** 54 13N 5 54W
Newcastle Emlyn **10 C5** 52 2N 4 29W
Newcastle-under-Lyme **7 F4** 53 2N 2 15W
Newcastle-upon-Tyne **6 C5** 54 59N 1 37W
Newcastle West **14 D4** 52 27N 9 3W
Newham **9 C9** 51 31N 0 2 E
Newhaven **9 E9** 50 47N 0 4 E
Newlyn **11 G2** 50 6N 5 33W
Newmarket, *Cork* **14 D5** 52 13N 9 0W
Newmarket, *Suffolk* **9 B9** 52 15N 0 23 E
Newmilns **4 C7** 55 36N 4 20W
Newport, *I. of W.* **8 E6** 50 42N 1 18W
Newport, *Mayo* **12 D2** 53 50N 9 31W
Newport, *Newp.* **11 D8** 51 35N 3 0W
Newport, *Shrops.* **7 G4** 52 47N 2 22W
Newport B. **12 D2** 53 52N 9 38W
Newport-on-Tay **5 B10** 56 27N 2 56W
Newport Pagnell **9 B7** 52 5N 0 42W
Newquay **11 G3** 50 24N 5 6W
Newry **13 C9** 54 10N 6 20W
Newton Abbot **11 F6** 50 32N 3 37W
Newton Aycliffe **6 C5** 54 36N 1 33W
Newton le Willows **7 F3** 53 28N 2 40W
Newton Stewart **4 E6** 54 57N 4 30W
Newtongrange **5 C9** 55 52N 3 4W
Newtonmore **3 H9** 57 4N 4 7W
Newtown **10 B7** 52 31N 3 19W
Newtownabbey **13 B10** 54 40N 5 55W
Newtownards **13 B10** 54 37N 5 40W
Newtownbarry = Bunclody **15 C9** 52 40N 6 40W
Newtownstewart **12 B7** 54 43N 7 22W
Neyland **10 D4** 51 43N 4 58W
Nidd —► **7 E6** 53 58N 1 28W
Nidderdale **6 D5** 54 5N 1 46W
Nigg B. **3 G9** 57 41N 4 5W
Nith —► **5 D8** 55 20N 3 5W
Nithsdale **5 D8** 55 14N 3 50W
Nore —► **15 D9** 52 24N 6 58W
Norfolk □ **9 A11** 52 39N 1 0 E
Norfolk Broads Nat. Park **9 A11** 52 45N 1 30 E
Normanton **7 E6** 53 41N 1 26W
North Ayrshire □ **4 C6** 55 38N 4 47W
North Berwick **5 B10** 56 4N 2 44W
North Channel **4 D4** 55 0N 5 30W
North Dorset Downs **8 E3** 50 50N 2 30W
North Downs **9 D9** 51 17N 0 30 E
North East Lincolnshire □ **7 E8** 53 35N 0 5W
North Esk —► **5 A11** 56 44N 2 25W
North Foreland **9 D11** 51 22N 1 28 E
North Harris **2 G4** 58 0N 6 55W
North Lanarkshire □ **4 C7** 55 52N 4 2W
North Lincolnshire □ **7 E7** 53 35N 0 38W
North Minch **2 F6** 58 5N 5 55W
North Roe **2 A15** 60 40N 1 22W
North Somerset □ **8 D3** 51 25N 2 45W
North Sd. **14 B3** 53 10N 9 48W
North Tyne —► **6 C4** 54 59N 2 7W
North Uist **2 G3** 57 40N 7 15W
North Walsham **9 A11** 52 49N 1 22 E
North West Highlands **2 G8** 57 35N 5 0W
North York Moors **6 D7** 54 25N 0 50W
North Yorkshire □ **6 D6** 54 15N 1 25W
Northallerton **6 D6** 54 20N 1 26W
Northampton **9 B7** 52 14N 0 54W
Northamptonshire □ **9 B7** 52 16N 0 55W
Northern Ireland □ **13 B8** 54 45N 7 0W
Northfleet **9 D9** 51 26N 0 20 E
Northumberland □ **6 B5** 55 12N 2 0W
Northwich **7 F3** 53 16N 2 31W
Norton **6 D7** 54 9N 0 48W
Norwich **9 A11** 52 38N 1 17 E
Noss Hd. **3 F11** 58 29N 3 4W
Nottingham **7 G6** 52 57N 1 10W
Nottinghamshire □ **7 F7** 53 10N 1 0W
Noup Hd. **3 D11** 59 20N 3 2W
Nowen Hill **14 E4** 51 42N 9 15W
Nuneaton **8 A6** 52 32N 1 29W

O

Oa, Mull of **4 C3** 55 35N 6 20W
Oadby **7 G6** 52 37N 1 7W
Oakengates **7 G4** 52 42N 2 29W
Oakham **7 G7** 52 40N 0 43W
Oban **4 B5** 56 25N 5 30W
Ochil Hills **5 B8** 56 14N 3 40W
Offaly □ **15 B7** 53 15N 7 30W
Okehampton **11 F5** 50 44N 4 1W
Old Bedford R. —► **9 A9** 52 36N 0 20 E
Old Fletton **7 G8** 52 34N 0 13W
Old Man of Hoy **3 E11** 58 53N 3 25W
Oldbury **8 C3** 51 38N 2 30W
Oldcastle **13 D7** 53 46N 7 10W
Oldham **7 E4** 53 33N 2 8W
Oldmeldrum **3 H13** 57 20N 2 19W
Olney **9 B7** 52 9N 0 42W
Omagh **12 B7** 54 36N 7 20W
Orford Ness **9 B12** 52 6N 1 31 E
Orkney □ **3 D11** 59 0N 3 0W
Ormskirk **7 E3** 53 35N 2 53W
Oronsay, Passage of **4 C3** 56 0N 6 10W
Orwell —► **9 B11** 52 2N 1 12 E
Ossett **7 E5** 53 40N 1 35W
Oswaldtwistle **7 E4** 53 44N 2 27W
Oswestry **7 G2** 52 52N 3 3W
Otley **7 E5** 53 54N 1 41W
Ottery St. Mary **11 F7** 50 45N 3 16W
Oughter, L. **12 C7** 54 2N 7 30W
Oughterard **14 B4** 53 26N 9 20W
Oundle **9 B8** 52 28N 0 28W
Ouse —► **7 E7** 53 33N 0 44W
Outer Hebrides **2 J2** 57 30N 7 40W
Owel, L. **12 D7** 53 34N 7 24W
Oxford **8 C6** 51 45N 1 15W
Oxfordshire □ **8 C6** 51 45N 1 15W
Oxted **9 D9** 51 14N 0 0 E
Oxwich Pt. **11 D5** 51 33N 4 8W
Oykel —► **3 G9** 57 55N 4 26W

P

Pabbay, Sd. of **2 G3** 57 45N 7 4W
Paddock Wood **9 D9** 51 13N 0 24 E
Padiham **7 E4** 53 48N 2 20W
Padstow **11 F4** 50 33N 4 57W
Paignton **11 G6** 50 26N 3 33W
Painshawfield **6 C5** 54 56N 1 54W
Paisley **4 C7** 55 51N 4 27W
Papa, Sd. of **2 B14** 60 19N 1 40W
Papa Sd. **3 D12** 59 20N 2 56W
Parrett —► **8 D3** 51 7N 3 0W
Partry Mts. **12 D3** 53 40N 9 28W
Parys Mt. **10 A5** 53 23N 4 18W
Passage West **14 E6** 51 52N 8 20W
Patna **4 D6** 55 21N 4 30W
Peak District Nat. Park **7 F5** 58 21N 1 6W
Peebles **5 C9** 55 40N 3 12W
Peel **13 C12** 54 13N 4 41W
Peel Fell **6 B3** 55 17N 2 35W
Pegwell B. **9 D11** 51 18N 1 22 E
Pembroke **10 D4** 51 41N 4 57W
Pembrokeshire □ **10 D4** 51 51N 4 56W
Pen-y-Ghent **6 D4** 54 10N 2 15W
Penarth **11 E7** 51 26N 3 11W
Pendle Hill **7 E4** 53 53N 2 18W
Penicuik **5 C9** 55 50N 3 14W
Penistone **7 E5** 53 31N 1 38W
Penkridge **7 G4** 52 44N 2 8W
Penmaenmawr **10 A6** 53 16N 3 55W
Pennines **6 C4** 54 50N 2 20W
Penrith **6 C3** 54 40N 2 45W
Penryn **11 G3** 50 10N 5 7W
Pentire Pt. **11 F4** 50 35N 4 57W
Pentland Firth **3 E11** 58 43N 3 10W
Pentland Hills **5 C9** 55 48N 3 25W
Penzance **11 G2** 50 7N 5 32W
Perranporth **11 G3** 50 21N 5 9W
Pershore **8 B4** 52 7N 2 4W
Perth **5 B9** 56 24N 3 27W
Perth & Kinross □ **5 A8** 56 45N 3 55W
Peterborough **7 G8** 52 35N 0 14W
Peterculter **3 H13** 57 5N 2 18W
Peterhead **3 G14** 57 30N 1 49W
Peterlee **6 C6** 54 45N 1 18W
Petersfield **9 D7** 51 0N 0 56W
Petworth **9 E7** 50 59N 0 37W
Pewsey, Vale of **8 D5** 51 20N 1 46W
Pickering **6 D7** 54 15N 0 46W
Pickering, Vale of **6 D7** 54 14N 0 45W
Pilsdon Pen **8 E3** 50 49N 2 51W
Pitlochry **5 A8** 56 43N 3 43W
Pittenweem **5 B10** 56 13N 2 43W
Plymouth **11 G5** 50 23N 4 9W
Plympton **11 G5** 50 24N 4 2W
Plymstock **11 G5** 50 22N 4 6W
Plynlimon = Pumlumon Fawr **10 C6** 52 29N 3 47W
Pocklington **7 E7** 53 56N 0 48W
Polegate **9 E9** 50 49N 0 15 E
Polperro **11 G4** 50 19N 4 31W
Pontardawe **10 D6** 51 43N 3 51W
Pontardulais **10 D5** 51 42N 4 3W
Pontefract **7 E6** 53 42N 1 19W
Ponteland **6 B5** 55 7N 1 45W
Pontypool **10 D7** 51 42N 3 1W
Pontypridd **11 D7** 51 36N 3 21W
Poole **8 E5** 50 42N 1 58W
Poole Harbour **8 E5** 50 41N 2 0W
Port Bannatyne **4 C5** 55 51N 5 4W
Port Ellen **4 C3** 55 38N 6 10W
Port Erin **13 C12** 54 5N 4 45W
Port Eynon Pt. **11 D5** 51 32N 4 12W
Port Glasgow **4 C6** 55 57N 4 40W
Port Isaac B. **11 F4** 50 36N 4 50W
Port Lairge = Waterford **15 D8** 52 16N 7 8W
Port Laoise **15 B8** 53 2N 7 20W
Port Talbot **11 D6** 51 35N 3 48W
Portadown **13 C9** 54 27N 6 26W
Portaferry **13 C10** 54 23N 5 32W
Portarlington **15 B8** 53 10N 7 10W
Porth Neigwl **10 B4** 52 48N 4 33W
Porthcawl **11 E6** 51 28N 3 42W
Porthleven **11 G3** 50 5N 5 19W
Porthmadog **10 B5** 52 55N 4 13W
Portishead **8 D3** 51 29N 2 46W
Portknockie **3 G12** 57 40N 2 52W
Portland, I. of **11 F9** 50 32N 2 25W
Portland Bill **11 F9** 50 31N 2 27W
Portmadoc = Porthmadog **10 B5** 52 55N 4 13W
Portpatrick **4 E5** 54 50N 5 7W
Portree **2 H5** 57 25N 6 11W
Portrush **13 A8** 55 13N 6 40W
Portslade **9 E8** 50 50N 0 11W
Portsmouth **8 E6** 50 48N 1 6W
Portsoy **3 G12** 57 41N 2 41W
Portstewart **13 A8** 55 12N 6 43W
Portumna **14 B6** 53 5N 8 12W
Potters Bar **9 C8** 51 42N 0 11W
Poulaphouca Res. **15 B10** 53 8N 6 30W
Poulton le Fylde **7 E3** 53 51N 2 59W
Powys □ **10 C7** 52 20N 3 20W
Prawle Pt. **11 G6** 50 13N 3 41W
Prestatyn **10 A7** 53 20N 3 24W
Prestbury **8 C4** 51 54N 2 2W
Presteigne **10 C7** 52 17N 3 0W
Preston **7 E3** 53 46N 2 42W
Prestonpans **5 C10** 55 58N 2 58W
Prestwich **7 E4** 53 32N 2 18W
Prestwick **4 D6** 55 30N 4 38W
Princes Risborough **9 C7** 51 43N 0 50W
Prudhoe **6 C5** 54 57N 1 52W
Pudsey **7 E5** 53 47N 1 40W
Pulborough **9 E8** 50 58N 0 30W
Pumlumon Fawr **10 C6** 52 29N 3 47W
Purbeck, I. of **8 E4** 50 40N 2 5W
Purfleet **9 D9** 51 29N 0 15 E
Pwllheli **10 B5** 52 54N 4 26W

Q

Quantock Hills **8 D2** 51 8N 3 10W
Queenborough **9 D10** 51 24N 0 46 E
Queensbury **7 E5** 53 46N 1 50W
Quendale, B. of **2 C15** 59 53N 1 20W
Quinag **2 F7** 58 13N 5 5W
Quoich, L. **2 H7** 57 4N 5 20W

R

Raasay **2 H5** 57 25N 6 4W
Radcliffe **7 E4** 53 35N 2 19W
Radcliffe-on-Trent **7 G6** 52 57N 1 3W
Radlett **9 C8** 51 41N 0 19W
Radnor Forest **10 C7** 52 17N 3 10W
Radstock **8 D4** 51 17N 2 25W
Rainham **9 D10** 51 22N 0 36 E
Rame Hd. **11 G5** 50 19N 4 14W
Ramsbottom **7 E4** 53 36N 2 20W
Ramsey, *Cambs.* **9 B8** 52 27N 0 6W
Ramsey, *I. of M.* **13 C13** 54 20N 4 21W
Ramsgate **9 D11** 51 20N 1 25 E
Randalstown **13 B9** 54 45N 6 20W
Rannoch **4 A7** 56 40N 4 20W
Rannoch, L. **4 A7** 56 41N 4 20W
Rannoch Moor **4 A6** 56 38N 4 48W
Rath Luirc **14 D5** 52 21N 8 40W
Rathdrum **15 C10** 52 57N 6 13W
Rathkeale **14 C5** 52 32N 8 57W
Rathlin I. **13 A9** 55 18N 6 14W
Rathmelton **12 A6** 55 3N 7 35W
Rattray **5 A9** 56 36N 3 20W
Rattray Hd. **3 G14** 57 38N 1 50W
Raunds **9 B7** 52 20N 0 32W
Ravenshead **7 F6** 53 5N 1 10W
Rawmarsh **7 F6** 53 27N 1 20W
Rawtenstall **7 E4** 53 42N 2 18W
Rayleigh **9 C10** 51 36N 0 38 E
Reading **9 D7** 51 27N 0 57W
Red B. **13 A9** 55 4N 6 2W
Red Wharf B. **10 A5** 53 18N 4 10W
Redbridge **9 C9** 51 35N 0 7 E
Redcar **6 C6** 54 37N 1 4W
Redditch **8 B5** 52 18N 1 57W
Redhill **9 D8** 51 14N 0 10W
Redruth **11 G3** 50 14N 5 14W
Ree, L. **12 D6** 53 35N 8 0W
Reigate **9 D8** 51 14N 0 11W
Renfrew **4 C7** 55 52N 4 24W
Renfrewshire □ **4 C6** 55 50N 4 31W
Renish Pt. **2 G4** 57 44N 6 59W
Retford **7 F7** 53 19N 0 55W
Rhayader **10 C7** 52 19N 3 30W
Rhinns Pt. **4 C3** 55 42N 6 29W
Rhois-Bheinn **2 J6** 56 50N 5 40W
Rhondda **10 D6** 51 39N 3 30W
Rhondda Cynon Taff □ **10 D7** 51 45N 3 27W
Rhosllanerchrugog **10 A7** 53 3N 3 4W
Rhossili B. **11 D5** 51 33N 4 15W
Rhum **2 J5** 57 0N 6 20W
Rhum, Sd. of **2 J5** 56 54N 6 14W
Rhyl **10 A7** 53 19N 3 29W
Rhymney **10 D7** 51 45N 3 17W
Ribble —► **7 E3** 53 46N 2 42W
Richmond **6 D5** 54 24N 1 43W
Richmond-upon-Thames **9 D8** 51 28N 0 18W
Rickmansworth **9 C8** 51 38N 0 28W
Ringwood **8 E5** 50 50N 1 48W
Ripley **7 F6** 53 3N 1 24W
Ripon **6 D5** 54 8N 1 31W
Risca **11 D7** 51 36N 3 6W
Rishton **7 E4** 53 46N 2 26W
Roag, L. **2 F4** 58 10N 6 55W
Roaringwater B. **14 F3** 51 30N 9 30W
Robin Hood's Bay **6 D7** 54 26N 0 31W
Rochdale **7 E4** 53 36N 2 10W
Rochester **9 D10** 51 22N 0 30 E
Rochford **9 C10** 51 36N 0 42 E
Rockingham Forest **9 B7** 52 28N 0 42W
Roe —► **13 A8** 55 10N 6 59W
Rogans Seat **6 D4** 54 25N 2 10W
Romney Marsh **9 D10** 51 4N 0 58 E
Romsey **8 E6** 51 0N 1 29W
Ronas Hill **2 A15** 60 33N 1 25W
Rora Hd. **3 E11** 58 51N 3 21W
Roscommon **12 D5** 53 38N 8 11W
Roscommon □ **12 D5** 53 40N 8 15W
Roscrea **14 C7** 52 58N 7 50W
Rose Ness **3 E12** 58 52N 2 50W
Ross-on-Wye **8 C3** 51 55N 2 34W
Rossall Pt. **7 E2** 53 55N 3 2W
Rossan Pt. **12 B4** 54 42N 8 47W
Rosscarbery B. **14 E5** 51 32N 9 0W
Rosses B. **12 A5** 55 2N 8 30W
Rosslare **15 D10** 52 17N 6 23W
Rosyth **5 B9** 56 2N 3 26W
Rotherham **7 F6** 53 26N 1 21W
Rothes **3 G11** 57 31N 3 12W
Rothesay **4 C5** 55 50N 5 3W
Rothwell, *Northants.* **9 B7** 52 25N 0 48W
Rothwell, *W. Yorks.* **7 E6** 53 46N 1 29W
Rottingdean **9 E8** 50 48N 0 3W
Rough Pt. **14 D2** 52 19N 10 2W
Royal Leamington Spa **8 B5** 52 18N 1 32W
Royal Tunbridge Wells **9 D9** 51 7N 0 16 E
Royston, *Herts.* **9 B8** 52 3N 0 1W
Royston, *S. Yorks.* **7 E6** 53 36N 1 27W
Royton **7 E4** 53 34N 2 7W
Rubh a' Mhail **4 C3** 55 55N 6 10W
Rubha Ardvule **2 H3** 57 17N 7 29W
Rubha Coigeach **2 F7** 58 6N 5 27W
Rubha Hunish **2 G5** 57 42N 6 20W
Rubha Robhanais = Lewis, Butt of **2 E5** 58 30N 6 12W
Rubh'an Dunain **2 H5** 57 10N 6 20W
Rugby **8 B6** 52 23N 1 16W
Rugeley **7 G5** 52 47N 1 56W
Runabay Hd. **13 A9** 55 10N 6 2W
Runcorn **7 F3** 53 20N 2 44W
Rush **13 D9** 53 31N 6 7W
Rushden **9 B7** 52 17N 0 37W
Rutherglen **4 C7** 55 50N 4 11W
Ruthin **10 A7** 53 7N 3 20W
Rutland □ **7 G7** 52 38N 0 40W
Rutland Water **7 G7** 52 38N 0 38W
Ryan, L. **4 E5** 55 0N 5 2W
Ryde **8 E6** 50 44N 1 9W
Rye **9 E10** 50 57N 0 46 E

S

Sacquoy Hd. **3 D11** 59 12N 3 5W
Saddle Hd. **12 C1** 54 1N 10 10W
Saffron Walden **9 B9** 52 2N 0 15 E
St. Abb's Hd. **5 C11** 55 55N 2 10W
St. Agnes Hd. **11 G3** 50 19N 5 14W
St. Albans **9 C8** 51 44N 0 19W
St. Alban's Hd. **8 E4** 50 34N 2 3W
St. Andrews **5 B10** 56 20N 2 48W
St. Ann's Hd. **10 D3** 51 41N 5 11W
St. Asaph **10 A7** 53 15N 3 27W
St. Austell **11 G4** 50 20N 4 48W
St. Bee's Hd. **6 C1** 54 30N 3 38W
St. Brides B. **10 D3** 51 48N 5 15W
St. Catherine's Hd. **8 E6** 50 36N 1 18W
St. Catherine's Pt. **8 E6** 50 34N 1 18W
St. David's **10 D3** 51 54N 5 16W
St. David's Hd. **10 D3** 51 55N 5 16W
St. Finan's B. **14 E2** 51 50N 10 22W
St. George's Channel **15 D11** 52 0N 6 0W
St. Govan's Hd. **11 D4** 51 35N 4 56W
St. Helens **7 F3** 53 28N 2 44W
St. Helier **11 J9** 49 11N 2 6W
St. Ives, *Cambs.* **9 B8** 52 20N 0 5W
St. Ives, *Corn.* **11 G3** 50 13N 5 29W
St. Ives B. **11 G3** 50 15N 5 27W
St. John's Pt., *Done.* **12 B5** 54 35N 8 26W
St. John's Pt., *Down* **13 C10** 54 14N 5 40W
St. Just **11 G2** 50 7N 5 41W
St. Leonards **9 E10** 50 51N 0 33 E
St. Magnus B. **2 B14** 60 25N 1 35W
St. Mary's Sd. **11 H1** 49 53N 6 19W
St. Mawes **11 G3** 50 10N 5 1W
St. Michael's Mount **11 G3** 50 7N 5 30W
St. Monance **5 B10** 56 13N 2 46W
St. Neots **9 B8** 52 14N 0 16W
St. Ouens B. **11 J9** 49 13N 2 14W
St. Peter Port **11 J8** 49 27N 2 31W
Saintfield **13 C10** 54 28N 5 50W
Salcombe **11 G6** 50 14N 3 47W
Sale **7 F4** 53 26N 2 19W
Salford **7 F4** 53 30N 2 17W
Salisbury **8 D5** 51 4N 1 48W
Salisbury Plain **8 D5** 51 13N 1 50W
Saltash **11 G5** 50 25N 4 13W
Saltburn by the Sea **6 C7** 54 35N 0 58W
Saltcoats **4 C6** 55 38N 4 47W
Sanday Sd. **3 D12** 59 11N 2 31W
Sandbach **7 F4** 53 9N 2 23W
Sandgate **9 D11** 51 5N 1 9 E
Sandness **2 B14** 60 18N 1 38W
Sandown **8 E6** 50 39N 1 9W
Sandringham **9 A10** 52 50N 0 30 E
Sandwich **9 D11** 51 16N 1 21 E
Sandy **9 B8** 52 8N 0 18W
Sanquhar **5 D8** 55 21N 3 56W
Sawbridgeworth **9 C9** 51 49N 0 10 E
Sawel **13 B7** 54 48N 7 5W
Saxmundham **9 B12** 52 13N 1 31 E
Scafell Pike **6 D2** 54 26N 3 14W
Scalby **6 D8** 54 18N 0 26W
Scalloway **2 B15** 60 9N 1 16W
Scalpay **2 H6** 57 18N 6 0W
Scapa Flow **3 E11** 58 52N 3 6W
Scarborough **6 D8** 54 17N 0 24W
Scavaig, L. **2 H5** 57 8N 6 10W
Schiehallion **4 A7** 56 40N 4 6W
Scilly, Isles of **11 H1** 49 55N 6 15W
Score Hd. **2 B15** 60 12N 1 5W
Scotch Corner **6 D5** 54 27N 1 40W
Scottish Borders □ **5 C10** 55 35N 2 50W
Scridain, L. **4 B3** 56 23N 6 7W
Scunthorpe **7 E7** 53 35N 0 38W
Seaford **9 E9** 50 46N 0 8 E
Seaforth, L. **2 G4** 57 52N 6 36W
Seaham **6 C6** 54 51N 1 20W
Seahouses **6 A5** 55 35N 1 39W
Seascale **6 D2** 54 24N 3 29W
Seaton **11 F7** 50 42N 3 3W
Sedbergh **6 D3** 54 20N 2 31W
Selby **7 E6** 53 47N 1 5W
Selkirk **5 C10** 55 33N 2 50W
Selsey **9 E7** 50 44N 0 47W
Selsey Bill **9 E7** 50 44N 0 47W
Settle **6 D4** 54 5N 2 18W
Seven Heads **14 E5** 51 35N 8 43W
Sevenoaks **9 D9** 51 16N 0 11 E
Severn —► **8 C3** 51 35N 2 38W
Sgurr a' Choire Ghlais **3 H8** 57 30N 4 56W
Sgurr Mor **3 G7** 57 42N 5 0W
Sgurr na Ciche **2 H7** 57 0N 5 29W
Sgurr na Lapaich **2 H7** 57 23N 5 5W
Shaftesbury **8 E4** 51 0N 2 12W
Shanklin **8 E6** 50 39N 1 9W
Shannon —► **14 C3** 52 35N 9 38W
Shannon Airport **14 C5** 52 42N 8 57W
Shapinsay Sd. **3 D12** 59 0N 2 51W
Sheelin, L. **12 D7** 53 48N 7 20W
Sheep Haven **12 A6** 55 12N 7 55W
Sheeps Hd. **14 E3** 51 32N 9 50W
Sheerness **9 D10** 51 26N 0 47 E
Sheffield **7 F6** 53 23N 1 28W
Shehy Mts. **14 E4** 51 47N 9 15W
Shell, L. **2 F5** 58 0N 6 28W
Shenfield **9 C9** 51 39N 0 21 E
Sheppey, I. of **9 D10** 51 23N 0 50 E
Shepshed **7 G6** 52 47N 1 18W
Shepton Mallet **8 D3** 51 11N 2 31W
Sherborne **8 E3** 50 56N 2 31W
Sheringham **9 A11** 52 56N 1 11 E
Sherwood Forest **7 F6** 53 5N 1 5W
Shetland □ **2 B15** 60 30N 1 30W
Shiant, Sd. of **2 G5** 57 54N 6 30W
Shiel, L. **2 J6** 56 48N 5 32W
Shildon **6 C5** 54 37N 1 39W
Shillelagh **15 C9** 52 46N 6 32W
Shin —► **3 G9** 57 58N 4 26W
Shin, L. **3 F8** 58 7N 4 30W
Shining Tor **7 F4** 53 15N 2 0W
Shipley **7 E5** 53 50N 1 47W
Shipston-on-Stour **8 B5** 52 4N 1 38W
Shirebrook **7 F6** 53 13N 1 11W
Shoeburyness **9 C10** 51 31N 0 49 E
Shoreham by Sea **9 E8** 50 50N 0 17W
Shotts **5 C8** 55 49N 3 47W
Shrewsbury **7 G3** 52 42N 2 45W
Shropshire □ **7 G3** 52 36N 2 45W
Sidlaw Hills **5 A9** 56 32N 3 10W
Sidmouth **11 F7** 50 40N 3 13W
Sighty Crag **6 B3** 55 8N 2 37W
Silloth **5 E9** 54 53N 3 25W
Silsden **7 E5** 53 55N 1 55W
Silvermine Mts. **14 C6** 52 47N 8 15W
Simonside **6 B5** 55 17N 1 58W
Sinclair's B. **3 E11** 58 30N 3 0W
Sion Mills **12 B7** 54 47N 7 29W
Sittingbourne **9 D10** 51 20N 0 43 E
Sixmilebridge **14 C5** 52 45N 8 46W
Sizewell **9 B12** 52 13N 1 38 E
Skaw Taing **2 B16** 60 23N 0 57W
Skegness **7 F9** 53 9N 0 20 E
Skelmersdale **7 E3** 53 34N 2 49W
Skelmorlie **4 C6** 55 52N 4 53W
Skelton **6 C7** 54 33N 0 59W
Skibbereen **14 E4** 51 33N 9 16W
Skiddaw **6 C2** 54 39N 3 9W
Skipton **7 E4** 53 57N 2 1W
Skokholm I. **10 D3** 51 42N 5 16W
Skomer I. **10 D3** 51 44N 5 19W
Skull **14 E3** 51 32N 9 40W
Skye **2 H5** 57 15N 6 10W
Slaney —► **15 D10** 52 20N 6 30W
Slea Hd. **14 D2** 52 7N 10 30W
Sleaford **7 F8** 53 1N 0 22W
Sleat, Pt. of **2 H5** 57 1N 6 0W
Sleat, Sd. of **2 H6** 57 5N 5 47W
Slieve Anierin **12 C6** 54 5N 7 58W
Slieve Aughty **14 B5** 53 4N 8 30W
Slieve Beagh **13 C7** 54 20N 7 12W
Slieve Bernagh **14 C5** 52 50N 8 30W
Slieve Donard **13 C10** 54 10N 5 57W
Slieve Elva **14 B4** 53 5N 9 16W

Place names on the turquoise-coded World Map section are to be found in the index at the rear of the book.

Slieve Foye · **Youghal**

Place names on the turquoise-coded World Map section are to be found in the index at the rear of the book.

WORLD MAPS

SETTLEMENTS

⬠ PARIS　　　■ Berne　　　◉ Livorno　　◉ Brugge　　◎ Algeciras　　◌ Frejus　　○ Oberammergau　○ Thira

Settlement symbols and type styles vary according to the scale of each map and indicate the importance
of towns on the map rather than specific population figures

∴ Ruins or Archæological Sites　　　　　˘ Wells in Desert

ADMINISTRATION

——— International Boundaries

– – – International Boundaries
(Undefined or Disputed)

⸱⸱⸱⸱⸱⸱⸱ Internal Boundaries

⬭ National Parks

Country Names

NICARAGUA

Administrative
Area Names

KENT

CALABRIA

International boundaries show the *de facto* situation where there are rival claims to territory

COMMUNICATIONS

——— Principal Roads

‿ Other Roads

⸱–⸱– Trails and Seasonal Roads

≍ Passes

✿ Airfields

‿ Principal Railways

⸱⸱⸱⸱ Railways
Under Construction

‿ Other Railways

⊐---⊏ Railway Tunnels

⸱⸱⸱⸱⸱⸱ Principal Canals

PHYSICAL FEATURES

~ Perennial Streams

⸱–⸱–⸱ Intermittent Streams

⬭ Perennial Lakes

⬭ Intermittent Lakes

Swamps and Marshes

Permanent Ice
and Glaciers

▲ 8848 Elevations in metres

▼ 8050 Sea Depths in metres

1134 Height of Lake Surface
Above Sea Level
in metres

ELEVATION AND DEPTH TINTS

Height of Land Above Sea Level　　　　　Land Below Sea Level　　　Depth of Sea

in metres	6000	4000	3000	2000	1500	1000	400	200	0						
in feet	18 000	12 000	9000	6000	4500	3000	1200	600		6000	12 000	15 000	18 000	24 000	in feet
									0	200	2000	4000	5000	6000	8000	in metres

Some of the maps have different contours to highlight and clarify the principal relief features

Projection: *Hammer Equal Area*

18
17
16
15
14
13
12
11
10

A R C T I C   O C E A N

20   40   60   70   80   100   120   140   160   180   80

Svalbard
(Nor.)

Severnaya
Zemlya

New Siberian Is.

Wrangel I.

A

Barents
Sea

Novaya
Zemlya

Kara
Sea

Laptev Sea

East Siberian
Sea

Arctic Circle

Murmansk

Norilsk

Verkhoyansk

Yenisey

Lena

Magadan

Bering
Sea

B

NORWAY
SWEDEN
FINLAND
Helsinki

Arkhangelsk

Salekhard

R U S S I A

Yakutsk

Okhotsk

Petropavlovsk-
Kamchatskiy

International
Date Line

Oslo
Stockholm
EST.
ST. PETERSBURG

Perm
Yekaterinburg
Tomsk
Krasnoyarsk

Sea of
Okhotsk

Ob

Sakhalin

Komsomolsk

DENMARK
Copenhagen
LATVIA
LITH.
MOSCOW
Kazan
Chelyabinsk
Omsk
Novosibirsk
Irkutsk
Ulan Ude
L. Baikal

Khabarovsk

mburg
NETH.
POLAND
BELARUS
Minsk
Volga
Samara
Saratov
Astana
Barnaul

Amur

Vladivostok
Sapporo

Amsterdam
GERMANY
Berlin
Prague
Warsaw
Kiev
UKRAINE
Volgograd
KAZAKSTAN
Karaganda
L. Balkhash

Ulan Bator

Harbin
Changchun

SHENYANG

JAPAN

40

Brussels
LUX.
Vienna
AUSTRIA
Budapest
ROMANIA
Bucharest
Astrakhan
Aral
Sea
Alma Ata
Bishkek
MONGOLIA

BEIJING
TIANJIN
NORTH
KOREA
Pyongyang
SEOUL
TŌKYŌ

PACIFIC

PARIS
Milan
CROATIA
Belgrade
YUG.
BULGARIA
Black
Sea
GEORGIA
Tbilisi
Yerevan
AZER.
Baku
UZBEKISTAN
Samarkand
KYRGYZSTAN
Tashkent
Dushanbe
Caspian
Sea
C H I N A
Lanzhou
Taiyuan
SOUTH
KOREA
Dalian
Osaka
Kitakyūshū

OCEAN

Marseilles
ITALY
Rome
Sofia
ARMENIA
TURKMENISTAN
Ashkhabad
Xi'an
Nanjing
SHANGHAI

C

Barcelona
Sardinia
Naples
Istanbul
Ankara
Izmir
GREECE
Athens
Tabriz
Mashhad
TAJIKISTAN
Chengdu
Wuhan
East China
Sea
Bonin Is.
(Japan)

Algiers
Sicily
Crete
CYPRUS
SYRIA
Damascus
Baghdad
TEHRAN
Esfahan
KABUL
AFGHANISTAN
Islamabad
T I B E T
Lhasa
CHONGQING
Hwang Ho
Fuzhou
Volcano Is.
(Japan)
Marcus I.
(Japan)
Tropic of Cancer

Tunis
TUNISIA
Mediterranean
Sea
Beirut
LEB.
Jerusalem
ISR.
Amman
JORDAN
IRAQ
IRAN
Shīrāz
PAKISTAN
Lahore
DELHI
NEPAL
Katmandu
BHUTAN
Kunming
GUANGZHOU
Taipei
Ryukyus
TAIWAN
Wake I.
(U.S.A.)

LIBYA
EGYPT
Aswân
Red
KUWAIT
BAHRAIN
QATAR
Riyadh
Abu Dhabi
U.A.E.
Muscat
New Delhi
Kanpur
I N D I A
BANGLA-
DESH
DACCA
CALCUTTA
(Kolkata)
BURMA
MYANMAR
Hanoi
HONG KONG
NORTHERN
MARIANAS
(U.S.A.)
20

Benghazi
Alexandria
CAIRO
SAUDI
ARABIA
Mecca
OMAN
Ahmadabad
Arabian
Sea
MUMBAI
(Bombay)
Nagpur
Hyderabad
Bay of
Bengal
Rangoon
Hainan
South
China
Sea
Manila

NIGER
CHAD
Omdurman
Khartoum
Asmara
ERITREA
YEMEN
Aden
Socotra
(Yemen)
Lakshadweep Is.
(India)
Bangalore
CHENNAI
(Madras)
Andaman Is.
(India)
BANGKOK
THAILAND
CAMBODIA
VIET-
NAM
Phnom
Penh
MANILA
PHILIPPINES
GUAM
(U.S.A.)
MARSHALL IS.
D

Niamey
NIGERIA
Abuja
Ibadan
Lagos
CAMEROON
Douala
Yaoundé
CENTRAL
AFRICAN
REP.
Bangui
SUDAN
Addis Ababa
ETHIOPIA
DJIBOUTI
SOMALI
REP.
Colombo
SRI LANKA
Nicobar Is.
(India)
Ho Chi Minh
City
MALAYSIA
Medan
PEN. MALAYSIA
Kuala Lumpur
BRUNEI
SABAH
Yap
FEDERATED STATES
Truk
Pohnpei
PALAU
Caroline Is.
Gilbert Is.

EQUATORIAL
GUINEA
SÃO TOME &
PRINCIPE
Libreville
GABON
CONGO
Brazzaville
CONGO
(DEM. REP.
OF THE)
Kisangani
Kampala
UGANDA
KENYA
L. Turkana
Mogadishu
MALDIVES
Equator
I N D I A N
SINGAPORE
Palembang
Sumatra
Borneo
Banjarmasin
IRIAN
JAYA
NAURU
KIRIBATI
0

Kinshasa
Kananga
Kigali
RWANDA
BURUNDI
Bujumbura
Nairobi
Mombasa
Zanzibar
TANZANIA
Dodoma
Dar es Salaam
SEYCHELLES
Amirante Is.
Diego Garcia
Chagos Arch.
(U.K.)
OCEAN
JAKARTA
Bandung
I N D O N E S I A
Ujung Pandang
Surabaya
Java
PAPUA
NEW
GUINEA
Port
Moresby
New
Ireland
New
Britain
SOLOMON
IS.
TUVALU

Luanda
ANGOLA
Benguela
Lubumbashi
L. Tanganyika
L. Malawi
Aldabra Is.
COMOROS
Mayotte
Agalega Is.
(Maur.)
Cargados Carajos
Christmas I.
(Austral.)
Cocos Is.
(Austral.)
York
VANUATU
Santa Cruz I.
E

ZAMBIA
Lusaka
MALAWI
Lilongwe
MADAGASCAR
Antananarivo
Rodriguez
MAURITIUS
RÉUNION I.
(Fr.)
Darwin
Cairns
Townsville
NEW
CALEDONIA
(Fr.)
FIJI

NAMIBIA
Windhoek
BOTSWANA
ZIMBABWE
Harare
Bulawayo
MOZAMBIQUE
Mozambique Channel
Tropic of Capricorn
Port Hedland
Alice Springs
AUSTRALIA
Rockhampton
Brisbane
Suva
20

Gaborone
Johannesburg
Pretoria
SWAZILAND
Maputo
SOUTH
AFRICA
LESOTHO
Durban
Amsterdam I.
(Fr.)
St. Paul (Fr.)
Geraldton
Perth
Fremantle
Kalgoorlie-
Boulder
Great
Australian
Bight
Adelaide
Newcastle
Sydney
Canberra
Lord Howe I.
(Austral.)
Norfolk I.
(Austral.)
F

Cape Town
C. of Good Hope
Port Elizabeth
Prince Edward Is.
(S.Africa)
Crozet Is.
(Fr.)
Kerguelen
(Fr.)
Melbourne
Tasmania
Tasman
Sea
NEW ZEALAND
Wellington
Auckland
North I.
40

Bouvet I.
(Nor.)
M.Donald Is.
(Austral.)
Heard Is.
(Austral.)
Hobart
Christchurch
South I.
Stewart I.
Bounty Is.
(N.Z.)
Antipodes Is.
(N.Z.)

S O U T H E R N   O C E A N

G

Antarctic Circle

60

Ross Sea

H

A n t a r c t i c a

20   40   60   80   100   120   140   160   180   80

East from Greenwich

10
11
12
13
14
15
16
17
18

Hanoi ● Capital Cities

CARTOGRAPHY BY PHILIP'S.

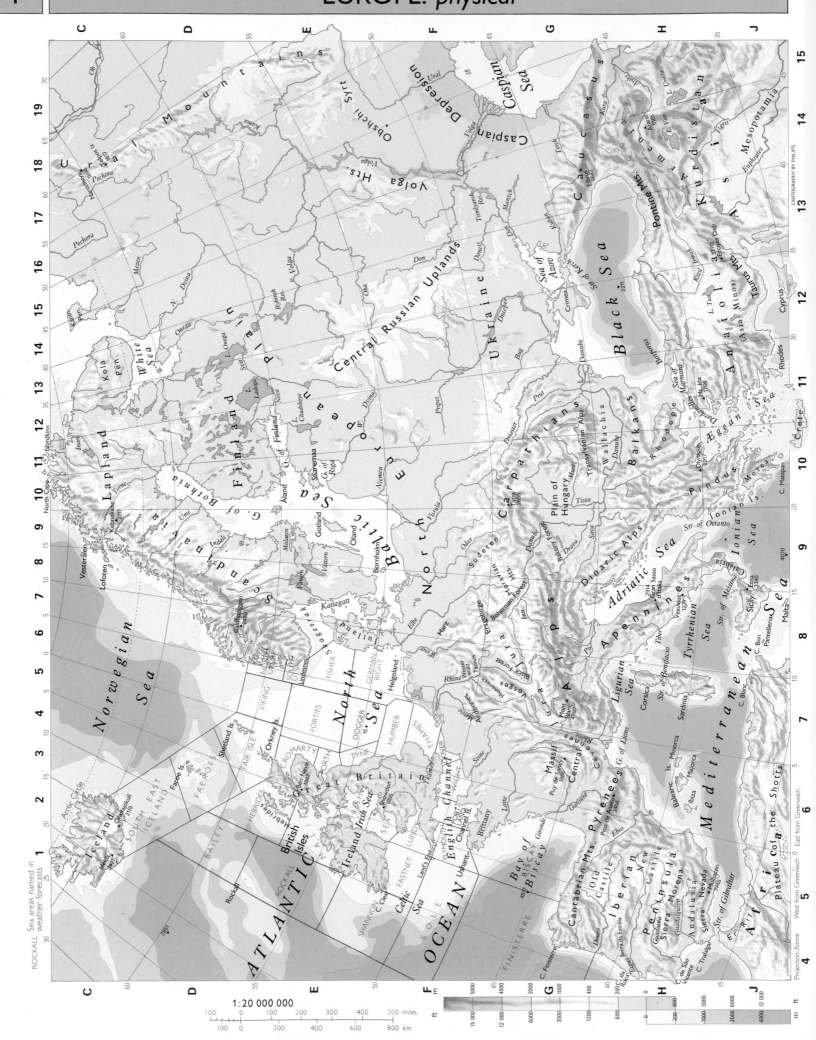

1:20 000 000

CARTOGRAPHY BY PHILIPS.

Projection: Bonne

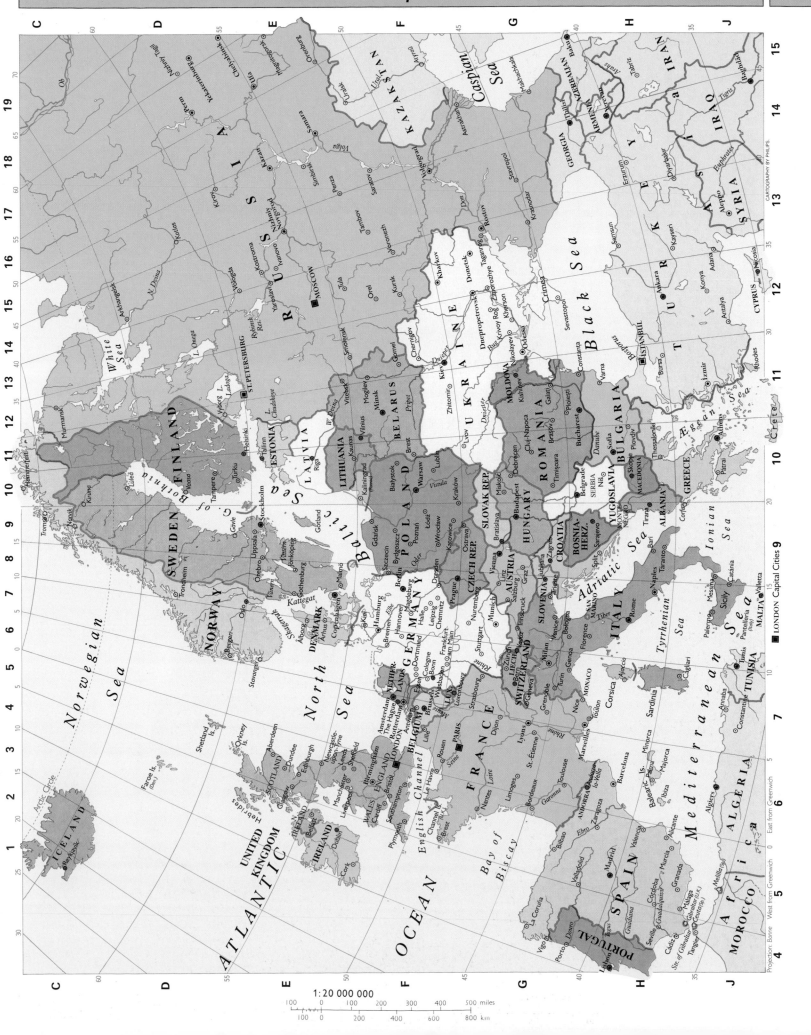

1:20 000 000

ICELAND
On the same scale

Projection : Conical with two standard parallels

East from Greenwich

COPYRIGHT GEORGE PHILIP & SON, LTD.

1:10 000 000

50   0   50   100   150   200   250 miles

50   0   50 100 150 200 250 300 350 400 km

Projection: Conical with two standard parallels

West from Greenwich

East from Greenwich

CARTOGRAPHY BY PHILIP'S.

1 : 5 000 000

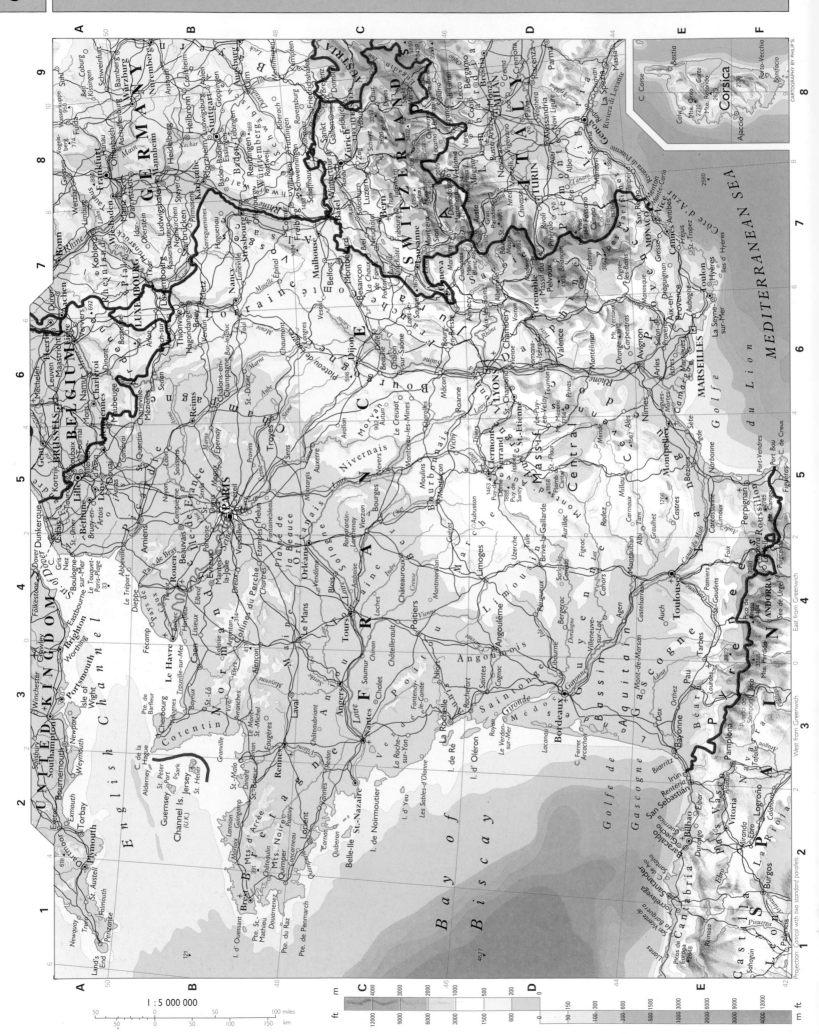

Corsica

CARTOGRAPHY BY PHILIPS.

MEDITERRANEAN SEA

1 : 5 000 000

Projection: Conical with two standard parallels

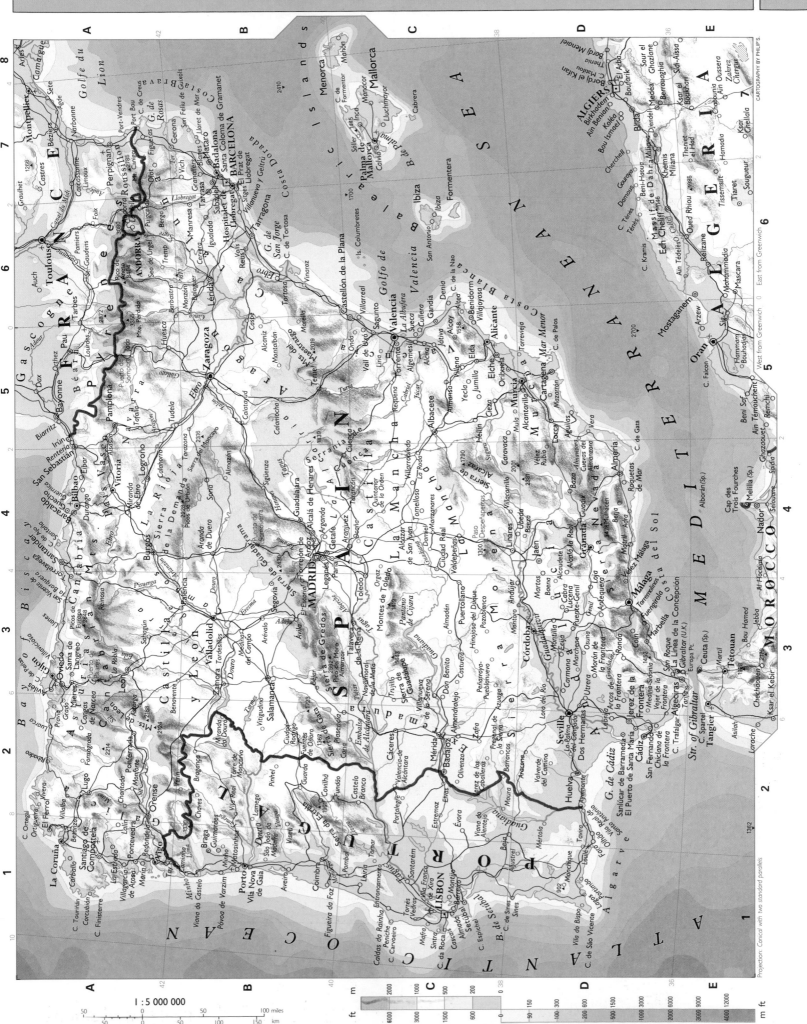

CARTOGRAPHY BY PHILIP'S.

Projection: Conical with two standard parallels

1 : 5 000 000

Projection: Conical with two standard parallels

Countries and seas:
NORTH SEA, BALTIC SEA, ADRIATIC SEA, UNITED KINGDOM, NETHERLANDS, BELGIUM, LUXEMBOURG, FRANCE, GERMANY, DENMARK, CZECH, AUSTRIA, SWITZERLAND, LIECHTENSTEIN, ITALY, SLOVENIA, POLAND

Selected cities:
HAMBURG, BERLIN, BRUSSELS, PARIS, PRAGUE, MUNICH, MILAN, TURIN, LYONS, MARSEILLES, MONACO, Amsterdam, Rotterdam, Cologne, Frankfurt, Stuttgart, Nuremberg, Dresden, Leipzig, Hannover, Bremen, Magdeburg, Szczecin, Ljubljana, Zagreb, Venice, Florence, Genoa, Zürich, Bern, Geneva, Strasbourg, Nancy, Dijon, Grenoble, Nice

Elevation scale:

ft	m
12000	4000
9000	3000
6000	2000
3000	1000
1500	500
600	200
0	0
150	50
300	100
600	200
1500	500
3000	1000
6000	2000

m ft

East from Greenwich

1 : 5 000 000

CARTOGRAPHY BY PHILIP'S

50   0   50   100 miles

50   0   50   100   150 km

1 2 3 4 5 6 7

SWITZERLAND
AUSTRIA
Steiermark
Graz
Lienz
Wolfsberg
Klagenfurt
Villach
Maribor
Nagykanizsa
Kärnten
Ljubljana
SLOVENIA
Triglav 2863
Karawanken
Kranj
Celje
Koprivnica
Bjelovar
Novo Mesto
Zagreb
Koper
Trieste
Virovitica
CROAT
Karlovac
Sisak
Krk
Senj
Una
Bosanska Gradiška
Banja Luka
Bihać

Rhône
Chur
Wildspitze
Badgastein
Gross Glockner 3797
Ortles 3899
Mte. Marmolada
Merano
Bolzano
Brenner P.
Bressanone
Davos
Sankt Moritz
Pizzo Bernina 4049
Piz Bernina
Ortler
Dolomiti
Belluno
Vittório Véneto
Udine
Gorizia
Pordenone
Conegliano
Treviso
Venice
Golfo di Venézia
Chióggia
Istra
Rovinj
Pula
Rt. Kamenjak
Cres
Lošinj
Pag
Zadar
Dugi Otok
Pasman
Šibenik
Split
Solta
Brač
Hvar
Vis
Korčula
Lastovo
Peljesac

FRANCE
Lyon
Annecy
Aix-les-Bains
Chambéry
Albertville
Chamonix
Mont Blanc 4807
Matterhorn 4478
Domodóssola
Verbánia
Aosta
Gran Paradiso 4061
Locarno
Lugano
Como
Lecco
Bérgamo
Brescia
Lago di Garda
Trento
Rovereto
Riva
Schio
Vicenza
Verona
Pádova
Bassano del Grappa
Legnago
Mántova
Adige
Rovigo
Ferrara
Comácchio
Ravenna

Grenoble
Massif du Pelvoux
Gap
Briançon
Modane
Turin
Piemonte
Pinerolo
Rivoli
Chivasso
Vercelli
Novara
Monza
MILAN
Lodi
Crema
Cremona
Pavia
Piacenza
Parma
Réggio nell'Emília
Módena
Carpi
Bologna
Imola
Faenza
Forlì
Cesena
Rímini

Valence
Montélimar
Mte. Viso 3841
Cuneo
Col di Tenda 1870
Alessándria
Novi Ligure
Asti
Bra
Alba
Mondovì
Savona
Genoa
Rapallo
Chiavari
La Spézia
Massa
Carrara
Pistóia
Prato
Lucca
Pisa
Livorno
Mte. Cimone 2165
Sassuolo

Orange
Carpentras
Avignon
Mt. Ventoux 1912
Digne-les-Bains
Alpes Maritimes
Riviera di Ponente
Impéria
San Remo
MONACO
Menton
Monte-Carlo
Nice
Antibes
Cannes
St-Tropez
Fréjus
Grasse
Draguignan
Riviera di Levante
Viaréggio

MARSEILLES
Toulon
La Seyne-sur-Mer
Hyères
Iles d'Hyères
Côte d'Azur
Golfo di Génova
LIGURIAN SEA
Provence
Salon-de-Provence
Istres
Martigues
Aubagne
Aix-en-Provence

C. Corse
C. Corse
Calvi
Bastia
Mte. Cinto 2710
Corte
Mte. Rotondo 2625
Corsica 2136
Ajaccio
Porto-Vecchio
Bonifácio
Maddalena
Capraia
Piombino
Portoferráio
Elba
Pianosa
Montecristo
Giglio
Orbetello

Rosignano Maríttimo
Volterra
Siena
L. Trasimeno
Toscana
Grosseto
Arezzo
Perúgia
Assisi
Città di Castello
Iesi
Ancona
Fabriano
Macerata
Fermo
Civitanova Marche
Ascoli Piceno
San Benedetto del Tronto
Chiusi
Orvieto
L. di Bolsena
Viterbo
Spoleto
Térni
Rieti
Gran Sasso d'Italia 2914
Teramo
Montesilvano Marina
Pescara
Chieti
Lanciano
Vasto
Térmoli

Asinara
C. Falcone
Porto Tórres
Sássari
Álghero
Bosa
Nuoro
Óbia
Golfo di Aranci
Sardinia
Oristano
Sórgono
Mti. del Gennargentu 1834
Arbatax
Lanusei
Iglésias
San Pietro
Sant'Antíoco
Portoscuso
Carbónia
Quartu Sant' Elena
Cágliari
C. Carbonara
C. Spartivento

Vatican City
ROME
Pomézia
Velletri
Frosinone
Isérnia
Campobasso
San Severo
Mte. Gargano 1056
Manfredónia
Foggia
Barletta
Trani
Molfetta
Bari
Andria
Corato
Monópoli
Altamura
Putignano
Matera
Potenza

Aprília
Latina
Fondi
Cassino
Terracina
Fórmia
Gaeta
Ísole Ponziane
Caserta
Benevento
Avellino
Avezzano
Ánzio
Ventotene
Pozzuoli
Aversa
NAPLES
Vesúvio
Torre del Greco
Ischia
Capri
Castellammare di Stábia
Nocera Inferiore
Battipáglia
Salerno
Sala Consilina
Ágri
Táranto
Golfo di Táranto

TYRRHENIAN SEA

Corigliano Cálabro
Rossano Cálabro
Cetraro
Cosenza
Crotone
Nicastro
Catanzaro
Vibo Valéntia
Palmi
Scilla

ADRIATIC SEA

Ustica (Italy)
Ísole Eólie
Strómboli
Salina
Lípari
Vulcano
Milazzo
Messina
Réggio di Calábria
Str. di Messina
C. Peloro
C. Spartivento

Ísole Égadi
Trápani
Érice
Palermo
Bagheria
Términi Imerese
Cefalù
Barcellona-Pozzo di Gotto
Partinico
Alcamo
Favignana
Marsala
Castelvetrano
Monti Nébrodi
Adrano
Etna 3340
Giarre
Acireale
Mazara del Vallo
Sciacca
Caltanissetta
Enna
Paternò
Catánia
Sicily
Porto Empédocle
Agrigento
Licata
Canicattì
Favara
Gela
Lentini
Augusta
Siracusa
Caltagirone
Vittória
Ragusa
Módica
Ispica
Avola
C. Passero

Pantelleria (Italy)

ALGERIA
El Mília
Collo
Skikda
Annaba
Azzaba
El Kala
Guelma
Constantine
El Khroub
Souk-Ahras
Sedrata
Aïn M'lila
Oum-el-Bouaghi
Aïn Beida
Tébessa
Khenchela
Aures
Chéria
Babar

TUNISIA
Bizerte
Menzel-Bourguiba
Mateur
Tabarka
Jendouba
Béja
Manouba
Ariana
La Marsa
Tunis
Soliman
Nabeul
Hammamet
Korba
Kélibia
Rass Mostefa
Menzel-Temime
Ben Arous
Bou Salem
El Kef
El Fahs
Zaghouan
Maktar
Kairouan
Sousse
Monastir
Moknine
Mahdia
El Djem
Kasserine
Sbeitla
Thala
Hammam Sousse

I. Linosa
Ísole Pelágie (Italy)
Lampione
Lampedusa
Linosa

Gozo
Valletta
Rabat
MALTA

MEDITER

Projection: Conical with two standard parallels

ft m
12000 4000
9000 3000
6000 2000
3000 1000
1500 500
600 200
0 0
50 150
100 300
200 600
500 1500
1000 3000
2000 6000
3000 9000
4000 12000
m ft

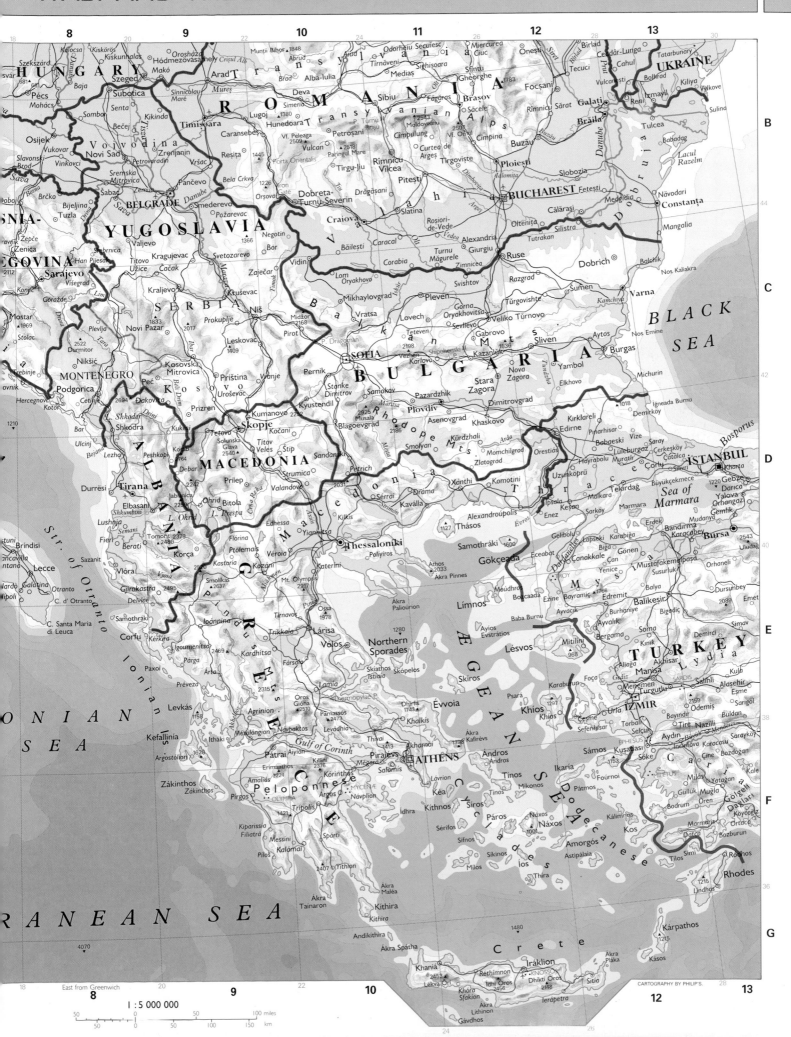

1. Crimea (Ukr.)
2. Adygea (Russ.)
3. Karachey-Cherkessia (Russ.)
4. Kabardino-Balkania (Russ.)
5. North Ossetia (Russ.)
6. Ingushetia (Russ.)
7. Chechenia (Russ.)
8. Nakhichevan (Azer.)

Karagiye Depression

9

COPYRIGHT: GEORGE PHILIP & SON LTD.

8

7

East from Greenwich   6

Projection: Conical with two standard parallels

Division between Greeks and Turks
in Cyprus, Turks to the North

1:10 000 000

50   0   50   100   150   200   250 miles

50   0   50   100   150   200   250   300   350   400 km

m   ft
4000   12,000
2000   6000
1000   3000
600   1200
400   600
200   0
0   200 - 600
       600 - 3000
       3000 - 6000
       6000 - 12,000
       12,000
m

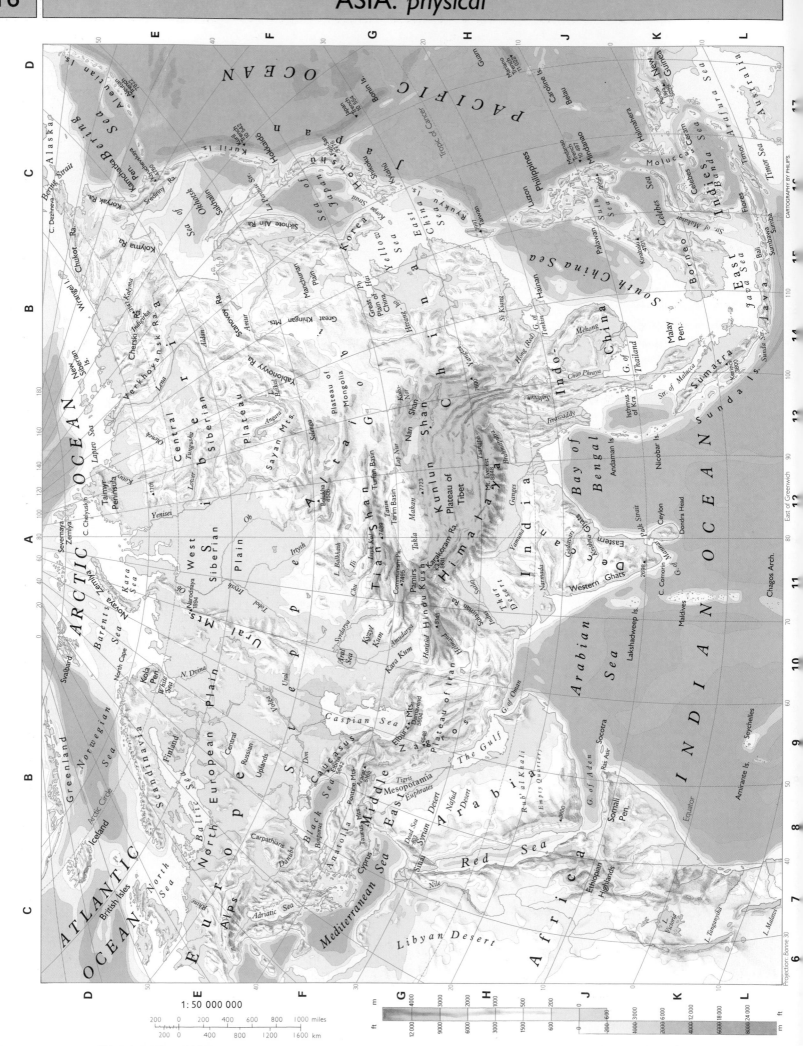

1 : 50 000 000

200   0   200   400   600   800   1000 miles

200   0   400   800   1200   1600 km

Projection: Bonne 30

CARTOGRAPHY BY PHILIP'S

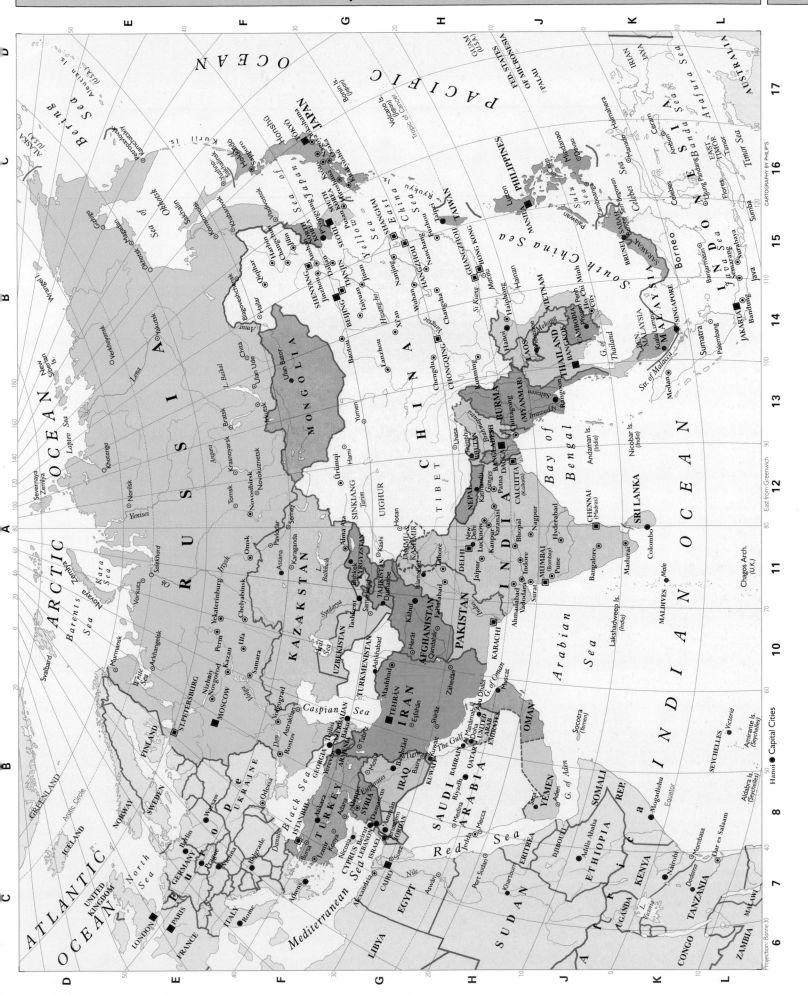

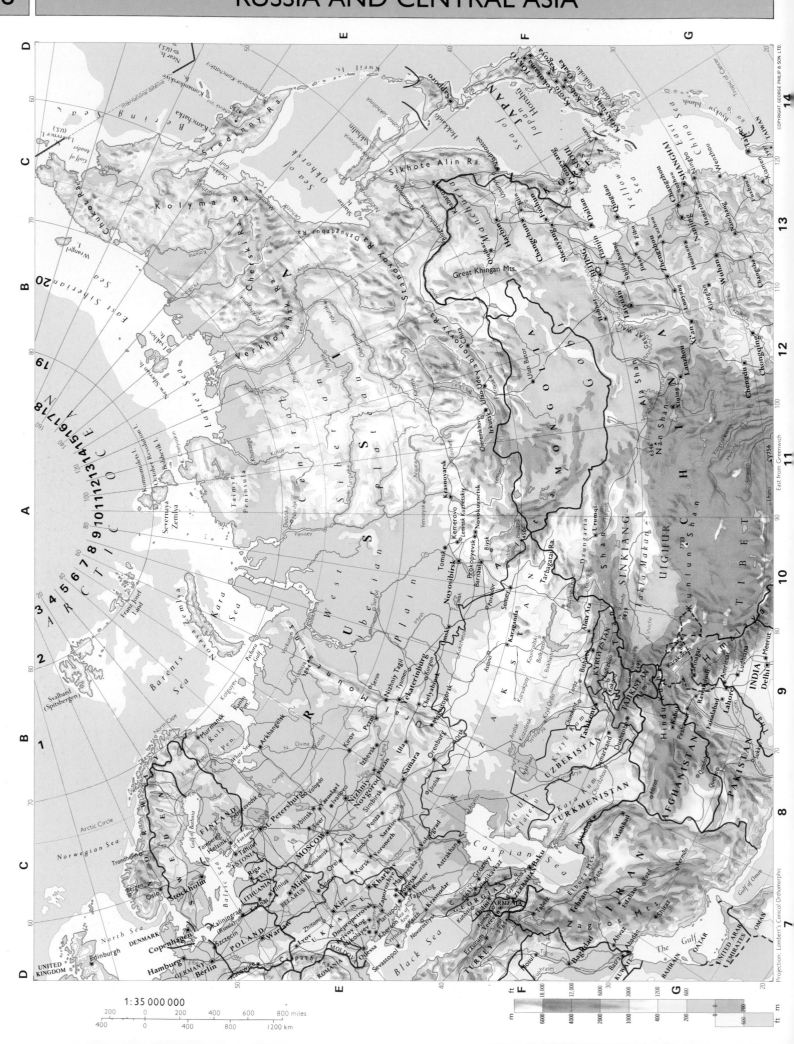

1:35 000 000

Projection: Lambert's Conical Orthomorphic

COPYRIGHT GEORGE PHILIP & SON LTD.

SOUTHERN HONSHU, KYUSHU AND SHIKOKU

1:5 000 000

1:10 000 000

JAPAN

COPYRIGHT, GEORGE PHILIP & SON, LTD.

CHINA AND KOREA

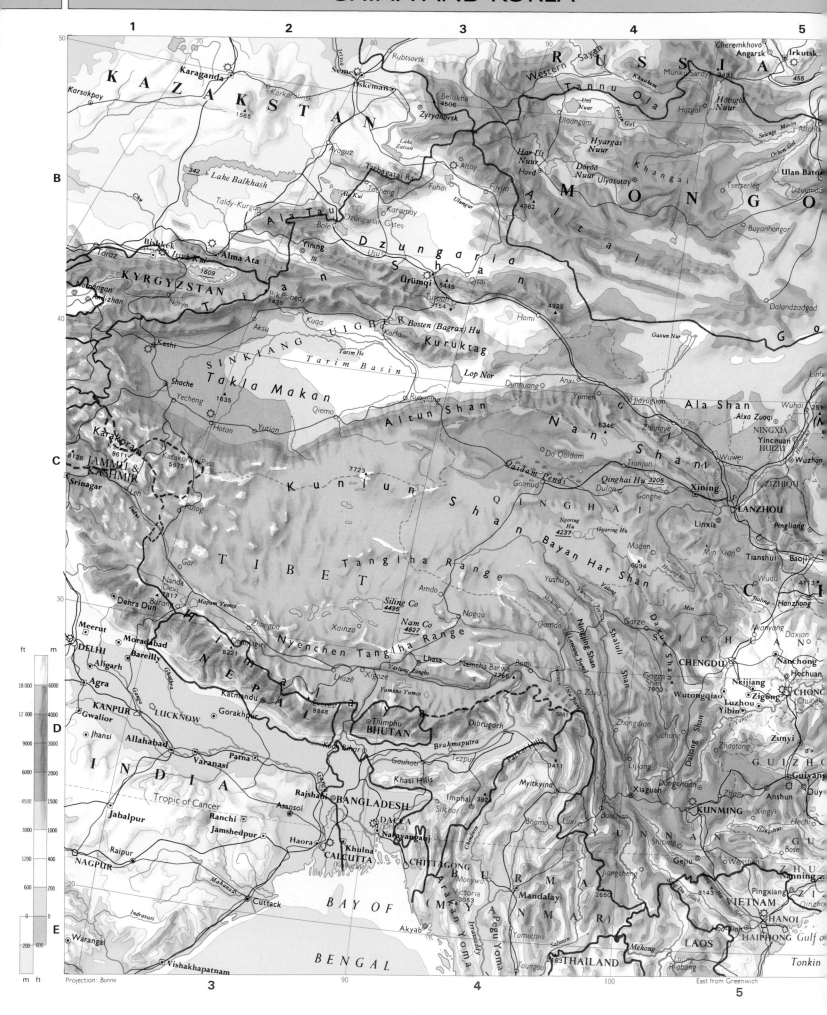

Projection: Bonne

East from Greenwich

7

6 8 9

120 130 140 50

Ulan Ude
Lake Baykal
Chita
Nerchinsk
Chegdomyn
Aleksandrovsk
C. Terpeniya
Yablonovyy Rang
Borzya
Orogen Zizhiqi
Blagoveshchensk
Svobodny
Komsomolsk
Poronaysk
Sakhalin

Manzhouli
Nenjiang
Little Khingan Mts.
Aihui
L. Bolon
Bikin
Yuzhno-Sakhalinsk

entiyn uruu
Hailar
Hulun Nur
Butha Qi
Bei'an
Yichun
Hegang
Hamusi
Shuangyashan
Khabarovsk
La Perouse Str.
Wakkanai
B

Choybalsan
Kerulen
Buir Nur
Qiqihar
Anda
Suihua
Mishan
Jixi
HARBIN
Mudanjiang
Lake Khanka
Ussuriysk
Asahigawa
2290
Otaru
Hokkaido
SAPPORO
Kushiro

Saynshand
Tao'an
Manchuria
CHANGCHUN
Jilin
Vladivostok
Nakhodka
Hakodate
C. Erimo

Dzamin Uud
Erenhot
Abagnar Qi
1949
Shuangliao
Songhua Lake
Yanji
Aomori
Hachinohe
40

INNER MONGOLIA
Chifeng
Tongliao
Siping
Liaoyuan
2744
Chongjin
Morioka
Akita

Hohhot
Zhangjiakou
Chengde
Fuxin
FUSHUN
SHENYANG
Tonghua
NORTH
SEA OF
Sado
Niigata
Koriyama
Utsunomiya

Baotou
Datong
Xuanhua
Chaoyang
Liaoyang
Benxi
Hungnam
JAPAN
Toyama
Kanazawa
TOKYO

Jining
Qinghuangdao
Jinzhou
Yingkou
ANSHAN
Dandong
Wonsan
KAWASAKI

BEIJING
Tangshan
G. of Liaodong
Liaodong Pen.
PYONGYANG
Kaesong
NAGOYA
YOKOHAMA
C

Baoding
DALIAN
Korea Bay
Haeju
SEOUL
Fuji 3776
Yokosuka

TAIYUAN
HEBEI
Cangzhou
G. of Chihli
INCHON
SOUTH
Okayama
KOBE
Shizuoka

Shijiazhuang
Yantai
Weihai
Taejon
KYOTO
OSAKA
Hamamatsu

JINAN
Weifang
YELLOW
TAEGU
PUSAN
Hiroshima
Sakai
Wakayama

Zibo
Masan
Shikoku
Kochi
Matsuyama

QINGDAO
SEA
Kwangju
1915
Shimonoseki

Tai'an
Jining
Lianyungang
KITAKYUSHU
FUKUOKA
Kyushu

Cheju Do
1950
Sasebo
Kumamoto

XI'AN
ZHENGZHOU
HENAN
JIANGSU
XUZHOU
Qingjiang
Nagasaki

Kagoshima
30

WUHAN
NANJING
SHANGHAI
Taneka

EAST CHINA
Amami-o-Shima

SEA
Okinawa
Naha
D

TAIWAN
Tropic of Cancer

TAIPEI
KAOHSIUNG
PACIFIC
20

HONG KONG
Macau

SOUTH CHINA
Batan Is.
E

SEA
Babuyan Is.

6 7 8

1:15 000 000

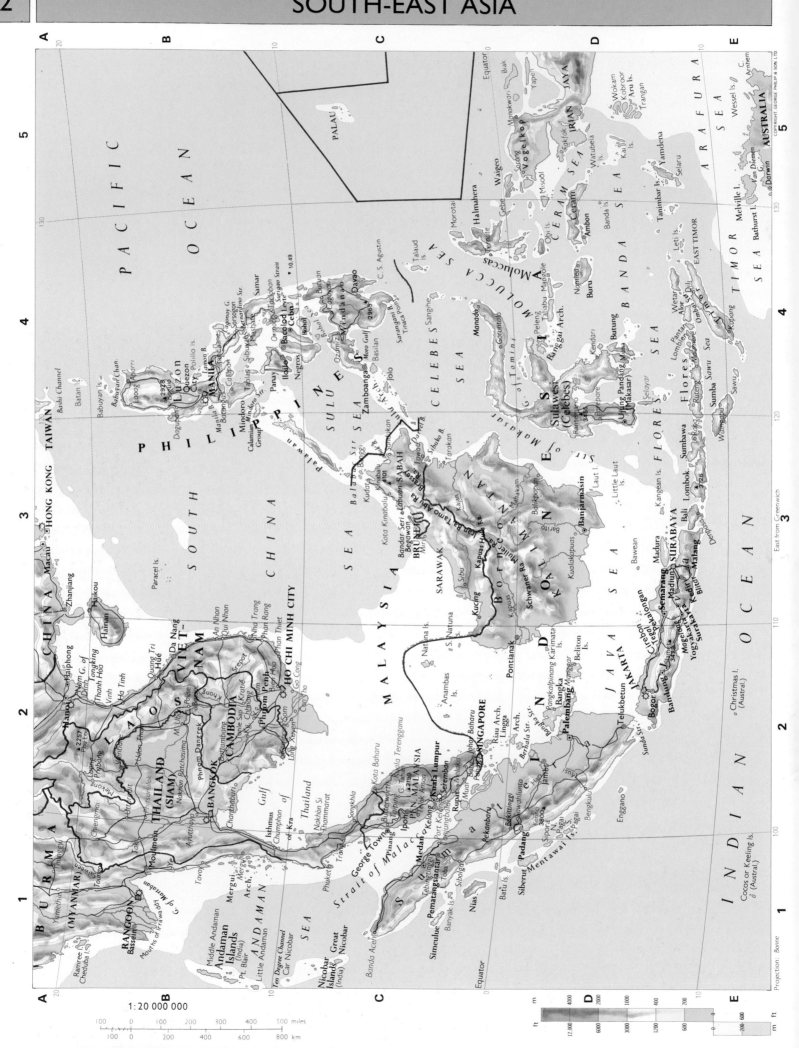

1:20 000 000

100   0   100   200   300   400   500 miles
100   0   200   400   600   800 km

Projection: Bonne

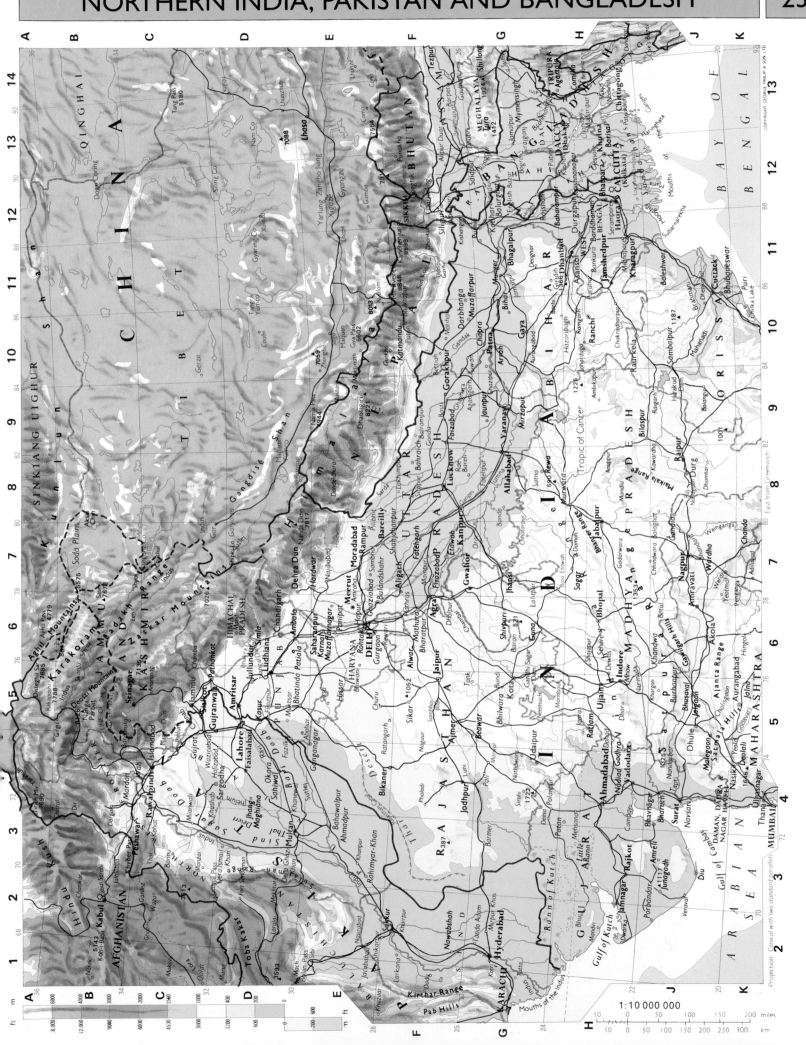

1   **2**   **3**   **4**   **5**

KAZAKSTAN

Borisovka
KAZ

UZBEKISTAN

TURKEY
Konya
Kayseri
Malatya
Mersin
Adana
Gaziantep
Diyarbakir
Erzurum
Yerevan
AZERBAIJAN
Baku

Urgench
Bukhara
Sam

CYPRUS
Nicosia
Tripoli
Latakia
Aleppo
Hama
Mosul
Urmia
Tabriz
Ardabil
Rasht
Krasnovodsk
Kara Bogaz Gol

TURKMENISTAN
Ashkhabad
Chardzhou
Mary
Bairam-Ali
Ter

ALEXANDRIA
Damanhur
Mansura
Dumyât
Port Said
Ismailia
Tanta
El Faiyum
Suez

LEBANON
Beirut
ISRAEL
Haifa
Tel Aviv-Jaffa
Tripoli
SYRIA
Homs
Damascus
Amman
JORDAN
Jerusalem

Zanjan
Qazvin
Qom
Tehran
Hamadan
Elburz Mountains
Babol
Anzali
Lenkoran
Caspian Sea

Mashhad
Maimana
Mazar-e Sharif

IRAQ
Ar Ramadi
Baghdad
Karbala
Hilla
An Najaf
Al Kut
Tigris
An Nâsiriyah
Basra

IRAN
Esfahan
Yazd
Kashan
Araq
Qom
Bakhtaran

Gonabad
Birjand
Tabas

Herat
Farah

AFGHANISTAN
Girishk
Qandahar

Sinai
2637

Dead Sea
Ma'an

Arabian Desert
Syrian Desert

KUWAIT
Kuwait
Ahvaz
Khorramshahr
Abadan
Bandar Khomeyni
Shatt al Arab

Shiraz
Busehr
Kazerun
Jahrom

Kerman
Zahedan

Helmand

PAKI
Quetta
Nushki
Shikarpur

EGYPT
Qena
Luxor
Bûr Safâga
El Quseir
Ras Banas
Yenbo
Halaib

Medina
W. Hamd
Al'Ula
Hail
N Buraydah

SAUDI ARABIA

Turabah
Al Qatif
Dammam
Mubarraz
BAHRAIN
QATAR
Doha

The Gulf
Bandar Abbas
Str. of Hormuz
Jask

Central Makran Ra.
Dasht
Bela
Nawabsh

Karachi
Indus Delta

SUDAN
Port Sudan
Suakin
2269

Jedda
Mecca
Taif

Riyadh
Al-Hufuf
Layla

Sharjah
Dubai
Abu Dhabi
UNITED ARAB EMIRATES
3048

Gulf of Oman
As Sohar
Muscat

Ormara
Pasni
Gwadar

Tropic of Cancer

Abha

Rub' al Khali
(Empty Quarter)

OMAN
Ras al Hadd

G. of Masirah
Ras al Madraka

Kuria Muria Is.
Mirbat

ERITREA
Asmera
Al Hudaydah
116
Massawa
Dahlak Arch.
Farasan Is.

Sana'
Shibam
Hadhramaut
YEMEN
Ta'izz
Mussa Al
2065
Bab el Mandeb
Aden
Shuqra
Madinat al Shaab
Mukalla

Ras Fartak
Sayhut

ETHIOPIA
Dese

DJIBOUTI
Djibouti
Dire Dawa
Harer
Hargeisa

Gulf of Aden

Socotra
(Yemen)

Ras Asir
(C. Guardafui)
Hordio

ARABIAN SEA

SOMALI REP.
Erigavo
Gabredarre
Ilig

Bender Beila

Juba
Shibeli
Obbia
Mogadishu

INDIA

East from Greenwich

ft | m
18,000 | 6000
12,000 | 4000
9000 | 3000
6000 | 2000
3000 | 1000
1200 | 400
600 | 200
0 | 0
200 | 600
m | ft

1:17 500 000

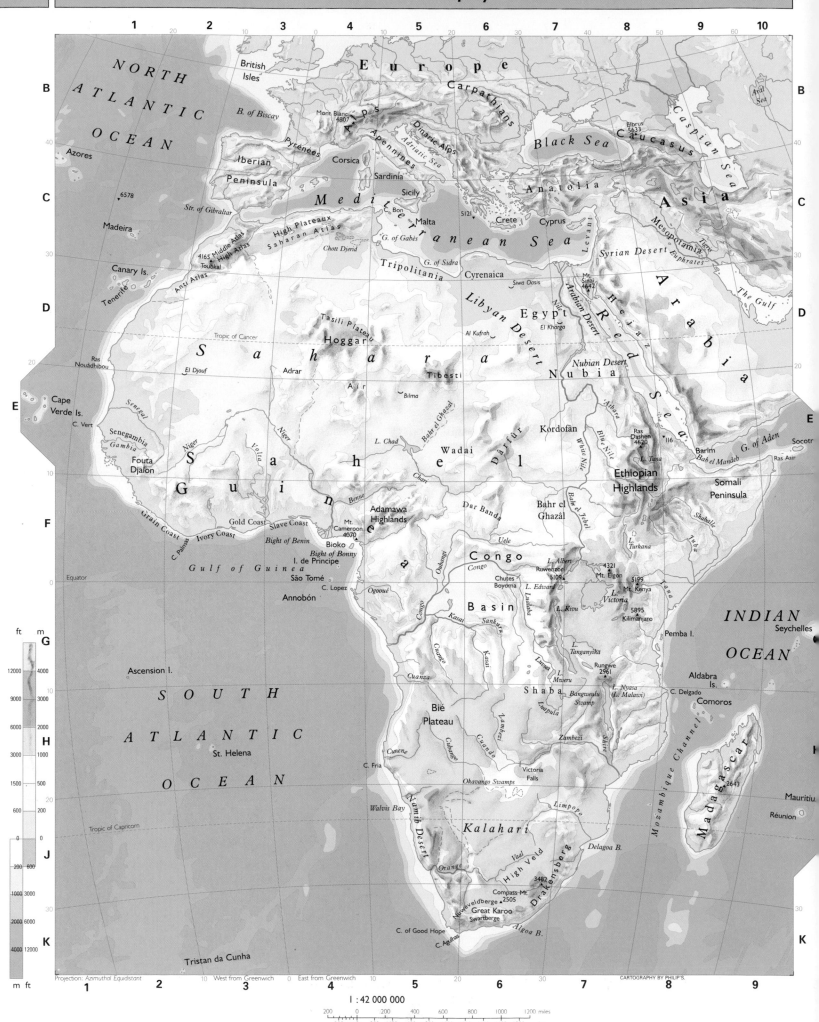

1 : 42 000 000

Projection: Azimuthal Equidistant   West from Greenwich   East from Greenwich   CARTOGRAPHY BY PHILIP'S.

200 0 200 400 600 800 1000 1200 miles
200 0 200 400 600 800 1000 1200 1400 1600 1800 km

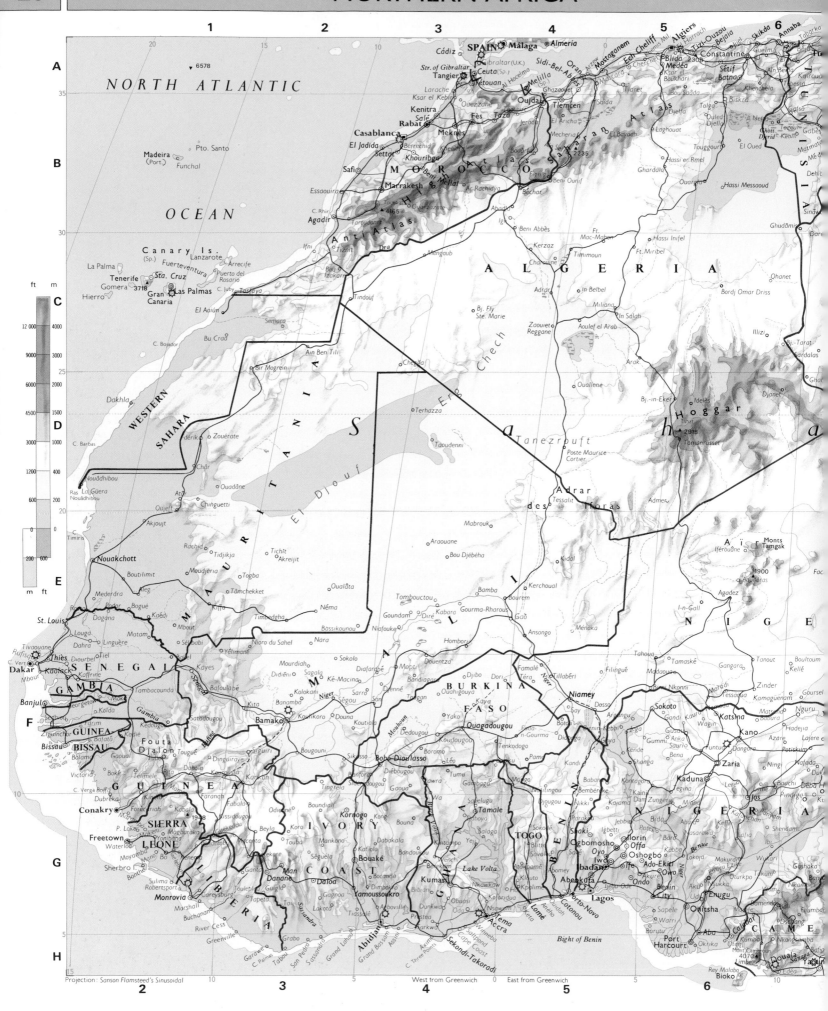

NORTH ATLANTIC

OCEAN

SPAIN

Madeira (Port.)

Canary Is. (Sp.)

WESTERN SAHARA

MAURITANIA

MOROCCO

ALGERIA

MALI

NIGER

Chech

Hoggar

Tanezrouft

El Djouf

SENEGAL

GAMBIA

GUINEA BISSAU

GUINEA

SIERRA LEONE

LIBERIA

IVORY COAST

BURKINA FASO

GHANA

TOGO

BENIN

NIGERIA

CAME

Bight of Benin

Projection: Sanson Flamsteed's Sinusoidal

West from Greenwich   East from Greenwich

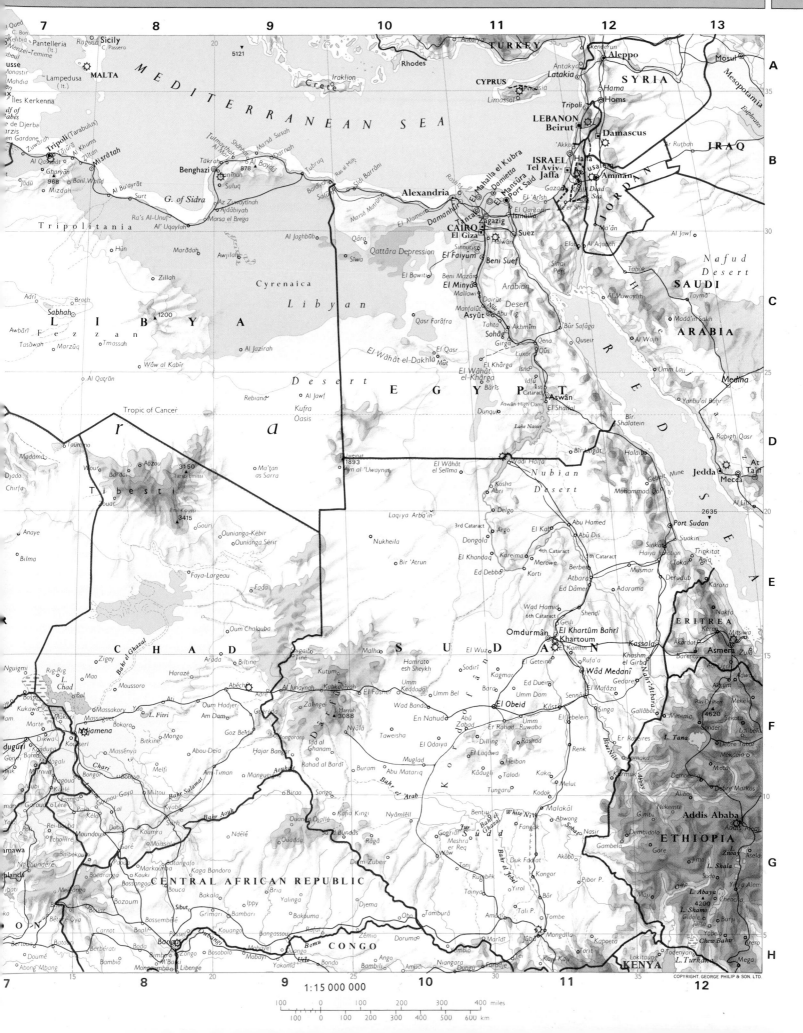

COPYRIGHT. GEORGE PHILIP & SON. LTD.

1:15 000 000

100   0   100   200   300   400 miles

100   0   100   200   300   400   500   600 km

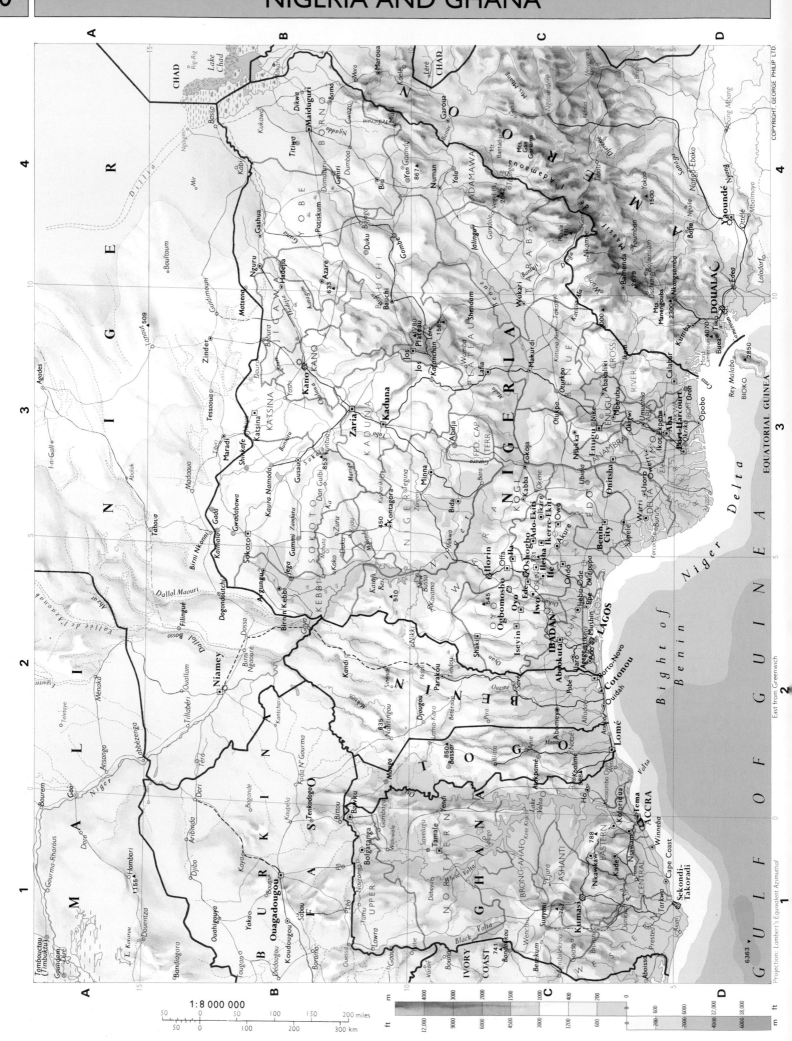

1:8 000 000

Projection: Lambert's Equivalent Azimuthal

East from Greenwich

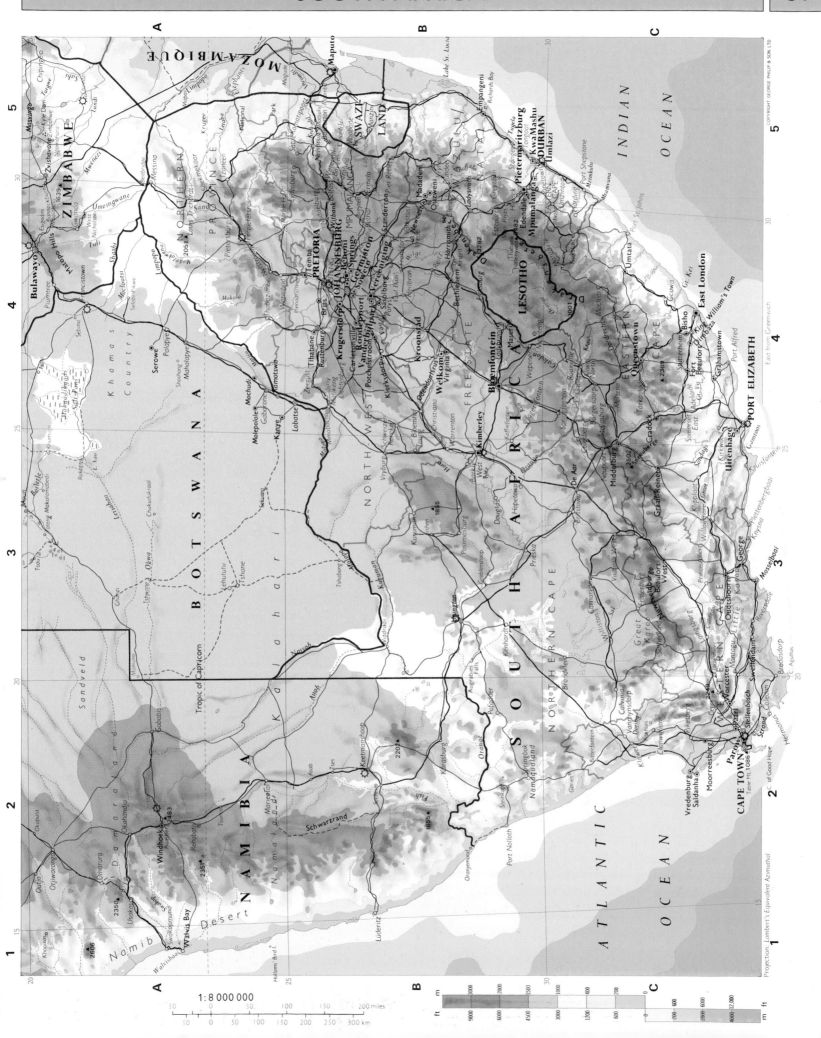

Projection: Lambert's Equivalent Azimuthal

East from Greenwich

COPYRIGHT GEORGE PHILIP & SON LTD

1:8 000 000

50   0   50   100   150   200 miles

50 0 50 100 150 200 250 300 km

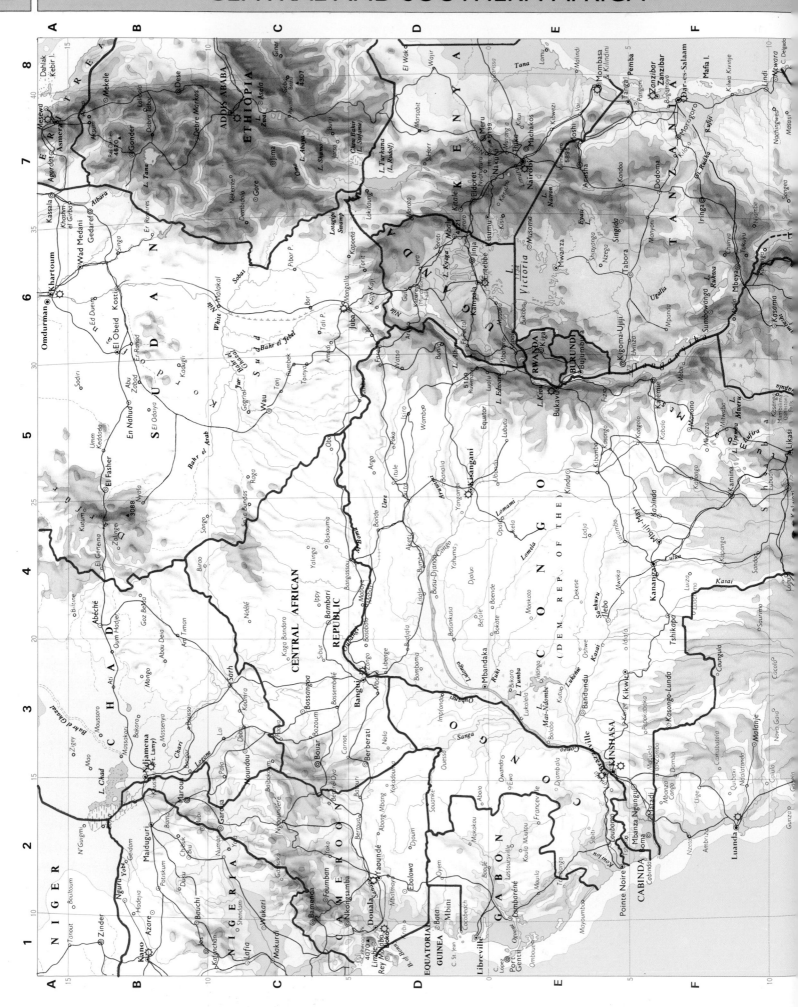

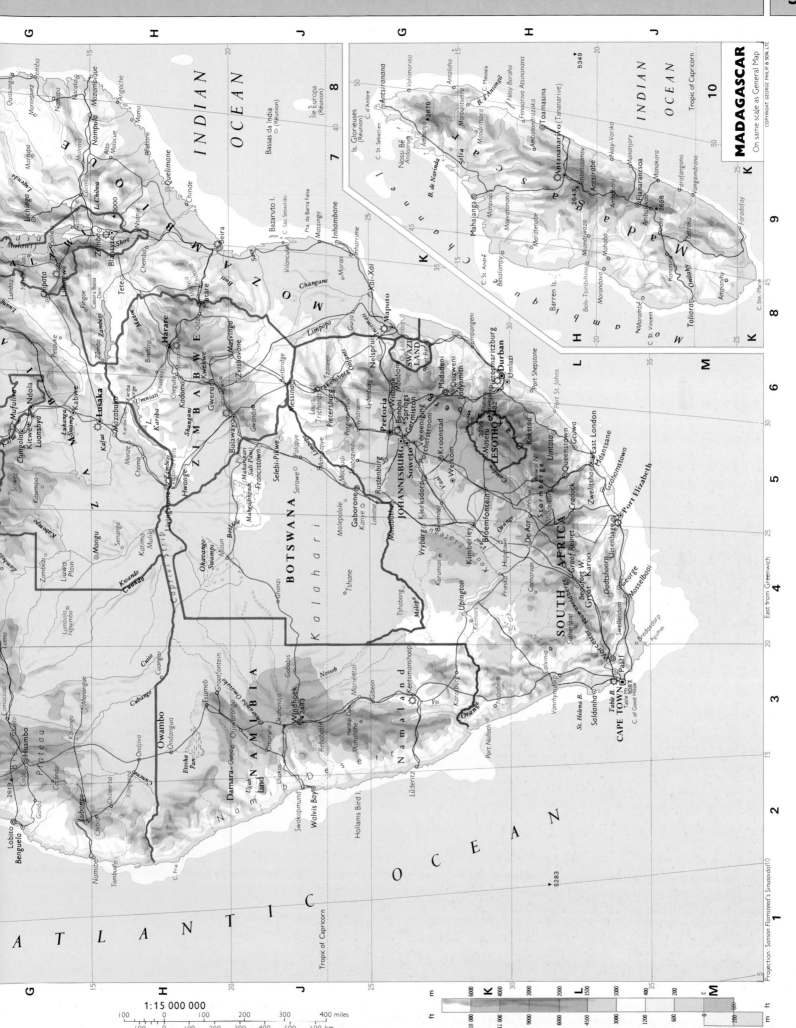

MADAGASCAR
On same scale as General Map

COPYRIGHT GEORGE PHILIP & SON LTD.

INDIAN OCEAN

ATLANTIC OCEAN

1:15 000 000

100   0   100   200   300   400 miles
100   0   100   200   300   400   500   600 km

Projection: Sanson Flamsteed's Sinusoidal

East from Greenwich

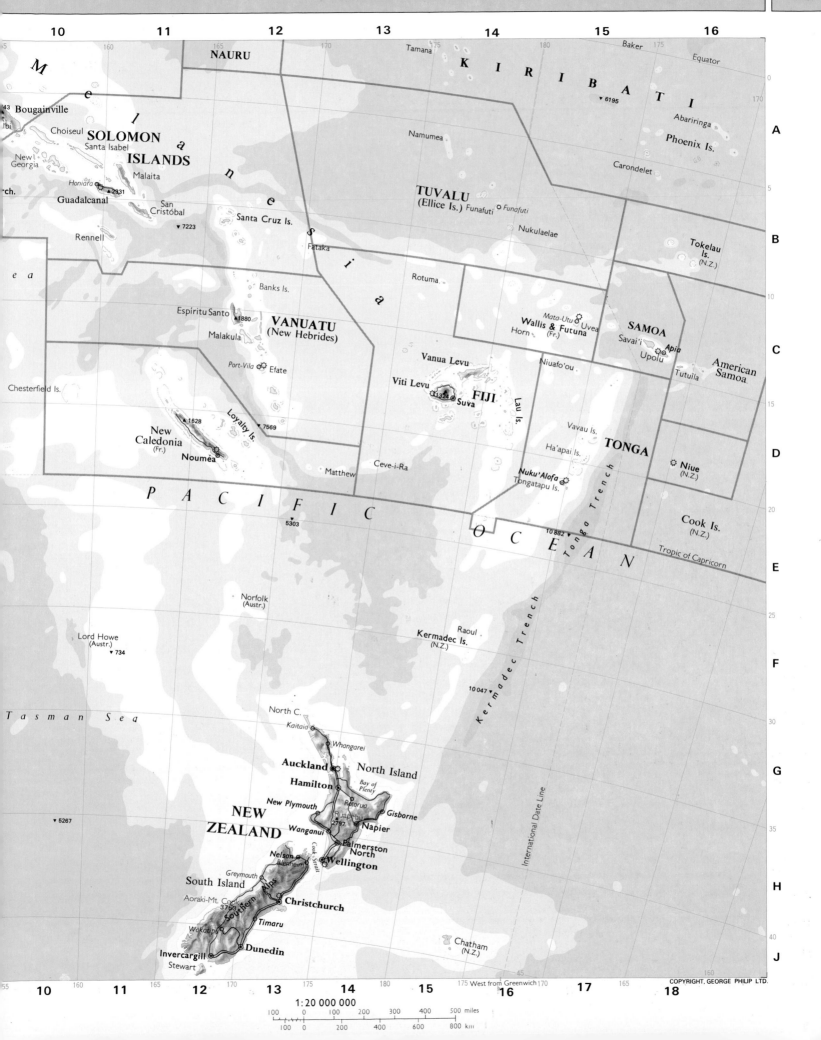

1:20 000 000

100   0   100   200   300   400   500 miles

100   0   200   400   600   800 km

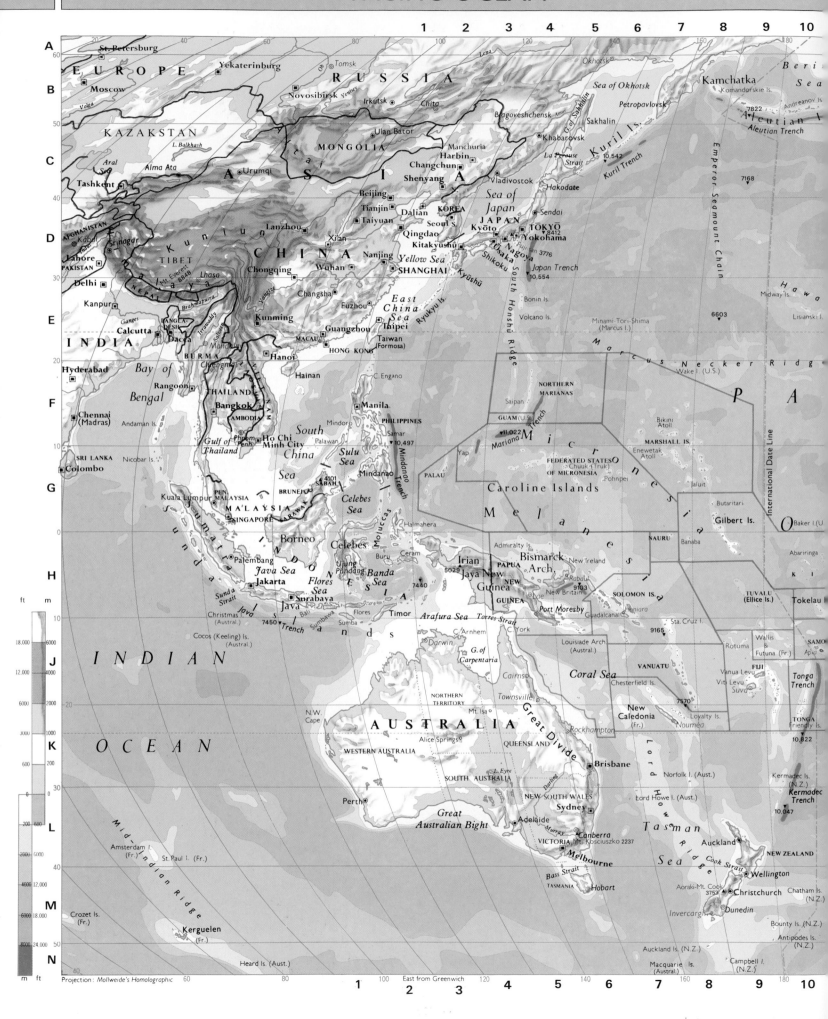

1:54 000 000

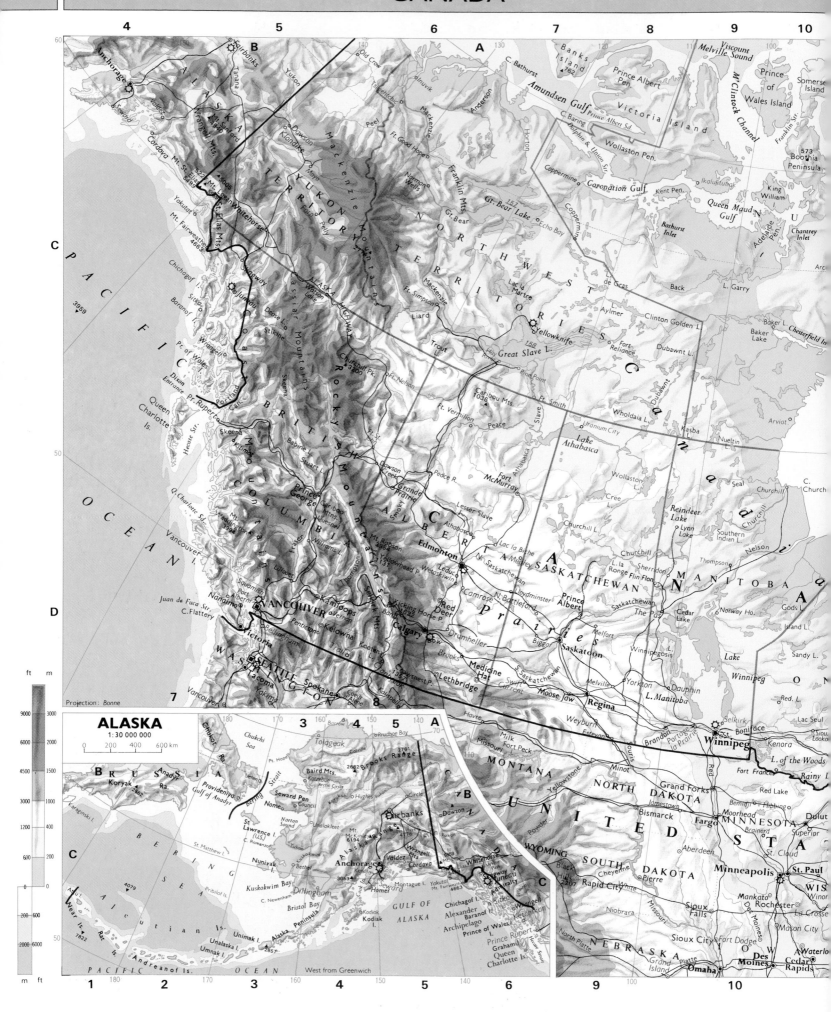

ALASKA

1:30 000 000

0   200   400   600 km

Projection: Bonne

ft	m
9000	3000
6000	2000
4500	1500
3000	1000
1200	400
600	200
0	0
600	200
6000	2000

m | ft

1:15 000 000

100   0   100   200   300   400 miles

100   0   100 200 300 400 500 600 km

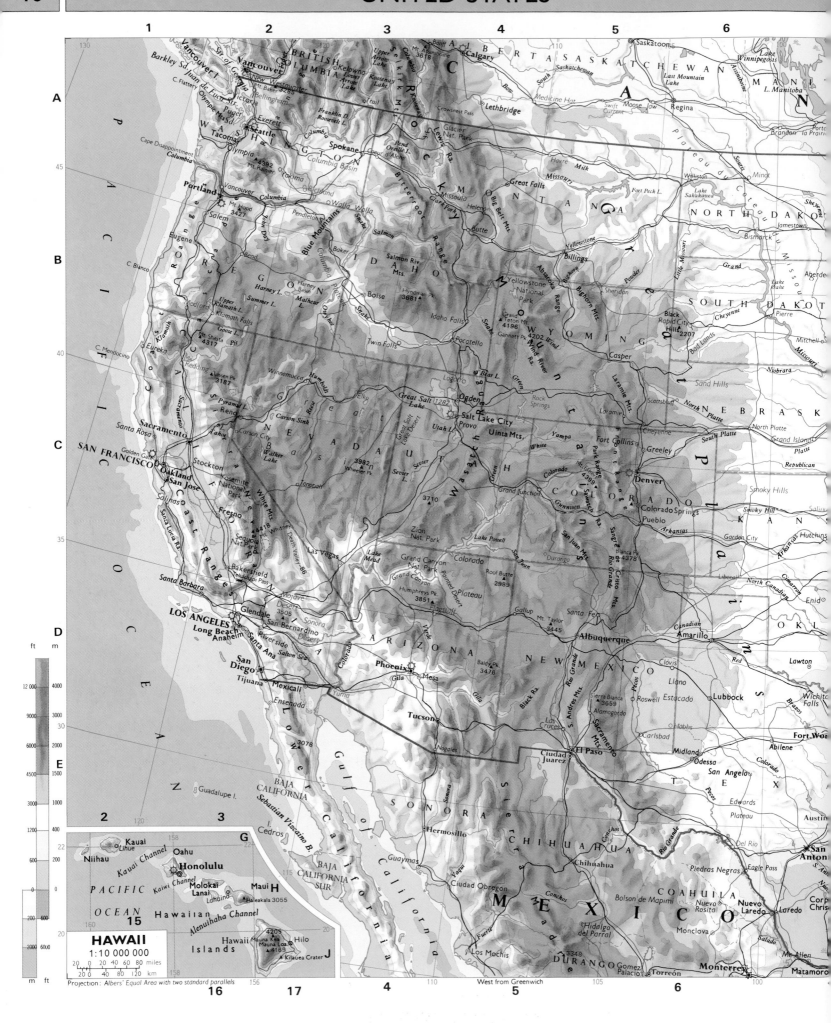

HAWAII
1:10 000 000

Projection: Albers' Equal Area with two standard parallels

1:12 000 000

COPYRIGHT. GEORGE PHILIP & SON. LTD.

50   0   50   100 150 200 250   300 miles

50   0   50 100 150 200 250 300 350 400 450 500 km

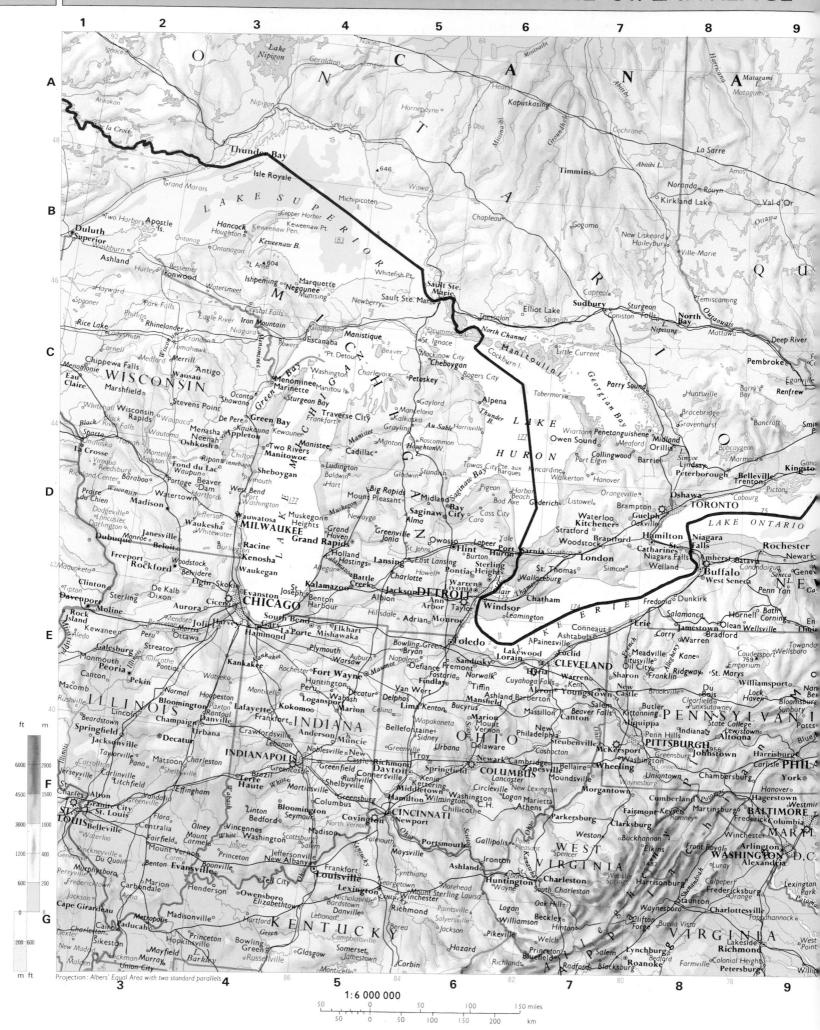

Projection: Albers' Equal Area with two standard parallels

1:6 000 000

NORTH AMERICA
Political 1 : 70 000 000

A

San Diego   Yuma
Tijuana   Mexicali
Ensenada
Pt. Baja
3078
Phoenix
Tucson
Nogales
Ciudad Juárez   El Paso
Agua Prieta
Carlsbad
3658
Wichita Falls
Fort Worth   Dallas
Shreveport   Jackson
Birmingham
Montgomery

B

Pt. Sta. Eugenia
Sta. Rosalia
Tiburón   Hermosillo
Guaymas
Empalme
Ciudad Obregón
Navojoa
3200
Villa Ahumada
Pecos
Abilene   Waco
Tyler
Monroe
Alexandria
Beaumont   Lake Charles
Baton Rouge   Mobile
Pensacola
C. San Blas
Chihuahua
Sta. Maria
Conchos
Grande
San Angelo
Austin   Houston
Brazos
Trinity
Sabine
Red
Port Arthur
New Orleans
Mississippi Delta
San Antonio
Piedras Negras
Eagle Pass
2896
Nueva Rosita
Sabinas
Delicias
Los Mochis
Guamúchil
3150
Laredo
Nuevo Laredo
Falcon Res.
Reynosa
Matagorda I.
Corpus Christi
Padre I.
Galveston

C

C. San Lucas
2406
Culiacan
Mazatlán
Rosario
S. Pedro
Gómez Palacio
Torreón   Saltillo
Monterrey
Monclova
Montemorelos
Concepcion del Oro
Brownsville
Rio Grande del Norte
Matamoros
Laguna de la Madre
GULF OF MEXICO
Durango
Elota
Nazas
Matehuala
4054
Ciudad Victoria
Fresnillo
Zacatecas
Ciudad Mante
Tropic of Cancer
Yucatan

D

PACIFIC OCEAN
Las Tres Marías
C. Corrientes
Tepic
3353
R. Grande de Santiago
Guadalajara
Ameca
Colima Vol.
3960
Colima
Manzanillo
Zamora
Léon
Irapuato
Celaya
L. de Chapala
Aguascalientes
San Luis Potosí
Panuco
Querétaro
Pachuca
C. Rojo
Tuxpan
Tampico
Ciudad Madero
Progreso
Mérida
Valladolid
I. de Cozumel
Peto
Gulf of

E

Morelia   MEXICO
Toluca
Cuernavaca
Balsas
Iguala
Chilpancingo
Acapulco
Ometepec
Popocatepetl 5452
Puebla   Orizaba
Mexcala
3703
Verde
Oaxaca
Citlaltepetl 5700
Jalapa Enriquez
Veracruz
Campeche
Ciudad del Carmen
Laguna de Terminos
Minatitlán
Coatzacoalcos
Villahermosa
Isthmus of Tehuantepec
3395
Salina Cruz
Juchitan
3139
Tonala
San Cristobal
Tuxtla Gutierrez
Usumacinta
Chetumal
Campeche
Yucatan
Belize
Belmopan
Turneffe Is.
BELIZE
Pto Barrios
Gulf of Ho
G. of Tehuantepec
Tapachula
4217
Quezaltenango
GUATEMALA
Guatemala
Sta. Ana
Pto Cortés
Telo
La Ceiba
Zacapa
S. Pedro Sula
HONDURAS
Comayagua
Tegucigalpa
San Salvador
EL SALVADOR
S. Miguel
Choluteca
Leon
NICARA
G. of Fonseca
Nicoya Pen.
Managua
Gra

PANAMA CANAL

14

Colón
Fort Sherman   Coco Solo
Cristobal   Margarita
Puerto Pilón
Zorra
Gatun
Gatun Locks
Gatun Dam
Juan Gallegos
El Limón
Frijoles
Escobal
Colorado I.
Darien
Gamboa
Madden L.
Madden Dam
Buenos Aires
The Gaillard Cut
Balboa Hill 350
Las Cascadas
Culebra
Pedro Miguel
Paraiso
Pedro Miguel Locks
Miraflores Locks
Corozal
Fort Clayton   Curundu
Balboa   Bay of
Arraiján
Fort Amador
La Chorrera
PANAMA
Panama

PANAMA CANAL
1:1 000 000
0   10   20km

H

JAMAICA

Montego Bay
Falmouth
St. Ann's Bay
Galina Point
Annotto Bay
Savanna la Mar
Mandeville
Port Antonio
KINGSTON
2256
Spanish Town
May Pen
Morant Point
Morant Bay
Portland Point

JAMAICA
1:5 000 000
0   50 km

15   **16**   **17**

TRINIDAD AND TOBAGO

Charlotteville
Tobago
Scarborough
Port of Spain
940
Arima
Sangre Grande
Gulf of Paria
San Fernando
Rio Claro
TRINIDAD
Point Fortin
Princes Town
Siparia
Serpent's Mouth

TRINIDAD AND TOBAGO
1:5 000 000
0   50 km

Projection: Bonne

19   **20**   **21**

LEEWARD ISLANDS

The Valley
Marigot
Anguilla (U.K.)
St. Martin (Fr.)
St. Maarten (Neth.)
St. Barthélemy (Fr.)
Saba (Neth.)
St. Eustatius (Neth.)
Codrington
Barbuda
ANTIGUA & BARBUDA
ST. KITTS-NEVIS
Basseterre
Charlestown
Redonda
St. John's
Antigua
Montserrat (U.K.)
Plymouth
Guadeloupe Passage
GUADELOUPE (Fr.)
Ste Rose
Grande Terre
Moule
Désirade (Fr.)
Basse Terre
Pointe-à-Pitre
Basse Terre
Marie-Galante (Fr.)
I. des Saintes
Grand Bourg
Dominica Passage
Portsmouth
Morne Diablotin
1490
Roseau
DOMINICA (Windward Is.)

LEEWARD ISLANDS
1:5 000 000
0   50 km

18   **19**   **20**   **21**

WINDWARD ISLANDS

Martinique Passage
Mt. Pelée 1397
Ste. Marie
St. Pierre
Fort de France   Le Francois
Lamentin
MARTINIQUE (Fr.)
Ste. Anne
St. Lucia Channel
Castries
St. LUCIA
Soufrière
Vieux Fort
St. Vincent Passage
Soufrière 1178
Georgetown
ST. VINCENT
Kingstown
& Bequia
THE GRENADINES
Mustique
Canouan
Union
Carriacou
Hillsborough
Ronde
St. George's
840
Grenville
GRENADA
BARBADOS
Speightstown
Bridgetown

WINDWARD ISLANDS
1:5 000 000
0   50 km

22

20   **21**

UNITED STATES
MEXICO
Sierra Madre
Gulf of California
Lower California

ft / m elevation scale:
12 000 / 4000
9000 / 3000
6000 / 2000
4500 / 1500
3000 / 1000
1200 / 400
600 / 200
0 / 0
200 / 200
2000 / 2000
m / ft

West from Greenwich

COPYRIGHT. GEORGE PHILIP & SON. LTD.

1:15 000 000

100   0   100   200   300   400 miles

100   0   100   200   300   400   600 km

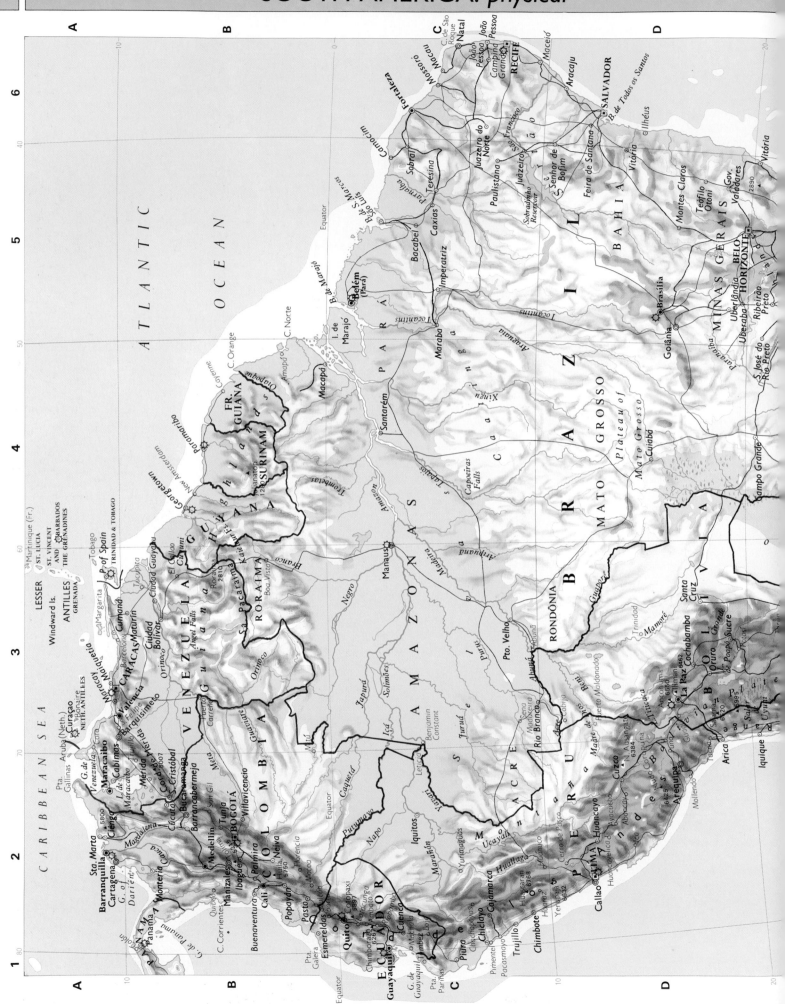

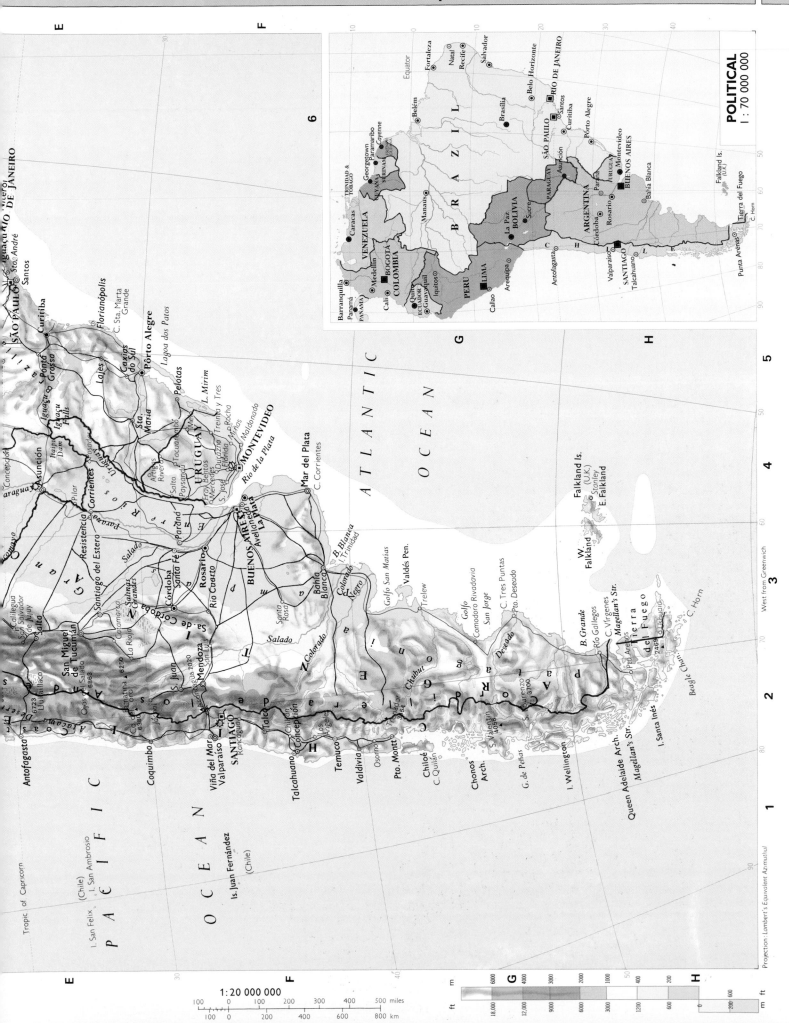

POLITICAL
1 : 70 000 000

Projection: Lambert's Equivalent Azimuthal

West from Greenwich

1 : 20 000 000

| 100 | 0 | 100 | 200 | 300 | 400 | 500 miles |

| 100 | 0 | 200 | 400 | 600 | 800 km |

Legend

- Ice cap
- Permanent ice shelf
- Maximum extent of sea ice
- March (Summer) extent of sea ice
- ▲3488 / 3700 — Surface elevation and depth of ice (in metres)
- ● Stanley (U.K.) — Permanent bases

Projection: Zenithal Equidistant

1 : 35 000 000

Scale:
200 0 200 400 600 800 miles
400 0 400 800 1200 km

West from Greenwich · East from Greenwich

Magnetic Pole 1990

COPYRIGHT. GEORGE PHILIP & SON. LTD.

(Full-page physical map showing the Arctic Ocean region — North America, Greenland, Svalbard, Russia, the Barents, Kara and Laptev Seas — and the continent of Antarctica with surrounding Southern Ocean, research bases, ice shelves, and elevation spot heights.)

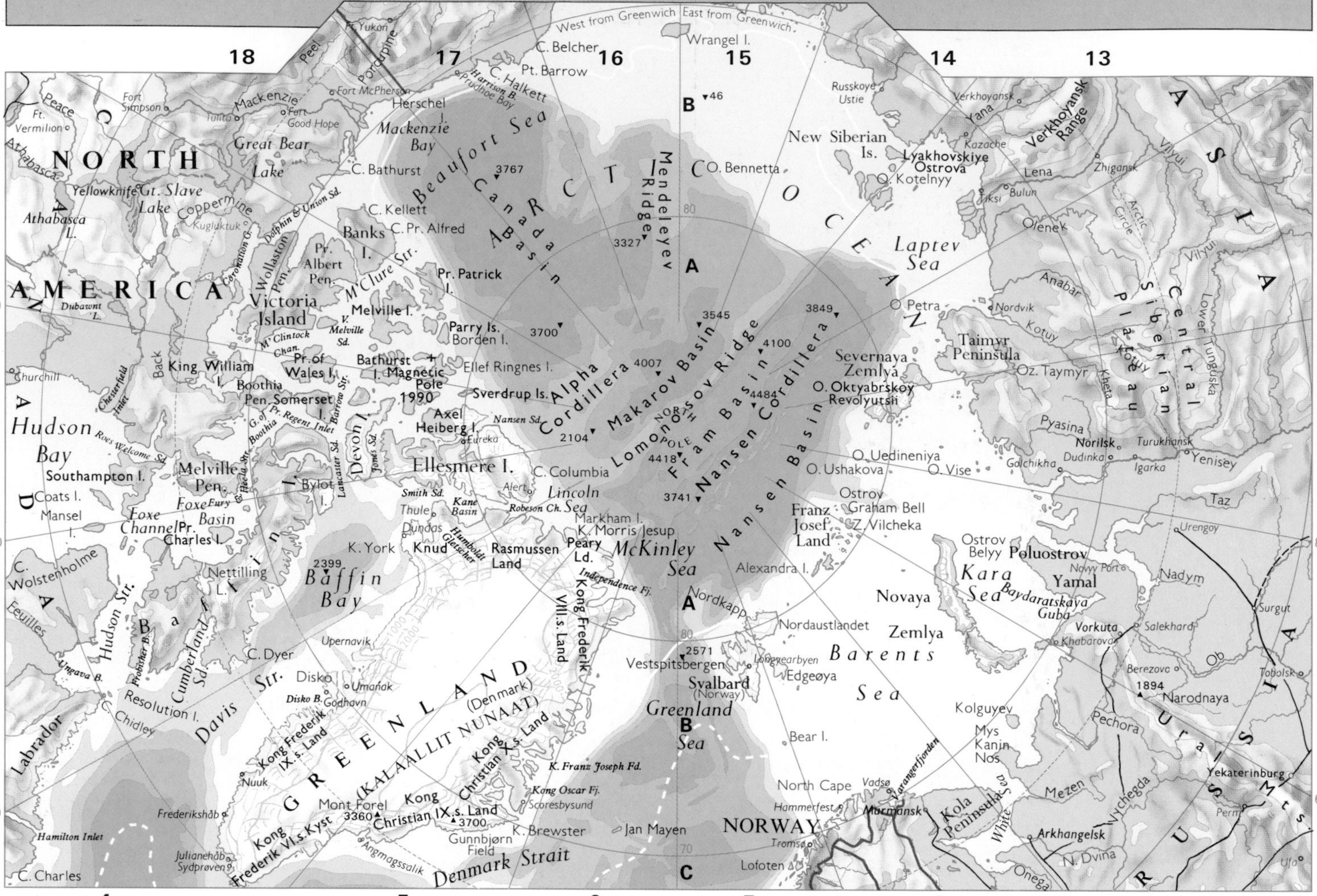

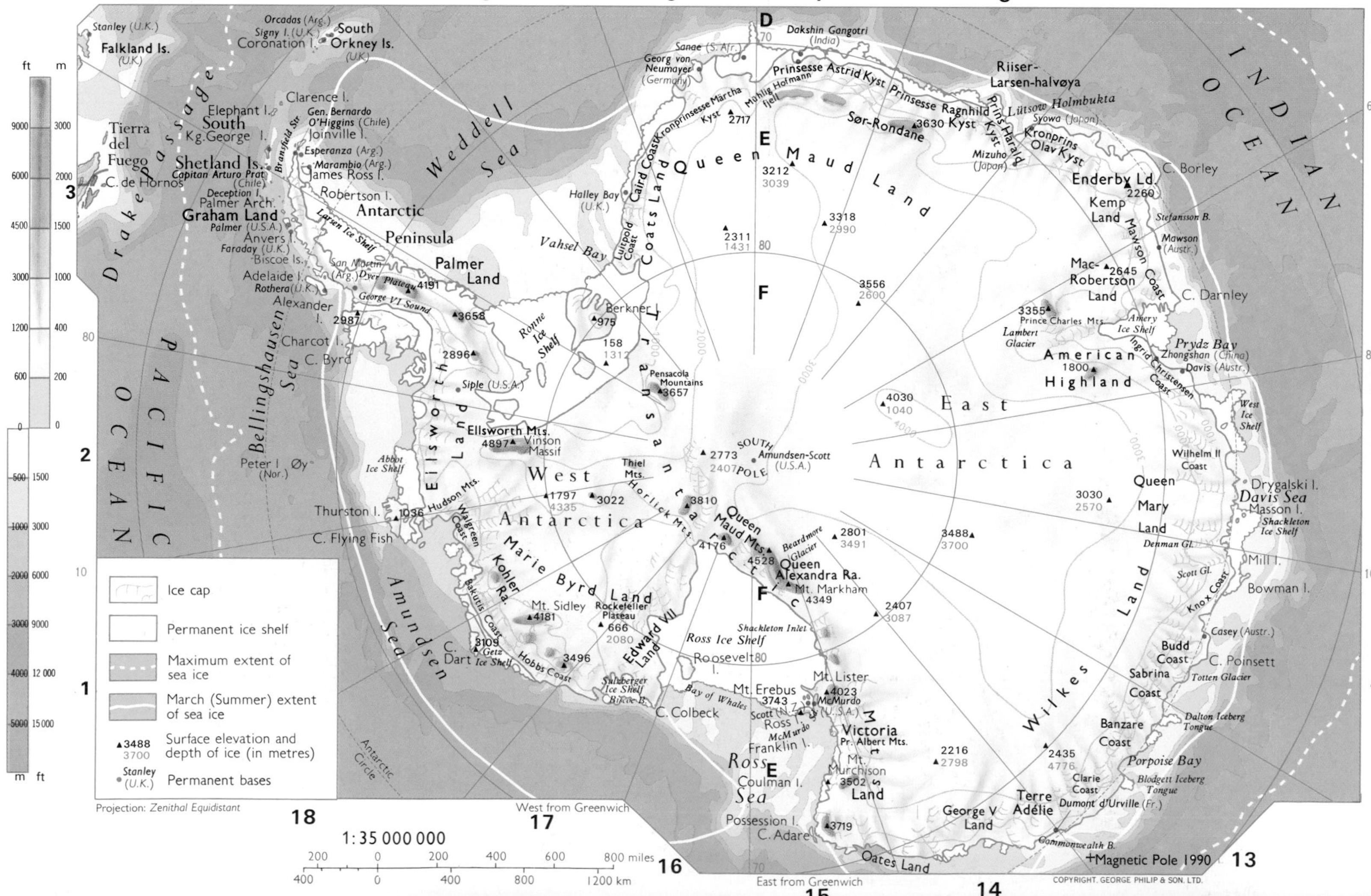

WORLD
THEMATIC MAPS

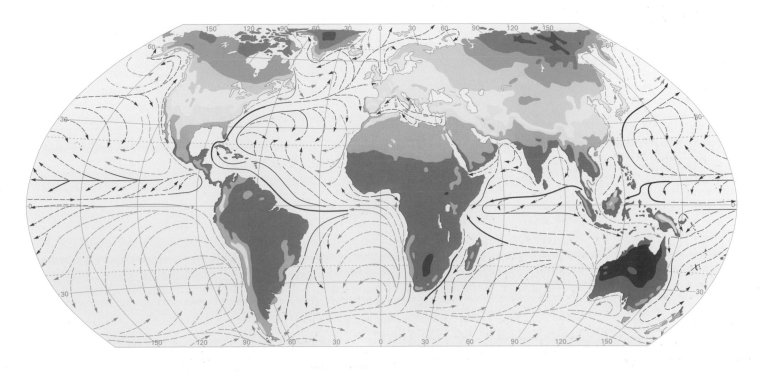

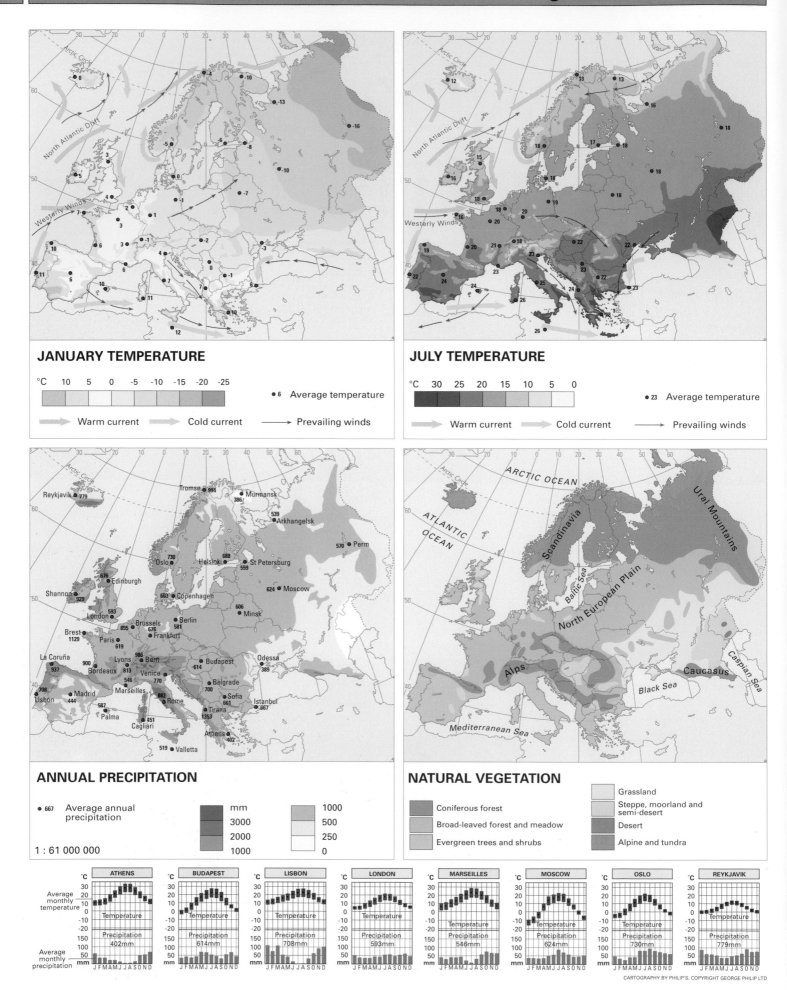

JANUARY TEMPERATURE

°C 10 5 0 -5 -10 -15 -20 -25

● 6 Average temperature

Warm current   Cold current   Prevailing winds

JULY TEMPERATURE

°C 30 25 20 15 10 5 0

● 23 Average temperature

Warm current   Cold current   Prevailing winds

ANNUAL PRECIPITATION

● 667 Average annual precipitation

1 : 61 000 000

mm	
3000	1000
2000	500
1000	250
	0

NATURAL VEGETATION

Coniferous forest

Broad-leaved forest and meadow

Evergreen trees and shrubs

Grassland

Steppe, moorland and semi-desert

Desert

Alpine and tundra

ATHENS — Temperature — Precipitation 402mm

BUDAPEST — Temperature — Precipitation 614mm

LISBON — Temperature — Precipitation 708mm

LONDON — Temperature — Precipitation 593mm

MARSEILLES — Temperature — Precipitation 546mm

MOSCOW — Temperature — Precipitation 624mm

OSLO — Temperature — Precipitation 730mm

REYKJAVIK — Temperature — Precipitation 779mm

Average monthly temperature °C 30 20 10 0 -10 -20

Average monthly precipitation mm 150 100 50

J F M A M J J A S O N D

CARTOGRAPHY BY PHILIP'S. COPYRIGHT GEORGE PHILIP LTD

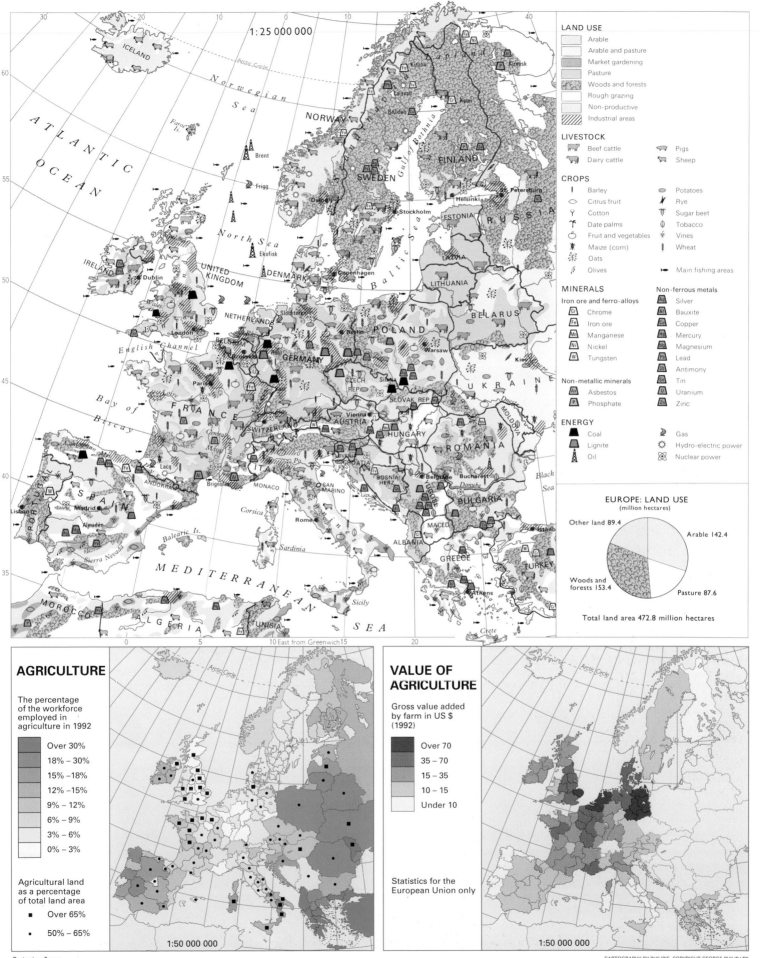

1 : 25 000 000

LAND USE
- Arable
- Arable and pasture
- Market gardening
- Pasture
- Woods and forests
- Rough grazing
- Non-productive
- Industrial areas

LIVESTOCK
- Beef cattle
- Dairy cattle
- Pigs
- Sheep

CROPS
- Barley
- Citrus fruit
- Cotton
- Date palms
- Fruit and vegetables
- Maize (corn)
- Oats
- Olives
- Potatoes
- Rye
- Sugar beet
- Tobacco
- Vines
- Wheat
- Main fishing areas

MINERALS

Iron ore and ferro-alloys
- Cr Chrome
- Fe Iron ore
- Mn Manganese
- Ni Nickel
- W Tungsten

Non-metallic minerals
- As Asbestos
- P Phosphate

Non-ferrous metals
- Ag Silver
- Al Bauxite
- Cu Copper
- Hg Mercury
- Mg Magnesium
- Pb Lead
- Sb Antimony
- Sn Tin
- U Uranium
- Zn Zinc

ENERGY
- Coal
- Lignite
- Oil
- Gas
- Hydro-electric power
- Nuclear power

EUROPE: LAND USE
(million hectares)

Other land 89.4
Arable 142.4
Woods and forests 153.4
Pasture 87.6

Total land area 472.8 million hectares

AGRICULTURE

The percentage of the workforce employed in agriculture in 1992

- Over 30%
- 18% – 30%
- 15% – 18%
- 12% –15%
- 9% – 12%
- 6% – 9%
- 3% – 6%
- 0% – 3%

Agricultural land as a percentage of total land area

- ■ Over 65%
- • 50% – 65%

1:50 000 000

VALUE OF AGRICULTURE

Gross value added by farm in US $ (1992)

- Over 70
- 35 – 70
- 15 – 35
- 10 – 15
- Under 10

Statistics for the European Union only

1:50 000 000

Projection: *Bonne*

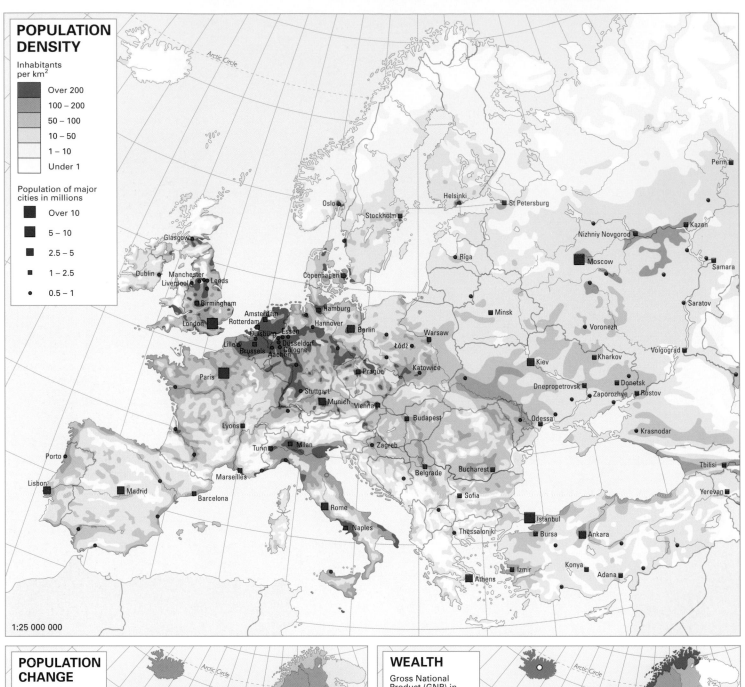

POPULATION DENSITY

Inhabitants per km²

- Over 200
- 100 – 200
- 50 – 100
- 10 – 50
- 1 – 10
- Under 1

Population of major cities in millions

- Over 10
- 5 – 10
- 2.5 – 5
- 1 – 2.5
- 0.5 – 1

1:25 000 000

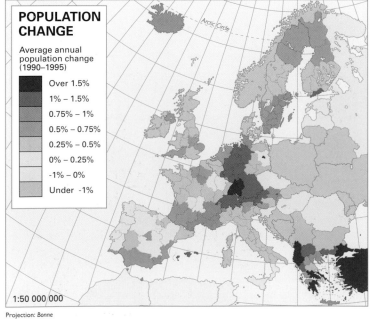

POPULATION CHANGE

Average annual population change (1990–1995)

- Over 1.5%
- 1% – 1.5%
- 0.75% – 1%
- 0.5% – 0.75%
- 0.25% – 0.5%
- 0% – 0.25%
- -1% – 0%
- Under -1%

1:50 000 000

Projection: *Bonne*

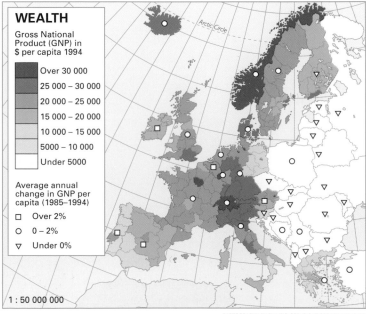

WEALTH

Gross National Product (GNP) in $ per capita 1994

- Over 30 000
- 25 000 – 30 000
- 20 000 – 25 000
- 15 000 – 20 000
- 10 000 – 15 000
- 5000 – 10 000
- Under 5000

Average annual change in GNP per capita (1985–1994)

- □ Over 2%
- ○ 0 – 2%
- ▽ Under 0%

1 : 50 000 000

CARTOGRAPHY BY PHILIP'S. COPYRIGHT GEORGE PHILIP LTD

E.U. BUDGET

billion ECU

Contributions to the E.U. 1993

Receipts from the E.U. 1993

Germany
France
Italy
U.K.
Spain
Netherlands
Belgium
Denmark
Greece
Portugal
Ireland
Luxembourg
Sweden
Finland
Austria

E.U. EXPENDITURE

Research, energy and technology 3.5%
Development co-operation 3.9%
Administration costs 4.6%
Social policy 8.0%
Regional policy and transport 13.2%
Agriculture and fisheries 63.5%
Others 3.3%

THE EUROPEAN UNION

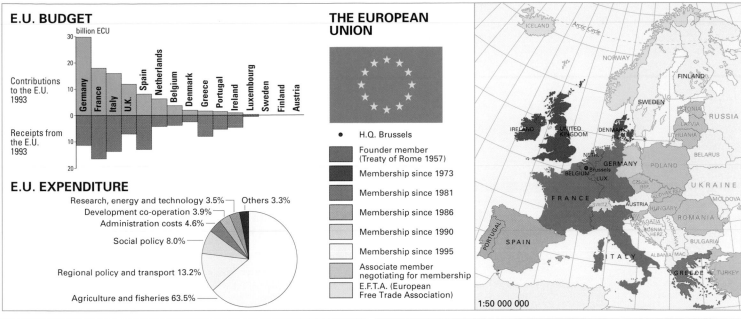

- H.Q. Brussels

Founder member (Treaty of Rome 1957)

Membership since 1973

Membership since 1981

Membership since 1986

Membership since 1990

Membership since 1995

Associate member negotiating for membership

E.F.T.A. (European Free Trade Association)

1:50 000 000

TRANSPORT

Airports with over 10 million passengers a year (1995)

- 50 million
- 25 million
- 10 million

— European high speed rail network built or planned for 2010

Planned journey times by rail from London

	1990	2010
Amsterdam	7 h 38	3 h 45
Barcelona	20 h 00	6 h 40
Berlin	16 h 35	8 h 25
Brussels	4 h 55	2 h 05
Bordeaux	9 h 48	4 h 45
Frankfurt	11 h 26	5 h 00
Lyons	9 h 04	4 h 00
Madrid	21 h 32	9 h 20
Paris	5 h 15	2 h 10
Venice	20 h 45	7 h 45

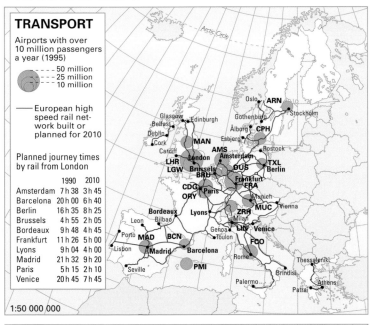

1:50 000 000

INDUSTRY

The percentage of the workforce employed in industry 1992

Over 40%
35 – 40%
30 – 35%
25 – 30%
20 – 25%
Under 20%

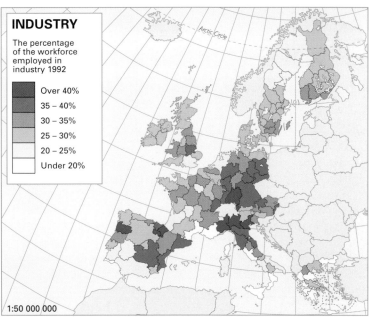

1:50 000 000

OUT OF WORK

The percentage of the work force unemployed in 1995

Over 20%
16 – 20%
12 – 16%
10 – 12%
8 – 10%
6 – 8%
Under 6%

Unemployment rate in 1995 for people under 25 years old

■ Over 30%
▪ 20 – 30%
• Under 20%

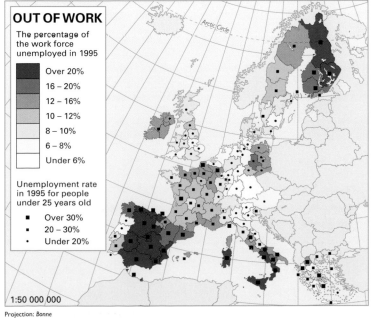

1:50 000 000

HEALTH AND EDUCATION

Number of doctors per thousand inhabitants

Over 4
3.5 – 4
3 – 3.5
2.5 – 3
2 – 2.5
1.5 – 2
Under 1.5

The percentage of people aged 15 – 24 in full time education

▲ Over 50 %
▽ Under 25 %

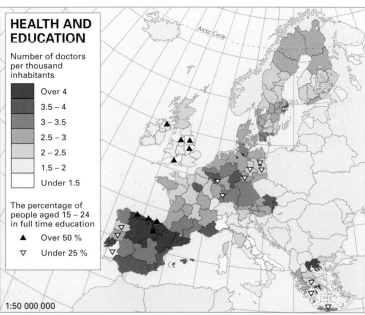

1:50 000 000

Projection: Bonne

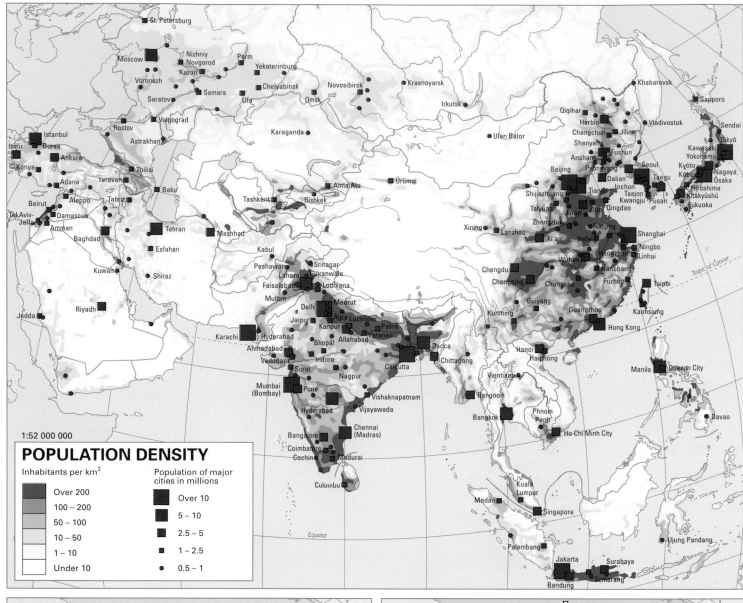

POPULATION DENSITY

1:52 000 000

Inhabitants per km²

	Over 200
	100 – 200
	50 – 100
	10 – 50
	1 – 10
	Under 10

Population of major cities in millions

	Over 10
	5 – 10
	2.5 – 5
	1 – 2.5
	0.5 – 1

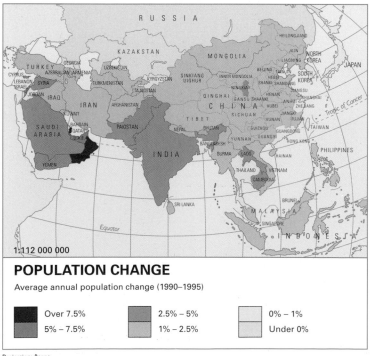

1:112 000 000

POPULATION CHANGE

Average annual population change (1990–1995)

Over 7.5%	2.5% – 5%	0% – 1%
5% – 7.5%	1% – 2.5%	Under 0%

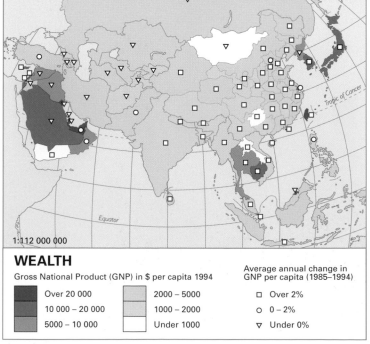

1:112 000 000

WEALTH

Gross National Product (GNP) in $ per capita 1994

Over 20 000	2000 – 5000
10 000 – 20 000	1000 – 2000
5000 – 10 000	Under 1000

Average annual change in GNP per capita (1985–1994)

□	Over 2%
○	0 – 2%
▽	Under 0%

Projection: Bonne

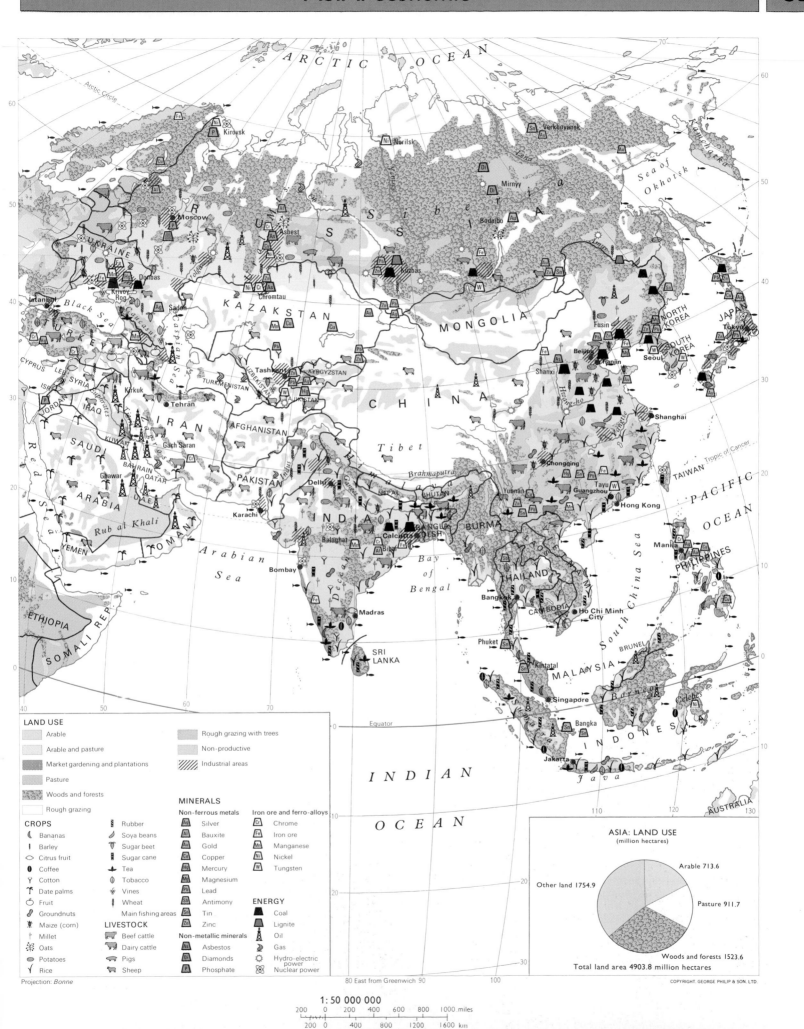

ARCTIC OCEAN

Arctic Circle

Kirovsk
Norilsk
Verkhoyansk
Sea of Okhotsk
Kamchatka

Moscow
Asbest
Mirnyy
Bodaibo

R U S S I A
S i b e r i a

Krivoy Rog
Donbas
Kuzbas
Amur

Istanbul
Black Sea
KAZAKSTAN
MONGOLIA
Sea of Japan

Chromtau
JAPAN
Tōkyō

Saden
NORTH KOREA
SOUTH KOREA
Seoul

TURKEY
CYPRUS
LEB
SYRIA
Caspian Sea
Fusin
Beijing
Tianjin
Shanxi
Hsüang-ho

Kirkuk
Tehran
TASHKENT
UZBEKISTAN
KYRGYZSTAN
TURKMENISTAN
C H I N A
Shanghai

JORDAN
IRAQ
I R A N
AFGHANISTAN
Tibet
Yangtse

SAUDI
KUWAIT
Gach Saran
Chongqing
Yunnan
Tayu
Guangzhou
TAIWAN
Tropic of Cancer

BAHRAIN
QATAR
PAKISTAN
Delhi
NEPAL
BHUTAN
Hong Kong
PACIFIC OCEAN

Ghawar
UAE
OMAN
Karachi
I N D I A
BANGLA DESH
BURMA

Red Sea
YEMEN
Rub al Khali
Balaghat
Calcutta
Bihar

ETHIOPIA
SOMALI REP.
Arabian Sea
Bombay
Deccan
Bay of Bengal
Manila
PHILIPPINES

Madras
THAILAND
Bangkok
CAMBODIA
Ho Chi Minh City
South China Sea

Phuket
Kintatal
BRUNEI
MALAYSIA
Borneo
Celebes

SRI LANKA
Singapore
Bangka
I N D O N E S I A

Equator
Jakarta
Java

I N D I A N
O C E A N
AUSTRALIA

LAND USE

Arable	Rough grazing with trees
Arable and pasture	Non-productive
Market gardening and plantations	Industrial areas
Pasture	
Woods and forests	
Rough grazing	

CROPS

Bananas
Barley
Citrus fruit
Coffee
Cotton
Date palms
Fruit
Groundnuts
Maize (corn)
Millet
Oats
Potatoes
Rice

Rubber
Soya beans
Sugar beet
Sugar cane
Tea
Tobacco
Vines
Wheat
Main fishing areas

LIVESTOCK

Beef cattle
Dairy cattle
Pigs
Sheep

MINERALS

Non-ferrous metals

Ag	Silver
Al	Bauxite
Au	Gold
Cu	Copper
Hg	Mercury
Mg	Magnesium
Pb	Lead
Sb	Antimony
Sn	Tin
Zn	Zinc

Non-metallic minerals

As	Asbestos
Di	Diamonds
P	Phosphate

Iron ore and ferro-alloys

Cr	Chrome
Fe	Iron ore
Mn	Manganese
Ni	Nickel
W	Tungsten

ENERGY

Coal
Lignite
Oil
Gas
Hydro-electric power
Nuclear power

ASIA: LAND USE
(million hectares)

Other land 1754.9
Arable 713.6
Pasture 911.7
Woods and forests 1523.6

Total land area 4903.8 million hectares

Projection: *Bonne*

80 East from Greenwich 90   100

COPYRIGHT. GEORGE PHILIP & SON. LTD.

1 : 50 000 000

200 0   200   400   600   800   1000 miles
200 0   400   800   1200   1600 km

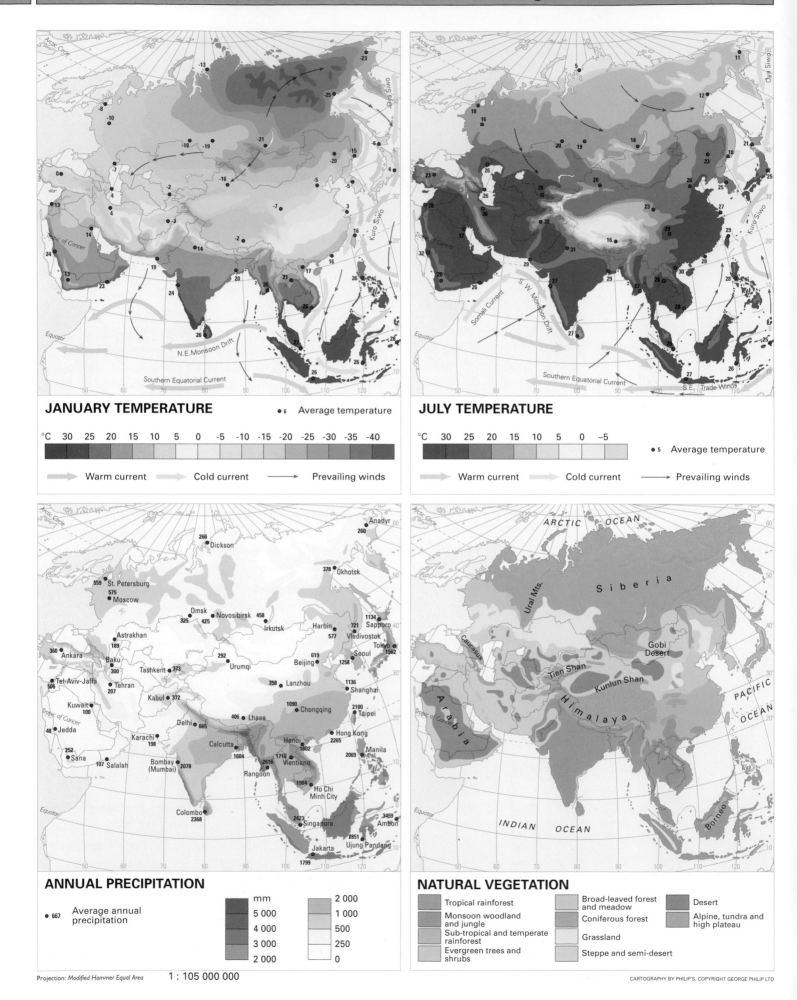

JANUARY TEMPERATURE

● 6 Average temperature

°C 30 25 20 15 10 5 0 −5 −10 −15 −20 −25 −30 −35 −40

⟹ Warm current   ⟹ Cold current   → Prevailing winds

JULY TEMPERATURE

°C 30 25 20 15 10 5 0 −5

● 5 Average temperature

⟹ Warm current   ⟹ Cold current   → Prevailing winds

ANNUAL PRECIPITATION

● 667 Average annual precipitation

	mm	
	5 000	2 000
	4 000	1 000
	3 000	500
	2 000	250
		0

NATURAL VEGETATION

- Tropical rainforest
- Monsoon woodland and jungle
- Sub-tropical and temperate rainforest
- Evergreen trees and shrubs
- Broad-leaved forest and meadow
- Coniferous forest
- Grassland
- Steppe and semi-desert
- Desert
- Alpine, tundra and high plateau

Projection: *Modified Hammer Equal Area*   1 : 105 000 000

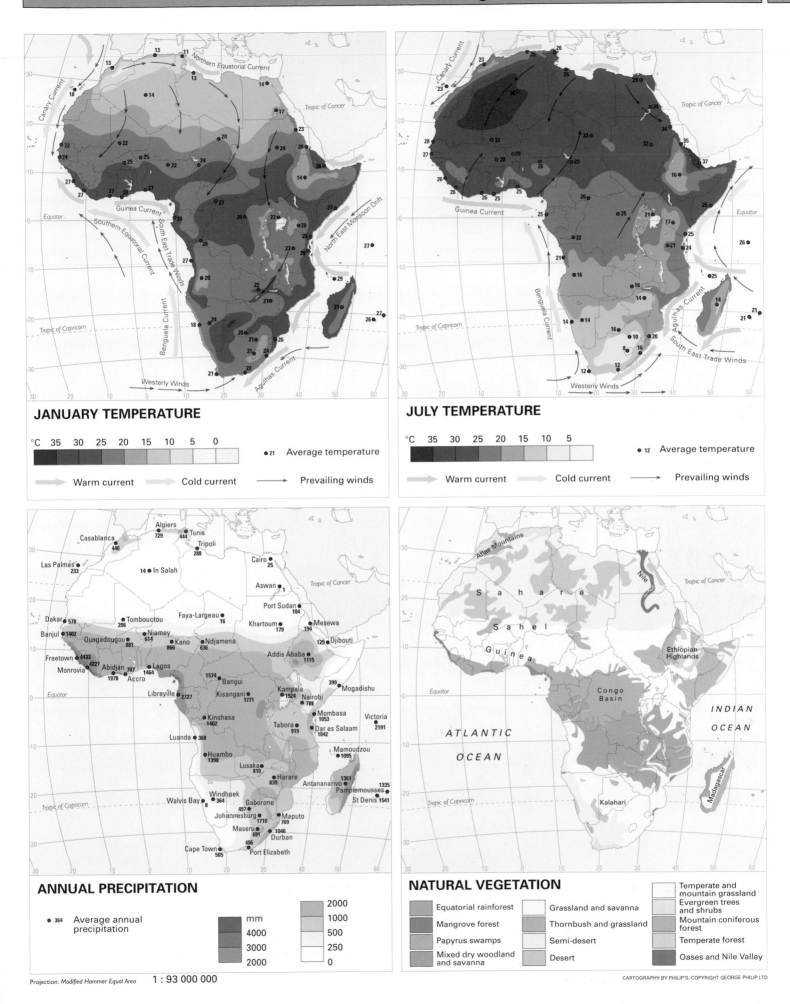

JANUARY TEMPERATURE

°C 35 30 25 20 15 10 5 0

•21 Average temperature

Warm current   Cold current   Prevailing winds

JULY TEMPERATURE

°C 35 30 25 20 15 10 5

•12 Average temperature

Warm current   Cold current   Prevailing winds

ANNUAL PRECIPITATION

•364 Average annual precipitation

mm
2000
1000
500
250
0

4000
3000
2000

NATURAL VEGETATION

Equatorial rainforest

Mangrove forest

Papyrus swamps

Mixed dry woodland and savanna

Grassland and savanna

Thornbush and grassland

Semi-desert

Desert

Temperate and mountain grassland

Evergreen trees and shrubs

Mountain coniferous forest

Temperate forest

Oases and Nile Valley

Projection: *Modified Hammer Equal Area*   1 : 93 000 000

CARTOGRAPHY BY PHILIP'S. COPYRIGHT GEORGE PHILIP LTD

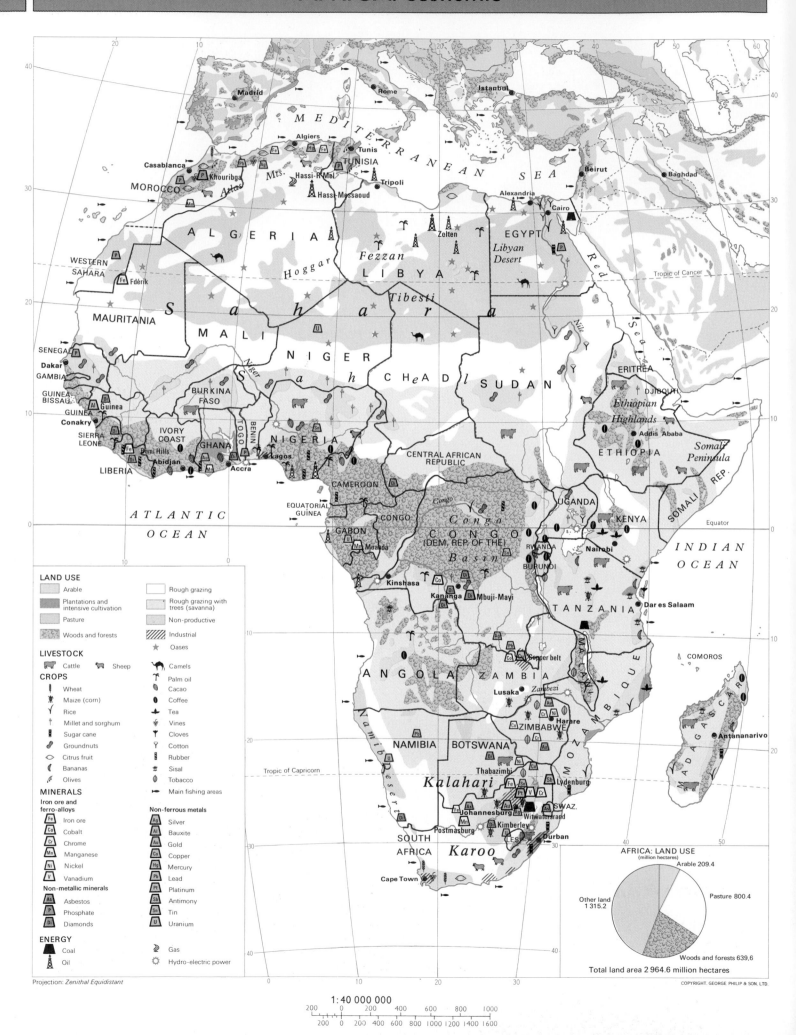

LAND USE

Arable	Rough grazing
Plantations and intensive cultivation	Rough grazing with trees (savanna)
Pasture	Non-productive
Woods and forests	Industrial
	Oases

LIVESTOCK

Cattle   Sheep   Camels

CROPS

Wheat
Maize (corn)
Rice
Millet and sorghum
Sugar cane
Groundnuts
Citrus fruit
Bananas
Olives

Palm oil
Cacao
Coffee
Tea
Vines
Cloves
Cotton
Rubber
Sisal
Tobacco
Main fishing areas

MINERALS

Iron ore and ferro-alloys

Fe Iron ore
Co Cobalt
Cr Chrome
Mn Manganese
Ni Nickel
V Vanadium

Non-metallic minerals

As Asbestos
P Phosphate
Di Diamonds

Non-ferrous metals

Ag Silver
Al Bauxite
Au Gold
Cu Copper
Hg Mercury
Pb Lead
Pt Platinum
Sb Antimony
Sn Tin
U Uranium

ENERGY

Coal   Gas
Oil   Hydro-electric power

AFRICA: LAND USE
(million hectares)

Arable 209.4
Pasture 800.4
Woods and forests 639.6
Other land 1 315.2

Total land area 2 964.6 million hectares

Projection: *Zenithal Equidistant*

COPYRIGHT. GEORGE PHILIP & SON, LTD.

1:40 000 000

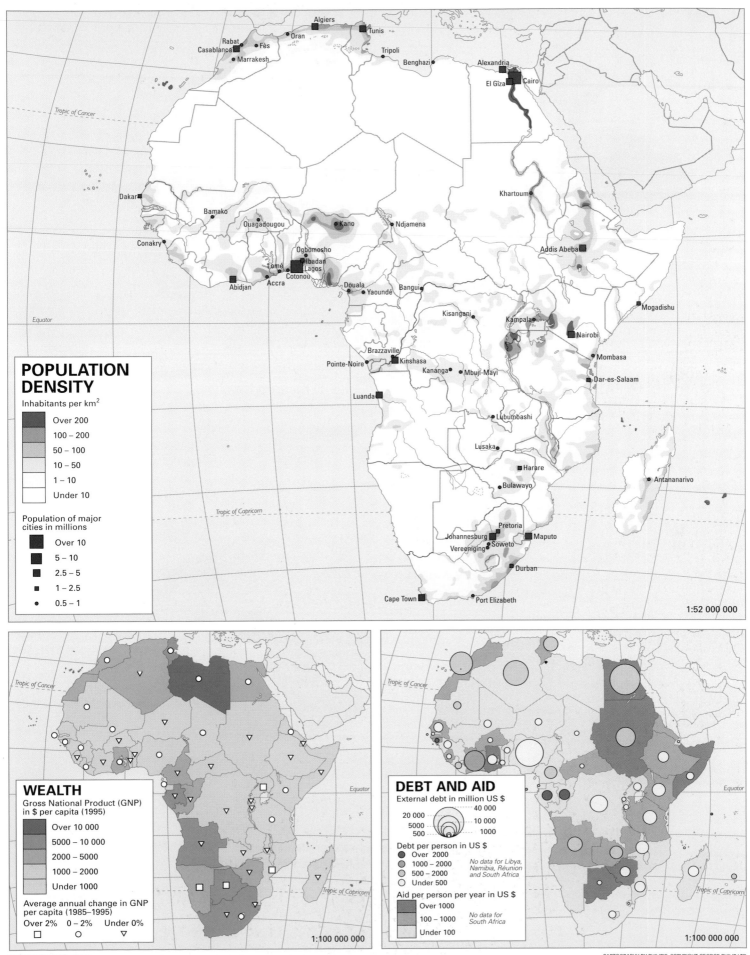

POPULATION DENSITY

Inhabitants per km²

	Over 200
	100 – 200
	50 – 100
	10 – 50
	1 – 10
	Under 10

Population of major cities in millions

■	Over 10
■	5 – 10
■	2.5 – 5
■	1 – 2.5
•	0.5 – 1

1:52 000 000

Algiers · Tunis · Oran · Rabat · Fès · Casablanca · Marrakesh · Tripoli · Benghazi · Alexandria · El Gîza · Cairo · Khartoum · Dakar · Bamako · Ouagadougou · Kano · Ndjamena · Conakry · Ogbomosho · Ibadan · Lagos · Lomé · Cotonou · Accra · Abidjan · Addis Abeba · Douala · Yaoundé · Bangui · Kisangani · Kampala · Mogadishu · Nairobi · Brazzaville · Kinshasa · Mombasa · Pointe-Noire · Kananga · Mbuji-Mayi · Dar-es-Salaam · Luanda · Lubumbashi · Lusaka · Harare · Antananarivo · Bulawayo · Pretoria · Maputo · Johannesburg · Soweto · Vereeniging · Durban · Cape Town · Port Elizabeth

Tropic of Cancer

Equator

Tropic of Capricorn

WEALTH

Gross National Product (GNP) in $ per capita (1995)

	Over 10 000
	5000 – 10 000
	2000 – 5000
	1000 – 2000
	Under 1000

Average annual change in GNP per capita (1985–1995)

Over 2%	0 – 2%	Under 0%
□	○	▽

1:100 000 000

DEBT AND AID

External debt in million US $

40 000 · 20 000 · 10 000 · 5000 · 1000 · 500

Debt per person in US $

●	Over 2000
◐	1000 – 2000
◔	500 – 2000
○	Under 500

No data for Libya, Namibia, Réunion and South Africa

Aid per person per year in US $

	Over 1000
	100 – 1000
	Under 100

No data for South Africa

1:100 000 000

Projection: *Zenithal Equidistant*

CARTOGRAPHY BY PHILIP'S. COPYRIGHT GEORGE PHILIP LTD

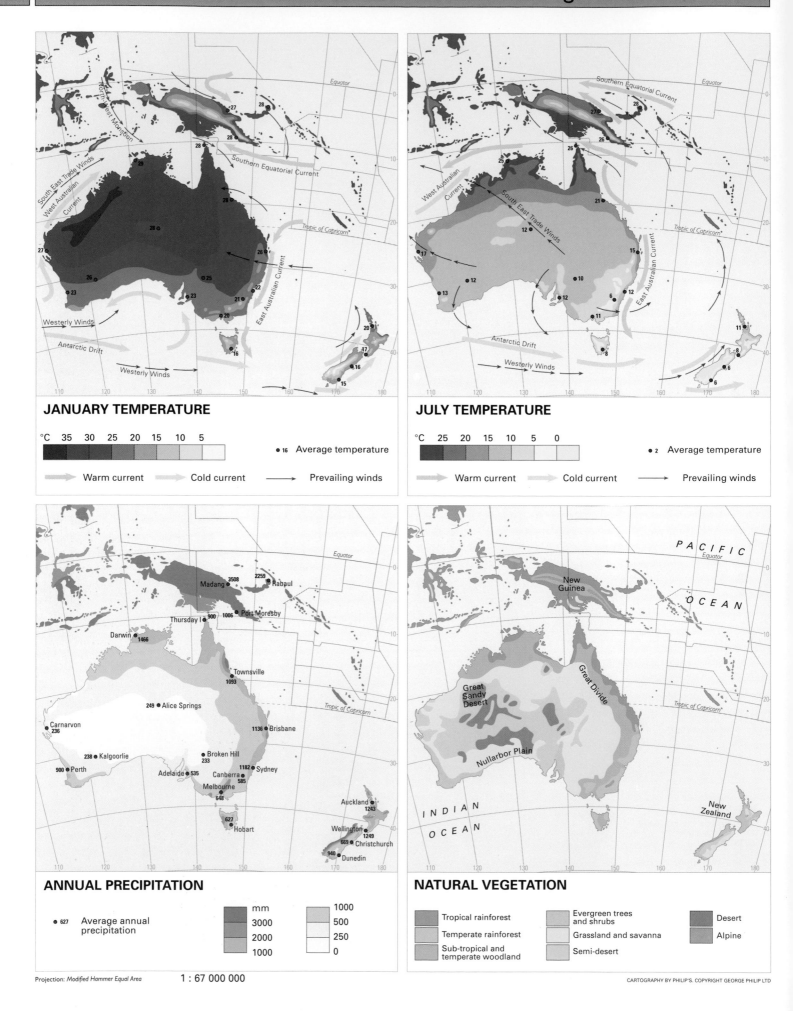

JANUARY TEMPERATURE

°C 35 30 25 20 15 10 5

● 16 Average temperature

⟹ Warm current   ⟹ Cold current   → Prevailing winds

JULY TEMPERATURE

°C 25 20 15 10 5 0

● 2 Average temperature

⟹ Warm current   ⟹ Cold current   → Prevailing winds

ANNUAL PRECIPITATION

● 627 Average annual precipitation

mm	
3000	1000
2000	500
1000	250
	0

NATURAL VEGETATION

Tropical rainforest

Temperate rainforest

Sub-tropical and temperate woodland

Evergreen trees and shrubs

Grassland and savanna

Semi-desert

Desert

Alpine

Annual precipitation labels:
Madang 3508 · 2259 · Rabaul
Thursday I 900 · 1006 Port Moresby
Darwin 1466
Townsville 1093
Alice Springs 249
Carnarvon 236
Brisbane 1136
Kalgoorlie 238
Broken Hill 233
Perth 900
Adelaide 535
Sydney 1182
Canberra 585
Melbourne 648
Hobart 627
Auckland 1243
Wellington 1249
Christchurch 669
Dunedin 940

Natural vegetation labels:
New Guinea, Great Divide, Great Sandy Desert, Nullarbor Plain, New Zealand, PACIFIC OCEAN, INDIAN OCEAN, Equator, Tropic of Capricorn

Projection: *Modified Hammer Equal Area*   1 : 67 000 000   CARTOGRAPHY BY PHILIP'S. COPYRIGHT GEORGE PHILIP LTD

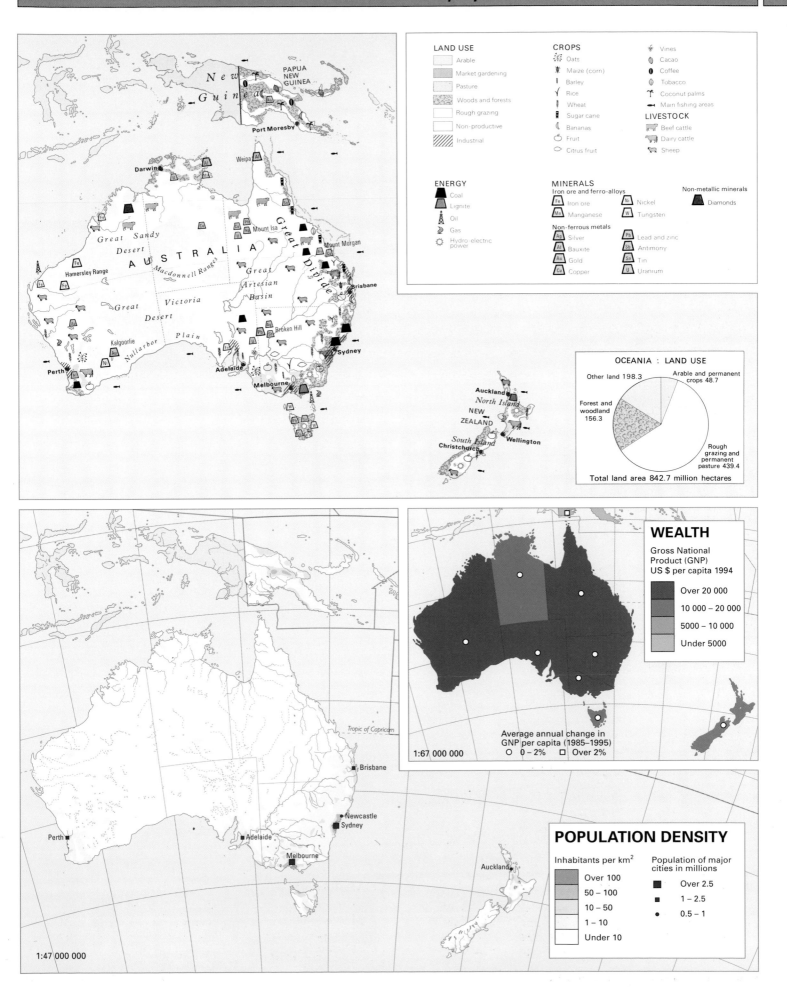

LAND USE
- Arable
- Market gardening
- Pasture
- Woods and forests
- Rough grazing
- Non-productive
- Industrial

CROPS
- Oats
- Maize (corn)
- Barley
- Rice
- Wheat
- Sugar cane
- Bananas
- Fruit
- Citrus fruit
- Vines
- Cacao
- Coffee
- Tobacco
- Coconut palms
- Main fishing areas

LIVESTOCK
- Beef cattle
- Dairy cattle
- Sheep

ENERGY
- Coal
- Lignite
- Oil
- Gas
- Hydro-electric power

MINERALS
Iron ore and ferro-alloys
- Fe Iron ore
- Mn Manganese
- Ni Nickel
- W Tungsten

Non-ferrous metals
- Ag Silver
- Al Bauxite
- Au Gold
- Cu Copper
- Pb Lead and zinc
- Sb Antimony
- Sn Tin
- U Uranium

Non-metallic minerals
- Diamonds

OCEANIA : LAND USE

Other land 198.3

Arable and permanent crops 48.7

Forest and woodland 156.3

Rough grazing and permanent pasture 439.4

Total land area 842.7 million hectares

WEALTH

Gross National Product (GNP)
US $ per capita 1994

- Over 20 000
- 10 000 – 20 000
- 5000 – 10 000
- Under 5000

Average annual change in GNP per capita (1985–1995)
- ○ 0 – 2%
- □ Over 2%

1:67 000 000

POPULATION DENSITY

Inhabitants per km²
- Over 100
- 50 – 100
- 10 – 50
- 1 – 10
- Under 10

Population of major cities in millions
- ■ Over 2.5
- ■ 1 – 2.5
- • 0.5 – 1

1:47 000 000

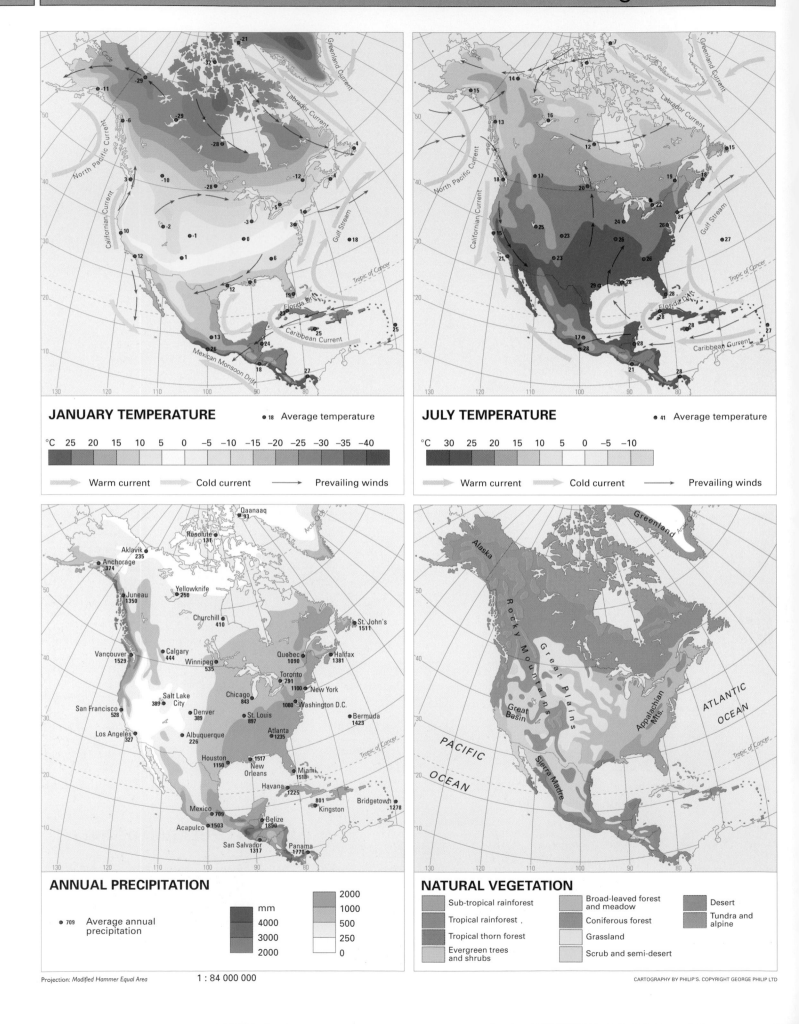

JANUARY TEMPERATURE

● 18 Average temperature

°C 25 20 15 10 5 0 −5 −10 −15 −20 −25 −30 −35 −40

Warm current   Cold current   Prevailing winds

JULY TEMPERATURE

● 41 Average temperature

°C 30 25 20 15 10 5 0 −5 −10

Warm current   Cold current   Prevailing winds

ANNUAL PRECIPITATION

● 709 Average annual precipitation

mm
2000
1000
500
250
0

4000
3000
2000

NATURAL VEGETATION

- Sub-tropical rainforest
- Tropical rainforest
- Tropical thorn forest
- Evergreen trees and shrubs
- Broad-leaved forest and meadow
- Coniferous forest
- Grassland
- Scrub and semi-desert
- Desert
- Tundra and alpine

Projection: *Modified Hammer Equal Area*   1 : 84 000 000

CARTOGRAPHY BY PHILIP'S. COPYRIGHT GEORGE PHILIP LTD

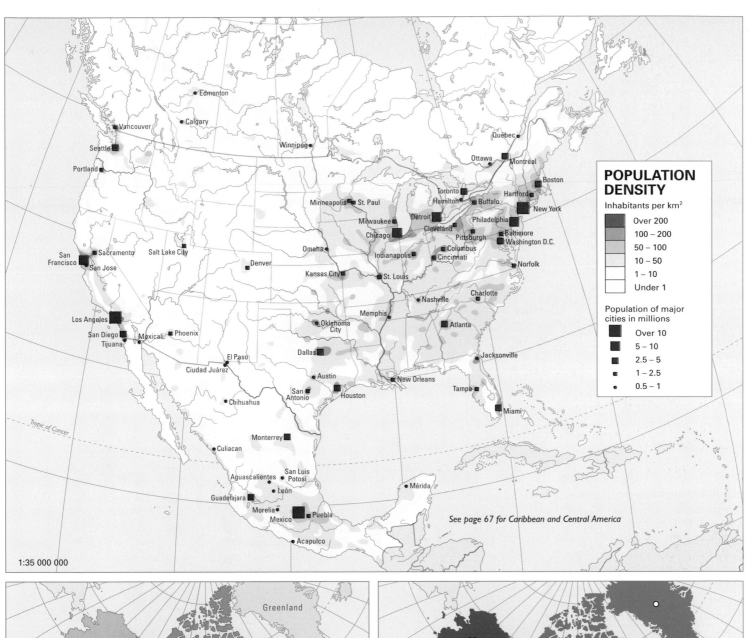

POPULATION DENSITY

Inhabitants per km²

- Over 200
- 100 – 200
- 50 – 100
- 10 – 50
- 1 – 10
- Under 1

Population of major cities in millions

- Over 10
- 5 – 10
- 2.5 – 5
- 1 – 2.5
- 0.5 – 1

See page 67 for Caribbean and Central America

1:35 000 000

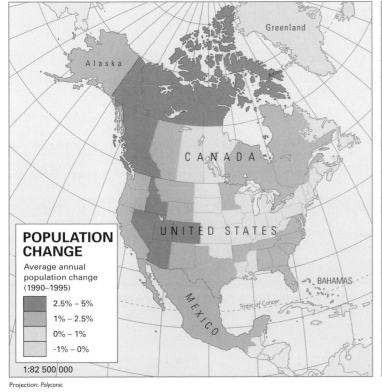

POPULATION CHANGE

Average annual population change (1990–1995)

- 2.5% – 5%
- 1% – 2.5%
- 0% – 1%
- -1% – 0%

1:82 500 000

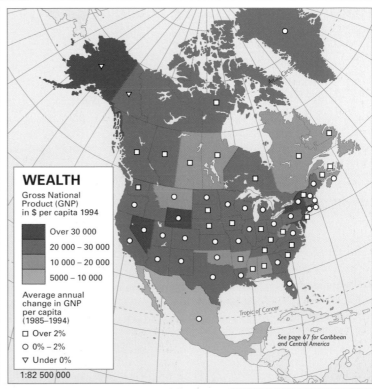

WEALTH

Gross National Product (GNP) in $ per capita 1994

- Over 30 000
- 20 000 – 30 000
- 10 000 – 20 000
- 5000 – 10 000

Average annual change in GNP per capita (1985–1994)

- □ Over 2%
- ○ 0% – 2%
- ▽ Under 0%

See page 67 for Caribbean and Central America

1:82 500 000

Projection: *Polyconic*

CARTOGRAPHY BY PHILIP'S. COPYRIGHT GEORGE PHILIP LTD

NORTH AMERICA: *economic*

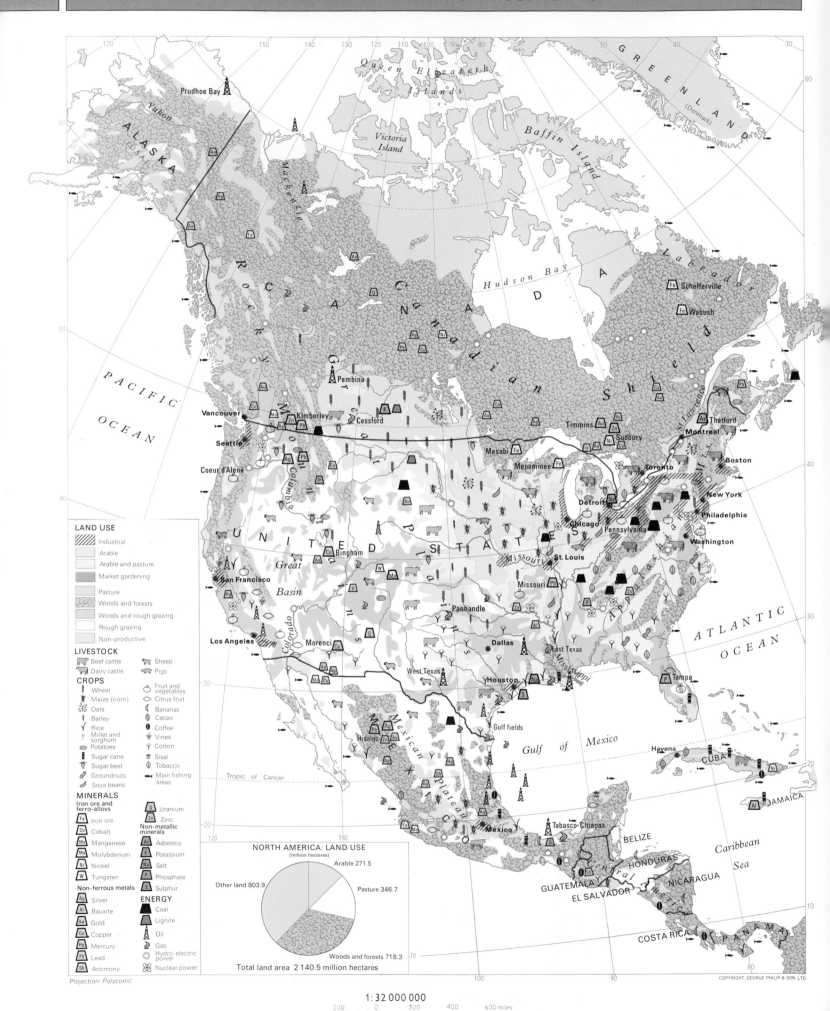

LAND USE
- Industrial
- Arable
- Arable and pasture
- Market gardening
- Pasture
- Woods and forests
- Woods and rough grazing
- Rough grazing
- Non-productive

LIVESTOCK
- Beef cattle
- Dairy cattle
- Sheep
- Pigs

CROPS
- Wheat
- Maize (corn)
- Oats
- Barley
- Rice
- Millet and sorghum
- Potatoes
- Sugar cane
- Sugar beet
- Groundnuts
- Soya beans
- Fruit and vegetables
- Citrus fruit
- Bananas
- Cacao
- Coffee
- Vines
- Cotton
- Sisal
- Tobacco
- Main fishing areas

MINERALS

Iron ore and ferro-alloys
- Fe Iron ore
- Co Cobalt
- Mn Manganese
- Mo Molybdenum
- Ni Nickel
- W Tungsten
- U Uranium
- Zn Zinc

Non-ferrous metals
- Ag Silver
- Al Bauxite
- Au Gold
- Cu Copper
- Hg Mercury
- Pb Lead
- Sb Antimony

Non-metallic minerals
- As Asbestos
- K Potassium
- Na Salt
- P Phosphate
- S Sulphur

ENERGY
- Coal
- Lignite
- Oil
- Gas
- Hydro-electric power
- Nuclear power

NORTH AMERICA: LAND USE
(million hectares)

Arable 271.5
Pasture 346.7
Woods and forests 718.3
Other land 803.9

Total land area 2 140.5 million hectares

Projection: *Polyconic*

COPYRIGHT. GEORGE PHILIP & SON, LTD.

1:32 000 000

200   0   200   400   600 miles
400   0   400   800 km

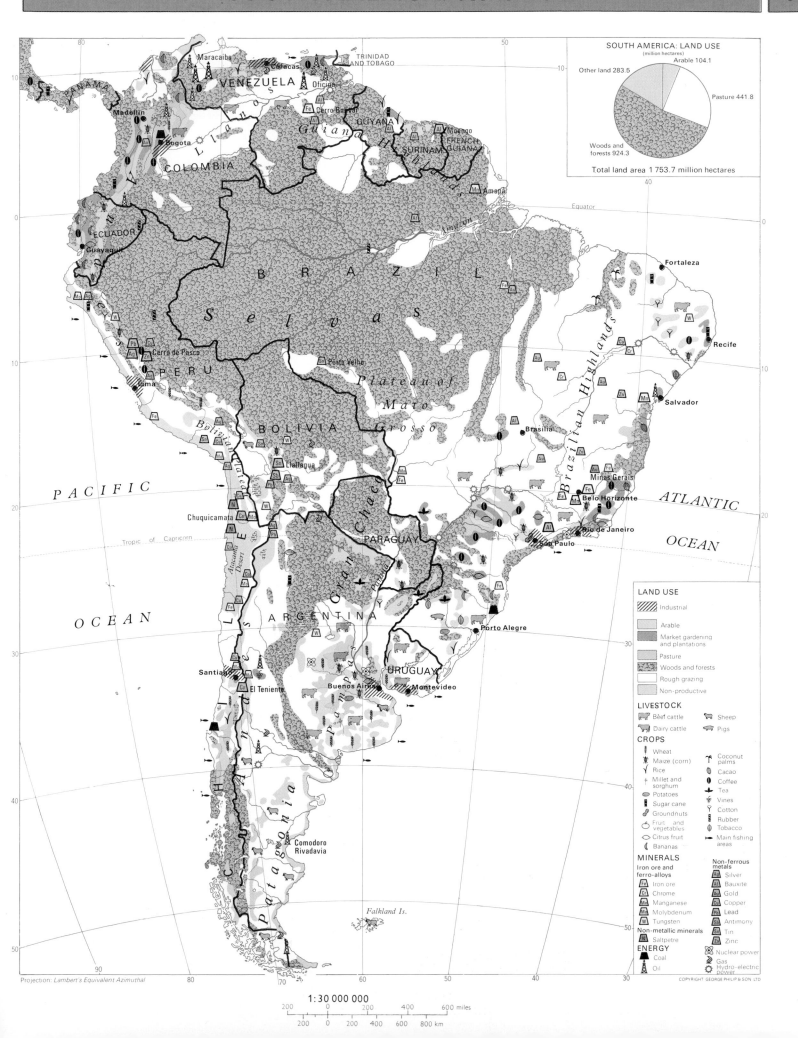

SOUTH AMERICA: LAND USE
(million hectares)

Other land 283.5   Arable 104.1

Pasture 441.8

Woods and
forests 924.3

Total land area 1 753.7 million hectares

LAND USE

Industrial

Arable

Market gardening
and plantations

Pasture

Woods and forests

Rough grazing

Non-productive

LIVESTOCK

Beef cattle   Sheep

Dairy cattle   Pigs

CROPS

Wheat   Coconut
                     palms
Maize (corn)
                     Cacao
Rice
                     Coffee
Millet and
sorghum   Tea

Potatoes   Vines

Sugar cane   Cotton

Groundnuts   Rubber

Fruit and   Tobacco
vegetables
                     Main fishing
Citrus fruit   areas

Bananas

MINERALS   Non-ferrous
Iron ore and   metals
ferro-alloys
                     Silver
Iron ore
                     Bauxite
Chrome
                     Gold
Manganese
                     Copper
Molybdenum
                     Lead
Tungsten
                     Antimony
Non-metallic minerals
                     Tin
Saltpetre
                     Zinc
ENERGY
                     Nuclear power
Coal
                     Gas
Oil   Hydro-electric
                     power

Projection: *Lambert's Equivalent Azimuthal*

COPYRIGHT GEORGE PHILIP & SON LTD

1:30 000 000

200   0   200   400   600 miles

200   0   200   400   600   800 km

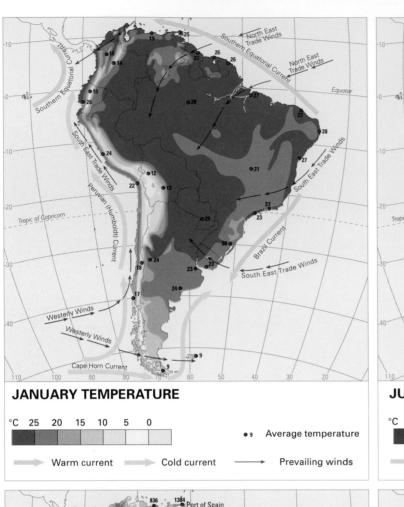

JANUARY TEMPERATURE

°C 25 20 15 10 5 0

• 9 Average temperature

➡ Warm current   ➡ Cold current   → Prevailing winds

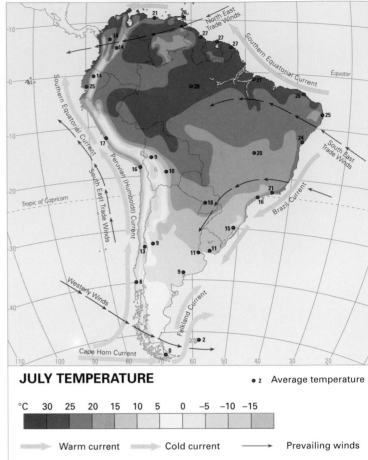

JULY TEMPERATURE

• 2 Average temperature

°C 30 25 20 15 10 5 0 −5 −10 −15

➡ Warm current   ➡ Cold current   → Prevailing winds

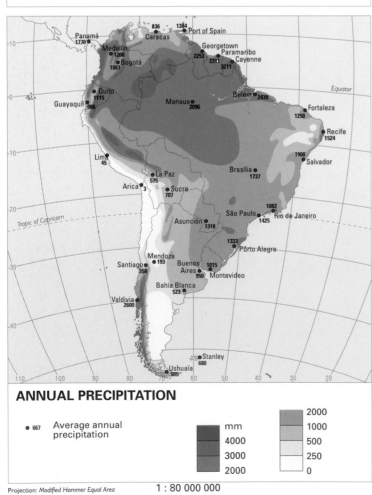

ANNUAL PRECIPITATION

• 667 Average annual precipitation

mm	
2000	
4000	1000
3000	500
2000	250
	0

Projection: *Modified Hammer Equal Area*

1 : 80 000 000

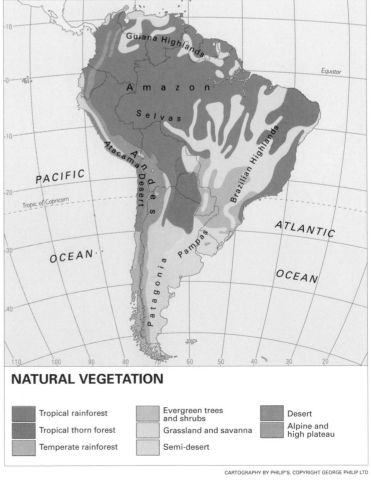

NATURAL VEGETATION

Tropical rainforest
Tropical thorn forest
Temperate rainforest

Evergreen trees and shrubs
Grassland and savanna
Semi-desert

Desert
Alpine and high plateau

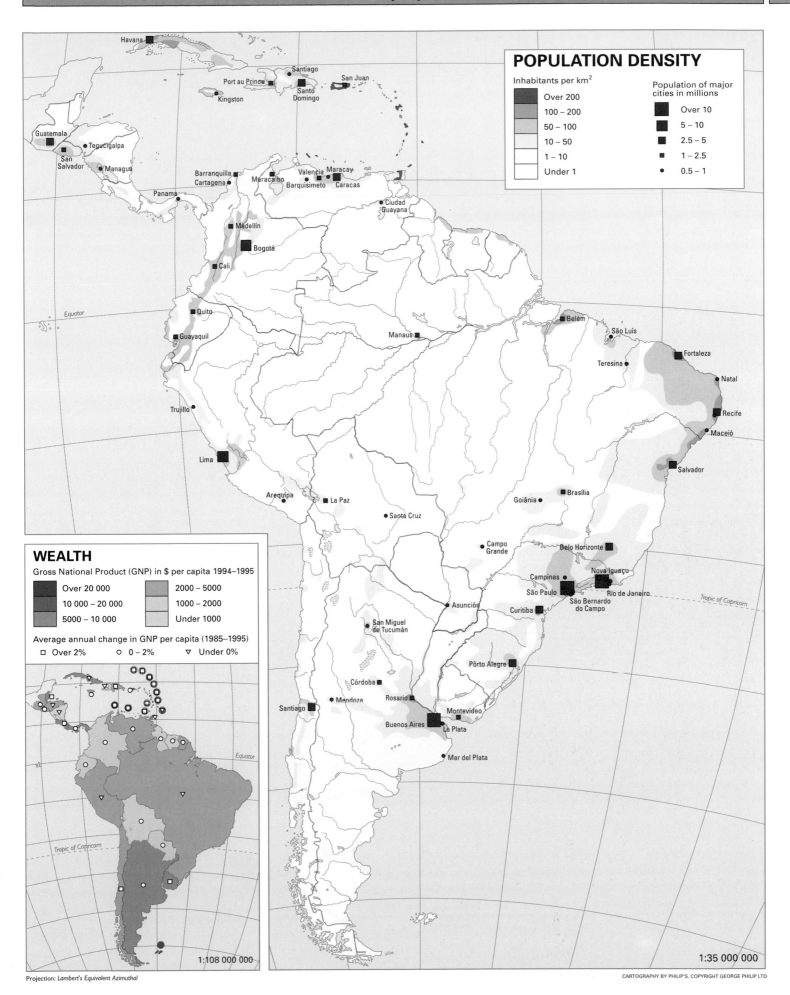

POPULATION DENSITY

Inhabitants per km²

Over 200
100 – 200
50 – 100
10 – 50
1 – 10
Under 1

Population of major cities in millions

Over 10
5 – 10
2.5 – 5
1 – 2.5
0.5 – 1

WEALTH

Gross National Product (GNP) in $ per capita 1994–1995

Over 20 000
10 000 – 20 000
5000 – 10 000
2000 – 5000
1000 – 2000
Under 1000

Average annual change in GNP per capita (1985–1995)

□ Over 2%   ○ 0 – 2%   ▽ Under 0%

1:108 000 000

1:35 000 000

Projection: *Lambert's Equivalent Azimuthal*

CARTOGRAPHY BY PHILIP'S. COPYRIGHT GEORGE PHILIP LTD

Map labels

Havana, Santiago, Port au Prince, San Juan, Kingston, Santo Domingo, Guatemala, Tegucigalpa, San Salvador, Managua, Panama, Barranquilla, Cartagena, Maracaibo, Valencia, Maracay, Caracas, Barquisimeto, Ciudad Guayana, Medellín, Bogotá, Cali, Quito, Guayaquil, Belém, São Luís, Manaus, Fortaleza, Teresina, Natal, Recife, Maceió, Trujillo, Lima, Salvador, Arequipa, La Paz, Santa Cruz, Brasília, Goiânia, Campo Grande, Belo Horizonte, Nova Iguaçu, Campinas, Rio de Janeiro, São Paulo, São Bernardo do Campo, Curitiba, Asunción, San Miguel de Tucumán, Pôrto Alegre, Córdoba, Mendoza, Rosario, Montevideo, Santiago, Buenos Aires, La Plata, Mar del Plata

Equator

Tropic of Capricorn

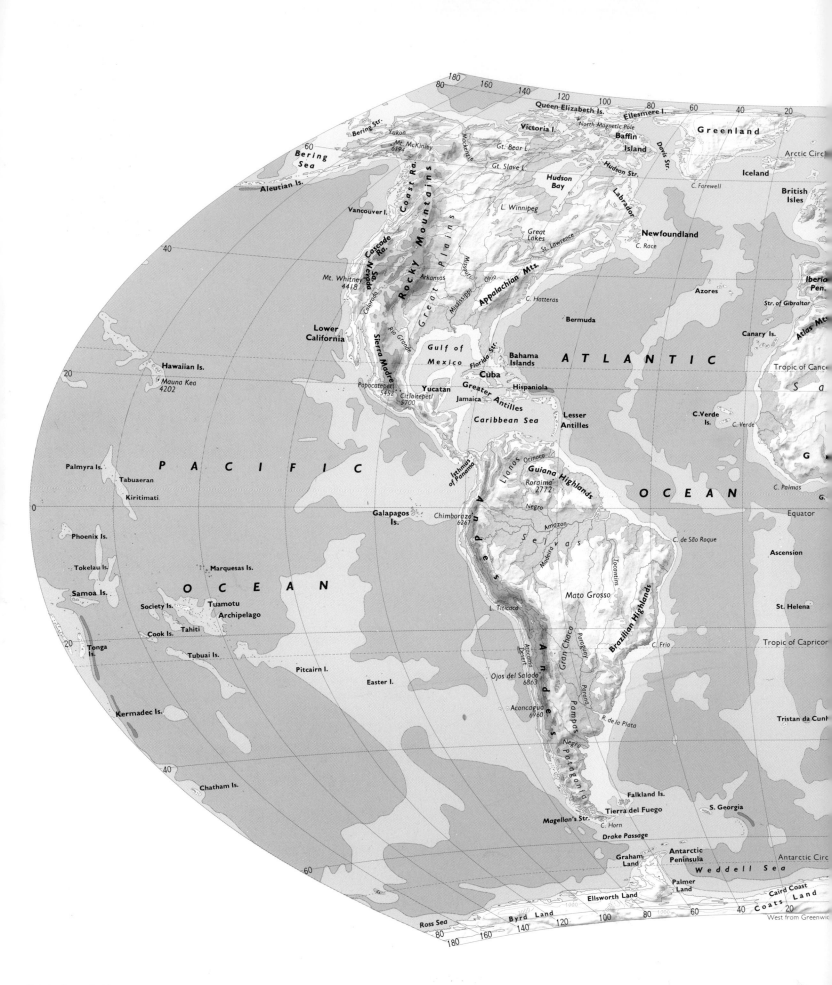

Projection: Hammer Equal Area

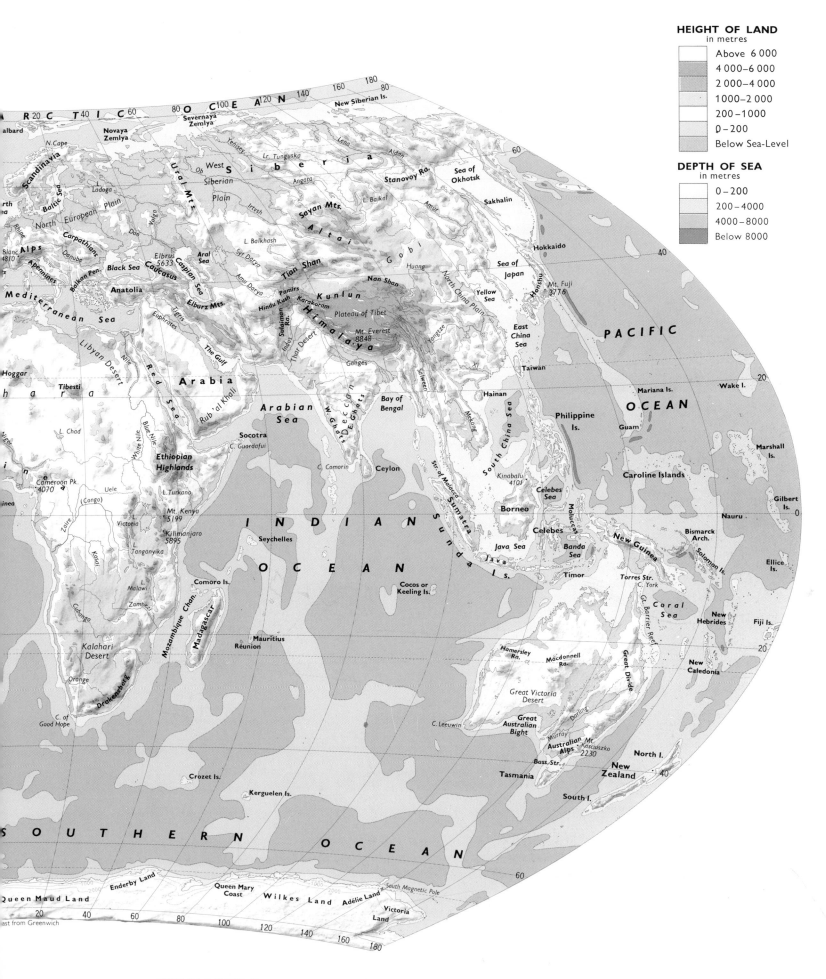

HEIGHT OF LAND
in metres

Above 6 000
4 000–6 000
2 000–4 000
1000–2 000
200–1000
0–200
Below Sea-Level

DEPTH OF SEA
in metres

0–200
200–4000
4000–8000
Below 8000

1 : 80 000 000

Copyright, George Philip & Son, Ltd.

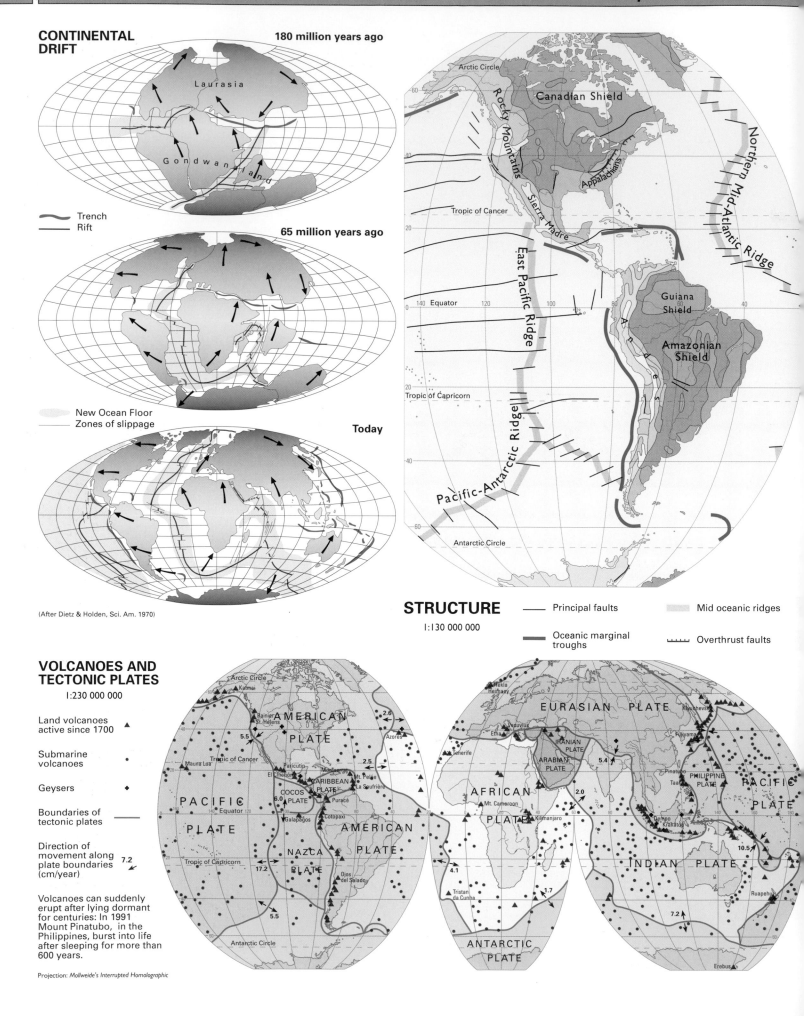

CONTINENTAL DRIFT

180 million years ago

Laurasia

Gondwanaland

~~~ Trench
— Rift

65 million years ago

New Ocean Floor
Zones of slippage

Today

(After Dietz & Holden, Sci. Am. 1970)

VOLCANOES AND TECTONIC PLATES

1:230 000 000

Land volcanoes active since 1700 ▲

Submarine volcanoes ·

Geysers +

Boundaries of tectonic plates —

Direction of movement along plate boundaries (cm/year) 7.2

Volcanoes can suddenly erupt after lying dormant for centuries: In 1991 Mount Pinatubo, in the Philippines, burst into life after sleeping for more than 600 years.

Projection: Mollweide's Interrupted Homolographic

STRUCTURE

1:130 000 000

— Principal faults

▬ Oceanic marginal troughs

▓ Mid oceanic ridges

⊥⊥⊥ Overthrust faults

Arctic Circle

Canadian Shield

Rocky Mountains

Appalachians

Sierra Madre

Tropic of Cancer

East Pacific Ridge

Equator

Guiana Shield

Andes

Amazonian Shield

Tropic of Capricorn

Pacific-Antarctic Ridge

Northern Mid-Atlantic Ridge

Antarctic Circle

Katmai
Rainier
St. Helens
Mauna Loa
Tropic of Cancer
Paricutin
El Chichon
Montserrat
COCOS PLATE
CARIBBEAN PLATE
Mt. Pelée
La Soufrière
Puracé
AMERICAN PLATE
PACIFIC PLATE
Galapagos
Cotopaxi
NAZCA PLATE
Ojos del Salado
Tropic of Capricorn
Antarctic Circle

Hekla
Heimaey
Etna
Vesuvius
Tenerife
EURASIAN PLATE
IRANIAN PLATE
ARABIAN PLATE
AFRICAN PLATE
Mt. Cameroon
Kilimanjaro
Tristan da Cunha
Klyuchevsk
Fujiyama
Pinatubo
Taal
PHILIPPINE PLATE
Dempo
Krakatoa
PACIFIC PLATE
INDIAN PLATE
Ruapehu
Erebus
ANTARCTIC PLATE

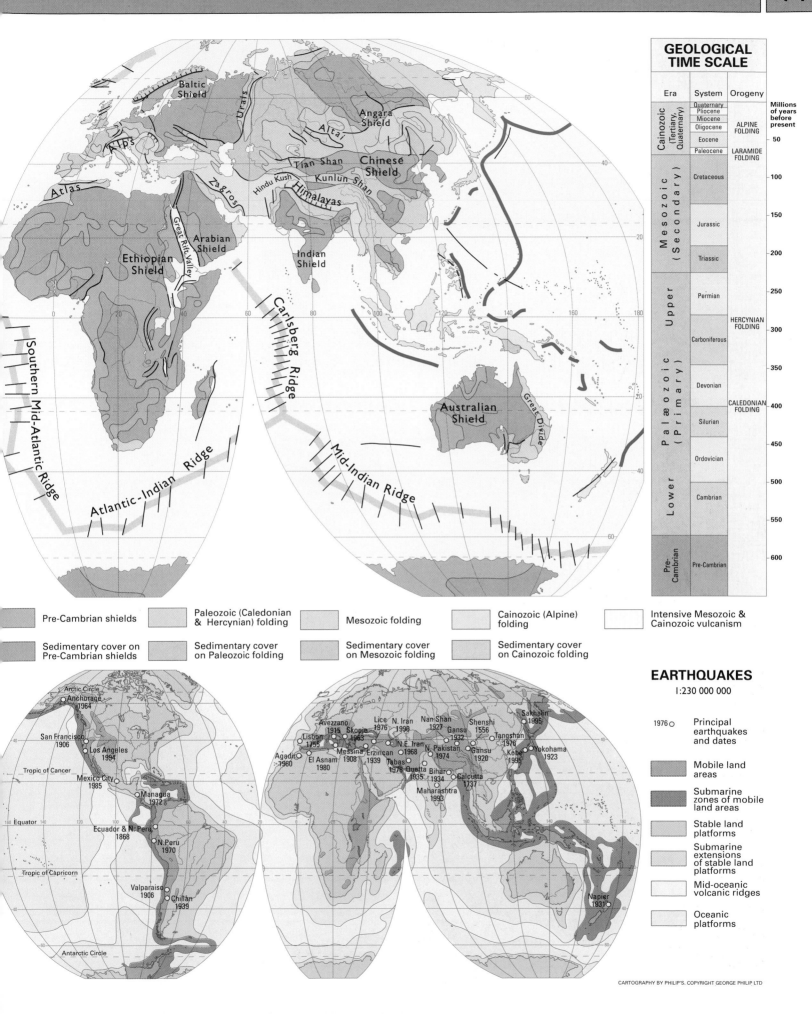

GEOLOGICAL TIME SCALE

Era	System	Orogeny	Millions of years before present
Cainozoic (Tertiary, Quaternary)	Quaternary		
	Pliocene	ALPINE FOLDING	
	Miocene		
	Oligocene		50
	Eocene		
	Paleocene	LARAMIDE FOLDING	
Mesozoic (Secondary)	Cretaceous		100
	Jurassic		150
	Triassic		200
Paleozoic (Primary) — Upper	Permian		250
	Carboniferous	HERCYNIAN FOLDING	300
	Devonian		350
Paleozoic (Primary) — Lower	Silurian	CALEDONIAN FOLDING	400
	Ordovician		450
	Cambrian		500
			550
Pre-Cambrian	Pre-Cambrian		600

Pre-Cambrian shields

Paleozoic (Caledonian & Hercynian) folding

Mesozoic folding

Cainozoic (Alpine) folding

Intensive Mesozoic & Cainozoic vulcanism

Sedimentary cover on Pre-Cambrian shields

Sedimentary cover on Paleozoic folding

Sedimentary cover on Mesozoic folding

Sedimentary cover on Cainozoic folding

EARTHQUAKES

1:230 000 000

1976 ○ Principal earthquakes and dates

Mobile land areas

Submarine zones of mobile land areas

Stable land platforms

Submarine extensions of stable land platforms

Mid-oceanic volcanic ridges

Oceanic platforms

CARTOGRAPHY BY PHILIP'S. COPYRIGHT GEORGE PHILIP LTD

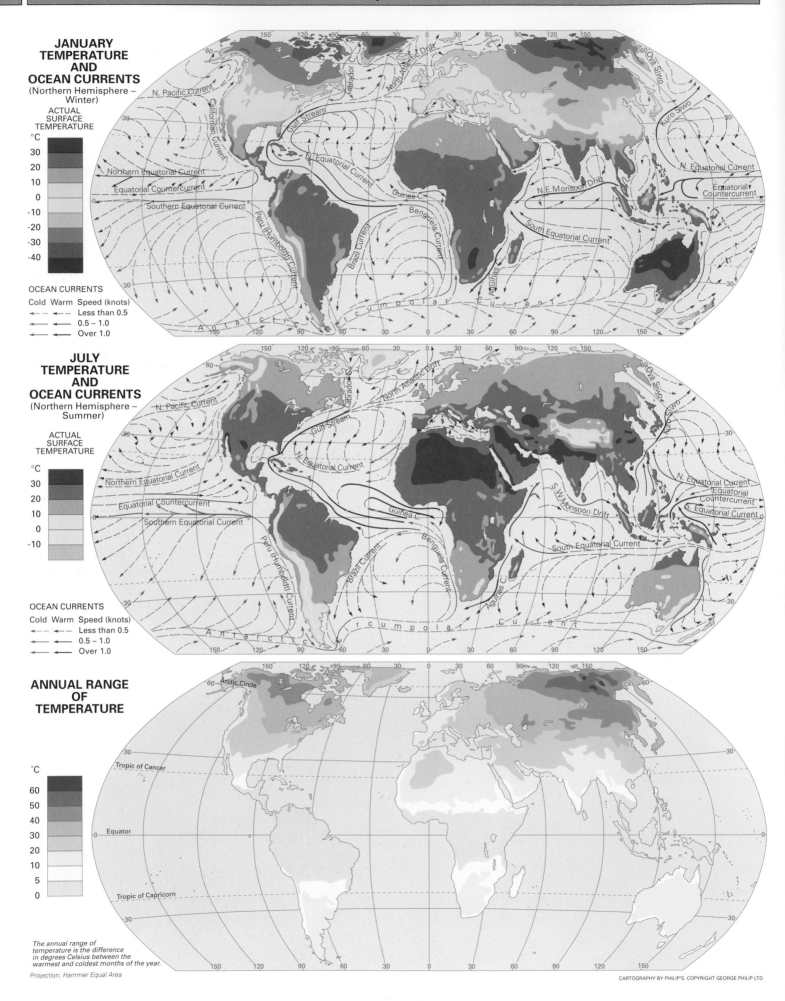

JANUARY TEMPERATURE AND OCEAN CURRENTS
(Northern Hemisphere – Winter)

ACTUAL SURFACE TEMPERATURE

°C
30
20
10
0
-10
-20
-30
-40

OCEAN CURRENTS

Cold Warm Speed (knots)
Less than 0.5
0.5 – 1.0
Over 1.0

JULY TEMPERATURE AND OCEAN CURRENTS
(Northern Hemisphere – Summer)

ACTUAL SURFACE TEMPERATURE

°C
30
20
10
0
-10

OCEAN CURRENTS

Cold Warm Speed (knots)
Less than 0.5
0.5 – 1.0
Over 1.0

ANNUAL RANGE OF TEMPERATURE

°C
60
50
40
30
20
10
5
0

The annual range of temperature is the difference in degrees Celsius between the warmest and coldest months of the year.

Projection: *Hammer Equal Area*

CARTOGRAPHY BY PHILIP'S. COPYRIGHT GEORGE PHILIP LTD

1 : 190 000 000

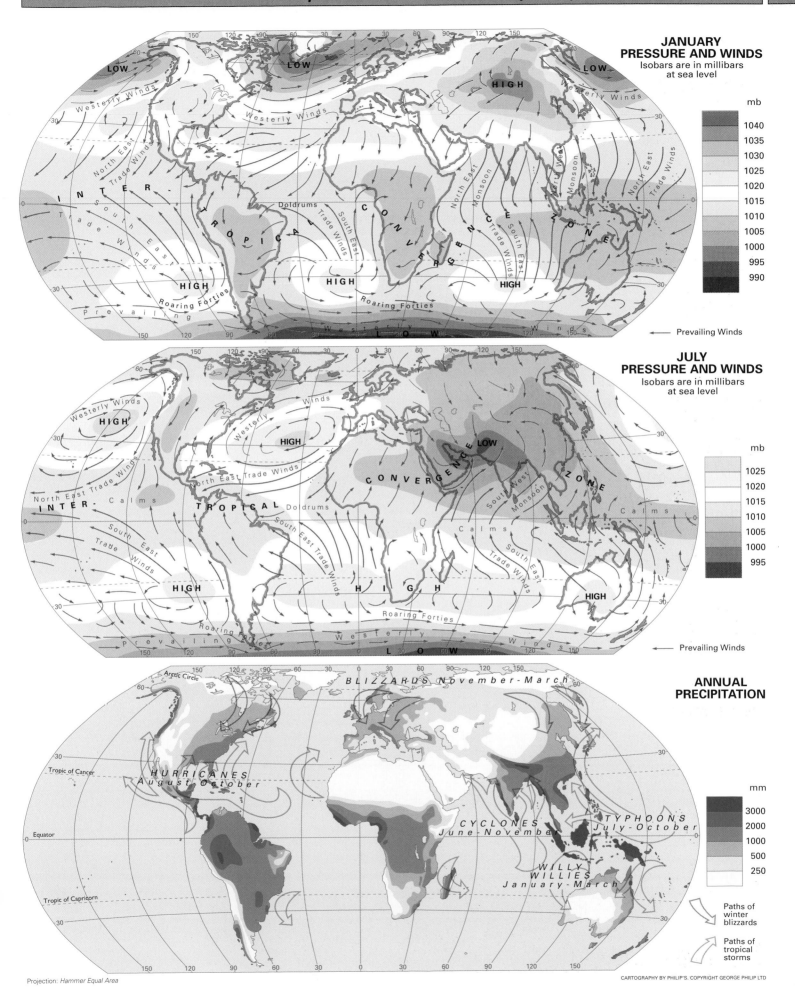

**JANUARY
PRESSURE AND WINDS**
Isobars are in millibars
at sea level

mb

1040
1035
1030
1025
1020
1015
1010
1005
1000
995
990

← Prevailing Winds

**JULY
PRESSURE AND WINDS**
Isobars are in millibars
at sea level

mb

1025
1020
1015
1010
1005
1000
995

← Prevailing Winds

**ANNUAL
PRECIPITATION**

mm

3000
2000
1000
500
250

⇨ Paths of
winter
blizzards

⇨ Paths of
tropical
storms

Projection: Hammer Equal Area

CARTOGRAPHY BY PHILIP'S. COPYRIGHT GEORGE PHILIP LTD

1 : 190 000 000

CLIMATIC REGIONS after Köppen

Köppen's classification recognises five major climatic regions corresponding broadly to the five principal vegetation types and these are designated by the letters A, B, C, D and E. Each one of these are subdivided on the basis of temperature and rainfall. This map shows a climate graph for a selected place within each of the 12 sub-regions.

TROPICAL RAINY CLIMATES A

Af	Rain Forest Climate	All mean monthly temperatures above 18°C and an annual variation in temperature of less than 6°C
Am	Monsoon Climate	
Aw	Savanna Climate	All monthly temperatures above 18°C but with an annual variation in temperature of less than 12°C

DRY CLIMATES B

BS	Steppe Climate	The principal difference between this grouping and groups A, C, D and E is the combination of a wide range of temperatures with low rainfall
BW	Desert Climate	

WARM TEMPERATE RAINY CLIMATES C

The climatic group is separated from group A by having the mean temperature of the coolest month below 18°C but above -3°C. The mean temperature of the warmest month is over 10°C.

Cw	Dry Winter Climate	The wettest month of summer has at least ten times as much rain as the driest winter month
Cs	Dry Summer Climate (Mediterranean)	The wettest month of winter has at least three times as much rain as the driest month of summer. The driest summer month itself has less than 30mm rainfall.
Cf	Climate with no Dry Season	Even rainfall throughout the year.

COLD TEMPERATE RAINY CLIMATES D

Dw	Dry Winter Climate	The mean temperature of the coldest month is below -3°C but the mean temperature of the warmest month is still over 10°C.
Df	Climate with no Dry Season	

POLAR CLIMATES E

ET	Tundra Climate	The mean temperature of the warmest month is below 10°C giving permanently frozen subsoil.
EF	Polar Climate	The mean temperature of the warmest month is below 0°C giving permanently ice and snow.

The classification is in some cases subdivided by the addition of the following letters after the major types :-

Used with groups C and D
- **a** Hot summer – mean temperature of the hottest month above 22°C and with more than four months of over 10°C.
- **b** Warm summer – mean temperature of the hottest month below 22°C but still with more than four months of over 10°C.
- **c** Cool short summer – mean temperature of the hottest month below 22°C but with less than four months of over 10°C.

Used with group D
- **d** Cool short summer and cold winter – mean temperature of the hottest month below 22°C and of the coolest month below -38°C.

Used with group B
- **h** Hot dry climate – mean annual temperature above 18°C.
- **k** Cool dry climate – mean annual temperature below 18°C.

Used with group E
- **H** Polar climate due to elevation being over 1500m.

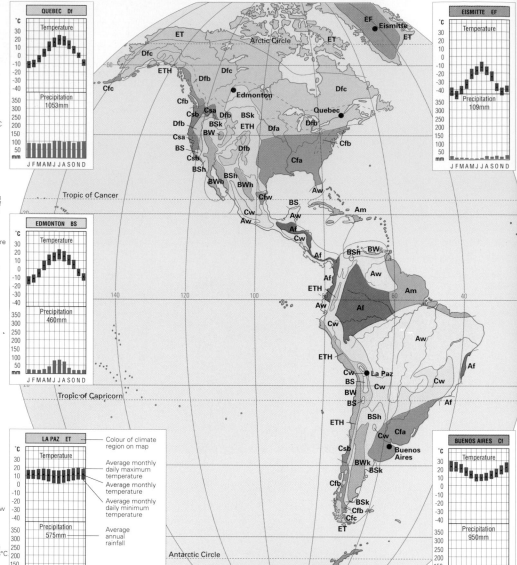

Colour of climate region on map
Average monthly daily maximum temperature
Average monthly temperature
Average monthly daily minimum temperature
Average annual rainfall
Average monthly rainfall
Months of the year

SOIL REGIONS

1:220 000 000

after Glinka, Stremme, Marbut, and others

	Tundra soil
	Podzols
	Brown forest soil
	Lightly leached dry forest soil
	Red and yellow sub-tropical forest soil
	Reddish savanna soil and tropical red earths
	Laterites
	Chernozem
	Degraded chernozem
	Black savanna soil
	Chestnut steppe soil
	Grey and brown desert steppe soils
	Alluvium
	Mountain and high plateau soils
	Oases soil
	Tropical and mangrove swamp

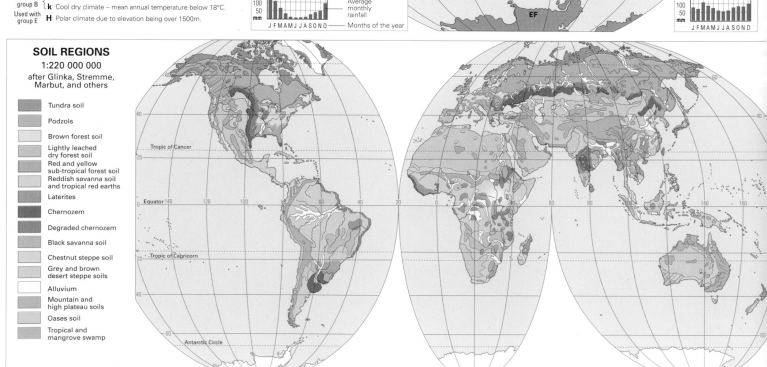

Projection: *Interrupted Mollweide's Homolographic*

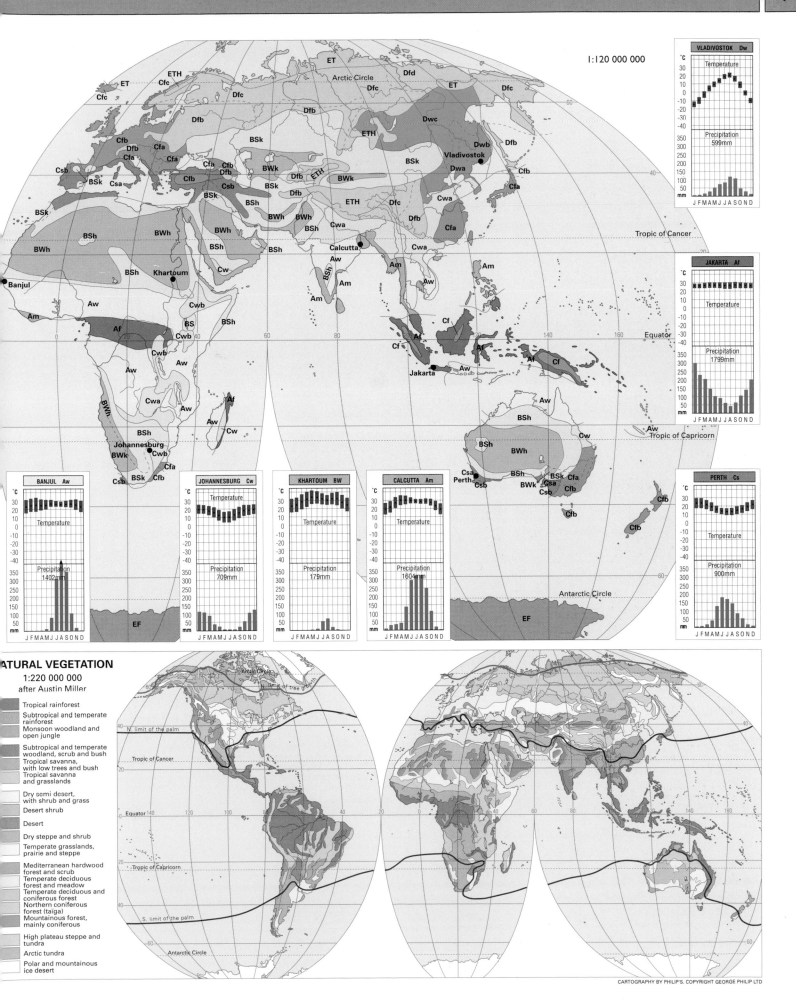

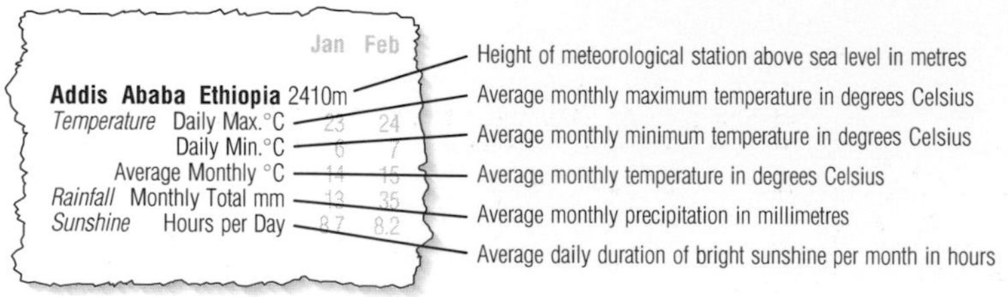
Jan Feb
Addis Ababa Ethiopia 2410m
Temperature Daily Max.°C 23 24
Daily Min.°C 6 7
Average Monthly °C 14 15
Rainfall Monthly Total mm 13 35
Sunshine Hours per Day 8.7 8.2
Height of meteorological station above sea level in metres
Average monthly maximum temperature in degrees Celsius
Average monthly minimum temperature in degrees Celsius
Average monthly temperature in degrees Celsius
Average monthly precipitation in millimetres
Average daily duration of bright sunshine per month in hours

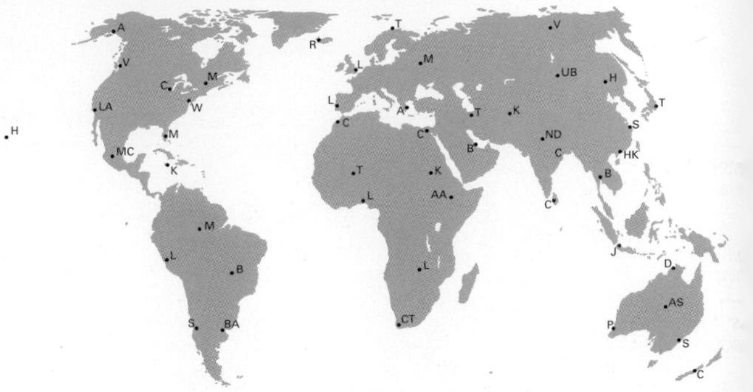

	Jan	Feb	Mar	Apr	May	June	July	Aug	Sep	Oct	Nov	Dec	Year
Addis Ababa Ethiopia 2410m													
Temperature Daily Max.°C	23	24	25	24	25	23	20	20	21	22	23	22	23
Daily Min.°C	6	7	9	10	9	10	11	11	10	7	5	5	8
Average Monthly °C	14	15	17	17	17	16	16	15	15	15	14	14	15
Rainfall Monthly Total mm	13	35	67	91	81	117	247	255	167	29	8	5	1115
Sunshine Hours per Day	8.7	8.2	7.6	8.1	6.5	4.8	2.8	3.2	5.2	7.6	6.7	7	6.4
Alice Springs Australia 580m													
Temperature Daily Max.°C	35	35	32	27	23	19	19	23	27	31	33	35	28
Daily Min.°C	21	20	17	12	8	5	4	6	10	15	18	20	13
Average Monthly °C	28	27	25	20	15	12	12	14	18	23	25	27	21
Rainfall Monthly Total mm	44	33	27	10	15	13	7	8	7	18	29	38	249
Sunshine Hours per Day	10.3	10.4	9.3	9.2	8	8	8.9	9.8	10	9.7	10.1	10	9.5
Anchorage USA 183m													
Temperature Daily Max.°C	-7	-3	0	7	13	18	19	17	13	6	-2	-6	-6
Daily Min.°C	-15	-12	-9	-2	4	8	10	9	5	-2	-9	-14	-2
Average Monthly °C	-11	-7	-4	3	9	13	15	13	9	2	-5	-10	-4
Rainfall Monthly Total mm	20	18	13	11	13	25	47	64	64	47	28	24	374
Sunshine Hours per Day	2.4	4.1	6.6	8.3	8.3	9.2	8.5	6	4.4	3.1	2.6	1.6	5.4
Athens Greece 107m													
Temperature Daily Max.°C	13	14	16	20	25	30	33	33	29	24	19	15	23
Daily Min.°C	6	7	8	11	16	20	23	23	19	15	12	8	14
Average Monthly °C	10	10	12	16	20	25	28	28	24	20	15	11	18
Rainfall Monthly Total mm	62	37	37	23	23	14	6	7	15	51	56	71	402
Sunshine Hours per Day	3.9	5.2	5.8	7.7	8.9	10.7	11.9	11.5	9.4	6.8	4.8	3.8	7.3
Bahrain City Bahrain 2m													
Temperature Daily Max.°C	20	21	25	29	33	36	37	38	36	32	27	22	30
Daily Min.°C	14	15	18	22	25	29	31	32	29	25	22	16	23
Average Monthly °C	17	18	21	25	29	32	34	35	32	29	25	19	26
Rainfall Monthly Total mm	18	12	10	9	2	0	0	0	0	0.4	3	16	70
Sunshine Hours per Day	5.9	6.9	7.9	8.8	10.6	13.2	12.1	12	12	10.3	7.7	6.4	9.5
Bangkok Thailand 10m													
Temperature Daily Max.°C	32	33	34	35	34	33	32	32	32	31	31	31	33
Daily Min.°C	20	23	24	26	25	25	25	24	24	24	23	20	24
Average Monthly °C	26	28	29	30	30	29	28	28	28	28	27	26	28
Rainfall Monthly Total mm	9	30	36	82	165	153	168	183	310	239	55	8	1438
Sunshine Hours per Day	8.2	8	8	10	7.5	6.1	4.7	5.2	5.2	6.1	7.3	7.8	7
Brasilia Brazil 910m													
Temperature Daily Max.°C	28	28	28	28	27	27	27	29	30	29	28	27	28
Daily Min.°C	18	18	18	17	15	13	13	14	16	18	18	18	16
Average Monthly °C	23	23	23	22	21	20	20	21	23	24	23	22	22
Rainfall Monthly Total mm	252	204	227	93	17	3	6	3	30	127	255	343	1560
Sunshine Av. Monthly Dur.	5.8	5.7	6	7.4	8.7	9.3	9.6	9.8	7.9	6.5	4.8	4.4	7.2
Buenos Aires Argentina 25m													
Temperature Daily Max.°C	30	29	26	22	18	14	14	16	18	21	25	28	22
Daily Min.°C	17	17	16	12	9	5	6	6	8	10	14	16	11
Average Monthly °C	23	23	21	17	13	10	10	11	13	15	19	22	16
Rainfall Monthly Total mm	79	71	109	89	76	61	56	61	79	86	84	99	950
Sunshine Hours per Day	9.2	8.5	7.5	6.8	4.9	3.5	3.8	5.2	6	6.8	8.1	8.5	6.6
Cairo Egypt 75m													
Temperature Daily Max.°C	19	21	24	28	32	35	35	35	33	30	26	21	28
Daily Min.°C	9	9	12	14	18	20	22	22	20	18	14	10	16
Average Monthly °C	14	15	18	21	25	28	29	28	26	24	20	16	22
Rainfall Monthly Total mm	4	4	3	1	2	1	0	0	1	1	3	7	27
Sunshine Hours per Day	6.9	8.4	8.7	9.7	10.5	11.9	11.7	11.3	10.4	9.4	8.3	6.4	9.5
Calcutta India 5m													
Temperature Daily Max.°C	27	29	34	36	35	34	32	32	32	32	29	26	31
Daily Min.°C	13	15	21	24	25	26	26	26	26	23	18	13	21
Average Monthly °C	20	22	27	30	30	30	29	29	29	28	23	20	26
Rainfall Monthly Total mm	10	30	34	44	140	297	325	332	253	114	20	5	1604
Sunshine Hours per Day	8.6	8.7	8.9	9	8.7	5.4	4.1	4.1	5.1	6.5	8.3	8.4	7.1
Cape Town South Africa 44m													
Temperature Daily Max.°C	26	26	25	23	20	18	17	18	19	21	24	25	22
Daily Min.°C	15	15	14	11	9	7	7	7	8	10	13	15	11
Average Monthly °C	21	20	20	17	14	13	12	12	14	16	18	20	16
Rainfall Monthly Total mm	12	19	17	42	67	98	68	76	36	45	12	13	505
Sunshine Hours per Day	11.4	10.2	9.4	7.7	6.1	5.7	6.4	6.6	7.6	8.6	10.2	10.9	8.4

	Jan	Feb	Mar	Apr	May	June	July	Aug	Sep	Oct	Nov	Dec	Year
Casablanca Morocco 59m													
Temperature Daily Max.°C	17	18	20	21	22	24	26	26	26	24	21	18	[illegible]
Daily Min.°C	8	9	11	12	15	18	19	20	18	15	12	10	[illegible]
Average Monthly °C	13	13	15	16	18	21	23	23	22	20	17	14	[illegible]
Rainfall Monthly Total mm	78	61	54	37	20	3	0	1	6	28	58	94	[illegible]
Sunshine Hours per Day	5.2	6.3	7.3	9	9.4	9.7	10.2	9.7	9.1	7.4	5.9	5.3	[illegible]
Chicago USA 186m													
Temperature Daily Max.°C	0.6	1.5	6.4	14.1	20.6	26.4	28.9	28	23.8	17.4	8.4	2.1	[illegible]
Daily Min.°C	-7	-6	-2	5	11	16	20	19	14	8	0	-5	[illegible]
Average Monthly °C	-3	-2	2	9	16	21	24	23	19	13	4	-2	[illegible]
Rainfall Monthly Total mm	47	41	70	77	96	103	86	80	69	71	56	48	[illegible]
Sunshine Hours per Day	4	5	6.6	6.9	8.9	10.2	10	9.2	8.2	6.9	4.5	3.7	[illegible]
Christchurch New Zealand 5m													
Temperature Daily Max.°C	21	21	19	17	13	11	10	11	14	17	19	21	[illegible]
Daily Min.°C	12	12	10	7	4	2	1	3	5	7	8	11	[illegible]
Average Monthly °C	16	16	15	12	9	6	6	7	9	12	13	16	[illegible]
Rainfall Monthly Total mm	56	46	43	46	76	69	61	58	51	51	51	61	[illegible]
Sunshine Hours per Day	7	6.5	5.6	4.7	4.3	3.9	4.1	4.7	5.6	6.1	6.9	6.3	[illegible]
Colombo Sri Lanka 10m													
Temperature Daily Max.°C	30	31	31	31	30	30	29	29	30	29	29	30	[illegible]
Daily Min.°C	22	22	23	24	25	25	25	25	25	24	23	22	[illegible]
Average Monthly °C	26	26	27	28	28	27	27	27	27	27	26	26	[illegible]
Rainfall Monthly Total mm	101	66	118	230	394	220	140	102	174	348	333	142	[illegible]
Sunshine Hours per Day	7.9	9	8.1	7.2	6.4	5.4	6.1	6.3	6.2	6.5	6.4	7.8	[illegible]
Darwin Australia 30m													
Temperature Daily Max.°C	32	32	33	33	33	31	31	32	33	34	34	33	[illegible]
Daily Min.°C	25	25	25	24	23	21	19	21	23	25	26	26	[illegible]
Average Monthly °C	29	29	29	29	28	26	25	26	28	29	30	29	[illegible]
Rainfall Monthly Total mm	405	309	279	77	8	2	0	1	15	48	108	214	[illegible]
Sunshine Hours per Day	5.8	5.8	6.6	9.8	9.3	10	9.9	10.4	10.1	9.4	9.6	6.8	[illegible]
Harbin China 175m													
Temperature Daily Max.°C	-14	-9	0	12	21	26	29	27	20	12	-1	-11	[illegible]
Daily Min.°C	-26	-23	-12	-1	7	14	18	16	8	0	-12	-22	[illegible]
Average Monthly °C	-20	-16	-6	6	14	20	23	22	14	6	-7	-17	[illegible]
Rainfall Monthly Total mm	4	6	17	23	44	92	167	119	52	36	12	5	[illegible]
Sunshine Hours per Day	6.4	7.8	8	7.8	8.3	8.6	8.6	8.2	7.2	6.9	6.1	5.7	[illegible]
Hong Kong China 35m													
Temperature Daily Max.°C	18	18	20	24	28	30	31	31	30	27	24	20	[illegible]
Daily Min.°C	13	13	16	19	23	26	26	26	25	23	19	15	[illegible]
Average Monthly °C	16	15	18	22	25	28	28	28	27	25	21	17	[illegible]
Rainfall Monthly Total mm	30	60	70	133	332	479	286	415	364	33	46	17	[illegible]
Sunshine Hours per Day	4.7	3.5	3.1	3.8	5	5.4	6.8	6.5	6.6	7	6.2	5.5	[illegible]
Honolulu Hawaii 5m													
Temperature Daily Max.°C	26	26	26	27	28	29	29	29	30	29	28	26	[illegible]
Daily Min.°C	19	19	19	20	21	22	23	23	23	22	21	20	[illegible]
Average Monthly °C	23	22	23	23	24	26	26	26	26	26	24	23	[illegible]
Rainfall Monthly Total mm	96	84	73	33	25	8	11	23	25	47	55	76	[illegible]
Sunshine Hours per Day	7.3	7.7	8.3	8.6	8.8	9.1	9.4	9.3	9.2	8.3	7.5	6.2	[illegible]
Jakarta Indonesia 10m													
Temperature Daily Max.°C	29	29	30	31	31	31	31	31	31	31	30	29	[illegible]
Daily Min.°C	23	23	23	24	24	23	23	23	23	23	23	23	[illegible]
Average Monthly °C	26	26	27	27	27	27	27	27	27	27	27	26	[illegible]
Rainfall Monthly Total mm	300	300	211	147	114	97	64	43	66	112	142	203	[illegible]
Sunshine Av. Monthly Dur.	6.1	6.5	7.7	8.5	8.4	8.5	9.1	9.5	9.6	9	7.7	7.1	[illegible]
Kabul Afghanistan 1791 m													
Temperature Daily Max.°C	2	4	12	19	26	31	33	33	30	22	17	8	[illegible]
Daily Min.°C	-8	-6	1	6	11	13	16	15	11	6	1	-3	[illegible]
Average Monthly °C	-3	-1	6	13	18	22	25	24	20	14	9	3	[illegible]
Rainfall Monthly Total mm	28	61	72	117	33	1	7	1	0	1	37	14	[illegible]
Sunshine Av. Monthly Dur.	5.9	6	5.7	6.8	10.1	11.5	11.4	11.2	9.8	9.4	7.8	6.1	[illegible]
Khartoum Sudan 380m													
Temperature Daily Max.°C	32	33	37	40	42	41	38	36	38	39	35	32	[illegible]
Daily Min.°C	16	17	20	23	26	27	26	25	25	25	21	17	[illegible]
Average Monthly °C	24	25	28	32	34	34	32	30	32	32	28	25	[illegible]
Rainfall Monthly Total mm	0	0	0	1	7	5	56	80	28	2	0	0	[illegible]
Sunshine Av. Monthly Dur.	10.6	11.2	10.4	10.8	10.4	10.1	8.6	8.6	9.6	10.3	10.8	10.6	[illegible]

	Jan	Feb	Mar	Apr	May	June	July	Aug	Sep	Oct	Nov	Dec	Year
ston Jamaica 35m													
erature Daily Max.°C	30	30	30	31	31	32	32	32	32	31	31	31	31
Daily Min.°C	20	20	20	21	22	24	23	23	23	23	22	21	22
Average Monthly °C	25	25	25	26	26	28	28	28	27	27	26	26	26
all Monthly Total mm	23	15	23	31	102	89	38	91	99	180	74	36	801
hine Av. Monthly Dur.	8.3	8.8	8.7	8.7	8.3	7.8	8.5	8.5	7.6	7.3	8.3	7.7	8.2
s Nigeria 40m													
erature Daily Max.°C	32	33	33	32	31	29	28	28	29	30	31	32	31
Daily Min.°C	22	23	23	23	23	22	22	21	22	22	23	22	22
Average Monthly °C	27	28	28	28	27	26	25	24	25	26	27	27	26
all Monthly Total mm	28	41	99	99	203	300	180	56	180	190	63	25	1464
hine Av. Monthly Dur.	5.9	6.8	6.3	6.1	5.6	3.8	2.8	3.3	3	5.1	6.6	6.5	5.2
Peru 120m													
erature Daily Max.°C	28	29	29	27	24	20	20	19	20	22	24	26	24
Daily Min.°C	19	20	19	17	16	15	14	14	14	15	16	17	16
Average Monthly °C	24	24	24	22	20	17	17	16	17	18	20	21	20
all Monthly Total mm	1	1	1	1	5	5	8	8	8	3	3	1	45
hine Av. Monthly Dur.	6.3	6.8	6.9	6.7	4	1.4	1.1	1	1.1	2.5	4.1	5	3.9
on Portugal 77m													
erature Daily Max.°C	14	15	17	20	21	25	27	28	26	22	17	15	21
Daily Min.°C	8	8	10	12	13	15	17	17	17	14	11	9	13
Average Monthly °C	11	12	14	16	17	20	22	23	21	18	14	12	17
all Monthly Total mm	111	76	109	54	44	16	3	4	33	62	93	103	708
hine Av. Monthly Dur.	4.7	5.9	6	8.3	9.1	10.6	11.4	10.7	8.4	6.7	5.2	4.6	7.7
on (Kew) United Kingdom 5m													
erature Daily Max.°C	6	7	10	13	17	20	22	21	19	14	10	7	14
Daily Min.°C	2	2	3	6	8	12	14	13	11	8	5	4	7
Average Monthly °C	4	5	7	9	12	16	18	17	15	11	8	5	11
all Monthly Total mm	54	40	37	37	46	45	57	59	49	57	64	48	593
hine Av. Monthly Dur.	1.7	2.3	3.5	5.7	6.7	7	6.6	6	5	3.3	1.9	1.4	4.3
Angeles USA 30m													
erature Daily Max.°C	18	18	18	19	20	22	24	24	24	23	22	19	21
Daily Min.°C	7	8	9	11	13	15	17	17	16	14	11	9	12
Average Monthly °C	12	13	14	15	17	18	21	21	20	18	16	14	17
all Monthly Total mm	69	74	46	28	3	3	0	0	5	10	28	61	327
hine Av. Monthly Dur.	6.9	8.2	8.9	8.8	9.5	10.3	11.7	11	10.1	8.6	8.2	7.6	9.2
ka Zambia 1154m													
erature Daily Max.°C	26	26	26	27	25	23	23	26	29	31	29	27	27
Daily Min.°C	17	17	16	15	12	10	9	11	15	18	18	17	15
Average Monthly °C	22	22	21	21	18	17	16	19	22	25	23	22	21
all Monthly Total mm	224	173	90	19	3	1	0	1	1	17	85	196	810
hine Av. Monthly Dur.	5.1	5.4	6.9	8.9	9	9	9.1	9.6	9.5	9	7	5.5	7.8
aus Brazil 45m													
erature Daily Max.°C	31	31	31	31	31	31	32	33	34	34	33	32	32
Daily Min.°C	24	24	24	24	24	24	24	24	24	25	25	24	24
Average Monthly °C	28	28	28	27	28	28	28	29	29	29	29	28	28
all Monthly Total mm	278	278	300	287	193	99	61	41	62	112	165	220	2096
hine Av. Monthly Dur.	3.9	4	3.6	3.9	5.4	6.9	7.9	8.2	7.5	6.6	5.9	4.9	5.7
ico City Mexico 2309m													
erature Daily Max.°C	21	23	26	27	26	25	23	24	23	22	21	21	24
Daily Min.°C	5	6	7	9	10	11	11	11	11	9	6	5	8
Average Monthly °C	13	15	16	18	18	18	17	17	17	16	14	13	16
all Monthly Total mm	8	4	9	23	57	111	160	149	119	46	16	7	709
hine Av. Monthly Dur.	7.3	8.1	8.5	8.1	7.8	7	6.2	6.4	5.6	6.3	7	7.3	7.1
mi USA 2m													
erature Daily Max.°C	24	25	27	28	30	31	32	32	31	29	27	25	28
Daily Min.°C	14	15	16	19	21	23	24	24	24	22	18	15	20
Average Monthly °C	19	20	21	23	25	27	28	28	27	25	22	20	24
all Monthly Total mm	51	48	58	99	163	188	170	178	241	208	71	43	1518
hine Av. Monthly Dur.	7.7	8.3	8.7	9.4	8.9	8.5	8.7	8.4	7.1	6.5	7.5	7.1	8.1
treal Canada 57m													
erature Daily Max.°C	-6	-4	2	11	18	23	26	25	20	14	5	-3	11
Daily Min.°C	-13	-11	-5	2	9	14	17	16	11	6	0	-9	3
Average Monthly °C	-9	-8	-2	6	13	19	22	20	16	10	3	-6	7
all Monthly Total mm	87	76	86	83	81	91	98	87	96	84	89	89	1047
hine Av. Monthly Dur.	2.8	3.4	4.5	5.2	6.7	7.7	8.2	7.7	5.6	4.3	2.4	2.2	5.1
cow Russia 156m													
erature Daily Max.°C	-6	-4	1	9	18	22	24	22	17	10	1	-5	9
Daily Min.°C	-14	-16	-11	-1	5	9	12	9	4	-2	-6	-12	-2
Average Monthly °C	-10	-10	-5	4	12	15	18	16	10	4	-2	-8	4
all Monthly Total mm	31	28	33	35	52	67	74	74	58	51	36	36	575
hine Av. Monthly Dur.	1	1.9	3.7	5.2	7.8	8.3	8.4	7.1	4.4	2.4	1	0.6	4.4
Delhi India 220m													
erature Daily Max.°C	21	24	29	36	41	39	35	34	34	34	28	23	32
Daily Min.°C	6	10	14	20	26	28	27	26	24	17	11	7	18
Average Monthly °C	14	17	22	28	33	34	31	30	29	26	20	15	25
all Monthly Total mm	25	21	13	8	13	77	178	184	123	10	2	11	665
hine Av. Monthly Dur.	7.7	8.2	8.2	8.7	9.2	7.9	6	6.3	6.9	9.4	8.7	8.3	8

	Jan	Feb	Mar	Apr	May	June	July	Aug	Sep	Oct	Nov	Dec	Year
Perth Australia 60m													
Temperature Daily Max.°C	29	30	27	25	21	18	17	18	19	21	25	27	23
Daily Min.°C	17	18	16	14	12	10	9	9	10	11	14	16	13
Average Monthly °C	23	24	22	19	16	14	13	13	15	16	19	22	18
Rainfall Monthly Total mm	8	13	22	44	128	189	177	145	84	58	19	13	900
Sunshine Av. Monthly Dur.	10.4	9.8	8.8	7.5	5.7	4.8	5.4	6	7.2	8.1	9.6	10.4	7.8
Reykjavik Iceland 18m													
Temperature Daily Max.°C	2	3	5	6	10	13	15	14	12	8	5	4	8
Daily Min.°C	-3	-3	-1	1	4	7	9	8	6	3	0	-2	3
Average Monthly °C	0	0	2	4	7	10	12	11	9	5	3	1	5
Rainfall Monthly Total mm	89	64	62	56	42	42	50	56	67	94	78	79	779
Sunshine Av. Monthly Dur.	0.8	2	3.6	4.5	5.9	6.1	5.8	5.4	3.5	2.3	1.1	0.3	3.7
Santiago Chile 520m													
Temperature Daily Max.°C	30	29	27	24	19	15	15	17	19	22	26	29	23
Daily Min.°C	12	11	10	7	5	3	3	4	6	7	9	11	7
Average Monthly °C	21	20	18	15	12	9	9	10	12	15	17	20	15
Rainfall Monthly Total mm	3	3	5	13	64	84	76	56	31	15	8	5	363
Sunshine Av. Monthly Dur.	10.8	8.9	8.5	5.5	3.6	3.3	3.3	3.6	4.8	6.1	8.7	10.1	6.4
Shanghai China 5m													
Temperature Daily Max.°C	8	8	13	19	24	28	32	32	27	23	17	10	20
Daily Min.°C	-1	0	4	9	14	19	23	23	19	13	7	2	11
Average Monthly °C	3	4	8	14	19	23	27	27	23	18	12	6	15
Rainfall Monthly Total mm	48	59	84	94	94	180	147	142	130	71	51	36	1136
Sunshine Av. Monthly Dur.	4	3.7	4.4	4.8	5.4	4.7	6.9	7.5	5.3	5.6	4.7	4.5	5.1
Sydney Australia 40m													
Temperature Daily Max.°C	26	26	25	22	19	17	17	18	20	22	24	25	22
Daily Min.°C	18	19	17	14	11	9	8	9	11	13	16	17	14
Average Monthly °C	22	22	21	18	15	13	12	13	16	18	20	21	18
Rainfall Monthly Total mm	89	101	127	135	127	117	117	76	74	71	74	74	1182
Sunshine Av. Monthly Dur.	7.5	7	6.4	6.1	5.7	5.3	6.1	7	7.3	7.5	7.5	7.5	6.8
Tehran Iran 1191m													
Temperature Daily Max.°C	9	11	16	21	29	30	37	36	29	24	16	11	22
Daily Min.°C	-1	1	4	10	16	20	23	23	18	12	6	1	11
Average Monthly °C	4	6	10	15	22	25	30	29	23	18	11	6	17
Rainfall Monthly Total mm	37	23	36	31	14	2	1	1	1	5	29	27	207
Sunshine Av. Monthly Dur.	5.9	6.7	7.5	7.4	8.6	11.6	11.2	11	10.1	7.6	6.9	6.3	8.4
Timbuktu Mali 269m													
Temperature Daily Max.°C	31	35	38	41	43	42	38	35	38	40	37	31	37
Daily Min.°C	13	16	18	22	26	27	25	24	24	23	18	14	21
Average Monthly °C	22	25	28	31	34	34	32	30	31	31	28	23	29
Rainfall Monthly Total mm	0	0	0	1	4	20	54	93	31	3	0	0	206
Sunshine Av. Monthly Dur.	9.1	9.6	9.6	9.7	9.8	9.4	9.6	9	9.3	9.5	9.5	8.9	9.4
Tokyo Japan 5m													
Temperature Daily Max.°C	9	9	12	18	22	25	29	30	27	20	16	11	19
Daily Min.°C	-1	-1	3	4	13	17	22	23	19	13	7	1	10
Average Monthly °C	4	4	8	11	18	21	25	26	23	17	11	6	14
Rainfall Monthly Total mm	48	73	101	135	131	182	146	147	217	220	101	61	1562
Sunshine Av. Monthly Dur.	6	5.9	5.7	6	6.2	5	5.8	6.6	4.5	4.4	4.8	5.4	5.5
Tromsø Norway 100m													
Temperature Daily Max.°C	-2	-2	0	3	7	12	16	14	10	5	2	0	5
Daily Min.°C	-6	-6	-5	-2	1	6	9	8	5	1	-2	-4	0
Average Monthly °C	-4	-4	-3	0	4	9	13	11	7	3	0	-2	3
Rainfall Monthly Total mm	96	79	91	65	61	59	56	80	109	115	88	95	994
Sunshine Av. Monthly Dur.	0.1	1.6	2.9	6.1	5.7	6.9	7.9	4.8	3.5	1.7	0.3	0	3.52
Ulan Bator Mongolia 1305m													
Temperature Daily Max.°C	-19	-13	-4	7	13	21	22	21	14	6	-6	-16	4
Daily Min.°C	-32	-29	-22	-8	-2	7	11	8	2	-8	-20	-28	-11
Average Monthly °C	-26	-21	-13	-1	6	14	16	14	8	-1	-13	-22	-4
Rainfall Monthly Total mm	1	1	2	5	10	28	76	51	23	5	5	2	209
Sunshine Av. Monthly Dur.	6.4	7.8	8	7.8	8.3	8.6	8.6	8.2	7.2	6.9	6.1	5.7	7.5
Vancouver Canada 5m													
Temperature Daily Max.°C	6	7	10	14	17	20	23	22	19	14	9	7	14
Daily Min.°C	0	1	3	5	8	11	13	12	10	7	3	2	6
Average Monthly °C	3	4	6	9	13	16	18	17	14	10	6	4	10
Rainfall Monthly Total mm	214	161	151	90	69	65	39	44	83	172	198	243	1529
Sunshine Av. Monthly Dur.	1.6	3	3.8	5.9	7.5	7.4	9.5	8.2	6	3.7	2	1.4	5
Verkhoyansk Russia 137m													
Temperature Daily Max.°C	-47	-40	-20	-1	11	21	24	21	12	-8	-33	-42	-8
Daily Min.°C	-51	-48	-40	-25	-7	4	6	1	-6	-20	-39	-50	-23
Average Monthly °C	-49	-44	-30	-13	2	12	15	11	3	-14	-36	-46	-16
Rainfall Monthly Total mm	7	5	5	4	5	25	33	30	13	11	10	7	155
Sunshine Av. Monthly Dur.	0	2.6	6.9	9.6	9.7	10	9.7	7.5	4.1	2.4	0.6	0	5.4
Washington USA 22m													
Temperature Daily Max.°C	7	8	12	19	25	29	31	30	26	20	14	8	19
Daily Min.°C	-1	-1	2	8	13	18	21	20	16	10	4	-1	9
Average Monthly °C	3	3	7	13	19	24	26	25	21	15	9	4	14
Rainfall Monthly Total mm	84	68	96	85	103	88	108	120	100	78	75	75	1080
Sunshine Av. Monthly Dur.	4.4	5.7	6.7	7.4	8.2	8.8	8.6	8.2	7.5	6.5	5.3	4.5	6.8

AGRICULTURAL PRODUCTION

Staple Crops

Wheat

China 18.9% | India 12.2% | U.S.A. 11.0% | France 5.7% | Russia 5.6% | Canada 4.6%

World total (1996): 584,874,000 tonnes

Rice

China 34.0% | India 21.7% | Indonesia 9.0% | Bangladesh 4.9% | Vietnam 4.5% | Thailand 3.8% | Burma 3.6%

World total (1996): 562,259,000 tonnes

Millet

India 33.2% | Nigeria 18.3% | China 16.1% | Niger 6.4%

World total (1996): 29,563,000 tonnes

Rye

Poland 27.7% | Germany 20.0% | Russia 18.1% | Belarus 9.5% | Ukraine 5.3%

World total (1996): 23,156,000 tonnes

Maize

U.S.A. 36.4% | China 21.8% | Brazil 7.0%

World total (1996): 576,821,000 tonnes

Potatoes

China 16.0% | Russia 14.0% | Poland 8.7% | U.S.A. 7.1% | India 6.3% | Ukraine 5.2% | Germany 3.6%

World total (1996): 294,834,000 tonnes

Soya

U.S.A. 47.1% | Brazil 20.4% | China 10.7% | Argentina 9.6%

World total (1996): 130,302,000 tonnes

Cassava

Nigeria 19.2% | Brazil 15.6% | Thailand 11.1% | Congo (Zaire) 10.7% | Indonesia 9.4% | Ghana 4.2% | India 3.7% | Tanzania 3.6%

World total (1996): 162,942,000 tonnes

Animal Products

Milk

U.S.A. 15.2% | Russia 8.4% | India 6.9% | Germany 6.0% | France 5.5% | Brazil 3.9% | Ukraine 3.7%

World total (1996): 466,317,000 tonnes

Butter

India 19.0% | U.S.A. 8.9% | Germany 7.2% | France 6.7% | Russia 6.2% | Pakistan 5.5% | New Zealand 4.6%

World total (1996): 6,565,000 tonnes

Lamb and Mutton

China 15.1% | Australia 8.5% | N. Zealand 7.9% | U.K. 5.2% | Turkey 3.8% | Iran 3.6% | Russia 3.6% | Pakistan 3.6%

World total (1996): 7,289,000 tonnes

Beef and Veal

U.S.A. 21.7% | Brazil 8.6% | China 6.5% | Russia 5.3% | Argentina 4.6% | France 3.6%

World total (1996): 53,956,000 tonnes

Pork

China 45.1% | U.S.A. 9.7% | Germany 4.3%

World total (1996): 85,761,000 tonnes

Sugars

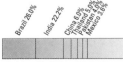

Sugarcane

Brazil 26.0% | India 22.2% | China 6.0% | Thailand 5.0% | Pakistan 5.0% | Mexico 3.8%

World total (1996): 1,192,555,000 tonnes

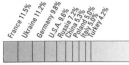

Sugar beet

France 11.5% | Ukraine 11.2% | Germany 9.8% | U.S.A. 9.6% | Russia 7.2% | China 5.3% | Poland 5.0% | Italy 5.0% | Turkey 4.2%

World total (1996): 255,500,000 tonnes

Projection: *Modified Hammer Equal Area*

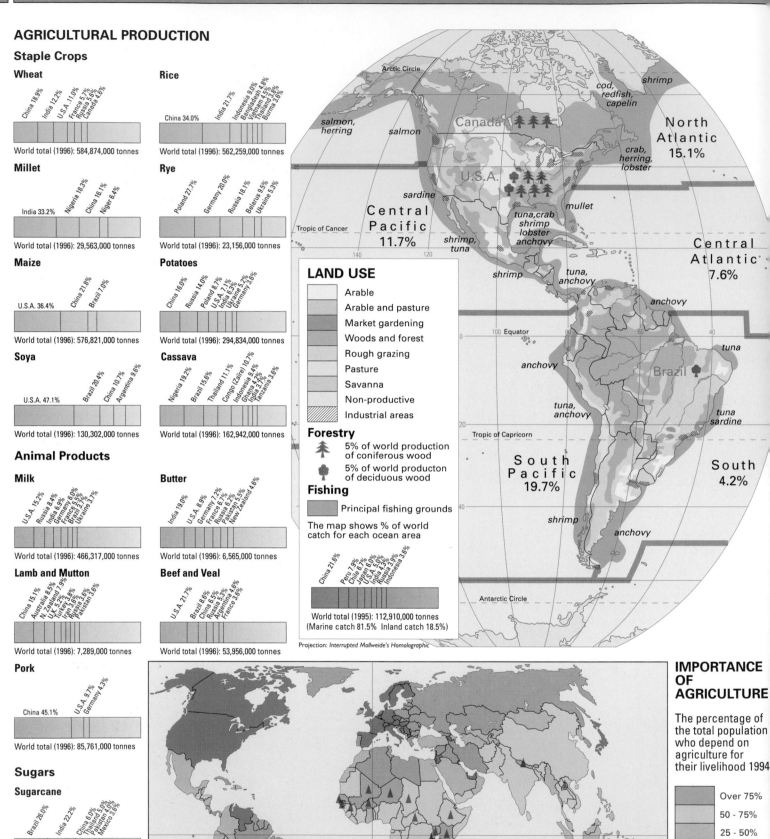

LAND USE

- Arable
- Arable and pasture
- Market gardening
- Woods and forest
- Rough grazing
- Pasture
- Savanna
- Non-productive
- Industrial areas

Forestry

- 5% of world production of coniferous wood
- 5% of world producton of deciduous wood

Fishing

- Principal fishing grounds

The map shows % of world catch for each ocean area

China 21.6% | Peru 7.9% | Chile 6.7% | Japan 6.0% | U.S.A. 5.0% | India 3.9% | Russia 3.9% | Indonesia 3.6%

World total (1995): 112,910,000 tonnes
(Marine catch 81.5% Inland catch 18.5%)

Projection: *Interrupted Mollweide's Homolographic*

IMPORTANCE OF AGRICULTURE

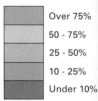

The percentage of the total population who depend on agriculture for their livelihood 1994

- Over 75%
- 50 - 75%
- 25 - 50%
- 10 - 25%
- Under 10%

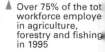

▲ Over 75% of the tot workforce employe in agriculture, forestry and fishing in 1995

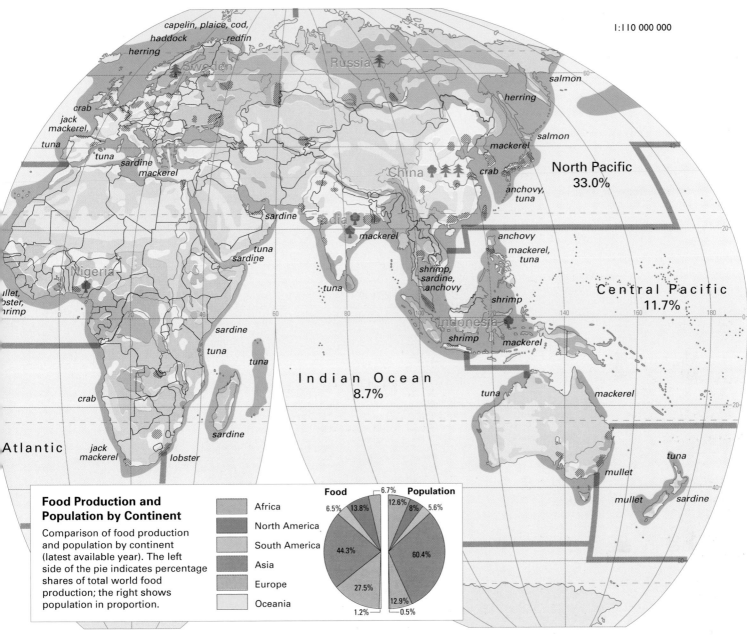

1:110 000 000

capelin, plaice, cod, haddock redfin
herring

Sweden

Russia

salmon

crab
jack
mackerel,
tuna

herring

tuna
sardine
mackerel

China

salmon

mackerel

crab

**North Pacific
33.0%**

anchovy,
tuna

sardine

India

mackerel

anchovy

mackerel,
tuna

ullet,
bster,
rimp

tuna
sardine

Nigeria

shrimp,
sardine,
anchovy

shrimp

**Central Pacific
11.7%**

tuna

sardine

Indonesia

shrimp

mackerel

tuna

sardine

tuna

crab

**Indian Ocean
8.7%**

tuna

mackerel

Atlantic

jack
mackerel

lobster

sardine

tuna

mullet

mullet

sardine

Food Production and Population by Continent

Comparison of food production and population by continent (latest available year). The left side of the pie indicates percentage shares of total world food production; the right shows population in proportion.

	Africa
	North America
	South America
	Asia
	Europe
	Oceania

Food 6.7% **Population**
6.5% 13.8% | 12.6% 8% 5.6%
44.3% | 60.4%
27.5% | 12.9%
1.2% 0.5%

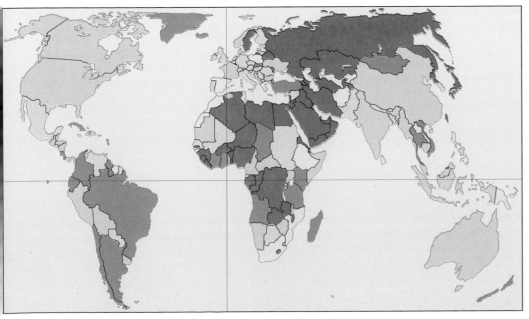

TRADE IN AGRICULTURAL PRODUCTS

Balance of trade in agricultural products (food and live animals) by value (latest available year)

- 50% more exports than imports
- 10% more exports than imports
- 10% either side
- 10% more imports than exports
- 50% more imports than exports

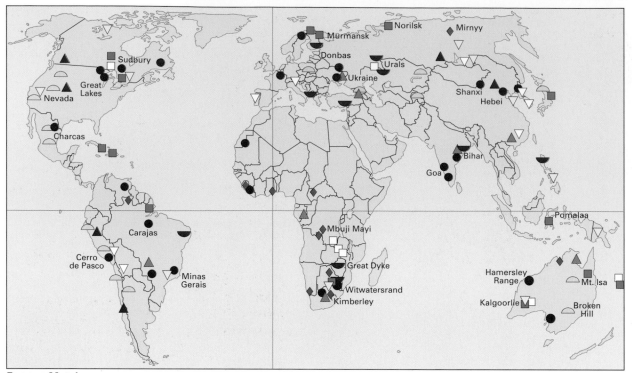

Precious Metals

▽ **Gold**
World total (1994)
2 290 tonnes

South Africa	25.3%
U.S.A.	14.2%
Australia	11.2%
Russia	6.4%
Canada	6.4%

◠ **Silver**
World total (1994)
13 900 tonnes

Mexico	16.8%
Peru	12.2%
U.S.A.	10.6%
Australia	7.6%
Chile	7.1%

◆ **Diamonds**
World total (1994)
106 000 000 carats

Australia	34.0%
Russia	18.9%
Congo (Zaïre)	16.8%
Botswana	15.6%
South Africa	8.0%

Ferrous Metals

● **Iron Ore**		■ **Nickel**		◗ **Chrome**		▲ **Manganese**		☐ **Cobalt**		▲ **Molybdenum**		▽ **Tungsten**	
World total (1994) 995 000 000 tonnes		World total (1994) 810 000 tonnes		World total (1994) 9 600 000 tonnes		World total (1994) 22 180 000 tonnes		World total (1994) 18 500 tonnes		World total (1994) 104 000 tonnes		World total (1994) 25 500 tonnes	
China	24.1%	Russia	22.2%	South Africa	37.4%	Ukraine	32.1%	Canada	23.4%	U.S.A.	45.0%	China	64.7%
Brazil	16.7%	Japan	13.7%	Kazakstan	21.0%	China	18.8%	Zambia	18.9%	China	16.8%	Russia	15.7%
Australia	12.9%	Canada	13.0%	India	9.5%	South Africa	14.4%	Russia	17.8%	Chile	15.4%	Portugal	3.9%
Russia	7.4%	Norway	8.4%	Turkey	8.2%	Gabon	10.9%	Australia	11.4%	Canada	9.2%	North Korea	3.5%
U.S.A.	5.9%	Australia	5.7%	Finland	6.0%	Brazil	7.7%	Congo (Zaïre)	10.8%	Russia	4.3%	Peru	3.1%

Fertilizers

■ **Nitrates**
World total (1993)
79 932 000 tonnes

China	20.0%
U.S.A.	17.2%
India	9.3%
Russia	7.1%
Canada	3.7%

△ **Phosphates**
World total (1994)
37 900 000 tonnes

U.S.A.	31.9%
China	18.5%
Morocco	15.6%
Russia	7.4%
Tunisia	4.3%

▼ **Potash**
World total (1994)
22 500 000 tonnes

Canada	35.7%
Germany	14.6%
Belarus	11.4%
Russia	11.0%
U.S.A.	6.2%

Non-Ferrous Metals

■ **Copper**		▲ **Lead**		● **Bauxite**		▽ **Tin**		◆ **Zinc**		◡ **Mercury**	
World total (1994) 9 750 000 tonnes		World total (1994) 5 380 000 tonnes		World total (1994) 107 000 000 tonnes		World total (1994) 199 000 tonnes		World total (1994) 7 360 000 tonnes		World total (1994) 1 760 tonnes	
U.S.A.	17.5%	U.S.A.	23.4%	Australia	39.0%	China	26.6%	China	13.2%	China	28.4%
Chile	13.1%	France	8.3%	Guinea	13.5%	Malaysia	21.1%	Japan	9.7%	Algeria	27.0%
Japan	11.5%	China	7.6%	Brazil	7.6%	Indonesia	15.6%	Canada	9.4%	Spain	17.0%
Russia	6.0%	U.K.	6.4%	India	5.0%	Brazil	15.2%	Germany	4.9%	Kyrgyzstan	11.4%
Canada	5.7%	Germany	6.2%	China	3.5%	Bolivia	7.7%	U.S.A.	4.8%	Finland	5.7%

Projection: *Modified Hammer Equal Area*

CARTOGRAPHY BY PHILIP'S. COPYRIGHT GEORGE PHILIP

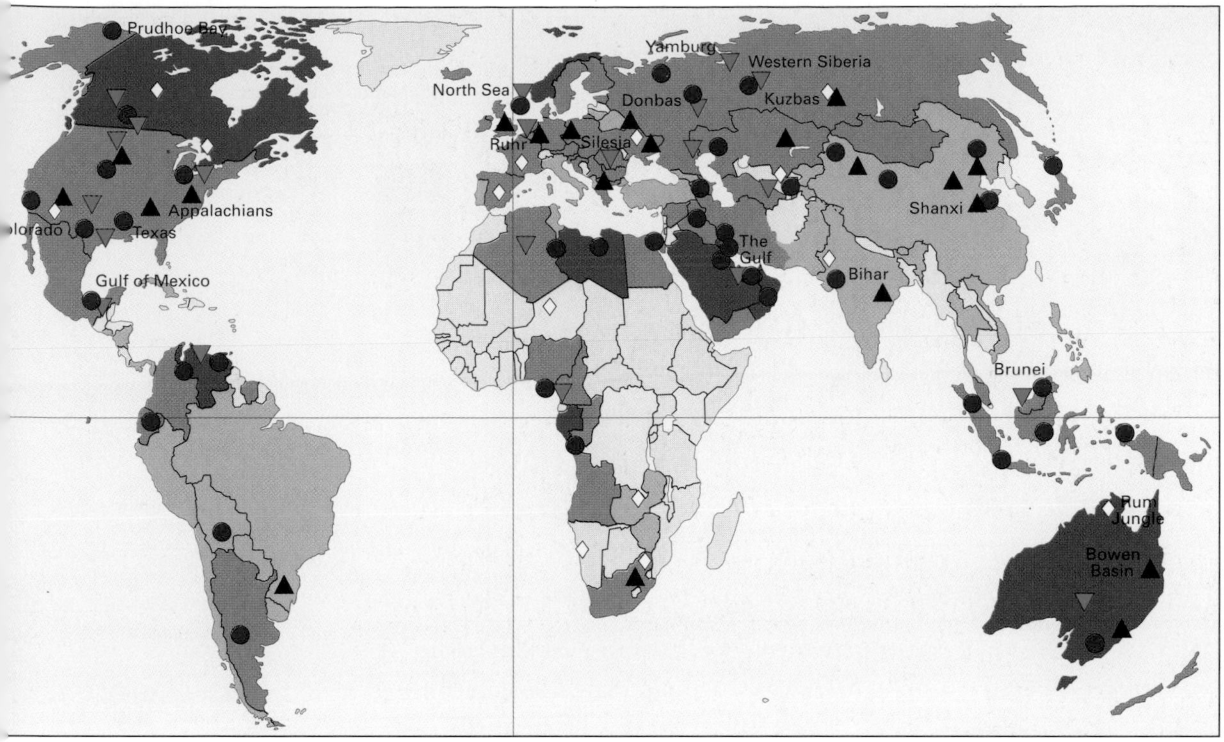

ENERGY PRODUCTION

Primary energy production
expressed in kilograms
of coal equivalent per
person 1994

Over 10 000 kg per person

1 000 – 10 000 kg per person

100 – 1 000 kg per person

10 – 100 kg per person

Under 10 kg per person

● Oil

▽ Natural gas

▲ Coal and lignite

◇ Uranium *(the fuel used to generate nuclear power)*

In developing countries traditional fuels are still very important. Sometimes called biomass fuels, they include wood, charcoal and dried dung. The pie graph for Nigeria at the foot of the page shows their importance.

Map labels: Prudhoe Bay, Colorado, Texas, Appalachians, Gulf of Mexico, North Sea, Ruhr, Silesia, Donbas, Yamburg, Western Siberia, Kuzbas, Shanxi, The Gulf, Bihar, Brunei, Rum Jungle, Bowen Basin

Oil	Natural Gas	Coal (bituminous)	Coal (lignite)	Uranium	Nuclear Power	Hydro-Electric Power
World total (1994) 183 500 000 tonnes	World total (1993) 2 658 000 000 tonnes of coal equivalent	World total (1993) 3 160 000 000 tonnes	World total (1993) 1 265 000 000 tonnes	World total (1993) 32 532 tonnes (metal content)	World total (1994) 820 000 000 tonnes of coal equivalent	World total (1994) 922 000 000 tonnes of coal equivalent
di Arabia 13.2%	Canada 28.2%	China 36.0%	U.S.A. 23.7%	Canada 28.2%	U.S.A. 31.0%	Canada 12.8%
.A. 12.6%	Nigeria 9.0%	U.S.A. 17.6%	Germany 17.5%	Niger 9.0%	France 16.3%	U.S.A. 12.2%
sia 9.9%	Kazakstan 8.3%	India 7.9%	Russia 9.1%	Kazakstan 8.3%	Japan 11.8%	Former U.S.S.R. 10.4%
5.7%	Uzbekistan 8.0%	Russia 6.3%	China 7.4%	Uzbekistan 8.0%	Former U.S.S.R. 7.9%	Brazil 10.3%
xico 4.9%	Russia 7.4%	Australia South Africa } 5.8%	Poland 5.4%	Russia 7.4%	Germany	China 6.9%

ENERGY CONSUMPTION

Primary energy consumption
expressed in kilograms
of coal equivalent per
person 1994

Over 10 000 kg per person

5 000 – 10 000 kg per person

1 000 – 5 000 kg per person

100 – 1 000 kg per person

Under 100 kg per person

Energy consumption by Continent 1991

		Change 1990-91
Europe*	38.3%	*(-0.2%)*
North America	30.0%	*(+2.4%)*
Asia	25.0%	*(+1.9%)*
South America	3.0%	*(-2.9%)*
Africa	2.4%	*(-0.4%)*
Australasia	1.3%	*(no change)*
includes former U.S.S.R.		

Projection: Modified Hammer Equal Area

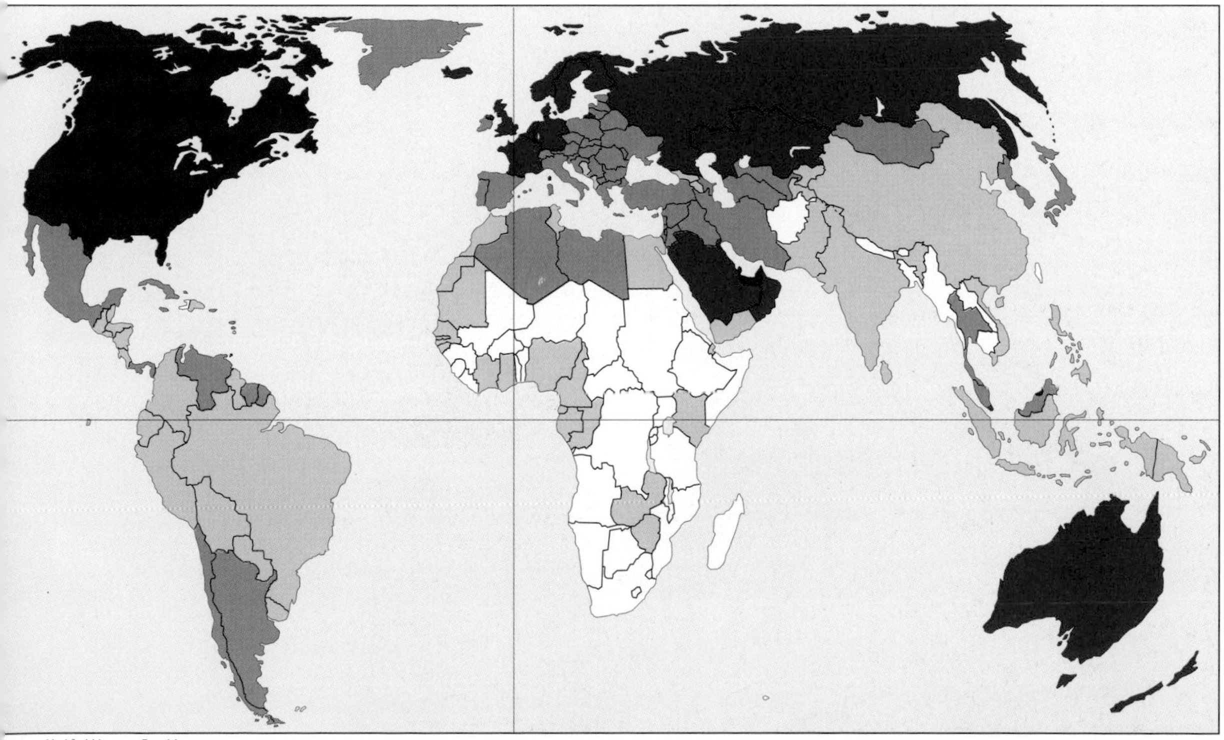

TYPE OF ENERGY CONSUMED BY SELECTED COUNTRIES 1993

Coal & Lignite

Oil

Natural gas

Hydro-electricity

Nuclear electricity

Traditional Fuels

NIGERIA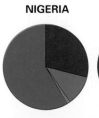

CHINA

JAPAN

FRANCE

USA

NORWAY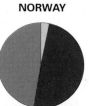

CARTOGRAPHY BY PHILIP'S. COPYRIGHT GEORGE PHILIP LTD

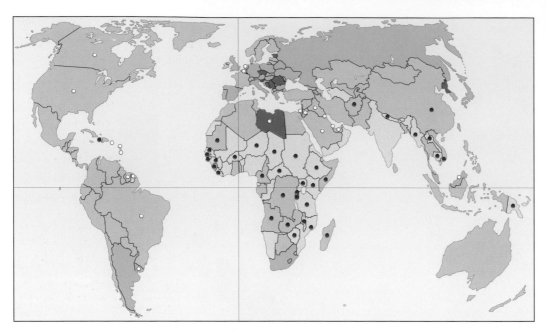

EMPLOYMENT IN INDUSTRY

Percentage of total workforce employed in manufacturing and mining 1995

- Over 30%
- 20 – 30%
- 10 – 20%
- Under 10%

● Over two thirds of total workforce employed in agriculture

○ Over a third of total workforce employed in service industries (work in offices, shops, tourism, transport, construction and government)

INDUSTRIAL PRODUCTION

Industrial output (mining, manufacturing, construction, energy and water production), top 40 nations, US $ billion (1991)

1.	U.S.A.	1,627	21.	Saudi Arabia	56
2.	Japan	1,412	22.	Indonesia	48
3.	Germany	614	23.	Spain	47
4.	Italy	380	24.	Argentina	46
5.	France	348	25.	Poland	39
6.	U.K.	324	26.	Norway	38
7.	Former U.S.S.R.	250	27.	Finland	37
8.	Brazil	161	28.	Thailand	36
9.	China	155	29.	Turkey	33
10.	South Korea	127	30.	Denmark	31
11.	Canada	117	31.	Israel	23
12.	Australia	93	32.	Iran	20
	Netherlands	93	33.	Ex- Czechoslovakia	19
14.	Taiwan	86	34.	Hong Kong	17
15.	Mexico	85		Portugal (1989)	17
16.	Sweden	70	36.	Algeria	16
17.	Switzerland (1989)	61		Greece	16
18.	India	60	38.	Iraq	15
19.	Austria	59		Philippines	15
	Belgium	59		Singapore	15

Graphs show the top ten producing countries for selected industrial goods.

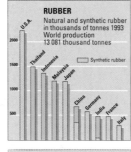

RUBBER Natural and synthetic rubber in thousands of tonnes 1993 World production 13 081 thousand tonnes — Synthetic rubber

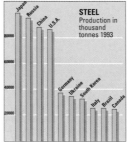

STEEL Production in thousand tonnes 1993

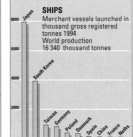

SHIPS Merchant vessels launched in thousand gross registered tonnes 1994 World production 16 340 thousand tonnes

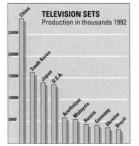

TELEVISION SETS Production in thousands 1992

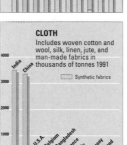

CLOTH Includes woven cotton and wool, silk, linen, jute, and man-made fabrics in thousands of tonnes 1991 — Synthetic fabrics

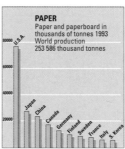

PAPER Paper and paperboard in thousands of tonnes 1993 World production 253 586 thousand tonnes

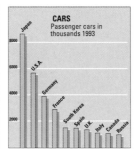

CARS Passenger cars in thousands 1993

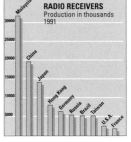

RADIO RECEIVERS Production in thousands 1991

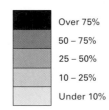

INDUSTRY AND TRADE

Manufactured goods (inc. machinery & transport) as a percentage of total exports (latest available year)

- Over 75%
- 50 – 75%
- 25 – 50%
- 10 – 25%
- Under 10%

The Far East and South-East Asia (Japan 98.3%, Macau 97.8%, Taiwan 92.7%, Hong Kong 93.0%, South Korea 93.4%) are most dominant, but many countries in Europe (e.g. Slovenia 92.4%) are also heavily dependent on manufactured goods.

Projection: *Modified Hammer Equal Area*

DEPENDENCE ON TRADE

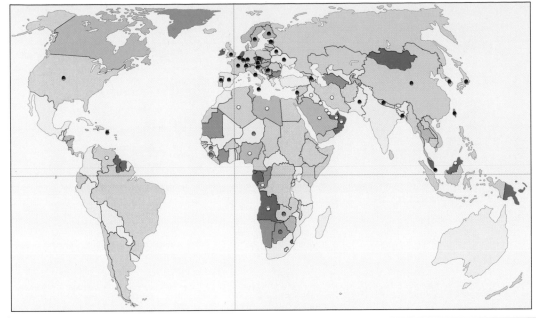

Value of exports as a percentage of G.N.P. (Gross National Product) 1995

Over 50% G.N.P. from exports

40 – 50% G.N.P. from exports

30 – 40% G.N.P. from exports

20 – 30% G.N.P. from exports

10 – 20% G.N.P. from exports

Under 10% G.N.P. from exports

- Most dependent on industrial exports (over 75% of total exports)

○ Most dependent on fuel exports (over 75% of total exports)

● Most dependent on metal and mineral exports (over 75% of total exports)

BALANCE OF TRADE

Value of exports in proportion to the value of imports 1995

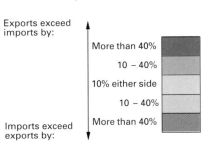

Exports exceed imports by:

More than 40%

10 – 40%

10% either side

10 – 40%

More than 40%

Imports exceed exports by:

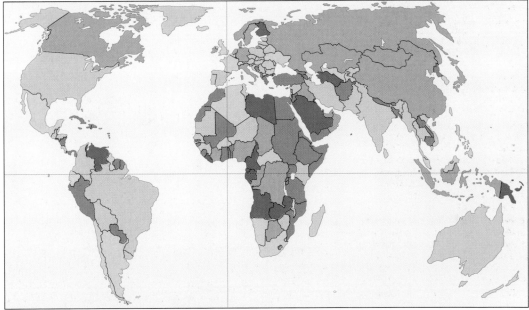

SHARE OF WORLD TRADE

Percentage share of total world exports by value 1995

Over 10% of world trade

5 – 10% of world trade

1 – 5% of world trade

0.5 – 1% of world trade

0.1 – 0.5% of world trade

Under 0.1% of world trade

Projection: *Modified Hammer Equal Area*

CARTOGRAPHY BY PHILIP'S. COPYRIGHT GEORGE PHILIP LTD

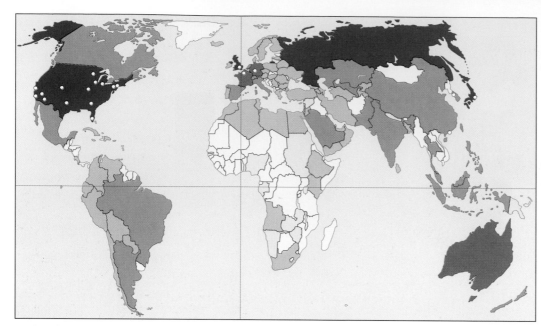

AIR TRAVEL

Passenger kilometres flown 1994

Passenger kilometres are the number of passengers (international and domestic) multiplied by the distance flown by each passenger from airport of origin.

- Over 100 000 million
- 50 000 – 100 000 million
- 10 000 – 50 000 million
- 1 000 – 10 000 million
- 500 – 1 000 million
- Under 500 million

o Major airports (handling over 25 million passengers in 1995)

World's busiest airports (total passengers)		World's busiest airports (international passengers)	
1. Chicago	(O'Hare)	1. London	(Heathrow)
2. Atlanta	(Hartsfield)	2. London	(Gatwick)
3. Dallas	(Dallas/Ft Worth)	3. Frankfurt	(International)
4. London	(Heathrow)	4. New York	(Kennedy)
5. Los Angeles	(Intern'l)	5. Paris	(De Gaulle)

TOURISM

Tourism receipts as a percentage of G.N.P. (Gross National Product) 1994

- Over 10% of G.N.P from tourism
- 5 – 10% of G.N.P. from tourism
- 2.5 – 5% of G.N.P. from tourism
- 1 – 2.5% of G.N.P. from tourism
- 0.5 – 1% of G.N.P. from tourism
- Under 0.5% of G.N.P. from tourism

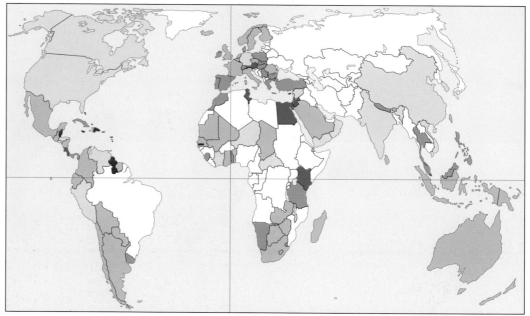

Countries spending the most on promoting tourism, millions of US $ (1996)		Fastest growing tourist destinations, % change in receipts (1994–5)	
Australia	88	South Korea	49%
Spain	79	Czech Republic	27%
U.K.	79	India	21%
France	73	Russia	19%
Singapore	54	Philippines	18%

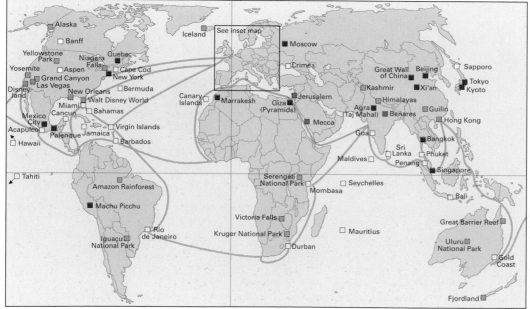

TOURIST DESTINATIONS

- ■ Cultural & historical centres
- □ Coastal resorts
- □ Ski resorts
- ▨ Centres of entertainment
- ■ Places of pilgrimage
- ▨ Places of great natural beauty

──── Popular holiday cruise routes

Projection: *Modified Hammer Equal Area*

CARTOGRAPHY BY PHILIP'S. COPYRIGHT GEORGE PHILIP LTD

TIME ZONES

Note: Certain of the time zones are affected by the incidence of "Summer Time" in countries where it is adopted.

Zones using Greenwich Mean Time	Half hour zones
Zones slow of Greenwich Mean Time	Zones fast of Greenwich Mean Time

- - - - - International boundaries
———— Time zone boundaries
———— International date line
———— Selected air routes

Actual Solar Time when noon at Greenwich is shown along the top of the map.

10 Hours slow or fast of Greenwich Mean Time

Equatorial scale: 1:220 000 000

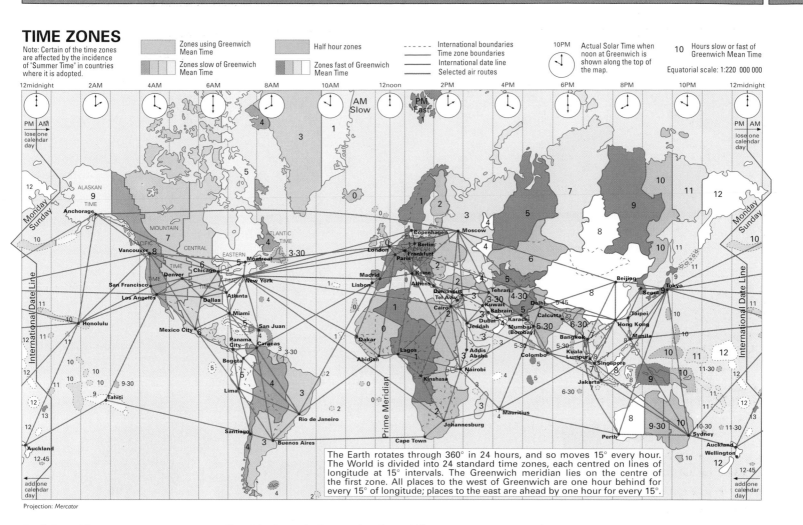

Projection: *Mercator*

The Earth rotates through 360° in 24 hours, and so moves 15° every hour. The World is divided into 24 standard time zones, each centred on lines of longitude at 15° intervals. The Greenwich meridian lies on the centre of the first zone. All places to the west of Greenwich are one hour behind for every 15° of longitude; places to the east are ahead by one hour for every 15°.

DISTANCE TABLE

The table shows air distances in miles and kilometres between twenty-four major cities. Known as 'Great Circle' distances, these measure the shortest routes between cities, which aircraft use where possible.

Kms	Beijing	Bogota	Buenos Aires	Cairo	Calcutta	Caracas	Chicago	Hong Kong	Honolulu	Johannesburg	Lagos	London	Los Angeles	Mexico City	Moscow	Nairobi	New York	Paris	Rio de Janeiro	Rome	Singapore	Sydney	Tokyo	Wellington	
		9263	11972	4688	2031	8947	6588	1220	5070	7276	7119	5057	6251	7742	3600	5727	6828	5106	10773	5049	2783	5561	1304	6700	**Beijing**
			2911	6971	10223	637	2710	10480	5697	7125	5319	5262	3478	1961	6758	7672	2481	5358	2820	5831	11990	8903	8851	7527	**Bogota**
				7341	10268	3167	5599	11481	7558	5025	4919	6917	6122	4591	8374	6463	5298	6867	1214	6929	9867	7332	11410	6202	**Buenos Aires**
Beijing					3541	6340	6127	5064	8838	3894	2432	2180	7580	7687	1803	2197	5605	1994	6149	1325	5137	8959	5947	10268	**Cairo**
Bogota	14908					9609	7978	1653	7048	5256	5727	4946	8152	9494	3438	3839	7921	4883	9366	4486	1800	5678	3195	7055	**Calcutta**
Buenos Aires	19268	4685					2502	10166	6009	6847	4810	4664	3612	2228	6175	7173	2131	4738	2825	5196	11407	9534	8801	8154	**Caracas**
Cairo	7544	11218	11814					5543	6669	7360	5980	7232	8775	4439	5453	8047	5984	11001	5769	1615	4582	1786	5857	**Chicago**
Calcutta	3269	16453	16524	5699					11934	10133	7228	2558	3781	7036	10739	4958	7437	8290	8026	6721	5075	3854	4669	**Hong Kong**
Caracas	14399	1026	5096	10203	15464					2799	5637	10362	9063	5692	1818	7979	5426	4420	4811	5381	6860	8418	7300	**Honolulu**
Chicago	10603	4361	9011	9860	12839	4027					3118	7713	6879	3886	2366	5268	2929	3750	2510	6925	9643	8376	9973	**Johannesburg**
Hong Kong	1963	16865	18478	8150	2659	16360	12526					5442	5552	1552	4237	3463	212	5778	889	6743	10558	5942	11691	**Lagos**
Honolulu	8160	9169	12164	14223	11343	9670	6836	8921					1549	6070	9659	2446	5645	6310	6331	8776	7502	5475	6719	**London**
Johannesburg	11710	11467	8088	6267	8459	11019	13984	10732	19206					6664	9207	2090	5717	4780	6365	10321	8058	7024	6897	**Los Angeles**
Lagos	11457	8561	7916	3915	9216	7741	9612	11845	16308	4505					3942	4666	1545	7184	1477	5237	9008	4651	10283	**Mexico City**
London	8138	8468	11131	3508	7961	7507	6356	9623	11632	9071	5017					7358	4029	5548	3350	4635	7552	6996	8490	**Moscow**
Los Angeles	10060	5596	9852	12200	13120	5812	2804	11639	4117	16676	12414	8758					3626	4832	4280	9531	9935	6741	8951	**Nairobi**
Mexico City	12460	3156	7389	12372	15280	3586	2726	14122	6085	14585	11071	8936	2493					5708	687	6671	10539	6038	11798	**New York**
Moscow	5794	10877	13477	2902	5534	9938	8000	7144	11323	9161	6254	2498	9769	10724					5725	9763	8389	11551	7367	**Paris**
Nairobi	9216	12347	10402	3536	6179	11544	12883	8776	17282	2927	3807	6819	15544	14818	6344					6229	10143	6127	11523	**Rome**
New York	10988	3993	8526	9020	12747	3430	1145	12950	7980	12841	8477	5572	3936	3264	7510	11842					3915	3306	5298	**Singapore**
Paris	8217	8622	11051	3210	7858	7625	6650	9630	11968	8732	4714	342	9085	9200	2486	6485	5836					4861	1383	**Sydney**
Rio de Janeiro	17338	4539	1953	9896	15073	4546	8547	17704	13342	7113	6035	9299	10155	7693	11562	8928	7777	9187					5762	**Tokyo**
Rome	8126	9383	11151	2133	7219	8363	7739	9284	12916	7743	4039	1431	10188	10243	2376	5391	6888	1105	9214					**Wellington**
Singapore	4478	19296	15879	8267	2897	18359	15078	2599	10816	8660	11145	10852	14123	16610	8428	7460	15339	10737	15712	10025				**Miles**
Sydney	8949	14327	11800	14418	9138	15343	14875	7374	8168	11040	15519	16992	12073	12969	14497	12153	15989	16962	13501	16324	6300			
Tokyo	2099	14245	18362	9571	5141	14164	10137	2874	6202	13547	13480	9562	8811	11304	7485	11260	10849	9718	18589	9861	5321	7823		
Wellington	10782	12113	9981	16524	11354	13122	13451	9427	7513	11761	16050	18814	10814	11100	16549	13664	14405	18987	11855	18545	8526	2226	9273	

WEALTH

The value of total production in 1995 divided by the population. (The Gross National Product per capita)

- Over 400% of world average
- 200 – 400% of world average
- 100 – 200% of world average

World average wealth per person $5 714

- 50 – 100% of world average
- 25 – 50% of world average
- 10 – 25% of world average
- Under 10% of world average

Top 5 countries		Bottom 5 countries	
Luxembourg	$41 210	Mozambique	$80
Switzerland	$40 630	Ethiopia	$100
Japan	$39 640	Congo (Zaïre)	$120
Norway	$31 250	Tanzania	$120
Denmark	$29 890	Burundi	$160
		U.K.	$18 700

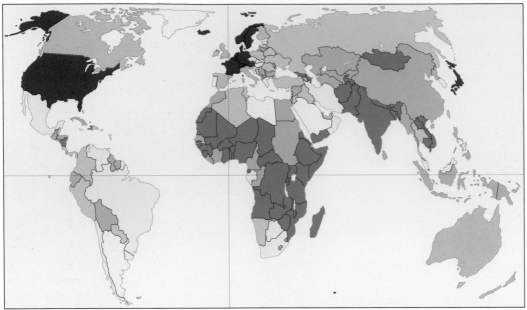

CAR OWNERSHIP

Number of people per car (latest available year)

- Over 1000 people per car
- 500 – 1000 people per car
- 100 – 500 people per car
- 25 – 100 people per car
- 5 – 25 people per car
- Under 5 people per car

Most people per car		Most cars (millions)	
Nepal	4247	U.S.A.	143.8
Bangladesh	2618	Germany	39.1
Cambodia	2328	Japan	39.0
Somalia	1790	Italy	29.6
Ethiopia	1423	France	24.0

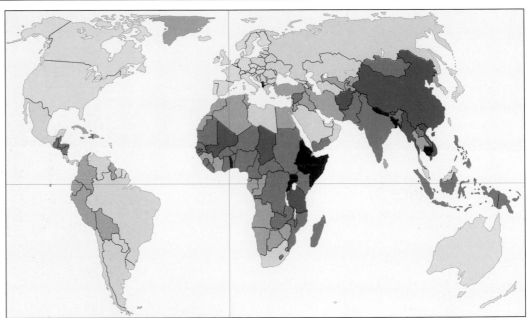

HUMAN DEVELOPMENT INDEX

The Human Development Index (H.D.I.) 1994 includes social and economic indicators and is calculated by the U.N. Development Programme as a measure of national human progress. Wealthy developed countries measure highest on the index.

- H.D.I. over 0.900
- H.D.I. 0.700 – 0.899
- H.D.I. 0.500 – 0.699
- H.D.I. 0.300 – 0.499
- H.D.I. under 0.299
- H.D.I. not available

Top 5 countries		Bottom 5 countries	
Canada	0.960	Mali	0.229
France	0.946	Burkina Faso	0.221
Norway	0.943	Niger	0.206
U.S.A.	0.942	Rwanda	0.187
Iceland	0.942	Sierra Leone	0.176
		U.K.	0.931

Projection: *Modified Hammer Equal Area*

HEALTH CARE

Number of people per doctor 1993

- Over 25 000 people per doctor
- 10 000 – 25 000 people per doctor
- 5 000 – 10 000 people per doctor
- 1 000 – 5 000 people per doctor
- 500 – 1 000 people per doctor
- Under 500 people per doctor

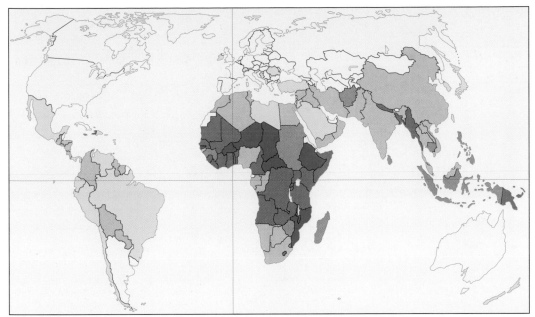

Most people per doctor 1993		Least people per doctor 1993	
Niger	53 986	Georgia	182
Malawi	44 205	Italy	207
Mozambique	36 225	Israel	220
Burkina Faso	34 804	Russia	222
Ethiopia	32 499	Ukraine	227
		U.K.	300

ILLITERACY & EDUCATION

Percentage of total population unable to read or write 1995

- Over 75% of population illiterate
- 50 – 75% of population illiterate
- 25 – 50% of population illiterate
- 10 – 25% of population illiterate
- Under 10% of population illiterate

• Less than 6 years compulsory education per child

Educational expenditure per person (latest available year)

Top five countries		Bottom five countries	
Norway	$2,820	Congo (Zaïre)	$1
Denmark	$2,450	Somalia	$2
Switzerland	$2,256	Sierra Leone	$2
Japan	$1,853	Nigeria	$3
Finland	$1,706	Haiti	$3
		U.K.	$1,009

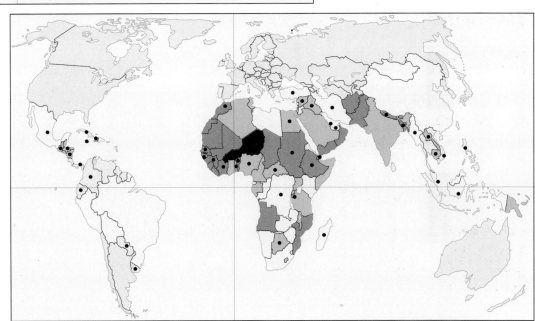

FERTILITY & EDUCATION

Fertility rates compared with female education, selected countries (1992–1995)

Fertility rate: average number of children borne per woman

Percentage of females aged 12 – 17 in secondary education

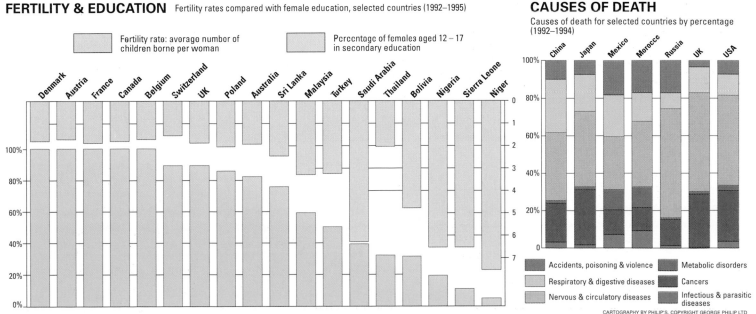

CAUSES OF DEATH

Causes of death for selected countries by percentage (1992–1994)

- Accidents, poisoning & violence
- Respiratory & digestive diseases
- Nervous & circulatory diseases
- Metabolic disorders
- Cancers
- Infectious & parasitic diseases

AGE DISTRIBUTION PYRAMIDS

The bars represent the percentage of the total population (males plus females) in the age group shown.

Developed countries such as the U.K. have populations evenly spread across age groups and usually a growing percentage of elderly people. Developing countries such as Kenya have the great majority of their people in the younger age groups, about to enter their most fertile years.

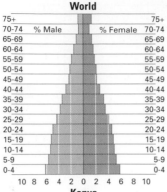

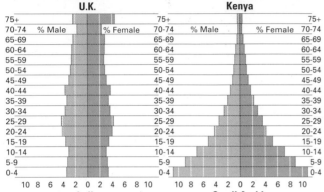

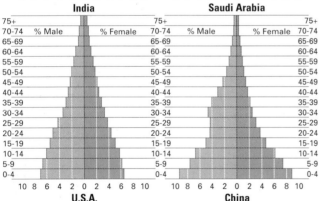

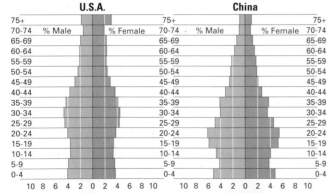

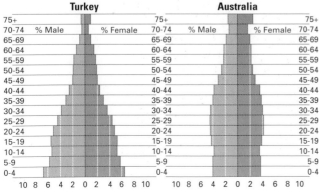

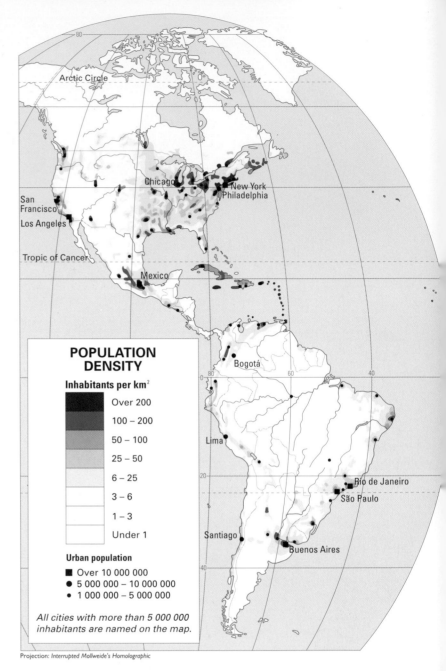

POPULATION DENSITY

Inhabitants per km²

- Over 200
- 100 – 200
- 50 – 100
- 25 – 50
- 6 – 25
- 3 – 6
- 1 – 3
- Under 1

Urban population

- ■ Over 10 000 000
- ● 5 000 000 – 10 000 000
- • 1 000 000 – 5 000 000

All cities with more than 5 000 000 inhabitants are named on the map.

Projection: *Interrupted Mollweide's Homolographic*

POPULATION CHANGE 1930-2020   Population totals are in millions

Figures in italics represent the percentage average annual increase for the period shown

	1930	1930-1960	1960	1960-1990	1990	1990-2020	2020
World	2013	*1.4%*	3019	*1.9%*	5292	*1.4%*	8062
Africa	155	*2.0%*	281	*2.85*	648	*2.7%*	1441
North America	135	*1.3%*	199	*1.1%*	276	*0.6%*	327
Latin America*	129	*1.8%*	218	*2.4%*	448	*1.6%*	719
Asia	1073	*1.5%*	1669	*2.1%*	3108	*1.4%*	4680
Europe	355	*0.6%*	425	*0.55*	498	*0.1%*	514
Oceania	10	*1.4%*	16	*1.75*	27	*1.1%*	37
C.I.S.†	176	*0.7%*	214	*1.0%*	288	*0.6%*	343

* South America plus Central America, Mexico, and the West Indies
† Commonwealth of Independent States, formerly the U.S.S.R.

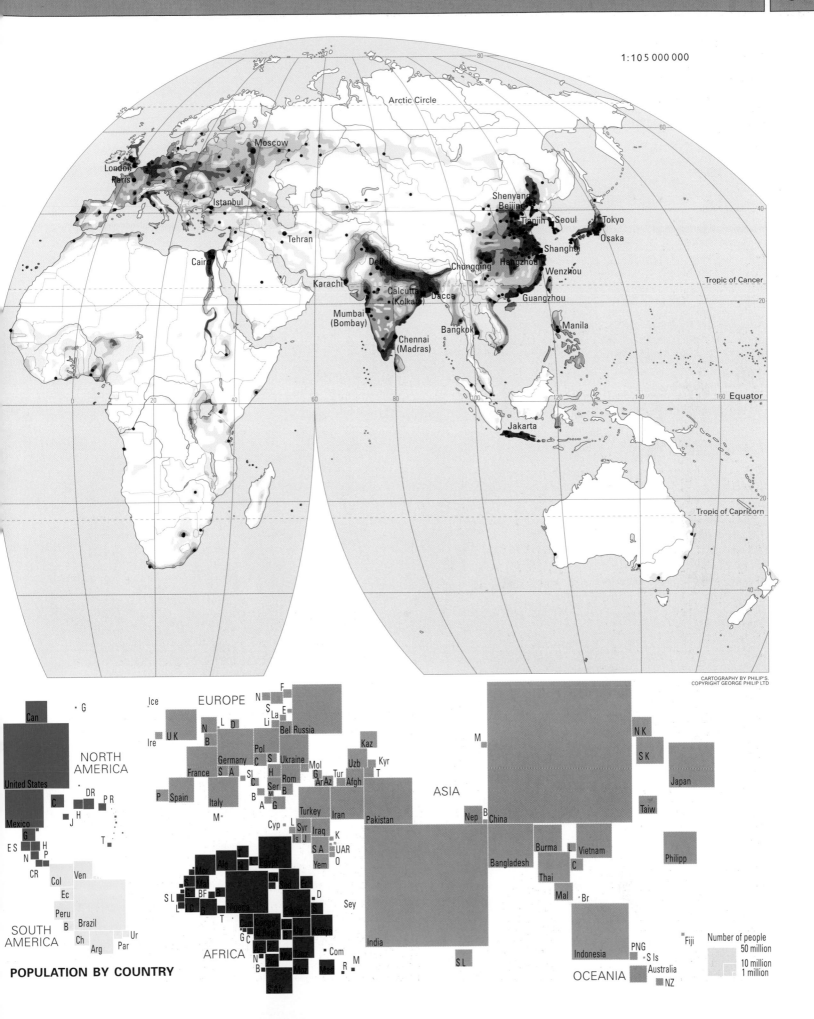

1:105 000 000

Arctic Circle

Moscow

London
Paris

Istanbul

Tehran

Shenyang
Beijing
Tianjin Seoul Tokyo
Osaka
Shanghai
Chongqing Hangzhou
Wenzhou

Cairo

Delhi

Tropic of Cancer

Karachi

Calcutta
(Kolkata) Dacca
Guangzhou

Mumbai
(Bombay)

Chennai
(Madras)

Bangkok

Manila

Equator

Jakarta

Tropic of Capricorn

CARTOGRAPHY BY PHILIP'S.
COPYRIGHT GEORGE PHILIP LTD

EUROPE

Ice

N   F

S   La   E
Li

Can   G

UK   N   L   D
Bel   Russia
Ire   B

Kaz

M

N K

S K

NORTH
AMERICA

Germany   Pol   Ukraine
France   S A   S   H   G   Mol
Ser   Rom   Ar Az   Uzb   Kyr

Japan

United States

P   Spain
Italy
A   G
M   Turkey   Iran

DR
C   P R
H
J

Cyp   L   Syr
Is   J   Iraq

Afgh   T

Pakistan

ASIA

Nep   B
China

Taiw

Mexico
G

Yem
S A   UAR
K   O

Burma   L   Vietnam
Bangladesh   C

Philipp

E S   H
N   P
CR

Col   Ven

Thai
Mal   Br

Ec

Peru

Ven

Sey

SOUTH
AMERICA

B   Brazil

Mor   Alg   Egypt
S L
BF   Sud   Er
Nigeria   D
Ethiop
Cam   Kenya
G   C   Tanz   Com   M
R   M
S Af

Ch   Arg   Par

AFRICA

India

S L

Indonesia   PNG
S ls
Australia
OCEANIA   NZ

Fiji   Number of people
50 million

10 million
1 million

POPULATION BY COUNTRY

POPULATION DENSITY BY COUNTRY

Density of people per square kilometre 1997

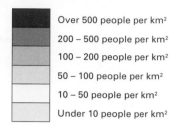

Over 500 people per km²

200 – 500 people per km²

100 – 200 people per km²

50 – 100 people per km²

10 – 50 people per km²

Under 10 people per km²

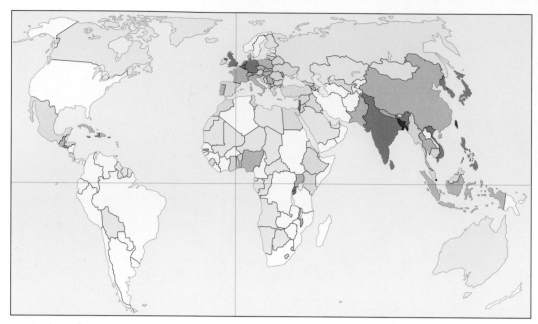

Top 5 countries		Bottom 5 countries	
Macau	22 111 per km²	Namibia	1.9 per km²
Monaco	20 805 per km²	French Guiana	1.5 per km²
Singapore	5 246 per km²	Mongolia	1.4 per km²
Malta	1 172 per km²	W. Sahara	0.8 per km²
Bangladesh	953 per km²	Greenland	0.2 per km²

U.K. 243 per km²

POPULATION CHANGE 1990-2000

The predicted population change for the years 1990-2000

Over 40% population gain

30 – 40% population gain

20 – 30% population gain

10 – 20% population gain

0 – 10% population gain

No change or population loss

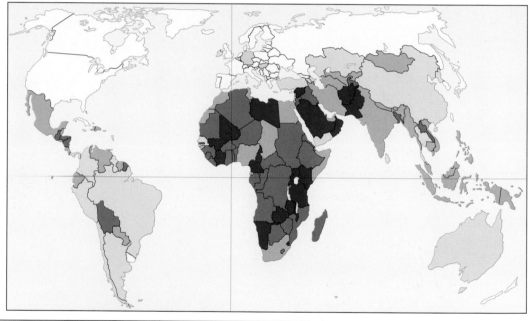

Top 5 countries		Bottom 5 countries	
Kuwait	+75.9%	Belgium	-0.1%
Namibia	+62.5%	Hungary	-0.2%
Afghanistan	+60.1%	Grenada	-2.4%
Mali	+55.5%	Germany	-3.2%
Tanzania	+54.6%	Tonga	-3.2%

U.K. +2.0%

URBAN POPULATION

Percentage of total population living in towns and cities 1995

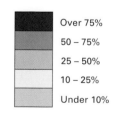

Over 75%

50 – 75%

25 – 50%

10 – 25%

Under 10%

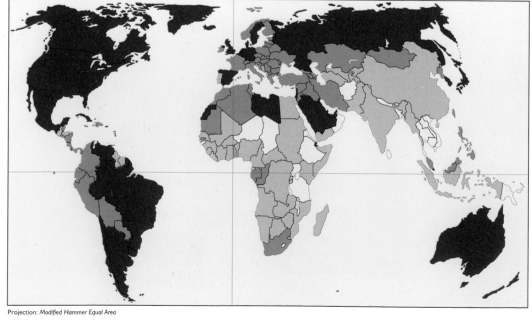

Most urbanized		Least urbanized	
Singapore	100%	Bhutan	6%
Belgium	97%	Rwanda	6%
Kuwait	97%	Burundi	7%
Iceland	92%	Uganda	12%
Venezuela	92%	Malawi	13%

U.K. 89%

Projection: *Modified Hammer Equal Area*

CHILD MORTALITY

The number of babies who died
under the age of one
(average 1990–95)

Over 150 deaths per 1 000 births

100 – 150 deaths per 1 000 births

50 – 100 deaths per 1 000 births

20 – 50 deaths per 1 000 births

10 – 20 deaths per 1 000 births

Under 10 deaths per 1 000 births

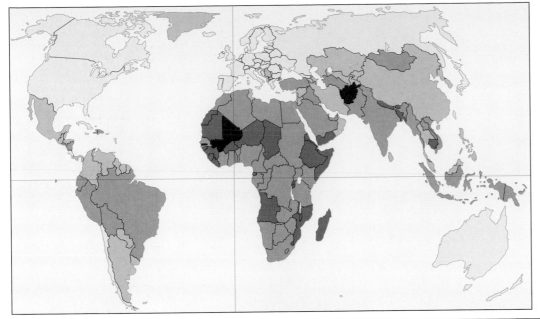

Highest child mortality		Lowest child mortality	
Afghanistan	162 deaths	Hong Kong	6 deaths
Mali	159 deaths	Denmark	6 deaths
Sierra Leone	143 deaths	Japan	5 deaths
Guinea-Bissau	140 deaths	Iceland	5 deaths
Malawi	138 deaths	Finland	5 deaths
		U.K.	8 deaths

LIFE EXPECTANCY

Average expected lifespan
of babies born in 1997

Over 75 years

70 – 75 years

65 – 70 years

60 – 65 years

55 – 60 years

50 – 55 years

Under 50 years

Highest life expectancy		Lowest life expectancy	
Iceland	81 years	Tanzania	42 years
Japan	80 years	Niger	41 years
Australia	80 years	Uganda	40 years
Canada	79 years	Rwanda	39 years
Luxembourg	79 years	Malawi	35 years
		U.K.	77 years

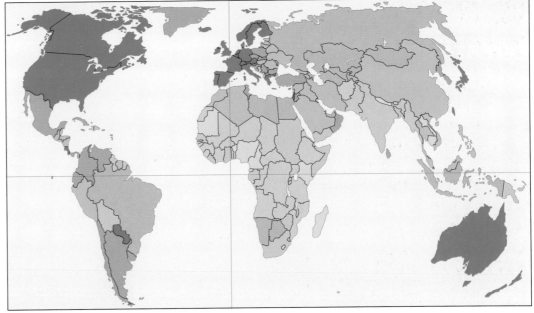

FAMILY SIZE

The average number of children a woman
can expect to bear during her lifetime 1995

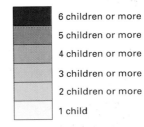

6 children or more

5 children or more

4 children or more

3 children or more

2 children or more

1 child

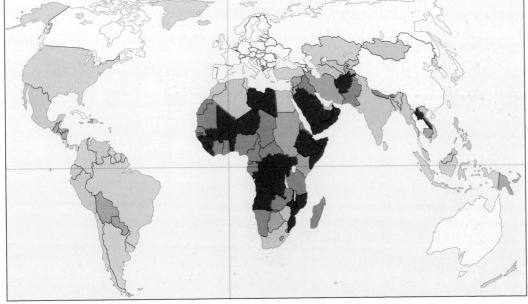

Most children per family

Yemen	7.4
Niger	7.4
Somalia	7.0
Oman	7.0
Ethiopia	7.0
U.K.	1.7

Projection: Modified Hammer Equal Area

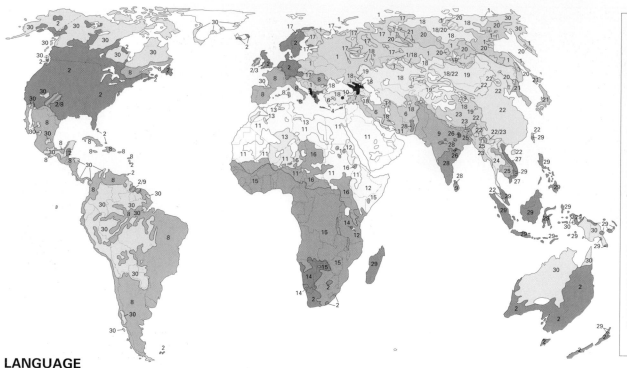

MOTHER TONGUES
Chinese 1069 million (Mandarin 864), English 443, Hindi 352, Spanish 341, Russian 293, Arabic 197, Bengali 184, Portuguese 173, Malay-Indonesian 142, Japanese 125, French 121, German 118, Urdu 92, Punjabi 84, Korean 71.

OFFICIAL LANGUAGES
English 27% of world population, Chinese 19%, Hindi 13.5%, Spanish 5.4%, Russian 5.2%, French 4.2%, Arabic 3.3%, Portuguese 3%, Malay 3%, Bengali 2.9%, Japanese 2.3%

Language can be classified by ancestry and structure . For example the Romance and Germanic groups are both derived from an Indo-European language believed to have been spoken 5000 years ago.

LANGUAGE

INDO-EUROPEAN FAMILY
- 1 Balto-Slavic group (incl. Russian, Ukrainian)
- 2 Germanic group (incl. English, German)
- 3 Celtic group
- 4 Greek
- 5 Albanian
- 6 Iranian group
- 7 Armenian
- 8 Romance group (incl. Spanish, Portuguese, French, Italian)
- 9 Indo-Aryan group (incl. Hindi, Bengali, Urdu, Punjabi, Marathi)
- 10 CAUCASIAN FAMILY

AFRO-ASIATIC FAMILY
- 11 Semitic group (incl. Arabic)
- 12 Kushitic group
- 13 Berber group
- 14 KHOISAN FAMILY
- 15 NIGER-CONGO FAMILY
- 16 NILO-SAHARAN FAMILY
- 17 URALIC FAMILY

ALTAIC FAMILY
- 18 Turkic group
- 19 Mongolian group
- 20 Tungus-Manchu group
- 21 Japanese and Korean

SINO-TIBETAN FAMILY
- 22 Sinitic (Chinese) languages
- 23 Tibetic-Burmic languages
- 24 TAI FAMILY

AUSTRO-ASIATIC FAMILY
- 25 Mon-Khmer group
- 26 Munda group
- 27 Vietnamese
- 28 DRAVIDIAN FAMILY (incl. Telugu, Tamil)
- 29 AUSTRONESIAN FAMILY (incl. Malay-Indonesian)
- 30 OTHER LANGUAGES

RELIGION

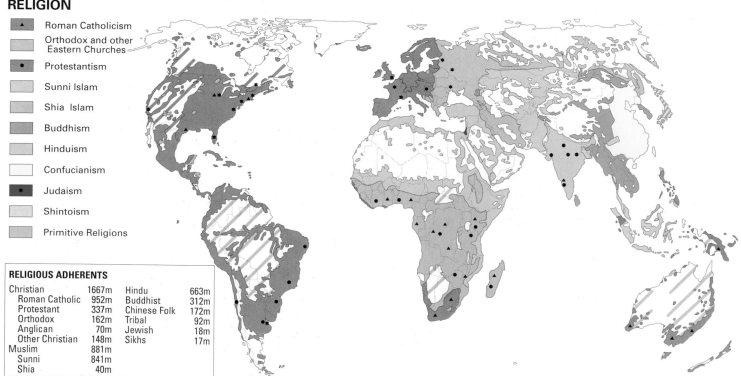

- Roman Catholicism
- Orthodox and other Eastern Churches
- Protestantism
- Sunni Islam
- Shia Islam
- Buddhism
- Hinduism
- Confucianism
- Judaism
- Shintoism
- Primitive Religions

RELIGIOUS ADHERENTS

Christian	1667m	Hindu	663m
Roman Catholic	952m	Buddhist	312m
Protestant	337m	Chinese Folk	172m
Orthodox	162m	Tribal	92m
Anglican	70m	Jewish	18m
Other Christian	148m	Sikhs	17m
Muslim	881m		
Sunni	841m		
Shia	40m		

UNITED NATIONS

Created in 1945 to promote peace and co-operation and based in New York, the United Nations is the world's largest international organization, with 185 members and an annual budget of US $2.6 billion (1996–97). Each member of the General Assembly has one vote, while the permanent members of the 15-nation Security Council – USA, Russia, China, UK and France – hold a veto. The Secretariat is the UN's principal administrative arm. The 54 members of the Economic and Social Council are responsible for economic, social, cultural, educational, health and related matters. The UN has 16 specialized agencies – based in Canada, France, Switzerland and Italy, as well as the USA – which help members in fields such as education (UNESCO), agriculture (FAO), medicine (WHO) and finance (IFC). By the end of 1994, all the original 11 trust territories of The Trusteeship Council had become independent.

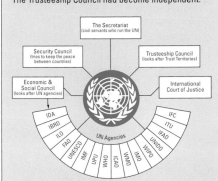

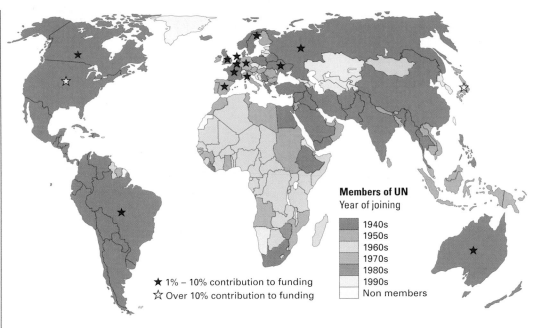

Members of UN
Year of joining

- 1940s
- 1950s
- 1960s
- 1970s
- 1980s
- 1990s
- Non members

★ 1% – 10% contribution to funding
☆ Over 10% contribution to funding

MEMBERSHIP OF THE UN In 1945 there were 51 members; by December 1994 membership had increased to 185 following the admission of Palau. There are 7 independent states which are not members of the UN – Kiribati, Nauru, Switzerland, Taiwan, Tonga, Tuvalu and the Vatican City. All the successor states of the former USSR had joined by the end of 1992. The official languages of the UN are Chinese, English, French, Russian, Spanish and Arabic.
FUNDING The UN budget for 1996–97 was US $ 2.6 billion. Contributions are assessed by the members' ability to pay, with the maximum 25% of the total, the minimum 0.01%. Contributions for 1996 were: USA 25.0%, Japan 15.4%, Germany 9.0%, France 6.4%, UK 5.3%, Italy 5.2%, Russia 4.5%, Canada 3.1%, Spain 2.4%, Brazil 1.6%, Netherlands 1.6%, Australia 1.5%, Sweden 1.2%, Ukraine 1.1%, Belgium 1.0%.

INTERNATIONAL ORGANIZATIONS

EU European Union (evolved from the European Community in 1993). The 15 members - Austria, Belgium, Denmark, Finland, France, Germany, Greece, Ireland, Italy, Luxembourg, Netherlands, Portugal, Spain, Sweden and the UK - aim to integrate economies, co-ordinate social developments and bring about political union. These members of what is now the world's biggest market share agricultural and industrial policies and tariffs on trade. The original body, the European Coal and Steel Community (ECSC), was created in 1951 following the signing of the Treaty of Paris.
EFTA European Free Trade Association (formed in 1960). Portugal left the original 'Seven' in 1989 to join what was then the EC, followed by Austria, Finland and Sweden in 1995. Only 4 members remain: Norway, Iceland, Switzerland and Liechtenstein.
ACP African-Caribbean-Pacific (formed in 1963). Members have economic ties with the EU.
NATO North Atlantic Treaty Organization (formed in 1949). It continues after 1991 despite the winding up of the Warsaw Pact. There are 19 member nations.
OAS Organization of American States (formed in 1948). It aims to promote social and economic co-operation between developed countries of North America and developing nations of Latin America.
ASEAN Association of South-east Asian Nations (formed in l967). Burma and Laos joined inJuly l997.
OAU Organization of African Unity (formed in 1963). Its 53 members represent over 94% of Africa's population. Arabic, French, Portuguese and English are recognized as working languages.
LAIA Latin American Integration Association (1980). Its aim is to promote freer regional trade.
OECD Organization for Economic Co-operation and Development (formed in 1961). It comprises the 29 major Western free-market economies. 'G7' is its' inner group' comprising the USA, Canada, Japan, UK, Germany, Italy and France. Russia attended the G7 summit in June 1997 ('Summit of the Eight').
COMMONWEALTH The Commonwealth of Nations evolved from the British Empire; it comprises 16 Queen's realms, 32 republics and 5 indigenous monarchies, giving a total of 53.
OPEC Organization of Petroleum Exporting Countries (formed in 1960). It controls about three-quarters of the world's oil supply. Gabon left the organization in 1996.

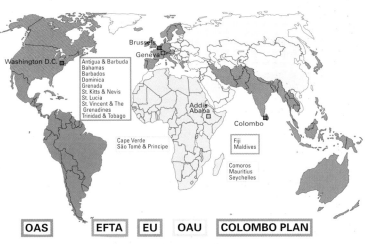

OAS **EFTA** **EU** **OAU** **COLOMBO PLAN**

ARAB LEAGUE (formed in 1945). The League's aim is to promote economic, social, political and military co-operation. There are 21 member nations.
COLOMBO PLAN (formed in 1951). Its 26 members aim to promote economic and social development in Asia and the Pacific.

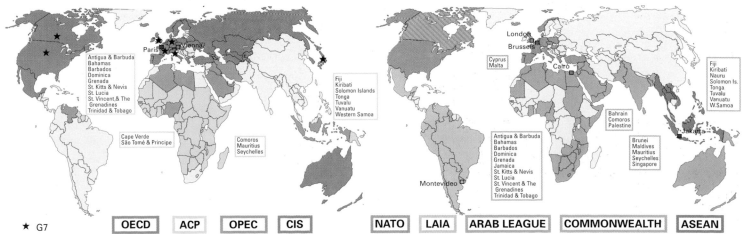

★ G7

OECD **ACP** **OPEC** **CIS**

NATO **LAIA** **ARAB LEAGUE** **COMMONWEALTH** **ASEAN**

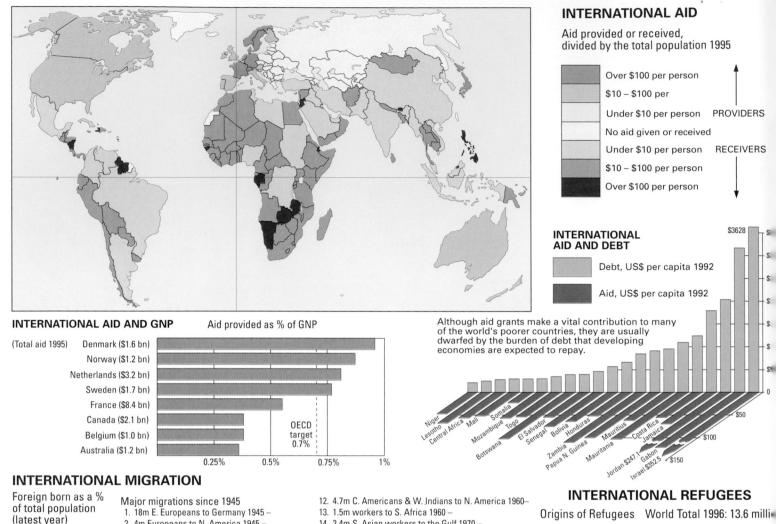

INTERNATIONAL AID

Aid provided or received,
divided by the total population 1995

- Over $100 per person
- $10 – $100 per
- Under $10 per person   PROVIDERS
- No aid given or received
- Under $10 per person   RECEIVERS
- $10 – $100 per person
- Over $100 per person

INTERNATIONAL AID AND DEBT

- Debt, US$ per capita 1992
- Aid, US$ per capita 1992

Although aid grants make a vital contribution to many
of the world's poorer countries, they are usually
dwarfed by the burden of debt that developing
economies are expected to repay.

$3628

Niger, Lesotho, Central Africa, Mali, Somalia, Mozambique, Togo, Botswana, El Salvador, Senegal, Bolivia, Honduras, Zambia, Papua N. Guinea, Mauritania, Mauritius, Costa Rica, Jordan $247.1, Jamaica, Gabon, Israel $352.5

$50 $100 $150

INTERNATIONAL AID AND GNP

Aid provided as % of GNP

(Total aid 1995)

Country	
Denmark ($1.6 bn)	
Norway ($1.2 bn)	
Netherlands ($3.2 bn)	
Sweden ($1.7 bn)	
France ($8.4 bn)	
Canada ($2.1 bn)	
Belgium ($1.0 bn)	
Australia ($1.2 bn)	

OECD target 0.7%

0.25%   0.5%   0.75%   1%

INTERNATIONAL MIGRATION

Foreign born as a %
of total population
(latest year)

- Over 7.5%
- 3 – 7.5%
- 1.5 – 3%
- Under 1.5%
- No available data

Major migrations since 1945

1. 18m E. Europeans to Germany 1945 –
2. 4m Europeans to N. America 1945 –
3. 2.4m Jews to Israel 1945 –
4. 2m Irish & Commonwealth to U.K. 1945 –
5. 2m Europeans to Australia 1945 –
6. 2m N. Africans & S. Europeans to France 1946 –
7. 5m Chinese to Japan & Korea 1947 –
8. 2.9m Palestinian refugees 1947
9. 25m Indian & Pakistani refugees 1947–
10. 9m Mexicans to N. America 1950 –
11. 5m Korean refugees 1950 – 54
12. 4.7m C. Americans & W. Indians to N. America 1960–
13. 1.5m workers to S. Africa 1960 –
14. 2.4m S. Asian workers to the Gulf 1970 –
15. 3m workers to Nigeria & Ivory Coast 1970 –
16. 2m Bangladeshi & Pakistani refugees 1972 –
17. 1.5m Vietnamese & Cambodian refugees 1975 –
18. 6.1m Afghan refugees 1979 –
19. 2.9m Egyptian workers to Libya & the Gulf 1980 –
20. 2m workers to Argentina 1980 –
21. 1.7m Mozambique refugees 1985 –
22. 1.7m Yugoslav refugees 1992 –
23. 2.6m Rwanda - Burundi refugees 1994–

INTERNATIONAL REFUGEES

Origins of Refugees   World Total 1996: 13.6 milli

- Palestine 27.1%
- Afghanistan 18
- Iraq 4.7%
- Other Asia 8.9%
- Liberia 5.4%
- Sudan 3.2%
- Somalia 3.2%
- Sierra Leone 2.5%
- Eritrea 2.5%
- Other Africa 9.1%
- Other Europe 7.0%
- Bosnia-Herz. 6.9%
- North & South America 0.7%

Refugee Destinations 1996

- Refugees in host country
- Refugees as a proportion of host country's population

Congo (Zaïre), Yugoslavia, Guinea, Gaza Strip, Pakistan, Jordan, Iran

500 000   1 000   1 500   2 000

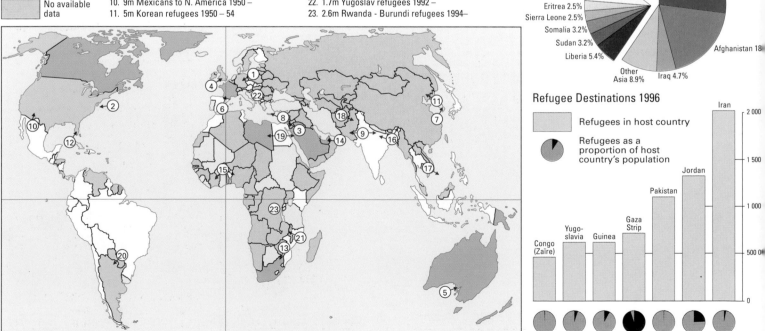

HOUSING

Number of people per household
(latest available year)

■	Over 6 people per household
■	5 – 6 people per household
■	4 – 5 people per household
■	3 – 4 people per household
■	2 – 3 people per household
■	Under 2 people per household

Expenditure on housing and energy as a
percentage of total consumer spending

▲   Over 20% spent

△   Under 5% spent

WATER SUPPLY

Percentage of total population with
access to safe drinking water
(average 1990 – 1996)

Over 90% with safe water	■
75 – 90% with safe water	■
60 – 75% with safe water	■
45 – 60% with safe water	■
30 – 45% with safe water	■
Under 30% with safe water	■

Least well provided countries

Afghanistan	23%	Papua New Guinea	28%
Chad	24%	Haiti	28%
Ethiopia	25%	Madagascar	29%

Average daily domestic water
consumption per person

◊   Under 80 litres   ▲   Over 320 litres

*80 litres of water a day is considered
necessary for a reasonable quality of life*

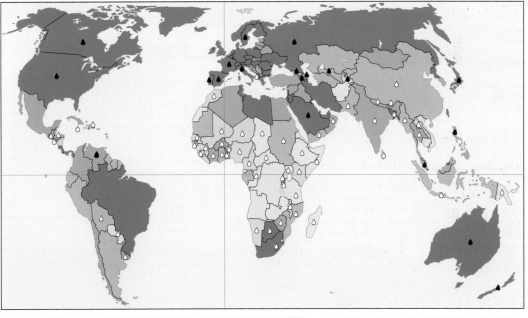

DAILY FOOD CONSUMPTION

Average daily food intake
in calories per person 1992

■	Over 3 500 cals. per person
■	3 000 – 3 500 cals. per person
■	2 500 – 3 000 cals. per person
■	2 000 – 2 500 cals. per person
■	Under 2 000 cals. per person
■	No available data

Top 5 countries		Bottom 5 countries	
Ireland	3 847	Mozambique	1 680
Greece	3 815	Liberia	1 640
Cyprus	3 779	Ethiopia	1 610
U.S.A.	3 732	Afghanistan	1 523
Spain	3 708	Somalia	1 499
	U.K.	3 317	

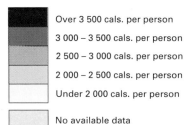

Malnutrition in children under 5 years

■   Over 50% of children

■   25 – 50% of children

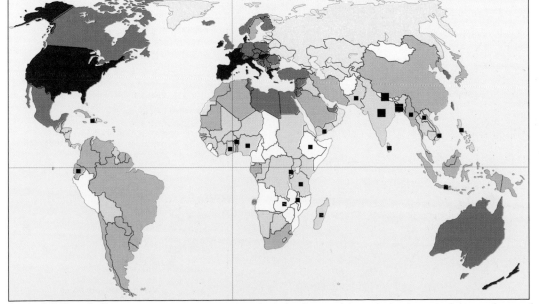

Projection: *Modified Hammer Equal Area*

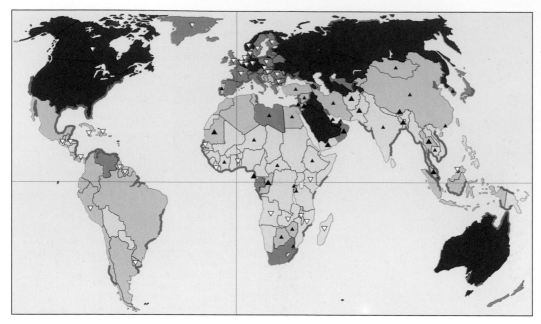

GLOBAL WARMING

Carbon dioxide emissions in tonnes per person per year (1992)

- Over 10 tonnes of CO_2
- 5 – 10 tonnes of CO_2
- 1 – 5 tonnes of CO_2
- Under 1 tonne of CO_2

Changes in CO_2 emissions 1980 – 1990

- ▲ Over 100% increase in emissions
- ▲ 50 – 100% increase in emissions
- ▽ Reduction in emissions
- ▬ Coasts in danger of flooding from rising sea levels caused by global warming

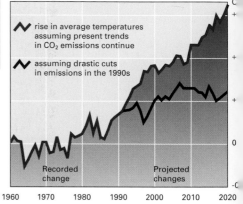

- rise in average temperatures assuming present trends in CO_2 emissions continue
- assuming drastic cuts in emissions in the 1990s

Recorded change   Projected changes

1960 1970 1980 1990 2000 2010 2020

5%   10%   15%   20%
U.S.A.
Former U.S.S.R.
China
Japan
Brazil
Germany
India
U.K.

Largest percentage share of total world greenhouse gas emissions 1992

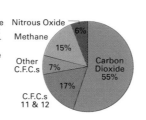

Contribution to the greenhouse effect by the major heat-absorbing gases in the atmosphere

Nitrous Oxide — 6%
Methane 15%
Other C.F.C.s 7%
Carbon Dioxide 55%
C.F.C.s 11 & 12 17%

THE GREENHOUSE EFFECT

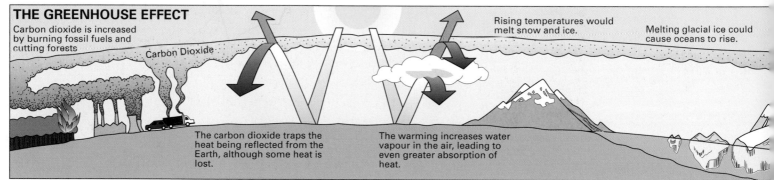

Carbon dioxide is increased by burning fossil fuels and cutting forests

Carbon Dioxide

Rising temperatures would melt snow and ice.

Melting glacial ice could cause oceans to rise.

The carbon dioxide traps the heat being reflected from the Earth, although some heat is lost.

The warming increases water vapour in the air, leading to even greater absorption of heat.

ACID RAIN

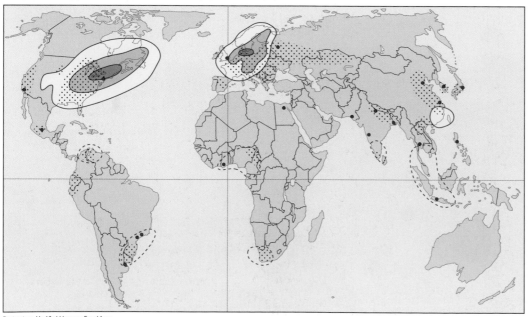

Acid rain is caused by high levels of sulphur and nitrogen in the atmosphere. They combine with water vapour and oxygen to form acids (H_2SO_4 and HNO_3) which fall as precipitation.

- Main areas of sulphur and nitrogen emissions (from the burning of fossil fuels)
- • Major cities with levels of air pollution exceeding World Health Organisation guidelines

Areas of acid deposition

(pH numbers measure acidity: normal rain is pH 5.6

- pH less than 4.0 (most acidic)
- pH 4.0 – 4.5
- pH 4.5 – 5.0
- ⌐ ⌐ Potential problem areas

WATER POLLUTION

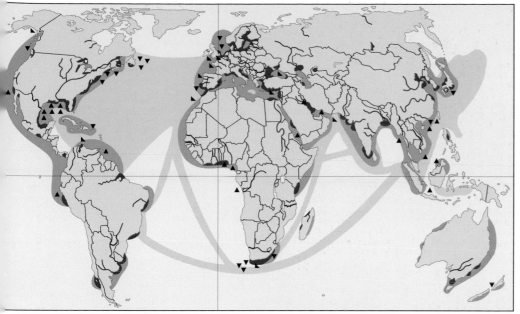

	Severely polluted sea areas and lakes
	Less polluted sea areas and lakes
	Areas of frequent oil pollution by shipping
◣	Major oil tanker spills
▲	Major oil rig blow-outs
▼	Offshore dumpsites for industrial and municipal waste
────	Severely polluted rivers and estuaries

Sources of marine oil pollution		Sources of river pollution	
Tanker operations	22%	Agriculture	64%
Municipal waste	22%	Mining	9%
Tanker accidents	13%	Land disposal	9%
River runoff	12%	Forestry	6%
Others	31%	Others	11%

DESERTIFICATION

	Existing deserts
	Areas with a high risk of desertification
	Areas with a moderate risk of desertification

DEFORESTATION IN THE TROPICS

	Former areas of rainforest
	Existing rainforest

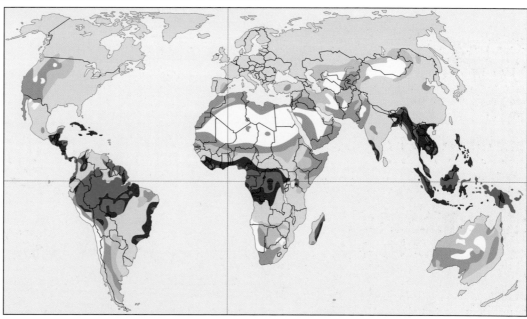

Deforestation 1990-1995

	Extent of forest cleared annually (thousand ha)	Annual deforestation rate (%)
Brazil	2554	0.5
Indonesia	1084	1.0
Congo (Zaire)	740	0.7
Bolivia	581	1.2
Mexico	508	0.9
Venezuela	503	1.1
Malaysia	400	2.4

NATURAL DISASTERS

	Earthquake zones
●	Major earthquakes since 1900 (with dates)
▲	Major volcanoes (notable eruptions since 1900 with dates)
	Areas liable to flood
⇨	Paths of tropical storms
⇨	Paths of winter blizzards
	Areas liable to invasion by locusts
■	Major famines since 1900 (with dates)
⑨	Major storms and floods

1	Texas 1900
2	Central America 1966,1974
3	West Indies 1928, 1963, 1979, 1988
4	Bangladesh 1960, 1963, 1965, 1970, 1985, 1988, 1989, 1991
5	Huang He 1887, 1931
6	Yangtze 1911, 1989, 1995
7	Hunan 1991
8	Haiphong 1881
9	Philippines 1970, 1991
10	Mississippi 1993

Projection: Modified Hammer Equal Area

	Population									Land and Agriculture					Energy	Trade	
	Population Total 1997	Population Density 1997	Average Annual Change 1970-80	Average Annual Change 1990-97	Birth Rate 1997	Death Rate 1997	Fertility Rate 1995	Life Expectancy Average 1997	Urban Population 1995	Land Area	Arable and Permanent Crops	Permanent grassland	Forest	Agriculture Population 1995	Consumption per capita 1994	Imports per capita 1995	Exports per capita 1995
	millions	persons per km²	%	%	births per thousand population	deaths per thousand population	children	years	%	thousand km²	% of land area	% of land area	% of land area	% of economically active pop.	tonnes of coal	US $	US $
Afghanistan	23	35	1.7	4.8	43	18	6.9	46	20	652	12	46	3	69	0.04	19	6
Albania	3.6	131	2.3	1.5	22	8	2.6	68	37	27.4	26	15	38	54	0.3	178	42
Algeria	29.3	12	3.1	2.3	28	6	3.5	69	56	2382	3	13	2	24	1.58	375	375
Angola	11.2	9	3.3	1.6	44	17	6.9	47	32	1247	3	43	18	74	0.08	198	309
Argentina	35.4	13	1.7	1.3	20	8	2.7	74	88	2737	10	52	19	11	2.15	579	603
Armenia	3.8	134	2	1.9	17	8	1.8	69	69	28.4	20	54	15	15	0.61	105	603
Australia	18.4	2	1.6	1.2	14	7	1.9	80	86	7644	6	54	19	5	7.61	3342	2942
Austria	8.2	99	0.1	1.1	11	10	1.5	77	65	82.7	18	24	39	7	4.16	8253	7166
Azerbaijan	7.7	89	1.8	1	22	9	2.3	65	56	86.1	23	52	11	30	2.6	105	86
Bahamas	0.3	28	2.1	1.5	18	6	2	73	85	10	1	0	32	5	2.97	4439	5418
Bangladesh	124	953	2.8	1	30	11	3.5	56	18	130	74	5	15	62	0.09	55	27
Barbados	0.3	616	0.4	0.6	15	8	1.8	75	46	0.43	37	5	12	6	1.58	2946	915
Belarus	10.5	51	0.7	0.3	11	13	1.4	69	69	208	31	14	34	18	3.38	297	243
Belgium	10.2	335	0.2	0.5	12	10	1.6	77	97	30.5	24	21	21	3	6.86	14702	16078
Benin	5.8	52	2.5	2.9	46	13	6	53	36	111	17	4	31	60	0.05	125	34
Bolivia	7.7	7	2.6	2.4	32	10	4.5	60	62	1084	2	24	53	45	0.49	192	149
Bosnia-Herzegovina	3.6	70	1	-2.7	6	7	1	60	41	51.2	16	24	39	10	0.36	204	12
Botswana	1.5	3	3.8	2.2	33	7	4.4	62	31	567	1	45	47	39	...	1153	1302
Brazil	159.5	19	2.4	1.4	20	9	2.4	62	78	8457	6	22	58	19	0.85	345	298
Bulgaria	8.6	77	0.4	-0.7	8	14	1.2	71	71	111	38	16	35	11	3.26	598	606
Burkina Faso	10.9	40	2.3	2.8	46	20	6.7	42	27	274	13	22	50	92	0.05	54	53
Burma	47.5	72	2.4	1.9	30	11	3.4	57	27	658	15	1	49	72	0.08	30	19
Burundi	6.3	243	1.6	0.5	42	15	6.5	49	7	25.7	46	39	13	91	0.02	39	18
Cambodia	10.5	59	-0.8	3.5	43	15	4.7	50	21	177	22	8	69	73	0.02	43	24
Cameroon	13.8	30	2.7	2.6	42	14	5.7	52	45	465	15	4	77	68	0.14	94	154
Canada	30.2	3	1.2	1.9	13	7	1.7	79	77	9221	5	3	54	3	11.21	5676	6491
Central African Rep.	3.4	5	2.3	1.8	40	18	5.1	45	39	623	3	5	75	79	0.04	54	52
Chad	6.8	5	2.1	2.5	44	17	5.9	48	22	1259	3	36	26	81	0.01	67	77
Chile	14.7	20	1.6	1.6	18	6	2.3	75	85	749	6	18	22	17	1.45	1121	1130
China	1210	130	1.8	1.2	17	7	1.9	70	29	9326	10	43	14	71	0.92	106	122
Colombia	35.9	35	2.3	1.2	21	5	2.8	73	73	1039	5	39	48	24	1	395	288
Congo	2.7	8	2.8	2.9	39	17	6	46	59	342	0	29	58	45	0.34	259	325
Congo (Zaïre)	47.2	21	2.9	4.1	48	17	6	47	29	2267	3	7	77	66	0.06	8	9
Costa Rica	3.5	69	2.8	2.2	23	4	2.8	76	50	51.1	10	46	31	22	0.87	977	811
Croatia	4.9	86	0.4	0.2	10	11	1.5	73	55	56.4	22	20	38	15	1.59	1586	969
Cuba	11.3	102	1.3	0.8	13	7	1.7	75	75	110	31	27	24	16	1.14	258	146
Cyprus	0.8	83	0.2	1.4	15	8	2.2	77	68	9.24	15	0	13	10	3.03	4986	1661
Czech Rep.	10.5	136	0.5	0.3	11	11	1.3	74	65	77	44	12	34	11	4.97	2450	2099
Denmark	5.4	126	0.4	0.3	12	10	1.8	78	86	42.4	56	7	10	4	5.15	8266	9378
Dominican Rep.	8.2	168	2.6	1.8	23	6	2.9	69	62	48.4	31	43	12	21	0.65	376	97
Ecuador	11.8	43	3	1.6	25	5	3.2	72	59	277	11	18	56	29	0.77	366	376
Egypt	63	63	2.1	2.6	28	9	3.4	62	45	995	4	0	0	33	0.66	199	58
El Salvador	6	287	2.3	1.8	27	6	3.7	69	52	20.7	35	29	5	32	0.5	504	176
Estonia	1.5	34	0.8	-1.1	12	14	1.3	68	73	43.2	27	7	48	14	4.9	1714	1240
Ethiopia	58.5	53	2.4	3.5	46	18	7	47	13	1101	11	20	13	86	0.03	19	7
Finland	5.2	17	0.4	0.6	11	11	1.8	76	63	305	9	0	76	7	7.4	5502	7744
France	58.8	107	0.6	0.7	13	9	1.7	79	74	550	35	19	27	4	5.15	4763	4941
Gabon	1.2	5	4.8	1.5	28	13	5.2	56	73	258	2	18	77	45	0.87	667	2055
Gambia, The	1.2	120	3.3	4.9	44	19	5.3	53	26	10	17	19	10	80	0.1	192	32
Georgia	5.5	78	0.8	0	14	9	1.9	68	58	69.7	16	24	33	25	0.85	39	22
Germany	82.3	236	0.1	0.5	9	11	1.2	76	87	349	34	15	31	3	5.48	5445	6227
Ghana	18.1	80	2.2	2.7	34	11	5.1	57	36	228	19	37	42	56	0.14	129	74
Greece	10.6	82	0.9	0.8	10	10	1.4	78	65	129	27	41	20	20	3.22	2056	899
Guatemala	11.3	104	2.8	2.9	33	7	4.7	66	42	108	18	24	54	51	0.29	310	203
Guinea	7.5	30	1.4	3.8	42	18	6.5	46	30	246	3	44	27	85	0.08	116	97
Guinea-Bissau	1.2	41	4.2	2.6	39	16	6	49	22	28.1	12	38	38	84	0.1	66	22
Guyana	0.8	4	0.7	-0.8	19	10	2.4	59	35	197	3	6	84	20	0.6	594	558
Haiti	7.4	269	1.7	1.8	33	15	4.4	50	32	27.6	33	18	5	66	0.04	91	16
Honduras	6.3	56	3.4	3	33	6	4.6	69	48	112	18	14	54	33	0.31	205	178
Hungary	10.2	110	0.4	-0.6	11	15	1.6	69	64	92.3	54	12	19	14	3.27	1472	1217
Iceland	0.3	3	1.1	1.2	17	6	2.1	81	92	100	0	23	1	10	6.7	6500	6678
India	980	330	2.2	2.5	25	9	3.2	60	27	2973	57	4	23	62	0.37	37	33
Indonesia	203.5	112	2.3	1.8	23	8	2.7	62	33	1812	17	7	62	53	0.47	211	234
Iran	69.5	42	3.2	3.5	33	6	4.5	68	58	1636	11	27	7	36	1.88	537	348
Iraq	22.5	51	3.6	2.5	43	6	5.4	67	73	437	12	9	4	12	1.76	278	383

Wealth							Social Indicators								Aid	
GNP 1995	GNP per capita 1995	Real GDP per capita 1995	Average Annual growth of Real GNP per capita 1985-95	GDP share Agriculture 1995	GDP share Industry 1995	GDP share services 1995	HDI Human Development Index 1994	Food Intake	Population per doctor 1993	% of GNP spent on health 1990-95	% of GNP spent on education 1993-94	%o GNP spent on military 1995	Adult Illiteracy Female	Adult Illiteracy Male	given (*) and received per capita 1994	
million US $	US $	US $	%	%	%	%		calories per day	persons	%	%	%	%	%	US $	
5000	300	800	-6	52	32	16	...	1523	7000	...	...	9.1	85	53	10	Afghanistan
2199	670	2750	-7	56	21	23	0.655	2605	735	2.7	3	2.8	0	0	21	Albania
44609	1600	5300	-2.6	13	47	40	0.737	2897	1062	4.6	5.6	2.5	51	26	11	Algeria
4422	410	1310	-6.1	12	59	29	0.335	1839	23725	4	...	4.8	71	44	40	Angola
278431	8030	8310	1.9	6	31	63	0.884	2880	330	10.6	3.8	1.7	4	4	7	Argentina
2752	730	2260	-15.1	44	35	21	0.651	...	261	7.8	7.3	4.4	2	1	27	Armenia
337909	18720	18940	1.4	3	28	69	0.931	3179	500	8.4	6	2.5	...	...	*62	Australia
216547	26890	21250	1.9	2	34	64	0.932	3497	231	9.7	5.5	1	0	0	*82	Austria
3601	480	1460	-16.3	27	32	41	0.636	...	257	7.5	5.5	5	4	1	3	Azerbaijan
3297	11940	14710	-1	3	9	88	0.894	2624	700	...	3.9	0.6	2	1	15	Bahamas
28599	240	1380	2.1	31	18	51	0.368	2019	12884	2.4	2.3	1.8	74	51	11	Bangladesh
1745	6560	10620	-0.2	5	17	78	0.907	3207	1000	5	7.5	0.7	3	2	...	Barbados
21356	2070	4220	-5.2	13	35	52	0.806	...	236	6.4	6.1	3.3	3	1	11	Belarus
250710	24710	21660	2.2	2	31	67	0.932	3681	274	8.2	5.6	1.7	0	0	*81	Belgium
2034	370	1760	-0.4	34	12	54	0.368	2532	14216	1.7	...	1.3	74	51	53	Benin
5905	800	2540	1.7	17	30	53	0.589	2094	2348	5	5.4	2.6	24	10	96	Bolivia
11650	2600	...	1.8	...	...	...	...	...	600	...	...	...	23	3	...	Bosnia-Herzegovina
4381	3020	5580	6	5	46	49	0.673	2266	5151	1.9	8.5	7.1	40	20	64	Botswana
579787	3640	5400	-0.7	14	37	49	0.783	2824	844	7.4	1.6	1.5	17	17	2	Brazil
11225	1330	4480	-2.2	13	34	53	0.78	2831	306	4	4.5	3.3	3	1	6	Bulgaria
2417	230	780	-0.1	34	27	39	0.221	2387	34804	5.5	3.6	2.4	91	71	48	Burkina Faso
45100	1000	1050	0.4	63	9	28	0.475	2598	12528	0.9	2.4	6.2	22	11	3	Burma
984	160	630	-1.3	56	18	26	0.247	1941	17153	0.9	3.8	5.3	78	51	46	Burundi
2718	270	1084	2	51	14	35	0.348	2021	9374	7.2	...	4.7	47	20	57	Cambodia
8615	650	2110	-7	39	23	38	0.468	1981	11996	1.4	3.1	1.8	48	25	35	Cameroon
573695	19380	21130	0.4	3	30	67	0.96	3094	464	9.8	7.6	1.6	2	2	*73	Canada
1123	340	1070	-2	44	13	43	0.355	1690	25920	1.7	2.8	1.8	48	32	50	Central African Rep.
1144	180	700	0.5	44	22	34	0.288	1989	30030	1.8	2.2	2.6	65	38	38	Chad
59151	4160	9520	6.1	8	34	58	0.891	2582	942	6.5	2.9	3.8	5	5	11	Chile
744890	620	2920	8	21	48	31	0.626	2727	1063	3.8	2.6	5.7	27	10	3	China
70263	1910	6130	2.8	14	32	54	0.848	2677	1105	7.4	3.7	2	9	9	6	Colombia
1784	680	2050	-3.2	10	38	52	0.5	2296	3713	6.8	8.3	1.7	33	17	50	Congo
5313	120	490	-8.5	51	16	33	0.381	2060	15150	2.4	1	2	32	13	4	Congo (Zaïre)
8884	2610	5850	2.9	17	24	59	0.889	2883	1133	8.5	4.7	0.3	5	5	8	Costa Rica
15508	3250	3960	-20	12	25	63	0.76	...	500	10.1	...	12.6	5	1	...	Croatia
13700	1250	3000	-10	...	...	...	0.723	2833	275	7.9	6.6	2.8	5	4	6	Cuba
8510	11500	13000	4.6	6	43	51	0.907	3779	450	3.9	4.3	4.5	7	2	30	Cyprus
39990	3870	9770	-1.8	6	39	55	0.882	...	273	9.9	5.9	2.8	0	0	5	Czech Rep.
156027	29890	21230	1.5	4	29	67	0.927	3664	360	6.6	8.5	1.8	0	0	*273	Denmark
11390	1460	3870	2.1	15	22	63	0.718	2286	949	5.3	1.9	1.3	18	18	16	Dominican Rep.
15997	1390	4220	0.8	12	36	52	0.775	2583	652	5.3	3	3.4	12	8	21	Ecuador
45507	790	3820	1.1	20	21	59	0.614	3335	1316	4.9	5	4.3	61	36	35	Egypt
9057	1610	2610	2.9	14	22	64	0.592	2663	1515	5	1.6	1.8	30	27	54	El Salvador
4252	2860	4220	-4.3	8	28	64	0.776	...	253	5.9	5.8	5.3	0	0	22	Estonia
5722	100	450	-0.5	57	10	33	0.244	1610	32499	1.1	6.4	2.1	75	55	16	Ethiopia
105174	20580	17760	-0.2	6	37	57	0.94	3018	406	8.3	8.4	2	0	0	*59	Finland
451051	24990	21030	1.5	2	27	71	0.946	3633	334	9.7	5.8	3.1	1	1	*137	France
3759	3490	3650	-1.6	9	59	32	0.562	2500	1987	0.5	3.2	1.7	47	26	138	Gabon
354	320	930	0.3	28	15	57	0.281	2360	14000	1.8	2.7	3.8	75	47	43	Gambia, The
2358	440	1470	-17	67	22	11	0.637	...	182	0.3	1.9	3.4	1	0	106	Georgia
2252343	27510	20070	1.9	1	30	69	0.924	3344	367	9.5	4.8	2	0	0	*81	Germany
6719	390	1990	1.5	46	16	38	0.468	2199	22970	3.5	3.1	1.2	47	24	38	Ghana
85885	8210	11710	1.2	21	36	43	0.923	3815	312	6.4	3	4.6	7	2	...	Greece
14255	1340	3340	0.3	25	19	56	0.572	2255	3999	2.7	1.6	1.4	51	38	21	Guatemala
3593	550	1100	1.4	24	31	45	0.271	2389	7445	0.9	2.2	1.4	78	50	62	Guinea
265	250	790	1.8	46	24	30	0.291	2556	3500	1.1	2.8	3	58	32	113	Guinea-Bissau
493	590	2420	0.8	50	35	15	0.649	2384	3000	10.4	5	1.1	2	1	...	Guyana
1777	250	910	-5.2	44	12	44	0.338	1706	10855	3.6	1.4	2.1	58	52	104	Haiti
3566	600	1900	0.2	21	33	46	0.575	2305	1266	5.6	4	1.3	27	27	75	Honduras
42129	4120	6410	-1	8	33	59	0.857	3503	306	7.3	6.7	1.4	1	1	7	Hungary
6686	24950	20460	0.3	13	29	58	0.942	3058	360	6.9	5.4	...	0	0	...	Iceland
319660	340	1400	3.1	29	29	42	0.446	2395	2459	3.5	3.8	2.5	62	35	2	India
190105	980	3800	6	17	42	41	0.668	2752	7028	1.5	1.3	1.6	22	10	7	Indonesia
328000	4800	5470	0.5	25	34	41	0.78	2860	3142	4.5	5.9	3.9	24	22	3	Iran
36200	1800	3150	...	28	20	52	0.531	2121	1659	...	5.1	14.8	55	29	16	Iraq

	Population									Land and Agriculture					Energy	Trade	
	Population Total 1997	Population Density 1997	Average Annual Change 1970-80	Average Annual Change 1990-97	Birth Rate 1997	Death Rate 1997	Fertility Rate 1995	Life Expectancy Average 1997	Urban Population 1995	Land Area	Arable and Permanent Crops	Permanent grassland	Forest	Agriculture Population 1995	Consumption per capita 1994	Imports per capita 1995	Exports per capita 1995
	millions	persons per km²	%	%	births per thousand population	deaths per thousand population	children	years	%	thousand km²	% of land area	% of land area	% of land area	% of economically active pop.	tonnes of coal	US $	US $
Ireland	3.6	53	1.4	0.5	13	9	1.9	76	58	68.9	19	45	5	13	4.31	9237	12469
Israel	5.9	286	2.7	3.6	20	6	2.4	78	91	20.6	21	7	6	3	3.26	5337	3436
Italy	57.8	196	0.5	0.2	10	10	1.2	78	67	294	38	15	23	7	3.95	3562	4038
Ivory Coast	15.1	47	4	3.4	42	17	5.3	45	46	318	12	41	34	57	0.26	231	301
Jamaica	2.6	240	1.3	0.8	22	6	2.4	75	53	10.8	20	24	17	24	1.66	1089	545
Japan	125.9	334	1.1	0.3	10	8	1.5	80	78	377	12	2	66	6	4.98	2684	3540
Jordan	5.6	63	2.4	4.9	36	4	4.8	73	72	88.9	5	9	1	15	1.01	680	325
Kazakstan	17	6	1.3	0.2	19	10	2.3	64	58	2670	13	70	4	21	5.93	40	70
Kenya	31.9	56	3.8	4.1	32	11	4.7	54	25	570	8	37	30	78	0.12	98	62
Korea, North	24.5	203	2.2	1.7	22	5	2.2	71	61	120	17	0	61	34	4.21	75	41
Korea, South	46.1	466	1.8	1.1	16	6	1.8	74	75	98.7	21	1	65	14	3.77	3013	2788
Kyrgyzstan	4.7	24	2	0.8	26	9	3.3	64	40	191	7	44	4	31	0.76	71	76
Laos	5.2	23	1.7	3.3	41	13	6.5	53	22	231	4	3	54	77	0.04	40	20
Latvia	2.5	38	0.7	-1.3	12	15	1.3	67	72	64.1	28	13	46	14	2.3	697	520
Lebanon	3.2	313	0.8	2.5	28	6	2.8	70	87	10.2	30	1	8	4	1.83	2058	197
Lesotho	2.1	69	2.3	2.7	32	14	4.6	52	23	30.4	11	66	0	39	...	520	58
Liberia	3	30	3.1	2.9	42	12	6.5	59	45	96.8	4	21	48	70	0.06	116	197
Libya	5.5	3	4.4	2.8	44	7	6.1	65	86	1760	1	8	0	6	3.34	1240	2596
Lithuania	3.7	57	0.9	-0.1	14	13	1.5	68	71	65.2	47	7	31	18	3.04	696	545
Luxembourg	0.4	163.5	0.7	1.9	13	8	1.7	79	88	2.6	...	...	...	...	12.82	20295	16090
Macedonia	2.2	86	1.6	0.9	13	9	2.2	72	60	24.9	26	25	39	17	1.9	600	500
Madagascar	15.5	27	2.7	4.8	42	14	5.8	53	27	582	5	41	40	76	0.04	36	25
Malawi	10.3	109	3.2	3.1	41	25	6.6	35	13	94.1	18	20	39	86	0.04	49	41
Malaysia	20.9	64	2.4	2.2	26	5	3.4	70	52	329	23	1	68	23	2.29	3751	3563
Mali	11	9	2.3	4.4	51	19	6.8	47	27	1220	2	25	10	84	0.02	70	42
Malta	0.4	1172	1.1	0.9	15	7	1.9	79	88	0.32	41	0	0	2	1.97	7951	5170
Mauritania	2.4	2	2.4	2.5	47	15	5.2	50	54	1025	0	38	4	49	0.61	284	223
Mauritius	1.2	569	1.6	1.1	19	7	2.2	71	44	2.03	52	3	22	12	0.7	1797	1410
Mexico	97.4	51	2.9	1.8	26	5	3	74	75	1909	13	39	26	24	2.03	508	520
Moldova	4.5	132	1.1	0.3	17	12	2	65	50	33.7	66	13	13	31	1.55	185	162
Mongolia	2.5	2	2.8	1.9	25	8	3.4	61	60	1567	1	75	9	29	1.55	158	208
Morocco	28.1	63	2.4	1.6	27	6	3.4	70	52	446	21	47	20	41	0.47	315	172
Mozambique	19.1	24	2.6	4.3	44	18	6.2	45	32	784	4	56	22	81	0.03	45	10
Namibia	1.7	2	2.5	2	37	8	5	65	34	823	1	46	15	45	...	916	881
Nepal	22.1	162	2.6	2.1	37	12	5.3	54	13	137	17	15	42	93	0.03	64	16
Netherlands	15.9	469	0.8	0.9	12	9	1.6	78	89	33.9	28	31	10	4	7.22	11419	12680
New Zealand	3.7	14	1	1.1	15	8	2.1	77	86	268	14	50	28	10	5.47	3951	3882
Nicaragua	4.6	39	3	2.5	33	6	4.1	66	63	119	10	45	26	23	0.36	212	115
Niger	9.7	8	3	3.3	54	24	7.4	41	16	1267	3	8	2	89	0.06	37	27
Nigeria	118	130	2.2	3.1	43	12	5.5	55	38	911	36	44	12	38	0.21	71	94
Norway	4.4	14	0.5	0.8	11	11	1.9	78	73	307	3	0	27	5	7.44	7563	9632
Oman	2.4	11	4.2	6.9	38	4	7	71	13	212	0	5	0	42	5.41	1994	2682
Pakistan	136	176	2.6	2.8	35	11	5.2	59	34	771	28	6	5	48	0.33	88	62
Panama	2.7	37	2.5	1.7	22	5	2.7	74	55	74.4	9	20	44	22	1.2	955	238
Papua New Guinea	4.4	10	2.5	1.8	33	10	4.8	58	16	453	1	0	93	78	0.29	357	651
Paraguay	5.2	13	3	2.8	30	4	4	74	52	397	6	55	32	35	0.38	669	196
Peru	24.5	19	2.7	1.3	24	6	3.1	70	72	1280	3	21	66	33	0.46	392	237
Philippines	73.5	247	2.6	2.4	29	7	3.7	66	52	298	31	4	46	42	0.43	403	249
Poland	38.8	127	0.9	0.1	12	10	1.6	72	64	304	48	13	29	26	3.51	753	593
Portugal	10.1	110	0.8	-0.3	11	10	1.4	76	36	92	32	11	36	14	2.13	3261	2280
Puerto Rico	3.8	432	1.7	1.4	18	8	2.1	75	77	8.86	9	26	16	3	3.07	4300	5900
Romania	22.6	98	0.9	-0.3	10	12	1.4	70	55	230	43	21	29	19	2.54	453	349
Russia	147.8	9	0.6	0	11	16	1.4	64	75	16996	8	5	45	12	6	261	427
Rwanda	7	284	3.3	-0.4	39	21	6.2	39	6	24.7	47	28	10	91	0.03	46	10
Saudi Arabia	19.1	9	5	4.4	38	5	6.2	70	79	2150	2	56	1	14	5.77	1539	2335
Senegal	8.9	46	2.9	2.8	45	11	5.7	57	42	193	12	30	39	74	0.16	156	103
Sierra Leone	4.6	64	2.1	1.5	47	18	6.5	48	35	71.6	8	31	28	67	0.05	30	6
Singapore	3.2	5246	1	2.5	16	5	1.7	79	100	0.61	2	0	5	1	9.67	41639	39553
Slovak Rep.	5.4	112	1.7	0.3	13	9	1.5	73	58	48.1	34	17	41	12	4.07	1250	1025
Slovenia	2	99	0.9	0.2	8	10	1.3	75	50	20.3	14	25	54	5	3.11	4793	4199
Somalia	9.9	16	3.8	1.9	44	13	7	56	27	627	2	69	26	74	0.05	26	5
South Africa	42.3	35	2.3	1.6	27	12	3.9	56	57	1221	11	67	7	11	2.73	718	653
Spain	39.3	79	1.1	0	10	9	1.2	79	77	499	40	21	32	9	3.01	2890	2334
Sri Lanka	18.7	289	1.7	1.2	18	6	2.3	73	22	64.6	29	7	32	47	0.16	290	212
Sudan	31	13	3	3	41	11	4.8	56	35	2376	5	46	18	68	0.06	44	21

Wealth							Social Indicators								Aid	
GNP 1995	GNP per capita 1995	Real GDP per capita 1995	Average Annual growth of Real GNP per capita 1985-95	GDP share Agriculture 1995	GDP share Industry 1995	GDP share services 1995	HDI Human Development Index 1994	Food Intake	Population per doctor 1993	% of GNP spent on health 1990-95	% of GNP spent on education 1993-94	%o GNP spent on military 1995	Adult Illiteracy Female	Adult Illiteracy Male	Aid given (*) and received per capita 1994	
million US $	US $	US $	%	%	%	%		calories per day	persons	%	%	%	%	%	US $	
52765	14710	15680	5.2	9	37	54	0.929	3847	632	7.9	6.4	1.2	0	0	*35	Ireland
37875	15920	16490	2.5	3	32	65	0.913	3050	220	4.1	6	9.2	7	3	226	Israel
38085	19020	19870	1.7	3	31	66	0.921	3561	207	8.3	5.2	1.8	4	2	*37	Italy
9548	660	1580	-4.3	31	20	49	0.368	2491	11739	3.4	...	1	70	50	87	Ivory Coast
3803	1510	3540	3.7	9	38	53	0.736	2607	6420	5.4	4.7	0.6	11	19	43	Jamaica
63587	39640	22110	2.9	2	38	60	0.94	2903	608	7	4.7	1.1	0	0	*106	Japan
6354	1510	4060	-2.8	8	27	65	0.73	3022	554	7.9	3.8	6.7	21	7	127	Jordan
22143	1330	3010	-8.6	12	30	58	0.709	...	254	2.2	5.4	3	4	1	2	Kazakstan
7583	280	1380	0.1	29	17	54	0.463	2075	21970	1.9	6.8	2.3	30	14	42	Kenya
24000	1000	4000	-8	...	...	...	0.765	2833	370	...	...	25.2	5	5	1	Korea, North
35137	9700	11450	7.6	7	43	50	0.89	3285	951	5.4	4.5	3.4	2	2	1	Korea, South
3158	700	1800	-6.9	44	24	32	0.635	...	303	3.5	6.8	3.5	4	1	19	Kyrgyzstan
1694	350	2500	2.7	52	18	30	0.459	2259	4446	2.6	2.3	4.2	56	31	66	Laos
5708	2270	3370	-6.6	9	31	60	0.711	...	278	3.7	6.5	3.2	0	0	14	Latvia
10673	2660	4800	2.7	7	24	69	0.794	3317	537	5.3	2	5.3	10	5	48	Lebanon
1519	770	1780	1.5	10	56	34	0.457	2201	24095	3.5	4.8	5.5	38	19	57	Lesotho
2300	850	1000	1.5	...	...	...	...	1640	25000	8.2	...	4.8	78	46	23	Liberia
38000	7000	6000	1	8	48	44	0.801	3308	957	...	9.6	5.5	37	12	1	Libya
7070	1900	4120	-11.7	11	36	53	0.762	...	235	4.8	4.5	2.4	2	1	14	Lithuania
16876	41210	37930	1	1	33	66	0.899	...	460	6.3	3.1	0.9	0	0	*148	Luxembourg
1813	860	4000	-15	19	44	37	0.748	...	427	7.7	5.6	...	16	6	...	Macedonia
3178	230	640	-2	34	13	53	0.35	2135	8385	1	1.9	1.1	27	12	23	Madagascar
1623	170	750	-0.7	42	27	31	0.32	1825	44205	2.3	3.4	1.2	58	28	40	Malawi
78321	3890	9020	5.7	13	43	44	0.832	2888	2441	1.4	5.3	4.5	22	11	6	Malaysia
2410	250	550	0.6	46	17	37	0.229	2278	18376	1.3	2.1	2.4	77	61	57	Mali
4070	11000	13000	5.1	3	28	69	0.887	3486	410	12.1	5.1	1.1	4	4	...	Malta
1049	460	1540	0.5	27	30	43	0.355	2685	15772	1.5	...	1.9	74	50	99	Mauritania
3815	3380	13210	5.7	9	33	58	0.831	...	1165	2.2	3.7	0.5	21	13	21	Mauritius
04596	3320	6400	0.1	8	26	66	0.853	3146	615	5.3	5.8	0.9	13	8	4	Mexico
3996	920	1600	-8.2	50	28	22	0.612	...	250	5.1	5.5	3.7	6	1	5	Moldova
767	310	1950	-3.8	21	46	33	0.661	1899	371	4.7	5.2	2.4	23	11	88	Mongolia
29545	1110	3340	0.8	14	33	53	0.566	2984	4665	3.4	5.4	4.3	69	43	19	Morocco
1353	80	810	3.6	33	21	46	0.281	1680	36225	4.6	6.2	3.7	77	42	66	Mozambique
3098	2000	4150	2.8	14	29	57	0.57	2134	4328	7.6	8.7	2.7	26	22	125	Namibia
4391	200	1170	2.4	42	22	36	0.347	1957	13634	5	2.9	1	86	59	21	Nepal
71039	24000	19950	1.8	3	27	70	0.94	3222	399	8.8	5.5	2.2	0	0	*172	Netherlands
51655	14340	16360	0.6	7	25	68	0.937	3669	518	7.5	7.3	1.7	1	1	*31	New Zealand
1659	380	2000	-5.8	33	20	47	0.53	2293	2039	7.8	3.8	1.8	33	35	155	Nicaragua
1961	220	750	-2.1	39	18	43	0.206	2257	53986	2.2	3.1	0.9	93	79	30	Niger
28411	260	1220	1.2	43	27	30	0.393	2124	5208	2.7	1.3	2.9	53	33	2	Nigeria
36077	31250	21940	1.6	3	36	61	0.943	3244	308	7.3	9.2	2.6	0	0	*255	Norway
10578	4820	8140	0.3	3	48	49	0.718	...	1131	2.5	4.5	15.1	76	42	29	Oman
59991	460	2230	1.2	26	24	50	0.445	2315	1923	0.8	2.7	6.5	76	50	6	Pakistan
7235	2750	5980	-0.4	11	18	71	0.864	2242	562	7.5	5.2	1.3	10	9	19	Panama
4976	1160	2420	2.1	26	38	36	0.525	2613	12754	2.8	...	1.3	37	19	88	Papua New Guinea
8158	1690	3650	1.1	24	22	54	0.706	2670	1231	4.3	2.9	1.4	9	7	30	Paraguay
55019	2310	3770	-1.6	7	38	55	0.717	1882	939	4.9	1.5	1.6	17	6	18	Peru
71865	1050	2850	1.5	22	32	46	0.672	2257	8273	2.4	2.4	1.6	6	5	109	Philippines
07829	2790	5400	-0.4	6	39	55	0.834	3301	451	4.6	5.5	2.5	2	1	40	Poland
96689	9740	12670	3.7	6	40	54	0.89	3634	353	7.6	5.4	2.9	13	13	*27	Portugal
27750	7500	7000	2.1	1	42	57	...	...	350	...	...	...	10	10	...	Puerto Rico
33488	1480	4360	-4	21	49	30	0.748	3051	538	3.3	3.1	3.1	5	1	3	Romania
31948	2240	4480	-5.1	7	38	55	0.792	...	222	4.8	4.4	7.4	3	0	12	Russia
1128	180	540	-5	37	17	46	0.187	1821	24967	1.9	3.8	4.4	48	30	92	Rwanda
33540	7040	9500	-1.9	6	51	43	0.774	2735	749	2.2	6.4	10.6	50	29	1	Saudi Arabia
5070	600	1780	-1.2	20	18	62	0.326	2262	18192	1.6	4.2	1.9	77	57	82	Senegal
762	180	580	-3.4	42	27	31	0.176	1694	11000	1.6	1.4	5.7	82	55	45	Sierra Leone
79831	26730	22770	6.2	0	36	64	0.9	...	714	3.5	3.3	5.9	14	4	6	Singapore
15848	2950	3610	-2.6	6	33	61	0.873	...	287	6.3	4.9	2.8	0	0	6	Slovak Rep.
16328	8200	10400	-1	5	39	56	0.886	...	500	7.9	6.2	1.5	0	0	...	Slovenia
4625	500	1000	-2.3	65	9	26	...	1499	13300	1.5	0.4	0.9	52	39	61	Somalia
30918	3160	5030	-1	5	31	64	0.716	2695	1500	7.9	7.1	2.9	18	18	10	South Africa
32347	13580	14520	2.6	3	31	66	0.934	3708	261	7.4	4.7	1.5	6	2	*31	Spain
12616	700	3250	2.7	23	25	52	0.711	2273	6843	1.9	3.2	4.9	13	7	31	Sri Lanka
20000	750	1050	0.6	36	18	46	0.333	2202	10000	0.3	...	4.3	65	42	8	Sudan

	Population									Land and Agriculture					Energy	Trade	
	Population Total 1997	Population Density 1997	Average Annual Change 1970-80	Average Annual Change 1990-97	Birth Rate 1997	Death Rate 1997	Fertility Rate 1997	Life Expectancy Average 1997	Urban Population 1995	Land Area	Arable and Permanent Crops	Permanent grassland	Forest	Agriculture Population 1995	Consumption per capita 1994	Imports per capita 1995	Exports per capita 1995
	millions	persons per km²	%	%	births per thousand population	deaths per thousand population	children	years	%	thousand km²	% of land area	% of land area	% of land area	% of economically active pop.	tonnes of coal	US $	US $
Surinam	0.5	3	-0.6	1.5	24	6	2.6	70	52	156	0	0	96	20	2.01	1565	873
Swaziland	1	55	3	3.1	43	10	4.6	58	29	17.2	11	62	7	34	...	1090	855
Sweden	8.9	22	0.3	0.7	11	11	1.7	78	84	412	7	1	68	4	6.79	7299	9051
Switzerland	7.1	180	0.2	1	11	10	1.5	78	61	39.6	11	29	32	5	4.5	10938	11088
Syria	15.3	83	3.5	2.9	39	6	4.8	67	52	184	30	45	3	33	1.28	325	280
Taiwan	21.7	603	2	0.9	15	6	1.8	76	76	36	26	11	52	19	2.5	4868	5238
Tajikistan	6	42	3	1.8	34	8	4.2	65	32	143	6	25	4	38	0.58	93	84
Tanzania	31.2	35	3.4	2.8	41	20	5.8	42	24	884	4	40	38	83	0.04	55	23
Thailand	60.8	119	2.7	0.9	17	7	1.8	69	19	511	41	2	26	60	1.07	1236	946
Togo	4.5	82	2.6	3.4	46	10	6.4	58	31	54.4	45	4	17	62	0.08	94	51
Trinidad & Tobago	1.3	253	1.1	0.2	16	7	2.1	70	70	5.13	24	2	46	9	7.53	1329	1904
Tunisia	9.2	59	2.2	1.9	24	5	2.9	73	57	155	32	20	4	24	0.75	886	614
Turkey	63.5	83	2.3	1.1	22	5	2.7	72	65	770	36	16	26	51	1.16	579	350
Turkmenistan	4.8	10	2.7	3.9	29	9	3.8	62	47	488	3	64	9	36	3.68	250	533
Uganda	20.8	104	3	2.4	45	21	6.7	40	12	200	34	9	32	83	0.03	50	22
Ukraine	51.5	85	0.6	-0.1	12	15	1.5	67	69	604	59	13	18	18	4.39	192	187
United Kingdom	58.6	243	0.1	0.3	13	11	1.7	77	90	242	25	46	10	2	5.33	4527	4130
United States	268	28	1.1	1	15	9	2.1	76	77	9573	20	25	30	3	11.39	2929	2222
Uruguay	3.3	19	0.4	0.7	17	9	2.2	75	90	175	7	77	5	14	0.78	899	660
Uzbekistan	23.8	56	2.9	2.1	29	8	3.7	65	42	425	11	50	3	34	2.94	111	138
Venezuela	22.5	26	3.5	1.9	24	5	3.1	72	92	882	4	20	34	11	3.75	553	854
Vietnam	77.1	237	2.3	2.1	22	7	3.1	67	20	325	21	1	30	69	0.16	30	30
Yemen	16.5	31	1.9	5.6	45	9	7.4	60	34	528	3	30	4	57	0.33	165	74
Yugoslavia	10.5	103	1	0.3	14	10	1.9	72	54	102	40	21	26	20	1.22	533	452
Zambia	9.5	13	3.2	2.4	44	24	5.7	45	45	743	7	40	43	74	0.19	12	94
Zimbabwe	12.1	31	3.1	3.7	32	19	3.8	60	32	387	7	44	23	67	0.7	231	183

	Land area thousand sq km	Population 1997 thousands		Land area thousand sq km	Population 1997 thousands		Land area thousand sq km	Population thousands
American Samoa	0.2	62	French Polynesia	3.66	226	Pitcairn I.	0.05	0.0
Andorra	0.45	75	Gaza Strip	0.36	900	Qatar	11	6
Anguilla	0.1	10	Gibraltar	0.01	28	Réunion	2.5	6
Antigua & Barbuda	0.44	66	Greenland	342	57	St Kitts-Nevis	0.36	
Aruba	0.19	70	Grenada	0.34	99	St Helena	0.3	
Ascension I.	0.09	1.1	Guadeloupe	1.69	440	St Lucia	0.61	
Bahrain	0.68	605	Guam	0.55	161	St Pierre & Miquelon	0.23	
Belize	22.8	228	Kiribati	0.73	85	St Vincent & the Grenadines	0.39	1
Bermuda	0.05	65	Kuwait	17.8	2050	San Marino	0.06	
Bhutan	47	1790	Liechtenstein	0.16	32	São Tomé & Principe	0.96	1
British Virgin Is.	0.15	13	Macau	0.02	450	Seychelles	0.45	
Brunei	5.27	300	Maldives	0.3	275	Solomon Is.	28	4
Cape Verde Is.	4.03	410	Marshall Is.	0.18	60	Svalbard	63	2
Cayman Is.	0.26	35	Martinique	1.06	405	Tokelau	0.01	
Cocos Is.	0.01	1	Mayotte	0.37	105	Tonga	0.72	
Comoros	2.23	630	Micronesia	0.7	127	Turks & Caicos Is.	0.43	
Cook Is.	0.23	20	Monaco	0.002	33	Tuvalu	0.03	
Djibouti	23.2	650	Montserrat	0.1	12	United Arab Emirates	83.6	24
Dominica	0.75	78	Nauru	0.02	53	US Virgin Is.	0.34	1
Equatorial Guinea	28.1	420	Netherlands Antilles	0.8	12	Vanuatu	12.2	1
Eritrea	101	3500	New Caledonia	18.3	210	Vatican City	0.0004	
Falkland Is.	12.2	2	Niue	0.26	192	Wallis & Futuna Is.	0.2	
Faroe Is.	1.4	45	Norfolk I.	0.04	2	West Bank	5.9	14
Fiji	18.3	800	Northern Marianas	0.48	2	Western Sahara	267	2
French Guiana	88.2	155	Palau	0.49	17	Western Samoa	2.83	1

Wealth							Social Indicators								Aid	
GNP 1995	GNP per capita 1995	Real GDP per capita 1995	Average Annual growth of Real GNP per capita 1985-95	GDP share Agriculture 1995	GDP share Industry 1995	GDP share services 1995	HDI Human Development Index 1994	Food Intake	Population per doctor 1993	% of GNP spent on health 1990-95	% of GNP spent on education 1993-94	%o GNP spent on military 1995	Adult Illiteracy Female %	Adult Illiteracy Male %	given (*) and received per capita 1994	
million US $	US $	US $	%	%	%	%		calories per day	persons	%	%	%	Female %	Male %	US $	
360	880	2250	0.7	22	23	55	0.792	2547	1200	2.9	3.6	3.9	9	5	183	Surinam
1051	1170	2880	0.6	10	25	65	0.582	2706	9250	7.2	6.8	...	24	22	59	Swaziland
09720	23750	18540	-0.1	2	32	66	0.936	2972	394	7.7	8.4	2.9	0	0	*189	Sweden
36014	40630	25860	0.2	3	32	65	0.93	3379	580	9.6	5.6	1.9	0	0	*135	Switzerland
15780	1120	5320	1	18	43	39	0.755	3175	1159	2.1	4.2	6.8	44	14	25	Syria
52000	12000	13000	7	3	42	55	...	3048	800	4.3		4.8	10	3	...	Taiwan
1976	340	920	-13	27	45	28	0.58	...	424	6.4	9.5	6.9	3	1	5	Tajikistan
3703	120	640	0.9	58	17	25	0.357	2018	22000	2.8	5	2.7	43	21	30	Tanzania
59630	2740	7540	8.4	11	40	49	0.833	2432	4416	5.3	3.8	2.5	8	4	15	Thailand
1266	310	1130	-2.8	38	21	41	0.365	2242	11385	1.7	6.1	2.5	63	33	47	Togo
4851	3770	8610	-1.6	3	42	55	0.88	2585	1520	3.9	4.5	1.3	3	1	20	Trinidad & Tobago
16369	1820	5000	1.8	12	29	59	0.748	3330	1549	5.9	6.3	2	45	21	8	Tunisia
69452	2780	5580	2.2	16	31	53	0.772	3429	976	4.2	3.3	3.6	28	8	5	Turkey
4125	920	3500	-9.6	31	31	38	0.723	...	306	2.8	7.9	1.9	3	1	3	Turkmenistan
4668	240	1470	2.8	50	14	36	0.328	2159	22399	3.9	1.9	2.6	50	26	43	Uganda
84084	1630	2400	-9.2	18	42	40	0.689	...	227	5.4	8.2	3	3	0	5	Ukraine
94734	18700	19260	1.4	2	32	66	0.931	3317	300	6.9	5.4	3.1	0	0	*53	United Kingdom
00007	26980	26980	1.4	2	26	72	0.942	3732	421	14.3	5.5	3.8	5	4	*33	United States
16458	5170	6630	3.3	9	26	65	0.883	2750	500	8.5	2.5	2.6	2	3	26	Uruguay
21979	970	2370	-3.9	33	34	33	0.662	...	282	3.5	11	3.6	4	1	1	Uzbekistan
65382	3020	7900	0.5	5	38	57	0.861	2618	633	7.1	5.1	1.1	10	8	4	Venezuela
17634	240	1200	4.2	28	30	42	0.557	2250	2279	5.2	...	4.3	9	4	8	Vietnam
4044	260	850	3.1	22	27	51	0.361	2203	4498	2.6	4.6	3.9	74	47	13	Yemen
14750	1400	4000	1.8	26	36	38	...	...	232	5.1	...	...	11	2	...	Yugoslavia
3605	400	930	-1	22	40	38	0.369	1931	10917	3.3	2.6	1.9	29	14	221	Zambia
5933	540	2030	-0.6	15	36	49	0.513	1985	7384	2.1	8.3	4.2	20	10	45	Zimbabwe

ny figures for Luxembourg are included in those Belgium.

energy, the figures for South Africa include those Botswana, Lesotho, Swaziland and Namibia.

e sign ... means that figures are not available.

pulation Total. This is an estimate for the mid-r, 1997.

pulation Density. This is the total population ided by the land area, both quoted in the table.

pulation Change. This shows the average ual percentage change for the two periods, 70-80 and 1990-97.

rth and Death Rates and Life Expectancy. ese are estimates from the US Census Bureau. e Birth and Death rates are the number of those currences per year, per thousand population. Life pectancy is the number of years that a child born ay can expect to live if the levels of mortality of day last throughout its life. The figure is the erage of that for men and women.

rtility Rate. This is the average number of ldren born to a woman in her lifetime.

ban Population. This is the percentage of the al population living in urban areas. The definition urban is that of the individual nations and often ludes quite small towns.

Land Area. This is the total area of the country less the area covered by major lakes and rivers.

Arable Land and Permanent Crops. This excludes fallow land but includes temporary pasture.

Forest and Woodland. This includes natural and planted woodland and land recently cleared of timber which will be replanted.

Agricultural Population. This is the percentage of the economically active population working in agriculture. It includes those working in forestry, hunting and fishing.

Energy. All forms of energy have been expressed in an approximate equivalent of tonnes of coal per person.

Trade. The trade figures are for 1994 or 1995. In a few cases the figure is older than this but is the latest available. The total Import and Export figures have been divided by the population to give a figure in US $ per capita.

Gross National Product (GNP). This figure is an estimate of the value of a country's production and the average production per person for 1995, in US $. The GNP measures the value of goods and services produced in a country, plus the balance, positive or negative, of income from abroad, for example, from investments, interest on capital, money returned from workers abroad, etc. The Gross Domestic Product (GDP), is the GNP less the foreign balances. The adjoining three columns show the percentage contribution to the GDP made by the

agricultural, mining and manufacturing and service sectors of the economy. The average annual rate of change is for the GNP per capita in PPP $ during the period 1985-95

Real GDP per capita. Using official exchange rates to convert national currencies into US $ makes no attempt to reflect the varying domestic purchasing powers of the local currency. The UN has made these estimates of Real GDP taking into account these local purchasing values and they are called Purchasing Power Parity $.

Human Development Index. This is a calculation made by the UN Development Programme, using 1994 data and takes into account not only national income, but also life expectancy, adult literacy and the years in education. It is a measure of national human progress. The wealthy developed countries have an index approaching 1, and the figures range down to some of the poorer with an index of less than 0.1.

Food Intake. The figures are the average intake per person in calories per day. They are for 1992 and are the latest estimates that are available.

Adult Illiteracy. This is the percentage of the male and female population aged 15 and over who cannot read or write a simple sentence.

Aid. The bulk of the table is concerned with aid received but aid given is shown by an asterisk.

To convert square kilometres to square miles multiply by 0.39.

AZIMUTHAL OR ZENITHAL PROJECTIONS

These are constructed by the projection of part of the graticule from the globe onto a plane tangential to any single point on it. This plane may be tangential to the equator (equatorial case), the poles (polar case) or any other point (oblique case). Any straight line drawn from the point at which the plane touches the globe is the shortest distance from that point and is known as a great circle. In its Gnomonic construction any straight line on the map is a great circle, but there is great exaggeration towards the edges and this reduces its general uses. There are five different ways of transferring the graticule onto the plane and these are shown below. The diagrams below also show how the graticules vary, using the polar case as the example.

MAP PROJECTIONS

A map projection is the systematic depiction of the imaginary grid of lines of latitude and longitude from a globe onto a flat surface. The grid of lines is called the graticule and it can be constructed either by graphical means or by mathematical formulae to form the basis of a map. As a globe is three dimensional it is not possible to depict its surface on a flat map without some form of distortion. Preservation of one of the basic properties listed below can only be secured at the expense of the others and the choice of projection is often a compromise solution.

Correct Area
In these projections the areas from the globe are to scale on the map. This is particularly useful in the mapping of densities and distributions. Projections with this property are termed Equal Area, Equivalent or Homolographic.

Correct Distance
In these projections the scale is correct along the meridians, or in the case of the Azimuthal Equidistant scale is true along any line drawn from the centre of the projection. They are called Equidistant.

Correct Shape
This property can only be true within small areas as it is achieved only by having a uniform scale distortion along both x and y axes of the projection. The projections are called Conformal or Orthomorphic.

Map projections can be divided into three broad categories - azimuthal, conic and cylindrical. Cartographers use different projections from these categories depending on the map scale, the size of the area to be mapped, and what they want the map to show.

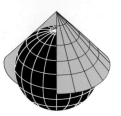

CONICAL PROJECTIONS

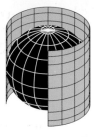

CYLINDRICAL AND OTHER WORLD PROJECTIONS

| Equidistant | Equal-Area | Orthographic | Gnomonic | Stereographic (conformal) |

These use the projection of the graticule from the globe onto a cone which is tangential to a line of latitude (termed the standard parallel). This line is always an arc and scale is always true along it. Because of its method of construction it is used mainly for depicting the temperate latitudes around the standard parallel i.e. where there is least distortion. To reduce the distortion and include a larger range of latitudes, the projection may be constructed with the cone bisecting the surface of the globe so that there are two standard parallels each of which is true to scale. The distortion is thus spread more evenly between the two chosen parallels.

This group of projections are those which permit the whole of the Earth's surface to be depicted on one map. They are a very large group of projections and the following are only a few of them. Cylindrical projections are constructed by the projection of the graticule from the globe onto a cylinder tangential to the globe. Although cylindrical projections can depict all the main land masses, there is considerable distortion of shape and area towards the poles. One cylindrical projection, Mercator overcomes this shortcoming by possesing the unique navigational property that any straight line drawn on it is a line of constant bearing (loxodrome). It is used for maps and charts between 15° either side of the equator. Beyond this enlargement of area is a serious drawback, although it is used for navigational charts at all latitudes.

Polar Case
The polar case is the simplest to construct and the diagram on the right shows the differing effects of all five methods of construction comparing their coverage, distortion etc., using North America as the example.

Simple Conical with one standard parallel

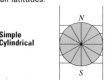

| Simple Cylindrical | | Cylindrical with two standard parallels |

Bonne
This is a modification of the simple conic whereby the true scale along the meridians is sacrificed to enable the accurate representation of areas. However scale is true along each parallel but shapes are distorted at the edges.

Mercator

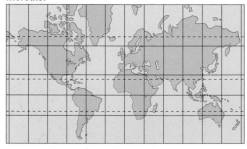

Oblique Case
The plane touches the globe at any point between the equator and poles. The oblique orthographic uses the distortion in azimuthal projections away from the centre to give a graphic depiction of the earth as seen from any desired point in space.

Albers Conical Equal Area
This projection uses two standard parallels. The selection of these relative to the land area to be mapped is very important. It is equal area and is especially useful for large land masses oriented East-West, for example the U.S.A.

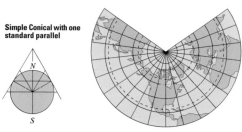

Eckert IV (pseudocylindrical equal area)

Equatorial Case
The example shown here is Lambert's Equivalent Azimuthal. It is the only projection which is both equal area and where bearing is true from the centre.

Hammer (polyconic equal area)

SATELLITE IMAGERY AND REMOTE SENSING

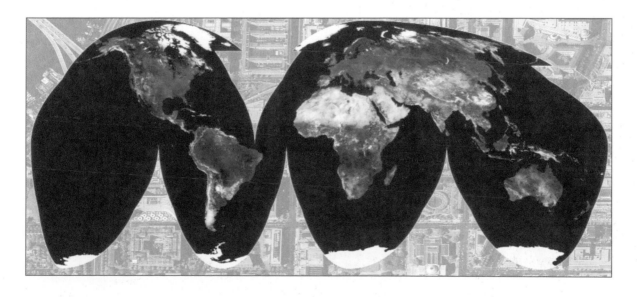

All satellite images in this section courtesy of NPA Group Limited, Edenbridge, Kent (www.satmaps.com)
Philip's would like to acknowledge the valuable assistance of Richard Chiles and the staff at NPA in the preparation of this section.

The first satellite to monitor our environment systematically was launched as long ago as April 1961. It was called TIROS-1 and was designed specifically to record atmospheric change. The first of the generation of Earth resources satellites was Landsat-1, launched in July 1972.

The succeeding two or three decades have seen a revolution in our ability to survey and map our global environment. Digital sensors mounted on satellites now scan vast areas of the Earth's surface day and night. They collect and relay back to Earth huge volumes of geographical data which is processed and stored by computers.

Satellite Imagery and Remote Sensing

Continuous development and refinement, and freedom from national access restrictions, have meant that sensors on these satellite platforms are increasingly replacing surface and airborne data-gathering techniques. Twenty-four hours a day, satellites are scanning and measuring the Earth's surface and atmosphere, adding to an ever-expanding range of geographic and geophysical data available to help us identify and manage the problems of our human and physical environments. Remote sensing is the science of extracting information from such images.

Satellite Orbits

Most Earth-observation satellites (such as the Landsat, SPOT and IRS series) are in a near-polar, Sun-synchronous orbit (*see diagram opposite*). At altitudes of around 700–900 km the satellites revolve around the Earth approximately every 100 minutes and on each orbit cross a particular line of latitude at the same local (solar) time. This ensures that the satellite can obtain coverage of most of the globe, replicating the coverage typically within 2–3 weeks. In more recent satellites, sensors can be pointed sideways from the orbital path, and 'revisit' times with high-resolution frames can thus be reduced to a few days.

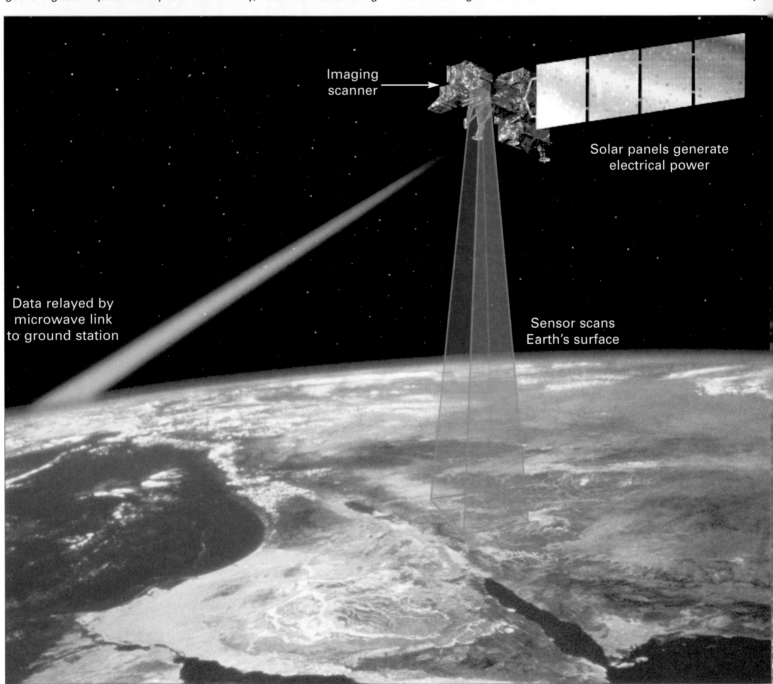

Imaging scanner

Solar panels generate electrical power

Data relayed by microwave link to ground station

Sensor scans Earth's surface

Landsat-7

This is the latest addition to the Landsat Earth-observation satellite programme, orbiting at 705 km above the Earth. With onboard recorders, the satellite can store data until it passes within range of a ground station. Basic geometric and radiometric corrections are then applied before distribution of the imagery to users.

Exceptions to these Sun-synchronous orbits include the geostationary meteorological satellites, such as Meteosat. These have a 36,000 km high orbit and rotate around the Earth every 24 hours, thus remaining above the same point on the equator. These satellites acquire frequent images showing cloud and atmospheric moisture movements for almost a full hemisphere.

In addition, there is the Global Positioning System (GPS) satellite 'constellation', which orbits at a height of 20,200 km, consisting of 24 satellites. These circle the Earth in six different orbital planes, enabling us to fix our position on the Earth's surface to an accuracy of a few centimetres. Although developed for military use, this system is now available to individuals through hand-held receivers and in-car navigation systems. The other principal commercial uses are for surveying and air and sea navigation.

Digital Sensors

Early satellite designs involved images being exposed to photographic film and returned to Earth by capsule for processing, a technique still sometimes used today. However, even the first commercial satellite imagery, from Landsat-1, used digital imaging sensors and transmitted the data back to ground stations (*see diagram opposite*).

Passive, or optical, sensors record the radiation reflected from the Earth for specific wavebands. Active sensors transmit their own microwave radiation, which is reflected from the Earth's surface back to the satellite and recorded. The SAR (synthetic aperture radar) Radarsat images on page 118 are examples of the latter.

Whichever scanning method is used, each satellite records image data of constant width but potentially several thousand kilometres in length. Once the data has been received on Earth, it is usually split into approximately square sections or 'scenes' for distribution.

Spectral Resolution, Wavebands and False-Colour Composites

Satellites can record data from many sections of the electromagnetic spectrum (wavebands) simultaneously. Since we can only see images made from the three primary colours (red, green and blue), a selection of any three wavebands needs to be made in order to form a picture that will enable visual interpretation of the scene to be made. When any combination other than the visible bands are used, such as near or middle infrared, the resulting image is termed a 'false-colour composite'. An example of this is shown on page 109.

The selection of these wavebands depends on the purpose of the final image – geology, hydrology, agronomy and environmental

GEOGRAPHIC INFORMATION SYSTEMS

A Geographic Information System (GIS) enables any available geospatial data to be compiled, presented and analysed using specialized computer software.

Many aspects of our lives now benefit from the use of GIS – from the management and maintenance of the networks of pipelines and cables that supply our homes, to the exploitation or protection of the natural resources that we use. Much of this is at a regional or national scale and the data collected from satellites form an important part of our interpretation and understanding of the world around us.

GIS systems are used for many aspects of central planning and modern life, such as defence, land use, reclamation, telecommunications and the deployment of emergency services. Commercial companies can use demographic and infrastructure data within a GIS to plan marketing strategies, identifying where their services would be most needed, and thus decide where best to locate their businesses. Insurance companies use GIS to determine premiums based on population distribution, crime figures and the likelihood of natural disasters, such as flooding or subsidence.

Whatever the application, all the geographically related information that is available can be input and prepared in a GIS, so that a user can display the specific information of interest, or combine data to produce further information which might answer or help resolve a specific problem. From analysis of the data that has been acquired, it is often possible to use a GIS to generate a 'model' of possible future situations and to see what impact might result from decisions and actions taken. A GIS can also monitor change over time, to aid the observation and interpretation of long-term change.

A GIS can utilize a satellite image to extract useful information and map large areas, which would otherwise take many man-years of labour to achieve on the ground. For industrial applications, including hydrocarbon and mineral exploration, forestry, agriculture, environmental monitoring and urban development, such dramatic and beneficial increases in efficiency have made it possible to evaluate and undertake projects and studies in parts of the world that were previously considered inaccessible, and on a scale that would not have been possible before.

requirements each have their own optimum waveband combinations. The following pages give an indication of the variety and detail provided by satellite imagery.

SELECTED REMOTE SENSING SATELLITES			
Year Launched	Satellite	Country	Repeat Cycle
Passive Sensors (Optical)			
1972	Landsat-1 MSS	USA	18 days
1975	Landsat-2 MSS	USA	18 days
1978	Landsat-3 MSS	USA	18 days
1978	NOAA AVHRR	USA	12 hours
1981	Cosmos TK-350	Russia	varied
1982	Landsat-4 TM	USA	16 days
1984	Landsat-5 TM	USA	16 days
1986	SPOT-1	France	26 days
1988	IRS-1A	India	22 days
1988	SPOT-2	France	26 days
1989	Cosmos KVR-1000	Russia	varied
1991	IRS-1B	India	22 days
1992	SPOT-3	France	26 days
1995	IRS-1C	India	24 days
1997	IRS-1D	India	24 days
1998	SPOT-4	France	26 days
1999	Landsat-7 ETM	USA	16 days
1999	UoSAT-12	UK	n/a
1999	IKONOS-2	USA	n/a
Active Sensors (Synthetic Aperture Radar)			
1991	ERS-1	Europe	up to 168 days
1992	JERS-1	Japan	44 days
1995	ERS-2	Europe	35 days
1995	Radarsat	Canada	16 days

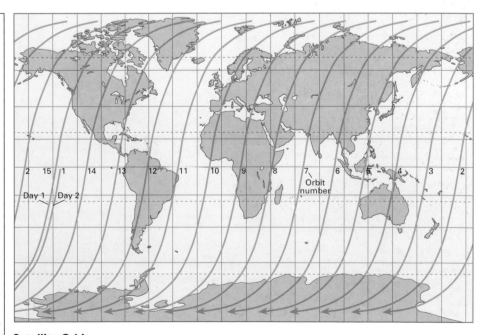

Satellite Orbits

Landsat-7 makes over 14 orbits per day in its Sun-synchronous orbit. During the full 16 days of a repeat cycle, coverage of the areas between those shown is achieved.

Natural-colour and false-colour composites
These images show the salt ponds at the southern end of San Francisco Bay, which now form the San Francisco Bay National Wildlife Refuge. They demonstrate the difference between 'natural colour' (*left*) and 'false colour' (*right*) composites.

The image on the left is made from visible red, green and blue wavelengths. The colours correspond closely to those one would observe from an aircraft. The salt ponds appear green or orange-red due to the colour of the sediments they contain. The urban areas appear grey and vegetation is either dark green (trees) or light brown (dry grass).

The right-hand image is made up of near-infrared, visible red and

visible green wavelengths. These wavebands are represented here in red, green and blue, respectively. Since chlorophyll in healthy vegetation strongly reflects near-infrared light, this is clearly visible as red in the image.

False-colour composite imagery is therefore very sensitive to the presence of healthy vegetation. The image above thus shows better discrimination between the 'leafy' residential urban areas, such as Palo Alto (south-west of the Bay) from other urban areas by the 'redness' of the trees. The high chlorophyll content of watered urban grass areas shows as bright red, contrasting with the dark red of trees and the brown of natural, dry grass. *(EROS)*

Europe at Night
This image was derived as part of the Defense Meteorological Satellite Program. The sensor recorded all the emissions of near-infrared radiation at night, mainly the lights from cities, towns and villages. Note also the 'lights' in the North Sea from the flares of the oil production platforms. This project was the first systematic attempt to record human settlement on a global scale using remote sensing. *(NOAA)*

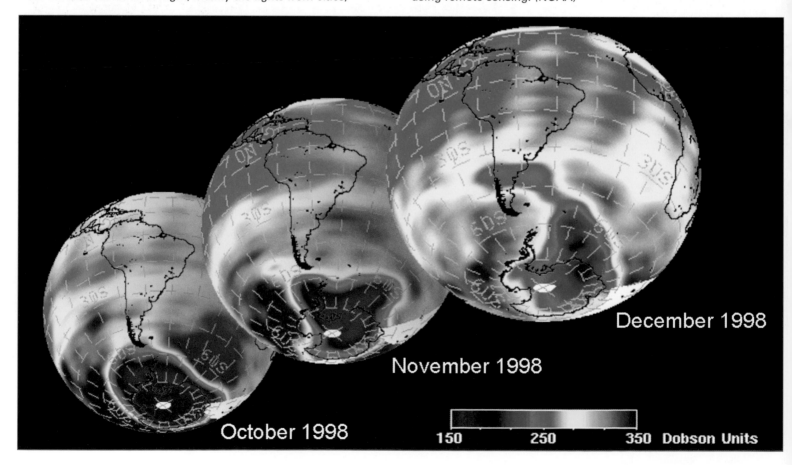

December 1998

November 1998

October 1998

150   250   350 **Dobson Units**

Ozone Distribution
The Global Ozone Monitoring Experiment (GOME) sensor was launched in April 1995. This instrument can measure a range of atmospheric trace constituents, in particular global ozone distributions. Environmental and public health authorities need this up-to-date information to alert people to health risks. Low ozone levels result in increased UV-B radiation, which is harmful and can cause cancers, cataracts and impact the human immune system. 'Dobson Units' indicate the level of ozone depletion (normal levels are around 280DU). *(DLR)*

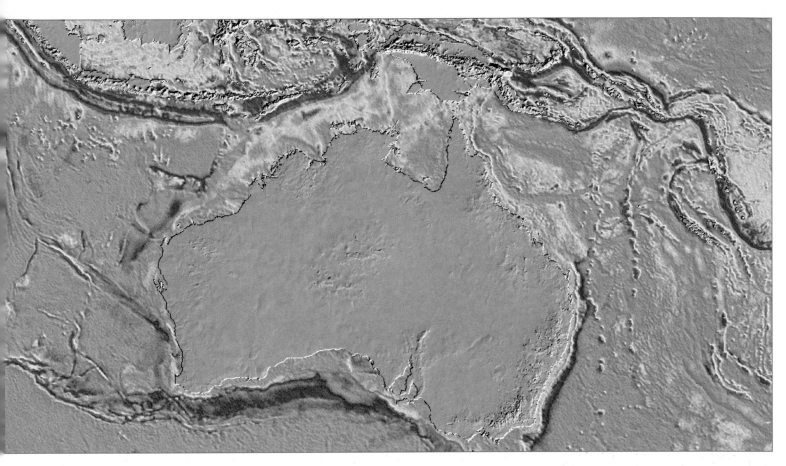

Gravitational Fields

The strength of the Earth's gravitational field at its surface varies according to the ocean depth and the density of local rocks. This causes local variations in the sea level. Satellites orbiting in precisely determined orbits are able to measure the sea level to an accuracy of a few centimetres. These variations give us a better understanding of the geological structure of the sea floor. Information from these sensors can also be used to determine ocean wave heights, which relate to surface wind speed, and are therefore useful in meteorological forecasting. *(NPA)*

Weather Monitoring

Geostationary and polar orbiting satellites monitor the Earth's cloud and atmospheric moisture movements, giving us an insight into the global workings of the atmosphere and permitting us to predict weather change. *(J-2)*

Hurricane Andrew

Although Hurricane Andrew, which hit Florida on 23 August 1992, was the most expensive natural disaster ever to strike the USA, its effects would have been far more disastrous had its path not been precisely tracked by large scale satellite images such as this from the AVHRR sensor. *(NOAA)*

Western Grand Canyon, Arizona, USA
This false-colour image shows in red the sparse vegetation on the limestone plateau, including sage, mesquite and grasses. Imagery such as this is used to monitor this and similar fragile environments. The sediment-laden river, shown as blue-green, can be seen dispersing into Lake Mead to the north-west. Side canyons cross the main canyon in straight lines, showing where erosion along weakened fault lines has occurred. *(EROS)*

Niger Delta, West Africa
The River Niger is the third longest river in Africa after the Nile and Congo. Deltas are by nature constantly evolving sedimentary features and often contain many ecosystems within them. In the case of the Niger Delta, there are also vast hydrocarbon reserves beneath it with associated wells and pipelines. Satellite imagery helps to plan activity and monitor this fragile and changing environment. *(EROS)*

Ayers Rock and Mt Olga, Northern Territory, Australia
These two huge outliers are the remnants of Precambrian mountain ranges created some 500 million years ago and then eroded away. Ayers Rock (*right*) rises 345 m above the surrounding land and has been a part of Aboriginal life for over 10,000 years. Their dramatic coloration, caused by oxidized iron in the sandstone, attracts visitors from around the world. The Yulara tourist resort (shown in blue) and the airport can be made out to the north of Ayers Rock. *(EROS)*

Mount St Helens, Washington, USA
A massive volcanic eruption on 18 May 1980 killed 60 people and devastated around 400 sq km of forest within minutes. The blast reduced the mountain peak by 400 m to its current height of 2550 m, and volcanic ash rose some 25 km into the atmosphere. The image shows Mount St Helens eight years after the eruption in 1988. The characteristic volcanic cone has collapsed in the north, resulting in the devastating 'liquid' flow of mud and rock. *(EROS)*

Kuwait City, Kuwait

This image shows Kuwait after the war with Iraq, which took place in 1991. During this conflict, more than 600 oil wells were set on fire and over 300 oil lakes were formed (visible as dark areas to the south). Satellite imagery helped reduce the costs of mapping these oil spills and enabled the level of damage to be determined prior to clean-up operations. *(Space Imaging)*

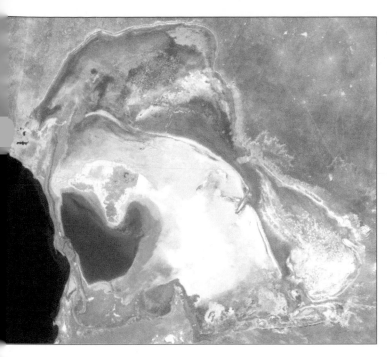

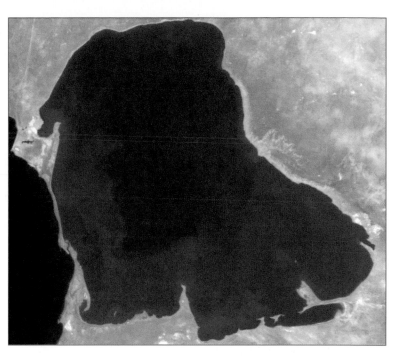

Kara-Bogaz-Gol, Turkmenistan

The Kara-Bogaz-Gol is a large, shallow lagoon joined by a narrow, steep-sided strait to the Caspian Sea. Evaporation makes it one of the most saline bodies of water in the world. Believing the Caspian sea level was falling, the straight was dammed by the USSR in 1980 with the intention of conserving the water to sustain the salt industry. However, by 1983 it had dried up completely (*left*), leading to widespread wind-blown salt, soil poisoning and health problems downwind to the east. In 1992 the Turkmenistan government began to demolish the dam to re-establish the flow of water from the Caspian Sea (*right*). Satellite imagery has helped monitor and map the Kara-Bogaz-Gol as it has fluctuated in size. *(EROS)*

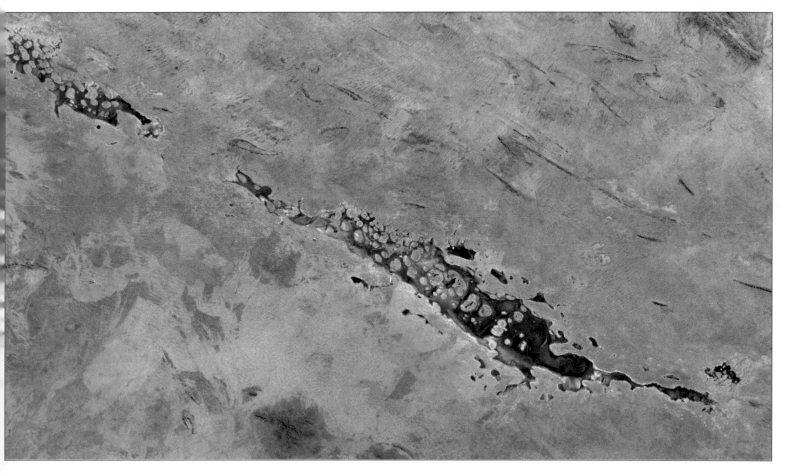

Lake Amadeus, Northern Territory, Australia

This is a saline lake system in the area between the Great Sandy Desert and Ayers Rock. An important wetland environment at the heart of one of the most arid areas in Australia, it supports a wide range of complex habitats and exists due to seepage from the central Australian groundwater system. Changes in its extent in an otherwise remote site can be monitored using satellite imagery such as this Landsat ETM scene. *(EROS)*

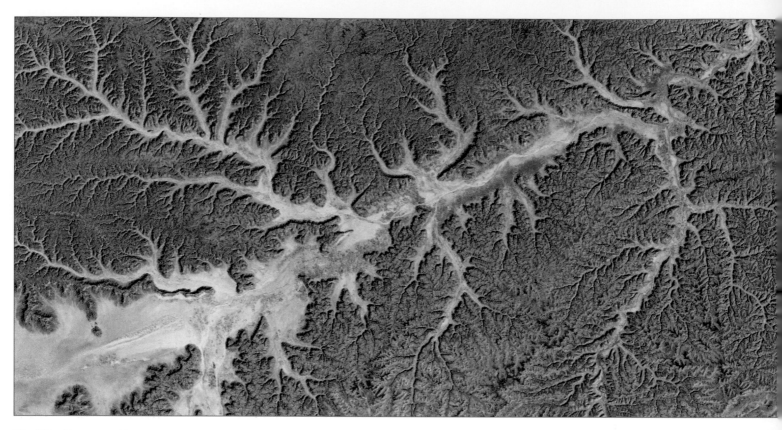

Wadi Hadhramaut, Yemen
Yemen is extremely arid – however, in the past it was more humid and wet, enabling large river systems to carve out the deep and spectacular gorges and dried-out river beds (*wadis*) seen in this image. The erosion has revealed many contrasting rock types. The image has been processed to exaggerate this effect, producing many shades of red, pink and purple, which make geological mapping easier and more cost-effective. *(EROS)*

North Anatolian Fault, Turkey
The east–west trending valley that runs through the centre of the image is formed by the North Anatolian wrench fault. It is the result of Arabia colliding with southern Eurasia, forcing most of Turkey westwards towards Greece. The valley was created by the Kelkit river removing the loosened rock formed by the two tectonic plates grinding together. This active fault has recently caused considerable damage further east in the Gulf of Izmit *(see page 120)*. *(EROS)*

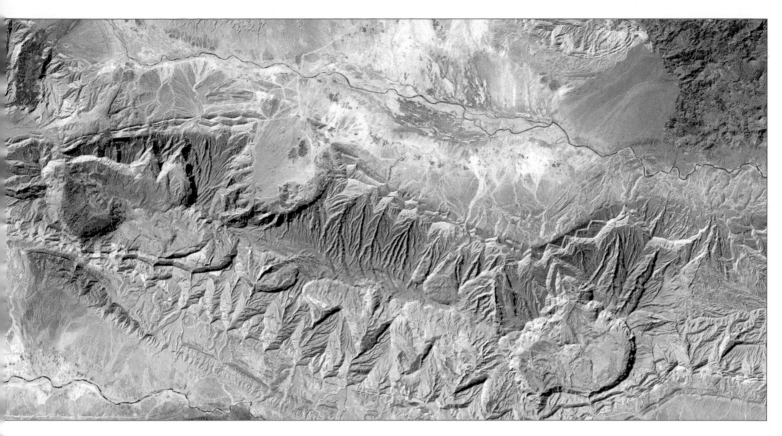

Zagros Mountains, Iran

These mountains were formed as Arabia collided with Southern Eurasia. The centre of this colour-enhanced image shows an anticline that runs east–west. The dark grey features are called *diapirs*, which are bodies of viscous rock salt that are very buoyant and sometimes rise to the surface, spilling and spreading out like a glacier. The presence of salt in the region is important as it stops oil escaping to the surface. *(EROS)*

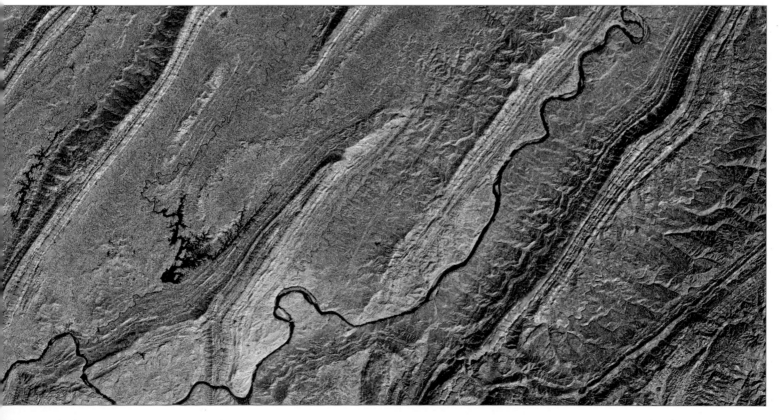

Sichuan Basin, China

The north-east/south-west trending ridges in this image are anticlinal folds developed in the Earth's crust as a result of plate collision and compression. Geologists map these folds and the lowlands between them formed by synclinal folds, as they are often the areas where oil or gas are found in commercial quantities. The river shown in this image is the Yangtze, near Chongqing. *(China RSGS)*

Montserrat, Caribbean Sea

Synthetic Aperture Radar (SAR) sensors send out a microwave signal and create an image from the radiation reflected back. The signal penetrates cloud cover and does not need any solar illumination. This image of Montserrat shows how the island can still be seen, despite clouds and the continuing eruption of the Soufrière volcano in the south. The delta visible in the sea to the east is being formed by lava flows pouring down the Tar River Valley. *(Radarsat)*

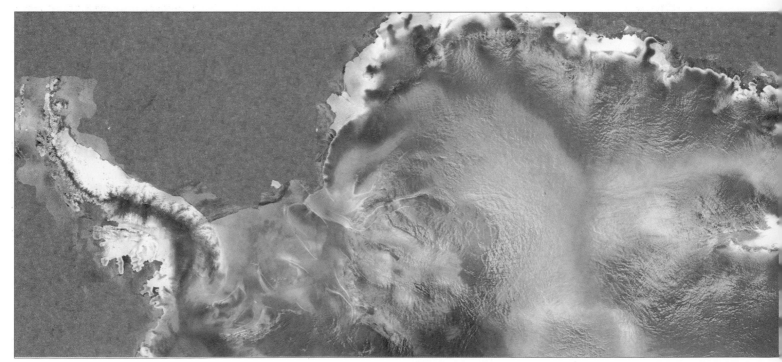

Antarctic Peninsula

SAR image brightness is dependent on surface texture. This image of part of Antarctica clearly shows the Antarctic ice tongues projecting from the Wilkins and George VI Ice Shelves at the south-west end of the peninsula as well as other coastal ice features. Images can be received, even during the winter 'night', and over a period of time form a valuable resource in our ability to monitor the recession of the ice and also the 'calving' of icebergs. *(Radarsat)*

Las Vegas, Nevada, USA

Two satellite images viewing the same area of ground from different orbits can be used to compile a Digital Elevation Model (DEM) of the Earth's surface. A computer compares the images and calculates the ground surface elevation to a vertical precision of 8–15 m, preparing this for thousands of square kilometres in just a few minutes. Overlaying a colour satellite image on to a DEM produced the picture of Las Vegas shown here. *(NPA)*

Urban (tall)
Urban dense
Urban
Industrial
Paved
Urban / Tree mix
Trees (coniferous)
Trees (deciduous)
Forest clearing
Grass or crops
Open
Water

Seattle, Washington, USA

Image processing software can use the differing spectral properties of land cover to 'classify' a multispectral satellite image. This classification of the area around Seattle was used together with elevation data to model the transmission of mobile phone signals before installation of the network. Microwave signals are affected by the absorption, reflection and scattering of the signal from vegetation and urban structures as well as the topography. *(NPA)*

Gulf of Izmit, north-west Turkey
On 17 August 1999 an earthquake measuring 7.4 on the Richter scale caused extensive damage and loss of life around Izmit. This image is a composite of two black-and-white images, one recorded on 7 August 1999 and the other on 24 September 1999. The colours in the image indicate change: orange highlights severely damaged buildings and areas where debris has been deposited during the rescue operation; blue indicates areas submerged beneath sea level as a result of the Earth's movement during the earthquake and fire-damaged oil tanks in the north-west. *(NPA)*

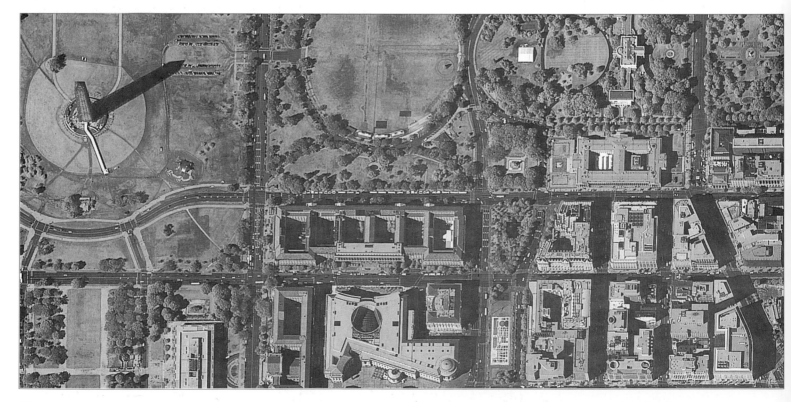

Washington D.C., USA
This image, with the White House seen at top right and the Washington Monument to the left, was recorded on 30 September 1999 by Space Imaging's IKONOS-2 satellite. It was the first satellite image to be commercially available with a ground-sampling interval (pixel size) of 1 m. With a directional sensor, image acquisition attempts can be made in as little as 1–3 days (cloud cover permitting). This level of resolution enables satellite imagery to be used as a data source for many applications that otherwise require expensive aerial surveys to be flown. In addition, data can readily be acquired for projects in remote regions of the world or areas where access is restricted. *(Space Imaging)*

INDEX TO
WORLD MAPS

The index contains the names of all the principal places and features shown on the World Maps. Each name is followed by an additional entry in italics giving the country or region within which it is located. The alphabetical order of names composed of two or more words is governed primarily by the first word and then by the second. This is an example of the rule:

New South Wales □, *Australia*..	**34**	**G8**	33 0S	146 0E
New York □, *U.S.A.*	**43**	**D10**	42 40N	76 0W
New York City, *U.S.A.*	**43**	**E11**	40 45N	74 0W
New Zealand ■, *Oceania*	**35**	**J13**	40 0S	176 0E
Newark, *U.S.A.*	**43**	**F10**	39 42N	75 45W

Physical features composed of a proper name (Erie) and a description (Lake) are positioned alphabetically by the proper name. The description is positioned after the proper name and is usually abbreviated:

Erie, L., *N. Amer.*	**42**	**D7**	42 15N	81 0W

Where a description forms part of a settlement or administrative name, however, it is always written in full and put in its true alphabetical position:

Mount Isa, *Australia*	**34**	**E6**	20 42S	139 26E

Names beginning with M' and Mc are indexed as if they were spelt Mac. Names beginning St. are alphabetized under Saint, but Santa and San are all spelt in full and are alphabetized accordingly. If the same placename occurs two or more times in the index and all are in the same country, each is followed by the name of the administrative subdivision in which it is located. The names are placed in the alphabetical order of the subdivision. For example:

Columbus, Ga., *U.S.A.*	**41**	**D10**	32 30N	84 58W
Columbus, Ind., *U.S.A.*	**42**	**F5**	39 14N	85 55W
Columbus, Ohio, *U.S.A.*	**42**	**F6**	39 57N	83 1W

The number in bold type which follows each name in the index refers to the number of the map page where that feature or place will be found. This is usually the largest scale at which the place or feature appears.

The letter and figure which are in bold type immediately after the page number give the grid square on the map page, within which the feature is situated. The letter represents the latitude and the figure the longitude. In some cases the feature itself may fall within the specified square, while the name is outside.

For a more precise location, the geographical co-ordinates which follow the letter-figure references give the latitude and the longitude of each place. The first set of figures represent the latitude, which is the distance north or south of the Equator measured as an angle at the centre of the Earth. The Equator is latitude 0°, the North Pole is 90°N, and the South Pole 90°S.

The second set of figures represent the longitude, which is the distance east or west of the prime meridian, which runs through Greenwich, England. Longitude is also measured as an angle at the centre of the Earth and is given east or west of the prime meridian, from 0° to 180° in either direction.

The unit of measurement for latitude and longitude is the degree, which is subdivided into 60 minutes. Each index entry states the position of a place in degrees and minutes, a space being left between the degrees and the minutes. The latitude is followed by N(orth) or S(outh) and the longitude by E(ast) or W(est).

Rivers are indexed to their mouths or confluences, and carry the symbol ⤳ after their names. A solid square ■ follows the name of a country, while an open square □ refers to a first order administrative area.

ABBREVIATIONS USED IN THE INDEX

Afghan. – Afghanistan	Conn. – Connecticut	Isla, Island, Isle(s)	Mo. – Missouri	Nebr. – Nebraska	Provincial	Sib. – Siberia
Ala. – Alabama	Cord. – Cordillera	Ill. – Illinois	Mont. – Montana	Neths. – Netherlands	Pt. – Point	St. – Saint, Sankt, Sint
Alta. – Alberta	Cr. – Creek	Ind. – Indiana	Mozam.– Mozambique	Nev. – Nevada	Pta. – Ponta, Punta	Str. – Strait, Stretto
Amer. – America(n)	D.C. – District of	Ind. Oc. – Indian Ocean	Mt.(s).– Mont, Monte,	Nfld. – Newfoundland	Pte. – Pointe	Switz. – Switzerland
Arch. – Archipelago	Columbia	Ivory C. – Ivory Coast	Monti, Montaña,	Nic. – Nicaragua	Qué. – Québec	Tas. – Tasmania
Ariz. – Arizona	Del. – Delaware	Kans. – Kansas	Mountain		Queens. – Queensland	Tenn. – Tennessee
Ark. – Arkansas	Domin. – Dominica	Ky. – Kentucky	N. – Nord, Norte, North,		R. – Rio, River	Tex. – Texas
Atl. Oc. – Atlantic Ocean	Dom. Rep. – Dominican	L. – Lac, Lacul, Lago,	Northern	Okla. – Oklahoma	R.I. – Rhode Island	Trin. & Tob. – Trinidad
B. – Baie, Bahia, Bay,	Republic	Lagoa, Lake, Limni,	N.B. – New Brunswick	Ont. – Ontario	Ra.(s). – Range(s)	& Tobago
Bucht, Bugt	E. – East	Loch, Lough	N.C. – North Carolina	Oreg. – Oregon	Reg. – Region	U.A.E. – United Arab
B.C. – British Columbia	El Salv. – El Salvador	La. – Louisiana	N. Cal. – New Caledonia	P.E.I. – Prince Edward	Rep. – Republic	Emirates
Bangla. – Bangladesh	Eq. Guin. – Equatorial	Lux. – Luxembourg	N. Dak. – North Dakota	Island	Res. – Reserve,	U.K. – United Kingdom
C. – Cabo, Cap, Cape,	Guinea	Madag. – Madagascar	N.H. – New Hampshire	Pa. – Pennsylvania	Reservoir	U.S.A. – United States
Coast	Fla. – Florida	Man. – Manitoba	N.J. – New Jersey	Pac. Oc. – Pacific Ocean	S. – San, South	of America
C.A.R. – Central African	Falk. Is. – Falkland Is.	Mass.– Massachusetts	N. Mex. – New Mexico	Papua N.G. – Papua	Si. Arabia – Saudi Arabia	Va. – Virginia
Republic	G. – Golfe, Golfo, Gulf	Md. – Maryland	N.S. – Nova Scotia	New Guinea	S.C. – South Carolina	Vic. – Victoria
C. Prov. – Cape	Ga. – Georgia	Me. – Maine	N.S.W. – New South	Pen. – Peninsula,	S. Dak. – South Dakota	Vol. – Volcano
Province	Guinea–Biss. –	Medit. S. –	Wales	Peninsule	S. Leone – Sierra Leone	Vt. – Vermont
Calif. – California	Guinea–Bissau	Mediterranean Sea	N.W.T. – North West	Phil. – Philippines	Sa. – Serra, Sierra	W. – West
Cent. – Central	Hd. – Head	Mich. – Michigan	Territory	Pk. – Park, Peak	Sask. – Saskatchewan	W. Va. – West Virginia
Chan. – Channel	Hts. – Heights	Minn. – Minnesota	N.Y. – New York	Plat. – Plateau	Scot. – Scotland	Wash. – Washington
Colo. – Colorado	I.(s). – Ile, Ilha, Insel,	Miss. – Mississippi	N.Z. – New Zealand	Prov. – Province,	Sd. – Sound	Wis. – Wisconsin

INDEX TO WORLD MAPS

Aachen — Banda

A

Aachen, *Germany* . . . **10 C4** 50 45N 6 6 E
Aalborg, *Denmark* . . . **6 G9** 57 2N 9 54 E
Aarau, *Switz.* . . . . **10 E5** 47 23N 8 4 E
Aare —►, *Switz.* . . . . **10 E5** 47 33N 8 14 E
Aarhus, *Denmark* . . . **6 G10** 56 8N 10 11 E
Abadan, *Iran* . . . . . . **24 B3** 30 22N 48 20 E
Abbeville, *France* . . . **8 A4** 50 6N 1 49 E
Abéché, *Chad* . . . . . **29 F9** 13 50N 20 35 E
Abeokuta, *Nigeria* . . . **30 C2** 7 3N 3 19 E
Aberdeen, *U.K.* **7 C5** 57 9N 2 5W
Abidjan, *Ivory C.* **28 G4** 5 26N 3 58W
Abitibi L., *Canada* . . . **42 A8** 48 40N 79 40W
Abkhazia □, *Georgia* **15 F7** 43 12N 41 5 E
Abohar, *India* . . . . . . **23 D5** 30 10N 74 10 E
Abu Dhabi, *U.A.E.* . . . **24 C4** 24 28N 54 22 E
Abuja, *Nigeria* . . . . . **30 C3** 9 16N 7 2 E
Acapulco, *Mexico* . . . **44 D5** 16 51N 99 56W
Accomac, *U.S.A.* . . . **43 G10** 37 43N 75 40W
Accra, *Ghana* **30 C1** 5 35N 0 6W
Acklins I., *Bahamas* . . **45 C10** 22 30N 74 0W
Aconcagua, *Argentina* **47 F3** 32 39S 70 0W
Acre □, *Brazil* **46 C2** 9 1S 71 0W
Adamawa Highlands,
Cameroon . . . . **29 G7** 7 20N 12 20 E
Adana, *Turkey* . . . . . **15 G6** 37 0N 35 16 E
Adapazarı, *Turkey* . . . **15 F5** 40 48N 30 25 E
Addis Ababa, *Ethiopia* **29 G12** 9 2N 38 42 E
Adelaide, *Australia* . . **34 G6** 34 52S 138 30 E
Adelaide, *S. Africa* . . **31 C4** 32 42S 26 20 E
Aden, *Yemen* . . . . . . **24 D3** 12 45N 45 0 E
Aden, G. of, *Asia* . . . **24 D3** 12 30N 47 30 E
Adirondack Mts.,
U.S.A. **43 D10** 44 0N 74 0W
Admiralty Is.,
Papua N. G. . . . . . **36 H6** 2 0S 147 0 E
Ado-Ekiti, *Nigeria* . . . **30 C3** 7 38N 5 12 E
Adoni, *India* . . . . **25 D6** 15 33N 77 18 E
Adour —►, *France* . . **8 E3** 43 32N 1 32W
Adrar, *Algeria* **28 C4** 27 51N 0 11W
Adrian, *U.S.A.* **42 E5** 41 54N 84 2W
Adriatic Sea, *Medit. S.* **12 C6** 43 0N 16 0 E
Ægean Sea, *Medit. S.* **13 E11** 38 30N 25 0 E
Afghanistan ■, *Asia* . **24 B5** 33 0N 65 0 E
'Afif, *Si. Arabia* . . . . **24 C3** 23 53N 42 56 E
Agadès, *Niger* . . . . . **30 A3** 16 58N 7 59 E
Agadir, *Morocco* **28 B3** 30 28N 9 55W
Agartala, *India* . . . . . **23 H13** 23 50N 91 23 E
Agen, *France* . . . . . . **8 D4** 44 12N 0 38 E
Agra, *India* . . . . **23 F6** 27 17N 77 58 E
Agrigento, *Italy* . . . . **12 F5** 37 19N 13 34 E
Aguascalientes,
Mexico **44 C4** 21 53N 102 12W
Agulhas, C., *S. Africa* **31 C3** 34 52S 20 0 E
Ahmadabad, *India* . . **23 H4** 23 0N 72 40 E
Ahmadnagar, *India* . . **25 D6** 19 7N 74 46 E
Ahmadpur, *Pakistan* . **23 E3** 29 12N 71 10 E
Ahvaz, *Iran* . . . . **24 B3** 31 20N 48 40 E
Ahvenanmaa Is.,
Finland . . . . **6 F11** 60 15N 20 0 E
Aïr, *Niger* . . . . **28 E6** 18 30N 8 0 E
Aisne —►, *France* . . . **8 B5** 49 26N 2 50 E
Aix-en-Provence,
France . . . . **8 E6** 43 32N 5 27 E
Aix-les-Bains, *France* **8 D6** 45 41N 5 53 E
Ajaccio, *France* . . . . **8 F8** 41 55N 8 40 E
Ajanta Ra., *India* . . . **23 J5** 20 28N 75 50 E
Ajaria □, *Georgia* . . . **15 F7** 41 30N 42 0 E
Ajmer, *India* . . . . **23 F5** 26 28N 74 37 E
Akashi, *Japan* . . . . . **19 B4** 34 45N 134 58 E
Akita, *Japan* . . . . . . **19 A7** 39 45N 140 7 E
Akola, *India* . . . . **23 J6** 20 42N 77 2 E
Akranes, *Iceland* . . . **6 B2** 64 19N 22 5W
Akron, *U.S.A.* **42 E7** 41 5N 81 31W
Aktyubinsk, *Kazakstan* **15 D10** 50 17N 57 10 E
Akure, *Nigeria* . . . . . **30 C3** 7 15N 5 5 E
Akureyri, *Iceland* . . . **6 B4** 65 40N 18 6W
Al Ḩudaydah, *Yemen* **24 D3** 14 50N 43 0 E
Al Hufūf, *Si. Arabia* . . **24 C3** 25 25N 49 45 E
Al Jawf, *Si. Arabia* . . **24 C2** 29 55N 39 40 E
Al Kut, *Iraq* . . . . **24 B3** 32 30N 46 0 E
Al Qatif, *Si. Arabia* . . **24 C3** 26 35N 50 0 E
Al 'Ula, *Si. Arabia* . . **24 C2** 26 35N 38 0 E
Alabama □, *U.S.A.* . . **41 D9** 33 0N 87 0W
Aland Is. =
Ahvenanmaa Is.,
Finland . . . . **6 F11** 60 15N 20 0 E
Alaska □, *U.S.A.* **38 B5** 64 0N 154 0W
Alaska, G. of, *Pac. Oc.* **38 C5** 58 0N 145 0W
Alaska Peninsula,
U.S.A. **38 C4** 56 0N 159 0W
Alaska Range, *U.S.A.* **38 B4** 62 50N 151 0W
Alba-Iulia, *Romania* . **11 E12** 46 8N 23 39 E
Albacete, *Spain* **9 C5** 39 0N 1 50W
Albania ■, *Europe* . . **13 D9** 41 0N 20 0 E
Albany, *Australia* . . . **34 H2** 35 1S 117 58 E
Albany, *Ga., U.S.A.* . . **41 D10** 31 35N 84 10W
Albany, *N.Y., U.S.A.* . **43 D11** 42 39N 73 45W
Albany —►, *Canada* . **39 C11** 52 17N 81 31W
Albert L., *Africa* . . . . **32 D6** 1 30N 31 0 E
Alberta □, *Canada* . . **38 C8** 54 40N 115 0W
Albertville, *France* . . **8 D7** 45 40N 6 22 E
Albi, *France* . . . . **8 E5** 43 56N 2 9 E
Albion, *U.S.A.* **42 D5** 42 15N 84 45W
Albuquerque, *U.S.A.* . **40 C5** 35 5N 106 39W
Albury, *Australia* . . . . **34 H8** 36 3S 146 56 E
Alcalá de Henares,
Spain **9 B4** 40 28N 3 22W
Aldabra Is., *Seychelles* **27 G8** 9 22S 46 28 E
Aldan —►, *Russia* . . . **18 C14** 63 28N 129 35 E
Aleksandrovsk-
Sakhalinskiy, *Russia* **18 D16** 50 50N 142 20 E
Alençon, *France* . . . . **8 B4** 48 27N 0 4 E
Alès, *France* . . . . **8 D6** 44 9N 4 5 E
Alessándria, *Italy* . . . **12 B3** 44 54N 8 37 E
Ålesund, *Norway* . . . **6 F9** 62 28N 6 12 E
Aleutian Is., *Pac. Oc.* **36 B10** 52 0N 175 0W
Alexander Arch.,
U.S.A. **38 C6** 56 0N 136 0W
Alexandria, *Egypt* . . . **29 B10** 31 13N 29 58 E
Alexandria, *La., U.S.A.* **41 D8** 31 18N 92 27W
Alexandria, *Va., U.S.A.* **42 F9** 38 48N 77 3W
Algarve, *Portugal* . . . **9 D1** 36 58N 8 20W
Algeciras, *Spain* **9 D3** 36 9N 5 28W
Algeria ■, *Africa* . . . . **28 C5** 28 30N 2 0 E
Algiers, *Algeria* . . . . . **28 A5** 36 42N 3 8 E
Alicante, *Spain* **9 C5** 38 23N 0 30W
Alice Springs, *Australia* **34 E5** 23 40S 133 50 E
Aligarh, *India* . . . . . . **23 F7** 27 55N 78 10 E
Alipur Duar, *India* . . . **23 F12** 26 30N 89 35 E
Aliquippa, *U.S.A.* . . . **42 E7** 40 37N 80 15W
Aliwal North, *S. Africa* **31 C4** 30 45S 26 45 E
Alkmaar, *Neths.* . . . . **10 B3** 52 37N 4 45 E
Allahabad, *India* . . . . **23 G8** 25 25N 81 58 E
Allegan, *U.S.A.* **42 D5** 42 32N 85 51W
Allegheny —►, *U.S.A.* **42 E8** 40 27N 80 1W
Allegheny Plateau,
U.S.A. **42 G7** 38 0N 80 0W
Allentown, *U.S.A.* . . . **43 E10** 40 37N 75 29W
Alleppey, *India* . . . . . **25 E6** 9 30N 76 28 E
Allier —►, *France* . . . **8 C5** 46 57N 3 4 E
Alma, *U.S.A.* **42 D5** 43 23N 84 39W
Almaty, *Kazakstan* . . **18 E9** 43 15N 76 57 E
Almelo, *Neths.* . . . . . **10 B4** 52 22N 6 42 E
Almería, *Spain* **9 D4** 36 52N 2 27W
Alor, *Indonesia* . . . . . **22 D4** 8 15S 124 30 E
Alpena, *U.S.A.* **42 C6** 45 4N 83 27W
Alps, *Europe* . . . . **10 E5** 46 30N 9 30 E
Alsace, *France* . . . . . **8 B7** 48 15N 7 25 E
Altai, *Mongolia* . . . . . **20 B4** 46 40N 92 45 E
Altay, *China* . . . . **20 B3** 47 48N 88 10 E
Altoona, *U.S.A.* **42 E8** 40 31N 78 24W
Altun Shan, *China* . . . **20 C3** 38 30N 88 0 E
Alwar, *India* . . . . **23 F6** 27 38N 76 34 E
Amadjuak L., *Canada* **39 B12** 65 0N 71 8W
Amagasaki, *Japan* . . **19 B4** 34 42N 135 20 E
Amarillo, *U.S.A.* **40 C6** 35 13N 101 50W
Amazon —►, *S. Amer.* **46 C4** 0 5S 50 0W
Ambala, *India* . . . . . . **23 D6** 30 23N 76 56 E
Ambikapur, *India* . . . **23 H9** 23 15N 83 15 E
Ambon, *Indonesia* . . . **22 D4** 3 35S 128 20 E
American Samoa □,
Pac. Oc. **35 C17** 14 20S 170 40W
Amiens, *France* . . . . . **8 B5** 49 54N 2 16 E
Amman, *Jordan* . . . . **24 B2** 31 57N 35 52 E
Amos, *Canada* **42 A8** 48 35N 78 5W
Amravati, *India* . . . . . **23 J6** 20 55N 77 45 E
Amreli, *India* . . . . **23 J3** 21 35N 71 17 E
Amritsar, *India* . . . . . **23 D5** 31 35N 74 57 E
Amroha, *India* . . . . . . **23 E7** 28 53N 78 30 E
Amsterdam, *Neths.* . . **10 B3** 52 23N 4 54 E
Amsterdam, *U.S.A.* . . **43 D10** 42 56N 74 11W
Amudarya —►,
Uzbekistan . . . . . . **18 E7** 43 58N 59 34 E
Amundsen Gulf,
Canada **38 A7** 71 0N 124 0W
Amundsen Sea,
Antarctica **48 E1** 72 0S 115 0W
Amur —►, *Russia* . . . **18 D16** 52 56N 141 10 E
An Najaf, *Iraq* . . . . . . **24 B3** 32 3N 44 15 E
An Nasiriyah, *Iraq* . . . **24 B3** 31 0N 46 15 E
An Nhon, *Vietnam* . . . **22 B2** 13 55N 109 7 E
Anadyr, *Russia* . . . . . **18 C19** 64 35N 177 20 E
Anadyr, G. of, *Russia* **18 C20** 64 0N 180 0 E
Anaheim, *U.S.A.* **40 D3** 33 50N 117 55W
Anambas Is.,
Indonesia . . . . **22 C2** 3 20N 106 30 E
Anantnag, *India* . . . . **23 C5** 33 45N 75 10 E
Anar, *Iran* . . . . **24 B4** 30 55N 55 13 E
Anatolia, *Turkey* . . . . **15 G5** 39 0N 30 0 E
Anchorage, *U.S.A.* . . . **38 B5** 61 13N 149 54W
Ancona, *Italy* . . . . . . **12 C5** 43 38N 13 30 E
Anda, *China* . . . . **21 B7** 46 24N 125 19 E
Andalucía □, *Spain* . . **9 D3** 37 35N 5 0W
Andaman Is., *Ind. Oc.* **25 D8** 12 30N 92 30 E
Anderson, *U.S.A.* . . . **42 E5** 40 10N 85 41W
Andes, *S. Amer.* **46 E3** 20 0S 68 0W
Andhra Pradesh □,
India . . . . **25 D6** 18 0N 79 0 E
Andorra ■, *Europe* . . **9 A6** 42 30N 1 30 E
Andreanof Is., *U.S.A.* **38 C2** 52 0N 178 0W
Ándria, *Italy* . . . . **12 D7** 41 13N 16 17 E
Andros I., *Bahamas* . **45 C9** 24 30N 78 0W
Angara —►, *Russia* . . **18 D11** 58 5N 94 20 E
Ånge, *Sweden* . . . . . **6 F11** 62 31N 15 35 E
Angel Falls, *Venezuela* **46 B3** 5 57N 62 30W
Angerman —►,
Sweden . . . . **6 F11** 62 40N 18 0 E
Angers, *France* **8 C3** 47 30N 0 35W
Anglesey, *U.K.* **7 E4** 53 17N 4 20W
Angola ■, *Africa* . . . . **33 G3** 12 0S 18 0 E
Angoulême, *France* . . **8 D4** 45 39N 0 10 E
Angoumois, *France* . . **8 D3** 45 50N 0 25 E
Anguilla ■, *W. Indies* **44 J18** 18 14N 63 5W
Anhui □, *China* . . . . . **21 C6** 32 0N 117 0 E
Anjou, *France* **8 C3** 47 20N 0 15W
Ankara, *Turkey* . . . . . **15 G5** 39 57N 32 54 E
Ann, C., *U.S.A.* **43 D12** 42 38N 70 35W
Ann Arbor, *U.S.A.* . . . **42 D6** 42 17N 83 45W
Annaba, *Algeria* . . . . **28 A6** 36 50N 7 46 E
Annapolis, *U.S.A.* . . . **42 F9** 38 59N 76 30W
Annecy, *France* . . . . . **8 D7** 45 55N 6 8 E
Annobón, *Atl. Oc.* . . . **27 G4** 1 25S 5 36 E
Anshun, *China* . . . . . . **20 D5** 26 18N 105 57 E
Antalya, *Turkey* . . . . . **15 G5** 36 52N 30 45 E
Antananarivo, *Madag.* **33 H9** 18 55S 47 31 E
Antarctic Pen.,
Antarctica **48 D4** 67 0S 60 0W
Antibes, *France* . . . . . **8 E7** 43 34N 7 6 E
Anticosti I., *Canada* . **43 A16** 49 30N 63 0W
Antigua & Barbuda ■,
W. Indies **44 K20** 17 20N 61 48W
Antofagasta, *Chile* . . **47 E2** 23 50S 70 30W
Antsiranana, *Madag.* . **33 G9** 12 25S 49 20 E
Antwerp, *Belgium* . . . **10 C3** 51 13N 4 25 E
Anyang, *China* . . . . . **21 C6** 36 5N 114 21 E
Aomori, *Japan* . . . . . **19 F12** 40 45N 140 45 E
Aoraki Mt. Cook, *N.Z.* **35 J13** 43 36S 170 9 E
Aparri, *Phil.* . . . . **22 B4** 18 22N 121 38 E
Apeldoorn, *Neths.* . . . **10 B3** 52 13N 5 57 E
Apennines, *Italy* . . . . **12 B4** 44 0N 10 0 E
Apia, *Samoa* **35 C16** 13 50S 171 50W
Appalachian Mts.,
U.S.A. **42 G7** 38 0N 80 0W
Appleton, *U.S.A.* **42 C3** 44 16N 88 25W
Aqmola = Astana,
Kazakstan . . . . **18 D9** 51 10N 71 30 E
Ar Ramadi, *Iraq* . . . . **24 B3** 33 25N 43 20 E
Arabian Desert, *Egypt* **29 C11** 27 30N 32 30 E
Arabian Gulf = Gulf,
The, *Asia* . . . . **24 C4** 27 0N 50 0 E
Arabian Sea, *Ind. Oc.* **24 D5** 16 0N 65 0 E
Aracaju, *Brazil* **46 D6** 10 55S 37 4W
Arad, *Romania* . . . . . **11 E11** 46 10N 21 20 E
Arafura Sea, *E. Indies* **22 D5** 9 0S 135 0 E
Aragón □, *Spain* **9 B5** 41 25N 0 40W
Araguaia —►, *Brazil* . **46 C5** 5 21S 48 41W
Arak, *Iran* . . . . **24 B3** 34 0N 49 40 E
Arakan Yoma, *Burma* **25 C8** 20 0N 94 40 E
Aral, *Kazakstan* . . . . **18 E8** 46 41N 61 45 E
Aral Sea , *Asia* . . . . . **18 E8** 44 30N 60 0 E
Arcachon, *France* . . . **8 D3** 44 40N 1 10W
Arctic Ocean, *Arctic* . **48 B17** 78 0N 160 0W
Arctic Red River,
Canada **38 B6** 67 15N 134 0W
Ardabil, *Iran* . . . . **24 B3** 38 15N 48 18 E
Ardennes, *Belgium* . . **10 D3** 49 50N 5 5 E
Arendal, *Norway* . . . . **6 G9** 58 28N 8 46 E
Arequipa, *Peru* **46 D2** 16 20S 71 30W
Argentan, *France* . . . **8 B3** 48 45N 0 1W
Argentina ■, *S. Amer.* **47 F3** 35 0S 66 0W
Arima, *Trin. & Tob.* . . **44 S20** 10 38N 61 17W
Arizona □, *U.S.A.* . . . **40 D4** 34 0N 112 0W
Arkansas □, *U.S.A.* . . **41 D8** 35 0N 92 30W
Arkansas —►, *U.S.A.* **41 D8** 33 47N 91 4W
Arkhangelsk, *Russia* . **14 B7** 64 38N 40 36 E
Arles, *France* . . . . **8 E6** 43 41N 4 40 E
Arlington, *U.S.A.* **42 F9** 38 53N 77 7W
Arlon, *Belgium* . . . . . **10 D3** 49 42N 5 49 E
Armenia ■, *Asia* . . . . **15 F7** 40 20N 45 0 E
Arnhem, *Neths.* . . . . . **10 C3** 51 58N 5 55 E
Arnhem Land,
Australia . . . . **34 C5** 13 10S 134 30 E
Arnprior, *Canada* . . . **42 C9** 45 26N 76 21W
Arrah, *India* . . . . **23 G10** 25 35N 84 32 E
Arran, *U.K.* **7 D4** 55 34N 5 12W
Arras, *France* . . . . . . **8 A5** 50 17N 2 46 E
Artois, *France* . . . . . . **8 A5** 50 20N 2 30 E
Aru Is., *Indonesia* . . . **22 D5** 6 0S 134 30 E
Arunachal Pradesh □,
India . . . . **25 C8** 28 0N 95 0 E
Arusha, *Tanzania* . . . **32 E7** 3 20S 36 40 E
Arviat, *Canada* **38 B10** 61 10N 94 15W
Asab, *Namibia* . . . . . **31 B2** 25 30S 18 0 E
Asahigawa, *Japan* . . **19 F12** 43 46N 142 22 E
Asansol, *India* . . . . . . **23 H11** 23 40N 87 1 E
Asbestos, *Canada* . . . **43 C12** 45 47N 71 58W
Asbury Park, *U.S.A.* . **43 E10** 40 13N 74 1W
Ascension I., *Atl. Oc.* **27 G2** 8 0S 14 15W
Ashkhabad,
Turkmenistan . . . . . **18 F7** 38 0N 57 50 E
Ashland, *Ky., U.S.A.* . **42 F6** 38 28N 82 38W
Ashland, *Ohio, U.S.A.* **42 E6** 40 52N 82 19W
Ashtabula, *U.S.A.* . . . **42 E7** 41 52N 80 47W
Asifabad, *India* . . . . . **23 K7** 19 20N 79 24 E
Asir □, *Si. Arabia* . . . **24 D3** 18 40N 42 30 E
Asmara, *Eritrea* . . . . **29 E12** 15 19N 38 55 E
Assam □, *India* . . . . . **23 F13** 26 0N 93 0 E
Assen, *Neths.* . . . . . . **10 B4** 53 0N 6 35 E
Assisi, *Italy* . . . . **12 C5** 43 4N 12 37 E
Astana, *Kazakstan* . . **18 D9** 51 10N 71 30 E
Asti, *Italy* . . . . **12 B3** 44 54N 8 12 E
Astrakhan, *Russia* . . . **15 E8** 46 25N 48 5 E
Asturias □, *Spain* . . . **9 A3** 43 15N 6 0W
Asunción, *Paraguay* . **47 E4** 25 10S 57 30W
Aswân, *Egypt* . . . . . . **29 D11** 24 4N 32 57 E
Atacama Desert, *Chile* **47 E3** 24 0S 69 20W
Atbara, *Sudan* . . . . . **29 E11** 17 42N 33 59 E
Atbara —►, *Sudan* . . **29 E11** 17 40N 33 56 E
Athabasca —►,
Canada **38 C8** 58 40N 110 50W
Athabasca, L., *Canada* **38 C9** 59 15N 109 15W
Athens, *Greece* . . . . . **13 F10** 37 58N 23 46 E
Athens, *U.S.A.* **42 F6** 39 20N 82 6W
Atikokan, *Canada* . . . **42 A2** 48 45N 91 37W
Atlanta, *U.S.A.* **41 D10** 33 45N 84 23W
Atlantic City, *U.S.A.* . **43 F10** 39 21N 74 27W
Atlantic Ocean **2 E9** 0 0 20 0W
Atyraū, *Kazakstan* . . . **18 E7** 47 5N 52 0 E
Au Sable —►, *U.S.A.* **42 C6** 44 25N 83 20W
Aube —►, *France* . . . **8 B5** 48 34N 3 43 E
Auburn, *Ind., U.S.A.* . **42 E5** 41 22N 85 4W
Auburn, *N.Y., U.S.A.* . **42 D9** 42 56N 76 34W
Aubusson, *France* . . . **8 D5** 45 57N 2 11 E
Auch, *France* . . . . **8 E4** 43 39N 0 36 E
Auckland, *N.Z.* . . . . . **35 H13** 36 52S 174 46 E
Aude —►, *France* . . . **8 E5** 43 13N 3 14 E
Augrabies Falls,
S. Africa . . . . **31 B3** 28 35S 20 20 E
Augsburg, *Germany* . . **10 D6** 48 25N 10 52 E
Augusta, *Ga., U.S.A.* **41 D10** 33 28N 81 58W
Augusta, *Maine*,
U.S.A. **43 C13** 44 19N 69 47W
Aunis, *France* **8 C3** 46 5N 0 50W
Aurangabad, *Bihar*,
India . . . . **23 G10** 24 45N 84 18 E
Aurangabad,
Maharashtra, India **23 K5** 19 50N 75 23 E
Aurillac, *France* . . . . . **8 D5** 44 55N 2 26 E
Aurora, *U.S.A.* **42 E3** 41 45N 88 19W
Austin, *U.S.A.* **40 D7** 30 17N 97 45W
Australia ■, *Oceania* **34 E5** 23 0S 135 0 E
Australian Capital
Territory □, *Australia* **34 H8** 35 30S 149 0 E
Austria ■, *Europe* . . . **10 E8** 47 0N 14 0 E
Autun, *France* . . . . . . **8 C6** 46 58N 4 17 E
Auvergne, *France* . . . **8 D5** 45 20N 3 15 E
Auxerre, *France* . . . . **8 C5** 47 48N 3 32 E
Avallon, *France* . . . . . **8 C5** 47 30N 3 53 E
Avellino, *Italy* . . . . . . **12 D6** 40 54N 14 47 E
Avignon, *France* . . . . **8 E6** 43 57N 4 50 E
Ávila, *Spain* **9 B3** 40 39N 4 43W
Avranches, *France* . . **8 B3** 48 40N 1 20W
Axiós —►, *Greece* . . **13 D10** 40 57N 22 35 E
Ayers Rock, *Australia* **34 F5** 25 23S 131 5 E
Ayr, *U.K.* **7 D4** 55 28N 4 38W
Azamgarh, *India* . . . . **23 F9** 26 5N 83 13 E
Azerbaijan ■, *Asia* . . **15 F8** 40 20N 48 0 E
Azores, *Atl. Oc.* **2 C8** 38 44N 29 0W
Azov, Sea of, *Europe* **15 E6** 46 0N 36 30 E
Azuero Pen., *Panama* **45 F8** 7 30N 80 30W

B

Babol, *Iran* . . . . **24 B4** 36 40N 52 50 E
Babuyan Chan., *Phil.* **22 B4** 18 40N 121 30 E
Bacău, *Romania* . . . . **11 E14** 46 35N 26 55 E
Bacolod, *Phil.* . . . . . . **22 B4** 10 40N 122 57 E
Bad Axe, *U.S.A.* **42 D6** 43 48N 83 0W
Badajoz, *Spain* **9 C2** 38 50N 6 59W
Badalona, *Spain* . . . . **9 B7** 41 26N 2 15 E
Baden-
Württemberg □,
Germany . . . . **10 D5** 48 20N 8 40 E
Baffin I., *Canada* **39 B12** 68 0N 75 0W
Baghdad, *Iraq* . . . . . . **24 B3** 33 20N 44 30 E
Baguio, *Phil.* . . . . **22 B4** 16 26N 120 34 E
Bahamas ■, *N. Amer.* **45 C10** 24 0N 75 0W
Baharampur, *India* . . **23 G12** 24 2N 88 27 E
Bahawalpur, *Pakistan* **23 E3** 29 24N 71 40 E
Bahía = Salvador,
Brazil **46 D6** 13 0S 38 30W
Bahía □, *Brazil* **46 D5** 12 0S 42 0W
Bahía Blanca,
Argentina **47 F3** 38 35S 62 13W
Bahraich, *India* . . . . . **23 F8** 27 38N 81 37 E
Bahrain ■, *Asia* . . . . . **24 C4** 26 0N 50 35 E
Baia Mare, *Romania* . **11 E12** 47 40N 23 35 E
Baie-St-Paul, *Canada* **43 B12** 47 28N 70 32W
Baikal, L., *Russia* . . . **18 D12** 53 0N 108 0 E
Baja California, *Mexico* **44 B2** 31 10N 115 12W
Bakersfield, *U.S.A.* . . **40 C3** 35 23N 119 1W
Bakhtaran, *Iran* . . . . . **24 B3** 34 23N 47 0 E
Baku, *Azerbaijan* . . . . **15 F8** 40 29N 49 56 E
Balabac Str., *E. Indies* **22 C3** 7 53N 117 5 E
Balaghat, *India* . . . . . **23 J8** 21 49N 80 12 E
Balaton, *Hungary* . . . **11 E9** 46 50N 17 40 E
Balboa, *Panama* **44 H14** 8 57N 79 34W
Baldwin, *U.S.A.* **42 D5** 43 54N 85 51W
Balearic Is., *Spain* . . . **9 C7** 39 30N 3 0 E
Baleshwar, *India* . . . . **23 J11** 21 35N 87 3 E
Bali, *Indonesia* . . . . . . **22 D3** 8 20S 115 0 E
Balıkeşir, *Turkey* . . . . **13 E12** 39 35N 27 58 E
Balikpapan, *Indonesia* **22 D3** 1 10S 116 55 E
Balkan Mts., *Bulgaria* **13 C10** 43 15N 23 0 E
Balkhash, L.,
Kazakstan . . . . **18 E9** 46 0N 74 50 E
Ballarat, *Australia* . . . **34 H7** 37 33S 143 50 E
Balqash, *Kazakstan* . . **18 E9** 46 50N 74 50 E
Balrampur, *India* . . . . **23 F9** 27 30N 82 20 E
Balsas —►, *Mexico* . . **44 D4** 17 55N 102 10W
Baltic Sea, *Europe* . . . **6 G11** 57 0N 19 0 E
Baltimore, *U.S.A.* . . . **42 F9** 39 17N 76 37W
Bam, *Iran* . . . . **24 C4** 29 7N 58 14 E
Bamako, *Mali* **28 F3** 12 34N 7 55W
Bamberg, *Germany* . . **10 D6** 49 54N 10 54 E
Bamenda, *Cameroon* . **30 C4** 5 57N 10 11 E
Bancroft, *Canada* . . . **42 C9** 45 3N 77 51W
Banda, *India* . . . . **23 G8** 25 30N 80 26 E

Place names on the yellow-coded large scale map section are to be found in the index at the end of that section

Place names on the yellow-coded large scale map section are to be found in the index at the end of that section

Brunei   **Comilla**

Place names on the yellow-coded large scale map section are to be found in the index at the end of that section

INDEX TO WORLD MAPS

Communism Pk. — Erfurt

Communism Pk., Tajikistan 18 F9 39 0N 72 2 E
Como, Italy 12 B3 45 47N 9 5 E
Como, L. di, Italy 12 B3 46 0N 9 11 E
Comodoro Rivadavia, Argentina 47 G3 45 50S 67 40W
Comorin, C., India 25 E6 8 3N 77 40 E
Comoros ■, Ind. Oc. 27 H8 12 10S 44 15 E
Compiègne, France 8 B5 49 24N 2 50 E
Conakry, Guinea 28 G2 9 29N 13 49W
Concepción, Chile 47 F2 36 50S 73 0W
Conchos →, Mexico 44 B3 29 32N 105 0W
Concord, U.S.A. 43 D12 43 12N 71 32W
Congo ■, Africa 32 E3 1 0S 16 0 E
Congo →, Africa 32 F2 6 4S 12 24 E
Congo, Dem. Rep. of the ■, Africa 32 E4 3 0S 23 0 E
Coniston, Canada 42 B7 46 29N 80 51W
Conneaut, U.S.A. 42 E7 41 57N 80 34W
Connecticut □, U.S.A. 43 E11 41 30N 72 45W
Connecticut →, U.S.A. 43 E11 41 16N 72 20W
Connellsville, U.S.A. 42 E8 40 1N 79 35W
Connersville, U.S.A. 42 F5 39 39N 85 8W
Constance, L., Europe 10 E5 47 35N 9 25 E
Constanţa, Romania 11 F15 44 14N 28 38 E
Constantine, Algeria 28 A6 36 25N 6 42 E
Conway, U.S.A. 43 D12 43 59N 71 7W
Cook, Aoraki Mt., N.Z. 35 J13 43 36S 170 9 E
Cook Is., Pac. Oc. 35 E17 17 0S 160 0W
Cook Strait, N.Z. 35 J13 41 15S 174 29 E
Copenhagen, Denmark 6 G10 55 41N 12 34 E
Copper Harbor, U.S.A. 42 B4 47 28N 87 53W
Coppermine = Kugluktuk, Canada 38 B8 67 50N 115 5W
Coppermine →, Canada 38 B8 67 49N 116 4W
Coral Sea, Pac. Oc. 36 J7 15 0S 150 0 E
Corbin, U.S.A. 42 G5 36 57N 84 6W
Córdoba, Argentina 47 F3 31 20S 64 10W
Córdoba, Spain 9 D3 37 50N 4 50W
Cordova, U.S.A. 38 B5 60 33N 145 45W
Corfu, Greece 13 E8 39 38N 19 50 E
Corinth, G. of, Greece 13 E10 38 16N 22 30 E
Cork, Ireland 7 F2 51 54N 8 29W
Corner Brook, Canada 39 D14 48 57N 57 58W
Corning, U.S.A. 42 D9 42 9N 77 3W
Cornwall, Canada 43 C10 45 2N 74 44W
Coromandel Coast, India 25 D7 12 30N 81 0 E
Coronation Gulf, Canada 38 B8 68 25N 110 0W
Corpus Christi, U.S.A. 40 E7 27 47N 97 24W
Corrientes, Argentina 47 E4 27 30S 58 45W
Corry, U.S.A. 42 E8 41 55N 79 39W
Corse, C., France 8 E8 43 1N 9 25 E
Corsica, France 8 F8 42 0N 9 0 E
Corte, France 8 E8 42 19N 9 11 E
Cortland, U.S.A. 43 D9 42 36N 76 11W
Cosenza, Italy 12 E7 39 18N 16 15 E
Coshocton, U.S.A. 42 E7 40 16N 81 51W
Costa Blanca, Spain 9 C5 38 25N 0 10W
Costa Brava, Spain 9 B7 41 30N 3 0 E
Costa del Sol, Spain 9 D3 36 30N 4 30W
Costa Dorada, Spain 9 B6 41 12N 1 15 E
Costa Rica ■, Cent. Amer. 45 F8 10 0N 84 0W
Côte d'Azur, France 8 E7 43 25N 7 10 E
Côte-d'Ivoire = Ivory Coast ■, Africa 28 G3 7 30N 5 0W
Cotentin, France 8 B3 49 15N 1 30W
Cotonou, Benin 30 C2 6 20N 2 25 E
Cotopaxi, Ecuador 46 C2 0 40S 78 30W
Cotswold Hills, U.K. 7 F5 51 42N 2 10W
Cottbus, Germany 10 C8 51 45N 14 20 E
Coudersport, U.S.A. 42 E8 41 46N 78 1W
Council Bluffs, U.S.A. 41 B7 41 16N 95 52W
Coventry, U.K. 7 E6 52 25N 1 28W
Covington, U.S.A. 42 F5 39 5N 84 31W
Cox's Bazar, Bangla. 23 J13 21 26N 91 59 E
Cradock, S. Africa 31 C4 32 8S 25 36 E
Craiova, Romania 11 F12 44 21N 23 48 E
Cranbrook, Canada 38 D8 49 30N 115 46W
Crawfordsville, U.S.A. 42 E4 40 2N 86 54W
Cremona, Italy 12 B4 45 7N 10 2 E
Crete, Greece 13 G11 35 15N 25 0 E
Creuse →, France 8 C4 47 0N 0 34 E
Crimea, Ukraine 15 E5 45 0N 34 0 E
Crişul Alb →, Romania 11 E11 46 42N 21 17 E
Crişul Negru →, Romania 11 E11 46 42N 21 16 E
Croatia ■, Europe 10 F9 45 20N 16 0 E
Crocodile →, Mozam. 31 B5 25 14S 32 18 E
Crystal Falls, U.S.A. 42 B3 46 5N 88 20W
Cuba ■, W. Indies 45 C9 22 0N 79 0W
Cubango →, Africa 33 H4 18 50S 22 25 E
Cúcuta, Colombia 46 B2 7 54N 72 31W
Cuenca, Ecuador 46 C2 2 50S 79 9W
Cuenca, Spain 9 B4 40 5N 2 10W
Cuernavaca, Mexico 44 D5 18 55N 99 15W
Cuiabá, Brazil 46 D4 15 30S 56 0W
Culiacán, Mexico 44 C3 24 50N 107 23W
Culpeper, U.S.A. 42 F9 38 30N 78 0W
Cumberland, U.S.A. 42 F8 39 39N 78 46W
Cumberland Plateau, U.S.A. 41 C10 36 0N 85 0W
Cúneo, Italy 12 B2 44 23N 7 32 E
Curitiba, Brazil 47 E5 25 20S 49 10W
Cuttack, India 23 J10 20 25N 85 57 E
Cuxhaven, Germany 10 B5 53 51N 8 41 E
Cuyahoga Falls, U.S.A. 42 E7 41 8N 81 29W
Cuzco, Peru 46 D2 13 32S 72 0W
Cyclades, Greece 13 F11 37 20N 24 30 E
Cynthiana, U.S.A. 42 F5 38 23N 84 18W
Cyprus ■, Asia 24 B2 35 0N 33 0 E
Czech Rep. ■, Europe 10 D8 50 0N 15 0 E
Częstochowa, Poland 11 C10 50 49N 19 7 E

D

Da Nang, Vietnam 22 B2 16 4N 108 13 E
Dacca, Bangla. 23 H13 23 43N 90 26 E
Dadra and Nagar Haveli □, India 23 J4 20 5N 73 0 E
Dadu, Pakistan 23 F1 26 45N 67 45 E
Dagestan □, Russia 15 F8 42 30N 47 0 E
Dagupan, Phil. 22 B4 16 3N 120 20 E
Dahod, India 23 H5 22 50N 74 15 E
Dakar, Senegal 28 F1 14 34N 17 29W
Dakhla, W. Sahara 28 D1 23 50N 15 53W
Dalhousie, Canada 43 A14 48 5N 66 26W
Dalian, China 21 C7 38 50N 121 40 E
Dallas, U.S.A. 41 D7 32 47N 96 49W
Dalmatia, Croatia 12 C7 43 20N 17 0 E
Daloa, Ivory C. 28 G3 7 0N 6 30W
Damaraland, Namibia 31 A2 21 0S 17 0 E
Damascus, Syria 24 B2 33 30N 36 18 E
Dammam, Si. Arabia 24 C4 26 20N 50 5 E
Dampier, Australia 34 E2 20 41S 116 42 E
Danbury, U.S.A. 43 E11 41 24N 73 28W
Dandeldhura, Nepal 23 E8 29 20N 80 35 E
Dandong, China 21 B7 40 10N 124 20 E
Dannemora, Sweden 6 F11 60 12N 17 51 E
Danube →, Europe 11 F15 45 20N 29 40 E
Danville, Ill., U.S.A. 42 E4 40 8N 87 37W
Danville, Ky., U.S.A. 42 G5 37 39N 84 46W
Dar-es-Salaam, Tanzania 32 F7 6 50S 39 12 E
Darbhanga, India 23 F10 26 15N 85 55 E
Dardanelles, Turkey 13 D12 40 17N 26 32 E
Dargai, Pakistan 23 B3 34 25N 71 55 E
Darjeeling, India 23 F12 27 3N 88 18 E
Darling →, Australia 34 G7 34 4S 141 54 E
Darling Ra., Australia 34 G2 32 30S 116 0 E
Darmstadt, Germany 10 D5 49 51N 8 39 E
Dartmouth, Canada 43 C16 44 40N 63 30W
Darwin, Australia 34 C5 12 25S 130 51 E
Dasht →, Pakistan 24 C5 25 10N 61 40 E
Dasht-e Lūt, Iran 24 B4 31 30N 58 0 E
Datong, China 21 B6 40 6N 113 18 E
Daulpur, India 23 F6 26 45N 77 59 E
Dauphin, Canada 38 C9 51 9N 100 5W
Dauphiné, France 8 D6 45 15N 5 25 E
Davao, Phil. 22 C4 7 0N 125 40 E
Davao, G. of, Phil. 22 C4 6 30N 125 48 E
Davenport, U.S.A. 41 B8 41 32N 90 35W
David, Panama 45 F8 8 30N 82 30W
Davis Str., N. Amer. 39 B14 65 0N 58 0W
Dawson, Canada 38 B6 64 10N 139 30W
Dawson Creek, Canada 38 C7 55 45N 120 15W
Dax, France 8 E3 43 44N 1 3W
Dayton, U.S.A. 42 F5 39 45N 84 12W
De Aar, S. Africa 31 C3 30 39S 24 0 E
De Pere, U.S.A. 42 C3 44 27N 88 4W
Dease Lake, Canada 38 C6 58 25N 130 6W
Death Valley, U.S.A. 40 C3 36 15N 116 50W
Debrecen, Hungary 11 E11 47 33N 21 42 E
Decatur, U.S.A. 42 E5 40 50N 84 56W
Deccan, India 25 D6 18 0N 79 0 E
Defiance, U.S.A. 42 E5 41 17N 84 22W
Dehra Dun, India 23 D7 30 20N 78 4 E
Delaware, U.S.A. 42 E6 40 18N 83 4W
Delaware □, U.S.A. 43 F10 39 0N 75 20W
Delaware →, U.S.A. 43 F10 39 15N 75 20W
Delhi, India 23 E6 28 38N 77 17 E
Delphos, U.S.A. 42 E5 40 51N 84 21W
Demavand, Iran 24 B4 35 47N 52 0 E
Den Helder, Neths. 10 B3 52 57N 4 45 E
Denizli, Turkey 15 G4 37 42N 29 2 E
Denmark ■, Europe 6 G9 55 30N 9 0 E
Denmark Str., Atl. Oc. 48 C5 66 0N 30 0W
Denpasar, Indonesia 22 D3 8 45S 115 14 E
Denver, U.S.A. 40 C5 39 44N 104 59W
Deoghar, India 23 G11 24 30N 86 42 E
Deolali, India 23 K4 19 58N 73 50 E
Deosai Mts., Pakistan 23 B5 35 40N 75 0 E
Dera Ghazi Khan, Pakistan 23 D3 30 5N 70 43 E
Dera Ismail Khan, Pakistan 23 D3 31 50N 70 50 E
Des Moines, U.S.A. 41 B8 41 35N 93 37W
Des Moines →, U.S.A. 41 B8 40 23N 91 25W
Dessau, Germany 10 C7 51 51N 12 14 E
Detour, Pt., U.S.A. 42 C4 45 40N 86 40W
Detroit, U.S.A. 42 D6 42 20N 83 3W
Deutsche Bucht, Germany 10 A5 54 15N 8 0 E
Deventer, Neths. 10 B4 52 15N 6 10 E
Dewas, India 23 H6 22 59N 76 3 E
Dhamtari, India 23 J8 20 42N 81 35 E
Dhanbad, India 23 H11 23 50N 86 30 E
Dhankuta, Nepal 23 F11 26 55N 87 40 E
Dhar, India 23 H5 22 35N 75 26 E
Dharwad, India 25 D6 15 22N 75 15 E
Dhaulagiri, Nepal 23 E9 28 39N 83 28 E
Dhenkanal, India 23 J10 20 45N 85 35 E
Dhuburi, India 23 F12 26 2N 89 59 E
Dhule, India 23 J5 20 58N 74 50 E
Diamantina →, Australia 34 F6 26 45S 139 10 E
Dieppe, France 8 B4 49 54N 1 4 E
Digby, Canada 43 C15 44 38N 65 50W
Digne-les-Bains, France 8 D7 44 5N 6 12 E
Dijon, France 8 C6 47 20N 5 3 E
Dili, Indonesia 22 D4 8 39S 125 34 E
Dillingham, U.S.A. 38 C4 59 3N 158 28W
Dimbaza, S. Africa 31 C4 32 50S 27 14 E
Dinajpur, Bangla. 23 G12 25 33N 88 43 E
Dinan, France 8 B2 48 28N 2 2W
Dinant, Belgium 10 C3 50 16N 4 55 E
Dinaric Alps, Croatia 12 C7 44 0N 16 30 E
Dir, Pakistan 23 B3 35 8N 71 59 E
Disteghil Sar, Pakistan 23 A5 36 20N 75 12 E
Diu, India 23 J3 20 45N 70 58 E
Diyarbakır, Turkey 15 G7 37 55N 40 18 E
Djakarta = Jakarta, Indonesia 22 D2 6 9S 106 49 E
Djibouti ■, Africa 24 D3 12 0N 43 0 E
Dneprodzerzhinsk, Ukraine 15 E5 48 32N 34 37 E
Dnepropetrovsk, Ukraine 15 E5 48 30N 35 0 E
Dnieper →, Ukraine 15 E5 46 30N 32 18 E
Dniester →, Europe 11 E16 46 18N 30 17 E
Dobreta-Turnu-Severin, Romania 11 F12 44 39N 22 41 E
Dobrich, Bulgaria 13 C12 43 37N 27 49 E
Dodecanese, Greece 13 F12 36 35N 27 0 E
Dodoma, Tanzania 32 F7 6 8S 35 45 E
Doha, Qatar 24 C4 25 15N 51 35 E
Dohazari, Bangla. 23 H14 22 10N 92 5 E
Dolbeau, Canada 43 A11 48 53N 72 18W
Dole, France 8 C6 47 7N 5 31 E
Dolomites, Italy 12 A4 46 23N 11 51 E
Dominica ■, W. Indies 44 M20 15 20N 61 20W
Dominican Rep. ■, W. Indies 45 D10 19 0N 70 30W
Don →, Russia 15 E6 47 4N 39 18 E
Dondra Head, Sri Lanka 25 E7 5 55N 80 40 E
Donetsk, Ukraine 15 E6 48 0N 37 45 E
Dongting, L., China 21 D6 29 18N 112 45 E
Dordogne →, France 8 D3 45 2N 0 36W
Dordrecht, Neths. 10 C3 51 48N 4 39 E
Dordrecht, S. Africa 31 C4 31 20S 27 3 E
Doring →, S. Africa 31 C2 31 54S 18 39 E
Dortmund, Germany 10 C4 51 30N 7 28 E
Douai, France 8 A5 50 21N 3 4 E
Douala, Cameroon 30 D3 4 0N 9 45 E
Doubs →, France 8 C6 46 53N 5 1 E
Douglas, S. Africa 31 B3 29 4S 23 46 E
Douro →, Europe 9 B1 41 8N 8 40W
Dover, U.K. 7 F7 51 7N 1 19 E
Dover, Del., U.S.A. 43 F10 39 10N 75 32W
Dover, N.H., U.S.A. 43 D12 43 12N 70 56W
Dover, Str. of, Europe 8 A4 51 0N 1 30 E
Dover-Foxcroft, U.S.A. 43 C13 45 11N 69 13W
Dovrefjell, Norway 6 F9 62 15N 9 33 E
Draguignan, France 8 E7 43 32N 6 27 E
Drakensberg, S. Africa 31 C4 31 0S 28 0 E
Drammen, Norway 6 G10 59 42N 10 12 E
Drava →, Croatia 13 B8 45 33N 18 55 E
Dresden, Germany 10 C7 51 3N 13 44 E
Dreux, France 8 B4 48 44N 1 23 E
Drina →, Bos.-H. 13 B8 44 53N 19 21 E
Drumheller, Canada 38 C8 51 25N 112 40W
Drummond I., U.S.A. 42 B5 46 1N 83 39W
Drummondville, Canada 43 C11 45 55N 72 25W
Du Bois, U.S.A. 42 E8 41 8N 78 46W
Dubai, U.A.E. 24 C4 25 18N 55 20 E
Dubbo, Australia 34 G8 32 11S 148 35 E
Dublin, Ireland 7 E3 53 21N 6 15W
Dubrovnik, Croatia 13 C8 42 39N 18 6 E
Dudinka, Russia 18 C10 69 30N 86 13 E
Duisburg, Germany 10 C4 51 26N 6 45 E
Duluth, U.S.A. 41 A8 46 47N 92 6W
Dumfries, U.K. 7 D5 55 4N 3 37W
Dun Laoghaire, Ireland 7 E3 53 17N 6 8W
Dundalk, Ireland 7 E3 54 1N 6 24W
Dundee, S. Africa 31 B5 28 11S 30 15 E
Dundee, U.K. 7 C5 56 28N 2 59W
Dunedin, N.Z. 35 K13 45 50S 170 33 E
Dunkerque, France 8 A5 51 2N 2 20 E
Dunkirk, U.S.A. 42 D8 42 29N 79 20W
Dunmore, U.S.A. 43 E10 41 25N 75 38W
Durance →, France 8 E6 43 55N 4 45 E
Durango, Mexico 44 C4 24 3N 104 39W
Durban, S. Africa 31 B5 29 49S 31 1 E
Düren, Germany 10 C4 50 48N 6 29 E
Durg, India 23 J8 21 15N 81 22 E
Durgapur, India 23 H11 23 30N 87 20 E
Durham, U.S.A. 41 C11 35 59N 78 54W
Durrësi, Albania 13 D8 41 19N 19 28 E
Dushanbe, Tajikistan 18 F8 38 33N 68 48 E
Düsseldorf, Germany 10 C4 51 14N 6 47 E
Duyun, China 20 D5 26 18N 107 29 E
Dvina, Severnaya →, Russia 14 B7 64 32N 40 30 E
Dwarka, India 23 H2 22 18N 69 8 E
Dzerzhinsk, Russia 14 C7 56 14N 43 30 E
Dzhambul = Taraz, Kazakstan 18 E9 42 54N 71 22 E
Dzhugdzhur Ra., Russia 18 D15 57 30N 138 0 E

E

Eagle L., U.S.A. 43 B13 46 20N 69 22W
East Beskids, Europe 11 D11 49 20N 22 0 E
East China Sea, Asia 21 C7 30 5N 126 0 E
East Indies, Asia 16 K15 0 0 120 0 E
East Lansing, U.S.A. 42 D5 42 44N 84 29W
East London, S. Africa 31 C4 33 0S 27 55 E
East Pt., Canada 43 B17 46 27N 61 58W
East Siberian Sea, Russia 18 B18 73 0N 160 0 E
East Timor □, Indonesia 22 D4 9 0S 125 0 E
Easter Islands, Pac. Oc. 37 K17 27 0S 109 0W
Eastern Ghats, India 25 D6 14 0N 78 50 E
Easton, Md., U.S.A. 43 F9 38 47N 76 5W
Easton, Pa., U.S.A. 43 E10 40 41N 75 13W
Eastport, U.S.A. 43 C14 44 56N 67 0W
Eau Claire, U.S.A. 41 B8 44 49N 91 30W
Ebro →, Spain 9 B6 40 43N 0 54 E
Ech Cheliff, Algeria 28 A5 36 10N 1 20 E
Echo Bay, Canada 38 B8 66 5N 117 55W
Ecuador ■, S. Amer. 46 C2 2 0S 78 0W
Ede, Nigeria 30 C2 7 45N 4 29 E
Edendale, S. Africa 31 B5 29 39S 30 18 E
Edinburgh, U.K. 7 D5 55 57N 3 13W
Edmonton, Canada 38 C8 53 30N 113 30W
Edmundston, Canada 43 B13 47 23N 68 20W
Edward, L., Africa 32 E5 0 25S 29 40 E
Effingham, U.S.A. 42 F3 39 7N 88 33W
Eganville, Canada 42 C9 45 32N 77 5W
Eger, Hungary 11 E11 47 53N 20 27 E
Egersund, Norway 6 G9 58 26N 6 1 E
Egypt ■, Africa 29 C11 28 0N 31 0 E
Eifel, Germany 10 C4 50 15N 6 50 E
Eindhoven, Neths. 10 C3 51 26N 5 28 E
El Aaiún, W. Sahara 28 C2 27 9N 13 12W
El Faiyûm, Egypt 29 C11 29 19N 30 50 E
El Fâsher, Sudan 29 F10 13 33N 25 26 E
El Jadida, Morocco 28 B3 33 11N 8 17W
El Mahalla el Kubra, Egypt 29 B11 31 0N 31 0 E
El Mansûra, Egypt 29 B11 31 0N 31 19 E
El Minyâ, Egypt 29 C11 28 7N 30 33 E
El Obeid, Sudan 29 F11 13 8N 30 10 E
El Paso, U.S.A. 40 D5 31 45N 106 29W
El Salvador ■, Cent. Amer. 44 E7 13 50N 89 0W
Elba, Italy 12 C4 42 46N 10 17 E
Elbasani, Albania 13 D9 41 9N 20 9 E
Elbe →, Europe 10 B5 53 50N 9 0 E
Elbeuf, France 8 B4 49 17N 1 2 E
Elbląg, Poland 11 A10 54 10N 19 25 E
Elbrus, Asia 15 F7 43 21N 42 30 E
Elburz Mts., Iran 24 B4 36 0N 52 0 E
Elche, Spain 9 C5 38 15N 0 42W
Eldoret, Kenya 32 D7 0 30N 35 17 E
Elephants →, Mozam. 31 A5 24 10S 32 40 E
Eleuthera, Bahamas 45 C9 25 0N 76 20W
Elgin, U.S.A. 42 D3 42 2N 88 17W
Elizabeth, U.S.A. 43 E10 40 40N 74 13W
Elizabethtown, U.S.A. 42 G5 37 42N 85 52W
Elkhart, U.S.A. 42 E5 41 41N 85 58W
Elkins, U.S.A. 42 F8 38 55N 79 51W
Elliot Lake, Canada 42 B6 46 25N 82 35W
Elmira, U.S.A. 42 D9 42 6N 76 48W
Eluru, India 25 D7 16 48N 81 8 E
Elyria, U.S.A. 42 E6 41 22N 82 7W
Emamrud, Iran 24 B4 36 30N 55 0 E
Emden, Germany 10 B4 53 21N 7 12 E
Emmen, Neths. 10 B4 52 48N 6 57 E
Empangeni, S. Africa 31 B5 28 50S 31 52 E
Emporium, U.S.A. 42 E8 41 31N 78 14W
Empty Quarter = Rub' al Khali, Si. Arabia 24 D3 18 0N 48 0 E
Ems →, Germany 10 B4 53 20N 7 12 E
Enderbury I., Kiribati 36 H10 3 8S 171 5W
Endicott, U.S.A. 43 D9 42 6N 76 4W
Engadin, Switz. 10 E6 46 45N 10 10 E
Enggano, Indonesia 22 D2 5 20S 102 40 E
England □, U.K. 7 E6 53 0N 2 0W
English Bazar, India 23 G12 24 58N 88 10 E
English Channel, Europe 8 A3 50 0N 2 0W
Enns →, Austria 10 D8 48 14N 14 32 E
Enschede, Neths. 10 B4 52 13N 6 53 E
Ensenada, Mexico 44 A1 31 50N 116 50W
Entebbe, Uganda 32 D6 0 4N 32 28 E
Enugu, Nigeria 30 C3 6 20N 7 30 E
Épernay, France 8 B5 49 3N 3 56 E
Épinal, France 8 B7 48 10N 6 27 E
Equatorial Guinea ■, Africa 32 D1 2 0N 8 0 E
Erbil, Iraq 24 B3 36 15N 44 5 E
Erfurt, Germany 10 C6 50 58N 11 2 E

Place names on the yellow-coded large scale map section are to be found in the index at the end of that section

Place names on the yellow-coded large scale map section are to be found in the index at the end of that section

Place names on the yellow-coded large scale map section are to be found in the index at the end of that section

Place names on the yellow-coded large scale map section are to be found in the index at the end of that section

INDEX TO WORLD MAPS

N

Place names on the yellow-coded large scale map section are to be found in the index at the end of that section

INDEX TO WORLD MAPS

Place names on the yellow-coded large scale map section are to be found in the index at the end of that section

Place names on the yellow-coded large scale map section are to be found in the index at the end of that section

INDEX TO WORLD MAPS

Place names on the yellow-coded large scale map section are to be found in the index at the end of that section

Place names on the yellow-coded large scale map section are to be found in the index at the end of that section